The New Middle Ages

Series Editor
Bonnie Wheeler, English and Medieval Studies, Southern
Methodist University, Dallas, TX, USA

The New Middle Ages is a series dedicated to pluridisciplinary studies of medieval cultures, with particular emphasis on recuperating women's history and on feminist and gender analyses. This peer-reviewed series includes both scholarly monographs and essay collections.

More information about this series at
http://www.palgrave.com/gp/series/14239

Donald J. Kagay

Elionor of Sicily, 1325–1375

A Mediterranean Queen of Two Worlds

Donald J. Kagay
University of Dallas
Dallas, TX, USA

The New Middle Ages
ISBN 978-3-030-71027-9   ISBN 978-3-030-71028-6   (eBook)
https://doi.org/10.1007/978-3-030-71028-6

© The Editor(s) (if applicable) and The Author(s), under exclusive license to Springer Nature Switzerland AG 2021
This work is subject to copyright. All rights are solely and exclusively licensed by the Publisher, whether the whole or part of the material is concerned, specifically the rights of translation, reprinting, reuse of illustrations, recitation, broadcasting, reproduction on microfilms or in any other physical way, and transmission or information storage and retrieval, electronic adaptation, computer software, or by similar or dissimilar methodology now known or hereafter developed.
The use of general descriptive names, registered names, trademarks, service marks, etc. in this publication does not imply, even in the absence of a specific statement, that such names are exempt from the relevant protective laws and regulations and therefore free for general use.
The publisher, the authors and the editors are safe to assume that the advice and information in this book are believed to be true and accurate at the date of publication. Neither the publisher nor the authors or the editors give a warranty, expressed or implied, with respect to the material contained herein or for any errors or omissions that may have been made. The publisher remains neutral with regard to jurisdictional claims in published maps and institutional affiliations.

Cover credit: Album/Alamy Stock Photo

This Palgrave Macmillan imprint is published by the registered company Springer Nature Switzerland AG
The registered company address is: Gewerbestrasse 11, 6330 Cham, Switzerland

Royal Houses

Sicilian Royal House
Pere I of Sicily
(1282–1285)
%
Pedro III of Aragon
(1276–1285)
%
Fadrique III of Sicily
(1296–1227)
%
Pietro II of Sicily
(1337–1342)
%
Queen Elionor of Aragon
(1349–1375)
%
Lodovico I of Sicily
(1342–1355)
%
Federico IV of Sicily
(1355–1377)
%

Maria I of Sicily
(1377–1402)
%
Martin I of Sicily
(1390–1409)
%
Martin II of Sicily
(1409–1410)

Aragonese Royal House
Jaime I of Aragon
(1214–1276)
%
Pedro III of Aragon
(1276–1285)
%
Alfonso III of Aragon
(1285–1291)
Jaime II of Aragon
(1291–1327)
%
Alfonso IV of Aragon
(1327–1336)
%
Pedro IV of Aragon
(1336–1387)
%
Juan I of Aragon
(1387–1395)
%
Martin I of Aragon
(1395–1410)

E'S SIBLINGS AND CHILDREN

Elionor's Siblings
Federico
(1324)
%
Beatrice
(1326–1365)
%
Constança
(unknown–1355)
%
Euphemia
(unknown)
%
Blanca
(unknown–1374)
%
Violante
(unknown)
%
Lodovico I of Sicily
(1338–1355)
%

viii E'SSIBLINGS AND CHILDREN

Giovani
(unknown–1353)
%
Federico IV of Sicily
(1342–1377)

Elionor's Children
Juan (Joan)
(1350–1396)
%
Martin (Martí)
(1356–1410)
%
Elionor
(1358–1377)
%
Alfonso (Alfóns)
(unknown–1364)

PREFACE

The period during which this work was written overlaps with the first frantic months during which the Covid-19 pandemic was introduced to the entire world. The author by prudent care or blind luck has avoided the terrible fate of many of his fellow citizens. Despite the disease's often dire consequences, the lockdown of business and life as usual that it has caused has made the production of this work much easier and has somehow wonderfully concentrated its organization. I will not thank the disease but would be remiss in not, at least, recognizing its effect on this small enterprise and that of the entire world.

Like the disparate effects of Covid-19 itself, this discussion of the life of Elionor of Sicily, the third wife of the long-lived king of Aragon, Pere III, is largely based on a remarkable number of fourteenth-century sources, but few of them have much connection to the normal building blocks of modern biography. The difficulty of bringing the Aragonese queen's life to the page is the often-frustrating lack of personal detail about her in contemporary chronicles of both Sicily and eastern Spain. On the other hand, from the amazing number of administrative documents that she dictated or wrote herself, the queen is clearly a significant player in the familial and political histories of the two regions she was long connected with. The difficulty these asymmetrical fonts of evidence produce for the biographer is not connected with Elionor's governmental, courtly, or wifely career, but rather with the determination of what kind of person she was. Despite these evidentiary problems, we can still see that

ix

the Aragonese queen as firmly "sundered" to her past, which extended forward as a "living history."[1]

Since a number of scholars have faced these same problems in regard to other Iberian queens down to the fifteenth century, I have fortunately been left a series of historical blueprints to follow in regard to the study of Queen Elionor. These studies concerning the Aragonese queens, Constanza and Violante who lived in the thirteenth century, Leonor of Castile, Sabilla de Fortia, and Violante de Bar in the fourteenth, and María de Luna, and María de Castile in the fifteenth have all helped in formulating this study on Pere III's most important wife. Important works on Navarrese female rulers of the fourteenth and fifteenth centuries have also helped to considerably lighten my organizational load for this work. For all of these fine studies, I would like to extend heartfelt thanks to the following accomplished scholars, some of whom I know, some of whom I do not, but all of whom I respect: Dawn Bratsch Prince, María del Carcía Herrero, Therea Earenfight, Lois Honeycutt, Nuría Muñoz i Soria, Sebastian Roebert, Cristina Segura Graino, Miriam Shadis, Nuría Silleras-Fernández, Marta VanLandingham; Theresa Vann, and Elena Woodacre.

In very specific terms, I would like to recognize the unfailing support of three close colleagues who have helped appreciably in bringing this and most of my other books into reality. I would first of all like to thank my mentor at Fordham University, Joseph F. O'Callaghan, who at age ninety-three is still a mighty force in Medieval Spanish Studies within Iberia and the United States. Secondly, I would like to thank my friend, Theresa Vann, with whom I have published two books and hope to publish another in the near future, whose advice on the study of Spanish queens in the Middle Ages is invaluable. Finally, I wish to express my gratitude to Andrew Villalon, my long-time partner in the publication of seven books on various aspects of military history in the Middle Ages, whose counsel has closely followed this book from its conception to its completion.

Dallas, USA

Donald J. Kagay

---

[1] *An Idea of History: Selected Essays of Américo Castro*, ed. and trans. Stephen Gilman and Edmund L. King (Columbus: Ohio State University Press, 1977), 6–7.

Contents

1	Introduction	1
2	The Many Faces of Medieval Mediterranean Queenship	23
3	Two Realms and a Marriage	41
4	Elionor and Her Departed Homeland	65
5	The Fiscal Support of Queen Elionor	91
6	Elionor of Sicily as Courtier and Administrator	111
7	Elionor of Sicily as a Wartime Leader	145
8	Elionor, a Personal Life	193
9	Elionor's Last Days	227
	Notes on Aragonese Money	237
	Bibliography	239
	Index	255

Abbreviations

Often-used titles of academic journals are abbreviated as are often-cited terms.

ACA	Achivo de la Corona de Aragón (Arxiu de la Corona d'Aragó)
AEM	*Anuario de Esdios Medievales*
AEEM	*Aragón de la Edad Media*
AHAM	*Acta Historica et Archaeologica Medievalia*
AHDE	*Anuario de Historia del Derecho Español*
AHR	*American Historical Review*
AUA	*Anales de la Univewrsidad de Alicante*
BD	*The Book of Deeds of James I of Aragon*
CHE	*Cuadernos de Historia Español*
CHJZ	*Cuadernos de Historia Jerónimo Zurita*
CHR	*Catholic Historical Review*
CSIC	*Concejo Superior de Investicaciones Científicas*
EEMCA	*Estudios de Edad Media de la Corona de Aragón*
EHR	*English Historical Review*
f.	folio
ff.	folios
JGAH	*Journal of the Georgia Association of Historians*
JMMH	*Journal of Medieval Military History*
MMM	*Miscelánea Medieval Murciana*
MS	*Mediterranean Studies*
R.	Register

CHAPTER 1

Introduction

No marriage occurs in a vacuum, but rather ties together the life history and experience of families in much the same way as it does for individuals bound in holy wedlock. In the medieval centuries, the bride took the longest to accommodate to this new lifestyle since she was invariably a stranger in the household in which she lived out her married life. As a result, historians catch few meaningful glimpses of wives in any such environment, whether peasant, urban, aristocratic, or royal. The literate view of such connubial existence which normally comes to us from the Middle Ages is oriented toward two extremes. The image of the good wife can do no better than emulate the existence of Christ's mother, Mary, whom the Church very early on portrayed as the protectress of a humanity living in total disarray.[1] That of the bad wife was easily assigned to Eve, the first woman whose oversexed nature cost her and her husband Paradise and replaced it with the sad reality of unavoidable death.[2] Between these two poles of theoretical reality, ancient and medieval women of all classes seemingly lived lives that provided scholars with little worthwhile evidence. Even clerical and royal women who lived in much more literate environments have often remained only partially known to investigators from the type and distribution of evidence about them that that remains.

The vast fonts of written evidence that remain from the medieval realms of the Crown of Aragon allow the researcher to study the life and

© The Author(s), under exclusive license to Springer Nature
Switzerland AG 2021
D. J. Kagay, *Elionor of Sicily, 1325–1375*, The New Middle Ages,
https://doi.org/10.1007/978-3-030-71028-6_1

1

career of one of the most important of the Aragonese queens of the late medieval period: Elionor, the third wife of the long-lived sovereign, Pere III (Pedro IV (r. 1336–1387)).

From their official nature, however, these vast documentary fonts often reveal more of Elionor's administrative career than the personal dynamics of an occasionally difficult marital union that endured from 1349 to 1375. She was the mother of three sons (two healthy and the other extremely short-lived) and a daughter; as such, she was considered a good and faithful wife by her husband and the royal courts she lived and worked in and temporarily helped to preside over. Even with the great amount of documentation produced and largely preserved from her twenty-six years of service as a wife, mother, and royal official, much of her life is still cast in various tones of darkness. The purpose of this work is to cast what light can be found on the life and career of a truly remarkable woman who deserves to be included in the pantheon of Iberian queens of the later Middle Ages, all of whose careers have been so thoroughly studied in the last few decades.[3]

1   ELIONOR IN CONTEMPORARY CHRONICLES

While Queen Elionor became a force within the government of the Crown of Aragon and had a long-range effect on her Sicilian homeland after she had left it never to return, her existence seemed to go all but unnoticed in the chronicles of the land of her birth, adolescence, and early adulthood. In the Sicilian historical works of the fourteenth and early fifteenth centuries, the Aragonese queen, who was also an important member of the Sicilian royal family during the reigns of her father, Pietro II (r. 1321–1342), and her brothers, Ludovico I "the Child" (r. 1342–1355) and Federico IV "the Simple" (r. 1355–1377), was never mentioned. In Sicily's principal chronicle of the era, *Cronica Sicilie* (Chronicle of Sicily) and lesser important annals of the island including the *Brevis Cronca de Factis Insulae Sicilie* (The Brief Chronicle of the Deeds of the Island of Sicily), the small appendix to the *Annales Siculi* (Sicilian Annals), and Nicolo de Marsala's *Cronica*, brief descriptions of reigns of Sicilian sovereigns from Frederick II (r. 1194–1250) to María (r. 1377–1399) as well as their Aragonese counterparts Pere II (Pedro III) (r. 1276–1285), Martí I (Martín I) (r. 1395–1410) were interlinked with general histories of Sicily and its neighbors, Genoa, Pisa, and Venice.[4]

1 INTRODUCTION 3

The same limited coverage of Elionor's life and accomplishments is obvious in her husband's own *Cronica*. Like his great-great-grandfather, Jaume I (Jaime I) (r. 1214–1276), Pere III had used his literate court officials to flesh out episodes of his own life and reign. He repeatedly edited their efforts, often expanding his own remembrances for them. His coverage of the crucial years 1349 to 1366, during which his third wife had emerged as a strong family leader and efficient royal administrator, distinctly gives his wife short shrift, except in her role as a mother.[5]

We first hear of the king's third wife at the end of the *Cronica*'s fourth book. In its sixty-fourth chapter, he talks of a delegation sent to Sicily in 1349 in order to search for a new bride to replace his second mate who had died of the Black Death the year before. Once the ambassadors finished their work, they accompanied Elionor back to the city of Valencia where the king solemnly took her as his wife "as corresponded to our royal dignity."[6] Two chapters later, the king refers to a trip of his court from Valenicia to Barcelona, and then across the Pyrenees on to Perpignan. On this long and tedious journey, he was accompanied by his heavily pregnant wife who gave birth to a son, Joan, on December 27, 1350.[7]

We only hear of the queen again four years later when she accompanied her husband to Sardinia to attempt to put down a lingering revolt on the island.[8] In Book Six, the king talks of a journey in February 1358 from Valencia city to the nearby shrine of Santa María del Puig where "Our most dear wife" gave birth to a daughter named Elionor after her mother.[9] The queen disappears from her husband's reminiscences until he mentions staying with her for a short time in the summer of 1364 at the Aragonese village of Sessa.[10] The king also talks of being with his wife at Barcelona in the same summer in which he headed a tribunal that judged Cabrera guilty of secretly conspiring with Pedro I of Castile (r. 1350–1366/69), Pere's constant enemy. The king provides little evidence of his wife's activities for the next nine years until he matter-of-factly announced that Elionor "passed from this life in the spring of 1375."[11] Pere's last mention of his third wife in his chronicle sought to explain the background for her death by saying that sadness and frustration had gripped her in the months before she passed away. In the king's opinion, the queen's anxiety about and opposition to their daughter's marriage with the son of the Castilian king, Enrique II (r.1366/1369–1379), and the sudden cancellation of a royal trip to her Sicilian homeland which she had long looked forward to had led to her steady decline and death.[12]

4   D. J. KAGAY

These skimpy references imbedded in the hundreds of pages that celebrate the glory of Pere III's reign and that of his realms do little to portray his third wife except in the most simplistic of terms. From the chronicle, we have no idea of her appearance and even less of her character. It is evident from the king's words that he considered Elionor a good wife and mother who had guaranteed that her husband's line would continue by giving birth to two male heirs who would extend the Barcelona dynasty for some decades to come after the king's death in 1387. From the *Cronica*, we learn that she loved "with all her heart" at least one of her offspring, her second son, Martí.[13] From these snippets the king leaves concerning his wife and the massive documental remains of her administrative career, we can characterize her with some confidence as a determined woman who was not afraid to unleash her temper to gain what she wanted or to accomplish what she thought was right. Despite her foreign upbringing, these qualities, in all likelihood, also gained the respect of her husband's corps of officials who clearly witnessed her administrative talents. For the modern reader, the thousands of documents she dictated or wrote herself bear ample testimony to her skills at governing. To gain an adequate understanding of how Queen Elionor functioned in this literate world, we must explore the remarkable archival culture that blossomed in eastern Spain from the eleventh century onward.

2   THE CROWN OF ARAGON'S ARCHIVAL ENVIRONMENT

With the dearth of evidence left to the modern scholar from the chronicle literature of the queen's period, we have no recourse but to turn to the voluminous medieval remains now maintained in the collections of the Archivo de la Corona de Aragón [hereafter ACA]. This singular institution with an official history extending back eight centuries was the end-result of document maintenance and copying which was clearly in the making from the twelfth century onward. When an *arxiu* finally came to exist in Barcelona in the fourteenth century, its activities were clearly in line with a much later understanding of how an archive should operate. The ACA from its beginnings was a "public place in which original papers and documents which contained the laws of the Prince and the individual subjects were protected."[14]

The first very small steps toward an archival culture in eastern Spain began in the northern Catalan counties during the ninth and tenth centuries. Clearly influenced by the literate, Carolingian culture that ultimately conquered from the Pyrenees to Barcelona to form the "Spanish March" (*marca hispanica*), Catalan rulers soon began producing official documents of all sorts. Rather than keeping these records in a central location, they stored them in various castles where they remained on bookcases and in portable chests with very little organization.[15] With the brutal attacks of the tenth-century, Muslim leader, al Mans©r, Barcelona fell and was sacked in 985. As a result, many of the Christian documents were destroyed and the remainder were seriously threatened with destruction.[16] When the Caliphate of Córdoba disintegrated in the early eleventh century into scattered and petty realms (*taifas*), Count Ramon Berenguer I of Barcelona (r. 1017–1035) began to issue new laws. In the following centuries, his actions eventually led to a new "constitutional order" for Catalonia.[17]

The codification of laws and the formalization of custom slowly advanced in Catalonia and Aragon until the battlefield death in 1134 of the great Aragonese warrior-king, Alfonso I (r. 1104–1134) with no offspring. With the strange testamentary directive that his realm should be left to the military order of the Hospital, the Aragonese nobility and clergy rose to head off a looming political disaster by rapidly choosing a new royal successor, Alfonso's brother, the monk and bishop-elect, Ramiro. They almost as rapidly arranged a marriage for the celibate sovereign with the noblewoman, Agnes of Poitier, and within a year the union was blessed with the birth of Princess Petronilla.[18]

After three years of rule, Ramiro abdicated in 1137, but not before he had married his two-year-old daughter to the count of Barcelona, Ramon Berenguer IV (r. 1131–1162). This critically important action tied the kingship of Aragon to the Catalan tradition of preserving documents and was highly significant for the establishment of archives in eastern Spain.[19]

The first step toward this archival culture began with the offspring of the Aragonese-Catalan union, Alfons I (Alfonso II), who took to heart the repeated emphasis on the significance of official documentation that he received from both of his parents. In the literate governmental culture he ruled over, Alfons took as political dogma the belief that the factual building blocks of his government would ultimately disappear unless they were carefully written down and just as carefully preserved.[20]

Among Alfons's clerical and lay courtiers, only a few had received advanced education. From this group, the first great legal milestone of the Crown of Aragon was to come about from luck and determination.

Like most other European royal governments of the time, Alfons's was not overly careful with the maintenance of its written records. As a result, many of the parchment deeds and bills of sales of important castles held by the king were pawned for ready cash with a Jewish moneylender in the early 1170 s. When some of these fortresses became the subject of litigation in the next few years, the Aragonese king was forced to redeem these records and then ordered them to be carefully organized by his court officials, especially two brothers, Porcell and Ramon de Caldes. The result was the *Liber Feudorum Maior*, two huge volumes containing complete records for almost all Catalan fortresses held by the crown. This notarial and judicial accomplishment now clearly equated the control and careful maintenance of such official records with the advancement of royal power.[21]

The *LFM* was the first of a number of cartularies used to defend the king's landed status. These examples of legal research were drawn from individual copies of documents which issued orders to officials, summoned armies and parliaments, followed the course of legal suits, and dealt with a myriad of other subjects. These documents were ultimately bound together in registers not according to their subjects but rather by the date on which they were produced. Their chronological order was not always perfect, however, and whole ranges of earlier or later documents sometimes sprang up, often playing havoc with a register's pagination. Each document was normally addressed with the name of the sender and the recipient. Scribes or notaries then folded and sealed the finished letter. The name of the addressee was written on the back side and was used by royal officials, normally the royal "doorman" (*porter*), to complete efficient delivery. The letter also bore the name of the scribe who had written it. The sent missives, however, comprised only half of this process; a copy was inserted into a quire of other messages and when these replicas were finished, they were bound into a register. Royal correspondence steadily increased during the long and eventful reign of Jaume I, the great Aragonese king and reconquest warrior who survived a troubled childhood to become one of Iberia's most powerful sovereigns of thirteenth-century Iberia.[22] The explosion of records production and preservation took place during Aragon's extension of power over the formerly Muslim territories of Majorca and Valencia as well as the rapid expansion of Catalan trade into the Mediterranean. In technical terms, the ready availability of high-grade paper from Muslim outposts such as Jativa (which Jaume I conquered in 1244) provided a perfect medium for the production of documents that proved the equal of parchment at a much lower cost.[23]

With the rapid expansion of his realms, the Conqueror found it prudent to emulate his predecessors' policy of keeping copies of official records. This was previously done in a piecemeal fashion and many of these documents remained unbound, even though their numbers doubled between the reigns of Ramon Berenguer IV and Jaime I.[24] Because of the peripatetic nature of his court, Jaume kept documents of all sorts in castles and monasteries throughout his lands. The Aragonese Hospitaller monastery of Santa María de Sixena served as a depository in which the king kept a "certain chest and box in which there were very many documents and other manuscripts."[25] The King was more than willing to entrust important documents including treaties to the protection of the Hospitallers. Despite the various way stations and the steady stream of documents that followed the king in his seemingly endless travels, Jaume eventually established what he called "our public archive" in his palace at Barcelona as the principal depository for the majority of his records.

Besides funding several permanent locations for the storage of the various types of records the governments of his realms normally produced, a new archival culture emerged as the years of Jaume's long reign passed. Besides using Latin, his notaries wrote in Aragonese, Castilian, Catalan, and Arabic, and did so in such a seamless way that his polyglot lands was served by one linguistic standard that did much to standardize the governments of his several realms. The production of thousands of documents issued by the king and his officials were also standardized in the look, spelling, punctuation and format. They were classified and indexed in such a way that names places, and other subjects could be cross-referenced and effectively made use of in royal litigation.[26]

Besides a growing number of unbound documents held in the king's different depositories, the Barcelona archive held several resettlements documents and new law codes of Majorca and Valencia.[27] The king's greatest accomplishment in archival terms was the selection of documents from his reign and that of his father, Pere II, into thirteen registers which in many ways preserved in one place the most significant governmental work of Aragonese kings and their notaries. According to Jaume's son-in-law, the Castilian king, Alfonso X (r. 1252–1282), the process of registering such documents preserved the remembrance of (granted) ordinances and privileges," especially those which had been damaged or

8   D. J. KAGAY

were illegible in some way.[28] The importance of this process for maintaining issued documents and ultimately providing crucially important historical records was clearly reinforced by their steady increase in the next Aragonese royal reigns.[29]

In the reigns of Pere II (Pedro III) (r. 1276–1285) and his son, Alfons II (Alfonso III) (r. 1285–1291), most of Jaume I's archival reforms continued as did the use of different depositories for official records. The basic archival headquarters remained in the royal palace at Barcelona which now housed rapidly increasing documentary collections of the royal chancery and a large number of unbound royal letters.[30]

With the ascent to the Aragonese throne of Pere II's second son, Jaume II (Jaime II) (r. 1291–1327), in the fall of 1291, the Crown of Aragon's archive became a much more professional institution that now bore the marks of Sicilian notarial practice. Having been the king of Sicily since 1286, the new sovereign adopted many of the administrative practices of Frederick II (r. 1194–1250) and the Angevin rulers that followed him. The depositories of former reigns were no longer as important since most documentary collections were removed to Barcelona where they were stored in the old royal palace or in the former Hostpitaller headquarters in the center of the city which would ultimately be adapted as a new royal palace. The stunning increase of documents and registers led Jaume II to expand the archival space in the old palace by adapting rooms such as one of its chapels that had fallen into a decrepit state. The new area, which the king called the "Royal Archive" (*Archivo Real*) was soon covered with shelves and desks to facilitate the work of royal notaries, scribes, and other officials. This burgeoning manuscript area was thus a kind of government office where regular citizens could only see these official records with royal permission.

Despite the many side and back steps toward a truly centralized archive for the Crown of Aragon, Jaume II' s reign truly marked the full accomplishment of this fact when in 1319 one of the king's financial officials issued a contract for the remodeling of the dilapidated Chapel of Santa Agueda to accommodate more efficiently the "registers, privileges, and other writings of the king's chancellery...[as well as his] jewels of gold and silver, clothes, and documents of his household."[31]

After the reign of Alfons III (Alfonso IV) (r. 1327–1336) which was largely unimportant for the advancement of the Aragonese royal archive, his son, Pere III oversaw the putting in place of the last piece of his realm's central archive. In 1346, the still relatively young king established the first central direction for an institution that was rapidly becoming known as the Arxiu de la Corona d'Aragó (Archivo de la Corona de Aragón) with the appointment of Pere de Passeya as the institution's first archivist. Paid a daily wage along with a yearly salary, the new official was also given funds for incidental expenses, including the production and copying of official documents. The entire archival collection, which would increase steadily with every reign, was now to be cared for as a whole and protected from the deleterious effect of "worms or other feeding insects."[32] Pere's actions in this regard show his concern for the safety and advancement of the remarkable institution the Barcelona archive had already become. The king's wife, Queen Elionor, was also seriously concerned with the future and improvement of the *arxiu*. She had become such a full-fledged administrator in her later life that she arranged to make changes in Barcelona's expanding archival culture, but not in the old royal palace. She rather arranged to use some of her operating funds to have shelves and a desk built within her chambers at the new royal palace built on the site of the Hospitaller' headquarters (*in domo Hospitalis*) in central Barcelona. This desire to have ready access to the many letters and official documents she produced as a royal official also led her to have a similar archive room installed in the house of one of her trusted "adviser and treasurer, Berenguer de Relat."[33]

The entire archival collection which would increase steadily quickly became overcrowded again until new royal archives were established for Valencia in 1419 and Majorca in 1461 and drew whole ranges of documents away from the Barcelona institution. The constant increase of paper documents continued within the original site in the Catalan capital until the old palace became increasingly run-down in the eighteenth century, leading all the official records to be transferred out of the Barrio Gotico to the *Palacio de la Generalitat* (a permanent agency of the Catalan *corts*). The archive remained there until 1836 when it was moved back into the medieval civic center again near the Gothic cathedral in the *Palacio de los Virreys*. Except for some transfers of the archive's collect during the Spanish Civil War (1936–1939), the ACA remained in the palace until 1993 when it was transferred to a newly built, extremely modern-looking site on the Calle de Los Almogaveres.[34]

3   The Queen's Documentary Voice

Over the past seven-hundred years, those familiar with the Barcelona archive such as Heinrich Finke, an important twentieth-century scholar of medieval history, especially that of the Crown of Aragon, declared that the ACA was "one of the most important archives in the world." One of the institution's former directors, Jesus Ernesto Martínez Ferrando, declared confidently that "no country of Europe can boast of a comparable documentary treasure."[35] Elionor of Sicily, who spent most of her married life in Barcelona when the Crown of Aragon's archive reached its first peak of importance, may not have fully agreed with such fulsome praise, but as a contributor to its burgeoning manuscript collection and lines of registers, would never deny its administrative importance. It many ways, it validated her existence, every bit as much as the children she gave birth to and presented to her husband.

It is hardly likely that the queen's childhood and adolescence in Sicily had instructed her, even in a basic way, concerning the intricacies of Sicily's administrative system. She surely knew even less about the accepted ways in which the Crown of Aragon governed and administered its various realms. From the age of twenty-four, however, this determined young woman never abandoned her agreed-upon role as wife and queen by loyally supporting her new husband and any children that might emanate from her marriage with him. This would establish her as the administrator of record for the legal rights to cities, towns, villages, castles, farmland, and even industrial concerns. To manage this complex network of tax-producing entities, Elionor was served by a veritable army of officials, lawyers, messengers, and envoys who often served as commissioners. These men advised, served, and represented the queen and were often viewed by the queen as her faithful servants.

Since Elionor's prime duty to her husband and by extension, to his realms was to provide him with healthy children, preferably of the male gender, she could hardly be blamed for neglecting matters of administration. This, however, Elionor would not do, since control of the sites that supplied her revenue was also a duty and one that could bring her power. In her middle years as queen in 1362, she emerged as a formidable stand-in for her husband who always held her immediate subjects responsible for carrying out their duties to her and the crown. In all such exchanges, she showed herself to be a strict taskmaster. In the military crisis that came to be called by later historians, the War of the Two Pedros (1356–1366),

1 INTRODUCTION   11

however, she could not ignore the suffering of her Christian, Jewish, and Muslim vassals, occasionally waiving their unpaid tax bills and other debts for a time. These clear examples of kindness could only go so far, and were often accompanied with the warning that their full tax bill would eventually have to be paid. Since we barely find the Aragonese queen discussed in either Iberian or Sicilian chronicles, the majority of the evidence for her adult life and work can principally be found in the orders, opinions, directives, and news that appear in each of her twenty-five registers of the Archivo de la Corona de Aragón. Besides their basic reason for being, these official records also tangentially express her anger, gratitude, excitement, disappointment, and sorrow concerning a myriad of subjects.

The earliest of the queen's registers bear the lowest numbers. They are included in her husband's document list in a series entitled "For Queen Elionor, wife of Pere III" (*Pro regina Elionora uxore Petri III*). In the registers numbered 1534 to 1537, the researcher can find a time capsule of the queen's dower rights which generally consisted of tax revenues of various cities, towns, villages, and hamlets located in most of the realms of the Crown of Aragon. These revenues that were due to annually supplied Elionor with operating funds for the maintenance of her household, those of her children, and that of the intended of her second son, Martí, Maria de Luna. With these funds, she also paid the salaries for each of the staff in these households, as well as those of her political and economic advisers.

Besides these urban revenues, the queen could count on annual taxes from Jewish and Muslim communities in her urban holdings as well as emergency grants. She also drew direct taxes from the Balearic Islands of Ibiza and Minorca. Elionor was also granted several salt mines which delivered a fairly constant income. Besides these sums that came to her in a piecemeal fashion throughout each year, she also received an annual stipend promised by the king and often voted by one of his parliaments. The list of such dower rights was never a constant one and could be changed if the king wished it. This normally occurred if the queen agreed to the wishes of her husband to place different communities on the dower list and remove others. She attempted to pawn some of these revenues for a limited time to receive a larger immediate pay-out. These funds that supported the queen began to decline drastically during the long conflict with Castile when Pedro I and his forces conquered many of her Aragonese and Valencian frontiers. In the last years of the war, 1365 and 1366, when Castilian forces began to pull out the regions they had conquered, Pere returned her captured sites along with tax revenues they had not paid her when under Castilian control. Elionor also received control of Valencian towns such as Murviedro (Sagunto) which had long been in Castilian hands. All of these actions by her husband were carried out to compensate the queen for her wartime losses.[36] Though the same type of financial and administrative documents exist in all of Elionor's first registers, the last of them, R. 1537 is unique in that it contains a small announcement of the Queen's death in spring, 1375 penned by one of her notaries as well as her complete last will and testament.[37]

The second archival division of the ACA with a larger selection of the queen's documental holdings is contained in a section of Pere III's archival list entitled "Leonor de Sicilia." This subdivision contains registers numbered 1563–1564 and 1570 which deal with the management of her households and courts, their finances and officials as well as a mixture of other subjects. These register books take the reader from 1349 to 1355 and from 1360 to 1362. Another one of these early volumes numbered 1564 and entitled "Of Court Officials" (*Officialium*) contains administrative documents which range from 1349 to 1368. By far the largest of these divisions which is labeled "Special Matters" (*Speciale*) include registers numbered 1566–1569, 1571 and 1573 all the way to 1585. The volumes of this section include examples of some of the queen's most significant administrative documents and the dates that each of these registers cover ranges of over two full years. Some, however, like R. 1568, R. 1574, and R. 1579 barely cover six months.[38] Though it is difficult to estimate the number of letter copies contained in the queen's registers because of their various sizes, we can hazard a guess at some 200 documents per register which would give a grand total of between 3,000 and 4,000 individual letters written in either Latin or Catalan. Though neither the queen nor her husband personally wrote most of these documents, but rather dictated them to a corps of scribes, this does not mean that either was unable to read or write. On the contrary, both routinely dictated such documents, occasionally perusing and appending short comments to such communiques.[39]

4 The Queen in Modern Works

Though not dealt with in as many secondary books and articles as her contemporary, the colorful queen of Naples, Joanna I (1326–1382),[40] studies of the less picturesque Elionor of Sicily were largely non-existent until the twentieth century and the publication of academic and popular works only saw a steady increase in the last decades of the previous century and into the present one. The undeniable beginning point of Elionor studies is the magisterial article of 1928 of the German scholar, Ulla Deibel.[41] She was a student in 1920 at Freiburg, receiving her training under Heinrich Finke, a famous medievalist and hispanicist who imbued in her a love of the "precious treasures of the Archive of the Crown of Aragon at Barcelona."[42] Her massive article, based on her Freiburg doctoral dissertation published in 1923, begins with a comparatively brief treatment of the queen's German ancestry, her Sicilian upbringing, and her married and family life with her husband and uncle, Pere III. The second part of Deibel's study is a very detailed review of the Aragonese queen's role as royal administrator of the many properties, urban sites, fortresses, and other types of possessions that supplied much of the funds for her upkeep. Deibel also studies the important offices Elionor held during her last decades; namely, that of Catalonia's governor and the king's direct representative or lieutenant. Her role as the head of several households and courts is also discussed in great detail with evidence from both sections of the queen's registers.

Since Elionor's registers reveal more about her life as a royal administrator than her personality or character, Deibel, like every scholar who attempts to see the queen more clearly through these sources, is largely a failure in doing so, despite the vast amount of archival documentation she plowed through in writing her seminal article. Despite this unavoidable failure, the German scholar provides the most detailed description to date of Elionor's royal career.

Despite the lack of truly personal information, the inferences from the primary sources she draws about the queen's character are surely on point. Her portrait of the two sides of Elionor's life—first as an extremely strong-willed *materfamilias* who always wanted, but did not always get her way with he husband and adult children and then as an efficient professional administrator who strongly supported Pere III and his government even when her help was not always asked for or appreciated—has clearly established a historiographical model essential for all subsequent investigators of the queen's life and work.

For a very long time, Deibels work was the only thing written about Pere III's third queen. In 1985, Nuria Muñoz i Soria published a dissertation at the University of Barcelona on Elionor's letters in the last years of her life (1374–1375).[43] Seven years later a team of scholars published

14   D. J. KAGAY

the four account books that trace the queen's spending in regard to the several households she managed for herself and her children.[44]

In the same period, there appeared several studies tangential to the direct study of Elionor, but important for paining a background of her era. In 1992, Mark Johnston wrote an article on political oratory in the medieval Crown of Aragon which discussed in some detail the famous speech Elionor delivered at the *corts* of Barcelona in 1365.[45] In 1995, Clifford Bachman wrote a monograph concerning the reign of Frederick (Federico) III (r. 1299–1337), Jaume II's brother and Elionor's grandfather whose reign marked the beginning of the long decline, during which the queen was attempting to maintain her influence on the island.[46] In 2003, Stephan Epstein, following up on an important article partially focusing on late medieval Sicilian cities that appeared nine years earlier, published a monograph that dealt with the economic and social changes that affected Elionor's homeland during her life as Aragonese queen.[47]

In 2005, two important articles began the outpouring of a great many studies, mostly in Catalan centering on various aspects of Elionor's life. Jaume Riera i Sans published an article that year which dealt with the largely unprecedented coronation of the Aragonese queen on September 5, 1352, three years after her marriage to Pere III. The initial reason for a formal meeting in the Cathedral of San Salvador at Zaragoza was to formally accept his infant son as his successor. Riera i Sans declares that the coronation ceremony was principally engaged in to ensure Joan's legitimate advancement to the throne when the time came. The coronation ceremony was a new one that seemingly advanced the king's power. As far as Elionor was concerned, her coronation may very well have been motivated by Pere's gratitude for her momentous accomplishment of giving him a healthy son.[48]

A volume dealing with the various forms of negotiation in the Middle Ages also appeared in 2005. In it, Manuel Sánchez Martínez published a chapter concerning the stormy *corts* of Barcelona of 1365. Left to face the angry Catalans in this meeting because the king was in the kingdom of Valencia seeking to protect its capital, Elionor supervised a Catalan assembly infuriated at the repeated taxes imposed on the eastern realm for the last two years whose representatives now faced her in the stormy meeting at Barcelona. Sánchez Martínez skillfully works through the complex interaction that ran from July to September 1365 and shows clearly how persistent an arbitrator Queen Elionor could be. Significantly, the author also publishes the crucial speech of September 21, 1365, which broke the back of Catalan opposition.[49]

Three recent works have focused on the office of lieutenant that several Aragonese queens, including Pere III's third wife, held as an important administrative post in which they acted directly for the king in significant missions that demanded his full and unquestioning trust. In the first, a dissertation published in 2014 at the University of Barcelona, Marina Aneas Hontangas discusses the female lieutenant's duties and then provides thumbnail sketches of the lieutenancies of Aragonese queens including Elionor.[50] In the second, a scholarly article published in 2017, Lledó Ruiz Domingo identifies the Aragonese queen as the first of the realm's female lieutenants who acted in place of the king who appointed them and insisted that both officials and other subjects recognized this fact. Any unwillingness to obey the lieutenant's commands could be considered treasonous both to the sovereign and to his mate.[51] In the third, another scholarly article published in 2018, Sebastian Roebert has provided a very complete discussion of the eight occasions between 1358 and 1374 on which Pere III granted his wife powers of the office of lieutenant general.[52]

Within the second decade of the twenty-first century, four articles written to explore certain phases of Elionor's life and career have appeared in Spanish academic journals. In 2015, Montse Aymerich Bassols published a study of the "rich clothing" that was in the Aragonese queen's closets, determining how long she wore such outfits, what they were made of, and who made then. Aymerich Bassols traced this lavish clothing from the expensive bolts of cloth, from which the dresses were made—much of which was bought outside of the queen's realms. She then follows the process the weavers and dressmakers who took the material and designed the gowns to fit the queen's tastes as well as her increasingly corpulent figure. These garments were also rendered suitable for both Catalonia's gloomy winter, the rainy weeks of spring, and the increasingly hot and dusty days of summer. Much simpler clothing was worn at home—which for Elionor meant the old and new palaces in Barcelona. In public, she and her ladies-in-waiting wore brightly colored and intricately decorated gowns that imitated French and Italian fashions. In her last years, the queen wore simpler and ever-larger garments in an attempt to conceal her growing obesity which was largely caused by a worsening inflammation of her kidneys. Because of Aymerich Bassols's careful research, the parade of Elionor's gowns take us unerringly from

16 D. J. KAGAY

the queen's wedding through her pregnancies down to her burial in 1375.[53]

Three other articles, all well-researched, well-organized, and well-written by the same author, Sebastian Roebert, deal with various aspects of Elionor's royal career. In 2014, using the Archivo de la Corona de Aragón, the provincial archive of Teruel, and other published documents, follows quite closely the founding and gradual growth of the Franciscan monastery of Santa Clara in Teruel and ties it carefully to the steady support Queen Elionor provided throughout the 1350 s until the institution was formally founded and its first phase of construction completed in the late 1360 s. This royal support consisted of direct grants and revenue transfers which faithfully continued down to the queen's death in 1375.[54] Roebert goes over much the same ground in a 2017 article which follows the queen's support of monasteries of different orders and varying grades of importance throughout the Crown of Aragon in her last years.[55]

In 2016, Roebert presented a brilliant assessment of the Aragonese queen's first ACA registers 1534 to 1537 generally named: "For Queen Elionor" (*Pro Regina Elionore*). As we have said before, these documents basically focus on the complex dower rights Pere III had granted to his third wife in the first decades of their marriage. The list of towns, villages, and castles supplying a constant flow of funds was itself hardly unchanging as new urban sites and the vassals living in them were added while the original sites and their residents were removed from the responsibility of the queen as their feudal lady. In the last years of her life, Queen Elionor saw this large font of power and money reduced because of the War of the Two Pedros and her husband's need to remove some of these communities from the formal assistance of his wife and then apply them to the aid of his male heirs, Joan and Martí.[56]

NOTES

1. Caroline Walker Bynum, *Jesus as Mother: Studies in the Spirituality of the High Middle Ages* (Berkeley: University of California Press, 1982); Luigi Gambero, *Mary in the Middle Ages: The Blessed Virgin Mary in the Thought of Medieval Latin Theologians* (Milan: Edizioni San Baolo, 2000); Beverly Roberts Gaventa, *Mary: Glimpses of the Mother of God* (Columbia, SC: University of South Carolina Press, 1995); Germain Grisez, "Mary, Mother of Jesus, Sketch of a Theology," *New Blackfriars* 78 (920) (October, 1997): 418–24; Diana Norman, *Siena and the Virgin: Art an*

Politics in a Late Medieval City-State (New Haven, CT: Yale University Press, 1999); Jeroslav Pelikan, et al., *Mary: Images of the Mother of Jesus in Jewish and Christian Perspective* (Minneapolis, MN: Fortress Press, 2005); Miri Rubin, *Emotion and Devotion: The Meaning of Mary in Medieval Religious Cultures* Budapest: CEU Press, 2009).

2. B. Bildhauer, *The Curse of Eve, The Wound of the Hero: Blood Gender and Medieval Literature* (Philadelphia: University of Pennsylvania Press, 2003); John Flood, *Representations of Eve in Antiquity and the English Middle Ages* (New York: Routledge, 2011)

3. See Chapter 2 for further discussion of these remarkable rulers.

4. *Cronache Siciliane inedito delle fine de medioevo*, ed. Francesco Giunta (Palermo: Della Società Siciliana per la storia patria, 1955), 89–92, 105–23, 410–49; Pietro Colletta (Roma: Nella de dell'istituto palazzo Baromini, 2011), 276, 278–82, 285–89 (docs. 14–16, 19, 24, 26–29, 33, 45–55, 60–61).

5. Pere III of Catalonia (Pedro IV of Aragon), *Chronicle*, trans. Mary Hillgarth, introduction, J. N. Hillgarth, 2 vols. (Toronto: Pontifical Institute of Mediaeval Studies, 1980), 1:61–65. For Pere III's composition of the work, see Jaume Aurell, *Authoring the Past: History, Aurobiography, and Politics in Medieval Catalonia* (Chicago: University of Chicago Press, 2012), 94–98; Ramon Gubern i Domench, "Notas sobre la reducció de la Cronica de Pere el Cerimoniós," *Estudis Romanics* 2 (1949–50): 135–43; L. J. Andrew Villalon and Donald J. Kagay, *To Win and Lose a Medieval Battle: Nájera (April 2, 1367), a Pyrrhic Victory for the Black Prince* (Leiden: Brill, 2017), 485–87.

6. Pere III, *Chronicle*, 2:449 (IV:63).

7. Ibid., 2:451 (IV:66). Except for his daughter, Elionor, the king neglects to mention the births of his other children—Martí in 1356 and the short-lived Alfons in 1362—and only refers to his second son and daughter when, by medieval standards, they were adults. Ibid., 2:495 (VI:2): 518 (VI:18); 533–34 (VI:30), 578–79 (VI:61), 583 (VI:64), 591, 595, 600 (Appendix:4), 613 (Appendix:10).

8. Ibid., 2:485, 488 (V:37, 39).

9. Ibid., 2:518 (VI:544).

10. Ibid., 2: 578 (VI:61).

11. Ibid., 2:583 (VI:64).

12. Ibid., 2:589-91 (Appendix:2).

13. Ibid., 2:591 (Appendix:2).

14. Carlos López Rodríguez, "Orígenes del Archivo de la Corona de Aragón (En tiempos, Archivo Real de Barcelona," *Hispania* 226 (mayo–augusto, 2007), 413–54, esp. 420. This definition is drawn from the *Diccionario de Autoridades* published by the Real Academia in 1726.

18   D. J. KAGAY

15. Lawrence J. McCrank, "Documenting Reconquest and Reform:: The Growth of Archives in the Medieval Crown of Aragon," *American Archivist* 56 (Spring, 1993), 256-318, esp. 266; Derek W. Lomax, *The Ronquest of Spain* (London: Longmans, 1978), 13, 33, 114; Roger Collins, *The Arab Conquest of Spain, 710–797* (London: Blackwell, 1989), 210–16.

16. Reinhart Pieter Anne Dozy, *Span ish Islam: A History of the Muslims in Spain*, trans. Francis Griffin Stokes (1913; reprint London: Frank Cass, 1972), 492–96; Manuel Rovira i Sola, "Notes documentales sobre alguns effectes de la presa de Barcelona per al-Mansur," *Acta Historica et Arqueológica Medievalia* 1 (1980): 31–45; Federico Udina Martorell, *El archivo condal de Barcelona en los siglos IX-X. Estudio crítico de sus fundos* (Barcelona: Consejo Superior de Investigaciones Cientificas [hereafter CSIC]), 1951, 8–12.

17. Thomas N. Bisson, "The Organized Peace in Southern France and Catalonia, ca. 1140–ca. 1230," *American Historical Review* [hereafter *AHR*], 82 (1977): 290–303, esp. 291; David Wasserstein, *The Rise and Fall of the Party-Kings* (Princeton, NJ: Princeton University Press, 1985), 38–39, 42–43.

18. "Chronica Adefonsi Imperatoris," in *The World of El Cid: Chronicles of the Spanish Reconquest*, trans. Simon Barton and Richard Fletcher (Manchester: Manchester University Press, 2000), 190–91 (Bk 1:64–65); Federico Balaguer, "La Chronica Adefonsi Imperatoris y la elevación de Ramiro al Trono Aragnés," *Estudios de Edad Media de la Corona de Aragón* [hereafter *EEMCA*], 6 (1952–1953): 7–33, esp. 28–29 (doc. 1); Sophie Hirel-Wouts, "Cuando abdicia la reina... Reflexiones sobre el papel pacificador de Petronilla, reina de Aragón y condesa de Barcelona (siglo XIII)," *e-Spania*, 20, http://journals.openedition.org/e-spania. 24344 (accessed February 27, 2017); William Clay Stalls, "Queenship and the Royal Patrimony in Twelfth-Century Iberia: The Example of Petronilla of Aragon," in *Queens, Regents, and Potentates*, ed. Theresa M. Vann (Dallas, TX.: Academia Press, 1993), 49–61. When accepting the Aragonese crown, Ramiro said he did so "not through ambition... nor desire for advancement but not only because of the needs of the people and the tranquillity of the Church."

19. *Liber Feudorum Maior* [hereafter *LFM*], ed. Francisco Miguel Rosell, 2 vols. (Barcelona: CSIC, 1945), 12–13 (doc. 7); McCrank, "Documenting Reconquest and Reform," 279; Joaquim Traggia, "Illustración del reynado de Don Ramiro II," *Memorias del Real Academia de História* 3 (1799): 497–592, esp. 586–89.

20. McCrank, "Documenting Reconquest and Reform," 279.

21. Thomas N. Bisson, *The Crisis of the Twelfth Century: Power, Lordship, and the Origins of European Government* (Princeton, NJ: Princeton University

Press, 2009), 372–73; idem, "Ramon de Caldes (c. 1135–1199: Dean of Barcelona and King's Minister," in *Medieval France and her Pyrenean Neighbors: Studies in Early Institutional History* (London: Hamdledon Press, 1989), 187–98, esp. 188–89; Adam Kosto, "The *Liber Feudorum Maior* of the counts of Barcelona: The Cartulary as an Expression of Power," *Journal of Medieval History* 27 (2001): 1–22; McCrank, "Documenting Reconquest and Reform," 282–90; Anscari M. Mundo, "El pacte de Cazola de 1179 I el "Liber feudorum maior". Notes paleogràfiques i diplmàtiques,"*Jaime I y su época*, 3 vols (Zaragoza: Institución "Fernando el Católico," 1979–1982, Comunicacions 1 y 2: 119–129.

22. For Jaume I's life and works, see *The Book of Deeds of James I of Aragon: A Translation of the Medieval Catalan "Llibre delos Feyts*, trans Damian Smith and Helena Buffery (Aldershot, Hampshire: Ashgate, 2003); Donald J. Kagay, "Jaime I of Aragon: Child and Master of the Spanish Reconquest," *Journal of Medieval Military History* [hereafter *JMMH*] 8 (2010): 69–108; F. Darwin Smith, *The Life and Times of James I the Conqueror, King of Aragon, Valencia, and Majorca, Count of Barcelond and Urgel, Lord of Montpellier* (Oxford, 1894) Ferran Soldevila, *Els primer temps de Jaime I* (Barcelona: Institut de Estudis Catalans, 1968).

23. Robert I. Burns, "The Paper Revolution in Europe: Crusader Valencia's Paper Industry: A Technological and Behavior Breakthrough," *Pacific Historical Review* 50 (1981): 1–30; idem, *Society and Documentation of the Crusader Valenia*, vol 1 of *Diplomatarium of the Crusade Kingdom of Valencia: The Registered Charters of its Conqueror, Jaume I, 1257–1276*, 4 vols. to date (Princeton, NJ: Princeton University Press, 1985 to date), 151–56; Oriols Valls i Subirà, *Paper and Watermarks in Catalonia*, 2 vols. (Amsterdam: Paper Publication Society, 1970; Josep Madurell i Mazrimon, *El paper a les terres caralans: contribuciio a la seva història*, 2 vols. (Barcelona: Fundacio Salvador Vives Casajuana, 1972).

24. Federico Udina Martorell, *Guía hustórica y descriptiva del Archivo de la Corona de Aragón* (Madrid: Ministerio de Cultura, 1986), 173–75.

25. Ibid., 79 Burns *Society*, 19; López Rodríguez, "Orígenes," 426–27, 433.

26. McCrank, "Documenting Reconquest and Reform," 292-93, 297. For notarial developments in Jaume I's lifetime, see Anton M. Aragó Cabañas, "Las escribanías reales catalano-aragonesas de Ramon Berenguer IV á la minoría de Jaume I," *Revista de archivos, bibvliotecas y museos* 80 (1977): 421–44; Josep Trenchs Odena, "Jaime Saccora y la escribaní de Jaume I," in *Jaume I y su època*, 2:607–21.

27. *CDACA*, 11:1–656; *Fori antiqui Valentiae*, 1–4; Chabas, *Genesis*, 17.

28. *Las Siete Partidas*, trans. Samuel Parsons Scott, ed. Robert I. Burns, S. J., 5 vols. (Philadelphia: University of Pennsylvania Press, 2001) 3:762

(Part. III, tit. 19, ley, 8); Burns, *Society*, 48-51; McCrank, "Documenting Reconquest and Reform," 293–95; Udina Martorell, *Guía*, 187.

29. This increase in registered document is obvious: Pere II: 20 registers; Alfons II (Alfonso III) (1285–1291); 22 registers; Jaume II (Jaime II) (1291–1327): 337 registers; Alfons III (Alfonso IV) (1327-1336): 156 registers; Pere III: 1615 registers.

30. Lópex, Rodríguez, "Orígenes," 437; Udina Martorell, *Guía*, 184–86, 221–22.

31. López Rodríguez, "Orígenes," 450.

32. McCrank, "Documenting Reconquest and Reform," 296–97. For Pere III's other intellectual pursuits besides the archive, see: Donald J. Kagay, "The Theory and Practice of War and Government Practis by King Pere III 'the Ceremonious' of Aragon, 1336–87," *Mediterranean Studies* 27, no. 1 (2019): 63–85.

33. ACA, CR, R. 1575, f. 105; R. 1581, f. 158v.

34. Udina Martorell, *Guía*, 83–87.

35. McCrank, "Documenting Reconquest and Reform," 296.

36. These first registers cover most of the queen's life, but in fairly technical fashion. R. 1534 runs from 1348 to 1377. R. 1535 contains documents dated from 1349 to 1368. The range of R. 1539 is from 1349 to 1375. For a full discussion of the queen's income guaranteed from her marriage with Pere III, see Chapter 5.

37. ACA, R. 1537, CR, ff. 139–56.

38. Udina Martorell, *Guía*, 193–94.

39. Salvador Sanpere y Miquel, *Las Damas d'Aragó* (Barcelona: Col. Biblioteca Popular de la Acenç, 1908), 15.

40. Nancy Goldstone, *Joanna: The Notorious Queen of Naples, Jerusalem & Sicily* (New York: Phoenix, 2010), 389–92.

41. Ulla Deibel, "La Reyna, Elionor de Sicilia," *Memorias, Real Academis de Buenas Letras de Barcelona* 10 (1928): 355–452.

42. Deibel, "Reyna Elionor, 353. For Finke see, Udina Martorell, *Guía*, 232–33.

43. Nuria Muñoz i Soria, "Las Cartes de la Reina Elionor de Sicilia" (PhD diss., University of Barcelona, 1985).

44. *Els quatre llibres de la reina Elionor de Sicilia a l'Arxiu de la Cadedral de Barcelona*, ed. Margarida Anglada, M. Àngels Fernandez, ConcepcióPetit Cibirain (Barcelona: Fundació Noguera, 1992).

45. Mark D. Johnston, Parliamentary Oratory in Medieval Aragon," *Rhetorica: A Jounal od the History of Rhetoric*, 10, no. 2 (Spring, 1992): 99–117.

46. Clifford R. Bachman. *The Decline and Fall of Medieval Sicily: Politics, Religion, and Economy in the Reign of Frederick III, 1296–1337* (Cambridge: Cambridge University Press, 1995).

47. Stephan R. Epstein, "Cities, Regions, and the late Medieval Crisis: Sicily and Tuscany Compared," *Past and Present* 130 (February, 1991): 50; idem, *An Island for Itself: Economic Development and Social Change in Late-Medieval Sicily* (Cambridge: Cambridge University Press, 2003).
48. Jaume Riera i Sans, "La Coronació de la Reina Elionor (1352)." *Acta historica et archaeologica mediaevalia* [Homenatge a la profesora Dra Carmen Batlle Girart] 26 (2005): 485–92). Concerning Pere III's theories and plans of self-coronation, see Jaume Aurell, "Strategies of Royal Self-fashioning: Iberian King's Self-coronations," in *Self-fashioning and Assumptions of Identity in Medieval and Early Modern Iberia*, ed. Laura Delbrugge (Leiden: Brill, 2016), 18–45, esp. 28–30.
49. Manuel Sánchez Martínez, "Negociación y fidcalidad en Cataluña a mediados de siglo XIV: Los Cortes de Barcelona de 1356." in *Necociar en la Edad Media/Négocier en la Moyen Âge. Actas de Colquio celedrada en Barcelona las dias 14, 15, 16 de Octubre de 2004*, ed. María Teresa Ferrer i Mallol, Jean-Maríe Moeglin; Stéphane Pequinot, and Manuel Sánchez Martínez (Barcelona: CSIC: Institución Milá y Fontanals, Depto de Estudios Medievales; Casa de Velásquez (Madrid); Université de Paris XII (Val de Marne, 2005), 123–64.
50. Marina Aneas Hontangas, "Les reines lloctinents a Corona d'Aragó" (Ph.D diss., University of Barcelona, July, 2014).
51. Lledó Ruiz Domingo, "'*Del qual tenim loch*,' Leonor de Scilia y el origen de la lugartenencia feminina en la Corona de Aragón," *Medievalismo* 27 (2017): 303–26.
52. Sebastian Roebert, "The Nominations of Elionor of Sicily as Queen-Lieutenant in the Crown of Aragon:Edition and Commentary," *Mediaeval Studies* 80 (2018): 171–229.
53. Montse Aymerich Bassols, "Les riques vestidures de la reina Elionor de Sicilia," *Summa: Revista de Cultures Medievals* 5 (Primavera, 2015): 24–50.
54. Sebastian Roebert, "Leonor de Sicilia y Santa Clara de Teruel: La foundación reginal de un convento de clarisas y su primer desarrollo," *Anuario de Estudios Medievales* [hereafter *AEM*], 44/1 (enero-junio de 2014), 141–78.
55. Sebastian Roebert, "'*Idcirco ad instar illius Zerobabell templum domini rehedifficantis*, La politica monastica de Elionora di Sicilia," *Edad Media. Revista de Historia* 18 (2017): 49–74.
56. Sebastgian Roebert, "'*Que nos tenemus a dicto domino rege pro camera assignata*,' The Development, Administration of the Queenly estate of Elionor of Sicily (1349-1375)," *AEM* 46/1 (enero-junio de 2016): 231–68.

CHAPTER 2

The Many Faces of Medieval Mediterranean Queenship

1 PRINCESSES INTO QUEENS

As one of the thousands of queens who paraded across the behavioral stages of royal life from the early medieval period to the dawn of the modern world, Elionor of Sicily lived a life she was trained for and surely would have expected. She and many of their fellow queens and princesses indeed would have come into a life in which her parents' expectations and those of the new family she had married into often removed most of the pivotal decisions of her existence from her own control and put them in the hands of people she might have barely known. The response to such an awful and seemingly unescapable imprisonment could lead a princess into one of three life paths: (1) the surrender to illness or insanity which in some ways bestowed a kind of agency on the young woman, (2) the taking of the long and often painful path to a stable wifely and maternal existence which promised some stability and at least some level of domestic power, and (3) the finding of a much more independent life within the confines of royal marriage by service in the government of her husband. Elionor's life decisions were a combination of the last two paths, but were by no means unique in the annals of royal life. Indeed, her decisions had much in common with other female rulers of the Middle Ages. To widen this aspect of royal women, I will review the lives and careers of such ruling women across the central Mediterranean and into the Iberian states between the thirteenth and late fourteenth century.

© The Author(s), under exclusive license to Springer Nature Switzerland AG 2021
D. J. Kagay, *Elionor of Sicily, 1325–1375*, The New Middle Ages,
https://doi.org/10.1007/978-3-030-71028-6_2

24   D. J. KAGAY

During this interesting and often terrifying time-span, queens had already gained a crucial difference from their counterparts in the early medieval centuries. Their upbringing had often readied them much better for their role as a partner for their husband in the business of ruling and for their own supervision of one or several households as well as for the overall care of their children. By the period in which Elionor lived, princesses had received some education and quite a few were functionally literate. Unlike earlier European queens, being a wife to a king was not enough. Producing legitimate heirs—especially males—was still essential, but these children had to be reared as members of the noble class, the purity of whose bloodlines was unassailable.[1]

Despite these changes that made the princess's approaching vocation seem a less fearful ordeal, the dangers of travel were never far away from the party of male and female officials and servants, muleteers, and soldiers who were given the terrible responsibility of safely delivering the princess to her new life in another royal court with a husband she had never seen before. A good example of the dangers that such a mission of state importance might encounter were soon apparent on such an official journey of 1348 when Edward III of England (r. 1327–1377) sent his favorite daughter, Joan, to marry Prince Pedro, son of the great Castilian warrior-king. Alfonso XI (r. 1327–1377). The trip across the English Channel and the Bay of Biscay presented few difficulties to the official party until it disembarked at Bordeaux. The port city, like most of France from Paris to the Pyrenees was under the dark cloud of the Black Death. In a very short time after the princess had landed on French soil, she contracted the horrific disease and within a few days died of it, leaving the heart-broken, English king to inform his Castilian counterpart that "destructive death, which seizes young and old alike… has lamentably snatched… our dearest daughter."[2]

Though such disasters seldom affected two royal families engaged in fulfilling marriage alliances, fear and loneliness were often the princess's traveling companions. Sometimes all but paralyzed by the thought of her future mate and mother-in-law who had earned the powerful position of queen mother by becoming pregnant as many times as possible and gracing her husband with healthy children who might live to assume the crown in time, the princess's anxiety might intensify from the initial ignorance of the language of the royal court in which she would spend so much of her adult life. Added to this isolation was the deep lonesomeness that the new bride—often a young girl no more than twelve years old—felt for her parents and siblings.[3]

Even new queens like Elionor, who had no language problems in her new courtly environment, still missed her family, most of whom she would never see for the rest of her life. Despite time and distance, the connection with the household a princess was born into was never broken and often allowed the queen she grew into to serve as a peacemaker and diplomat between her new and old families.[4] A good example of a queen's simultaneous influence on both her father and husband was apparent in 1264 when Violante, the daughter of Jaume I of Aragon and wife of Alfonso X of Castile addressed a crisis that may have turned back the steady advancement of Castilian arms against Spanish Islam which had begun in 1212 at the great Christian victory of Las Navas de Tolosa. After months of a massive uprising among the *mudejar* (Muslim) population of Seville and most of Andalusia which her husband could not contain even with the help of some of his local Muslim allies, Violante sent a number of letters to her father.

These missives grew more frantic as the frightened queen begged her parent for help. As a "good and loyal father," the Aragonese king answered this call from his loving daughter. While this parental impulse shows how strong a queen's appeal to her parent could be, it also demonstrates how nervous a father could be about the reaction of his son-in-law to military help which could be interpreted as unwanted interference.[5]

Beyond such rare involvements as an intermediary between her near and distant kin, the true and tested means of a queen's advancement was the delivery of healthy offspring. Since motherhood normally first came to a royal woman between age thirteen and fifteen, it could then be repeated as many as twelve times until she was in her thirties. Since infant mortality caused by diseases such as measles, scarlet fever, or whopping cough could kill up to twenty percent of infants under two, the great number of pregnancies seemed prudent, especially to a royal dynasty that may not survive without healthy children. As a result of dynastic pressures, royal couples could produce up to ten legitimate descendants. Unfortunately, they might lose two or three little ones in their swaddling stage.[6]

While the education of royal children was normally turned over to trustworthy nobles and clerics who trained princes for the future that would soon be on them and inculcated in their education the basic elements of Christianity. Princesses were trained by their aristocratic ladies-in-waiting in the elements of married life they would soon face. By the fourteenth century, some of the denizens of the royal court were literate and could occasionally write. Perhaps under the distant influence of contemporary scholars, kings and queens were slowly growing to think that the good of the realm demanded that their children have some kind of intellectual training. For princesses, this demanded a mixture of etiquette and at least a modicum of academic training for themselves and their aristocratic companions, all of whom in all likelihood would soon be in a foreign court.[7]

Even before a queen proved herself as a mother, her status was largely secure after she exchanged marriage oaths with her new husband in a public ceremony. When this union was being negotiated, the envoys of the princess's parents arranged for the terms of a dowry payment and her mate set up an endowment of dower rights which would supply his wife with a regular revenue from a string of urban sites, castles, and farmland. While the first of these payments—at least in Elionor's case—were not always easy to collect, the second gave the queen, even after she became a widow, a stable financial foundation on which to rely.[8]

With this strong landed support to depend on, as well as a positive reputation throughout the realm with her success in delivering healthy children, she evolved into the stage of queen mother. Now several public evocations were open to her and these occasionally advanced her reputation and power throughout the realm. As an administrator of her dower lands, the queen had to support her vassals in these holdings, even if such actions could put her on the opposite side of certain issues from the king. She managed her court, largely paying a coterie of officials and servants. When her husband was entangled in war, she could show herself to be an important figure in his realm who might generously use her funds to support the crown in the conflict. Power, which was occasionally undefined, came to a queen when the sovereign grew ill, insane, or was incapacitated in battle. In such cases, she could advance to a greater, albeit temporary, control, which was granted in the name of the king or of her children.[9] As one modern scholar has observed, the medieval queen was a chameleon of sorts, "stable and unstable, a passive body, but at the same time an active one, transmitting life onward."[10]

2 Castilian Queens

While the lives of all European queens of the medieval period contained many of the aspects discussed, the royal women of Spain and the western Mediterranean occasionally devised several different ruling solutions. To review these alterations and adaptations, we will explore some of the royal women of Castile, the Crown of Aragon, Navarre, and Naples.

Castile, the largest of the Iberian kingdoms by the thirteenth century, was also a leader in the theoretical and practical position of queens. Of the great cultural, educational, musical, religious, and legal accomplishments of the royal court of Alfonso X, one of the greatest was the *Siete Partidas* (the Seven Parts), which comprised both a law code and a legal encyclopedia.[11] In Book Two of the work, which focused on the theory and practice of the royal government, the king described the judicial and customary limits within which queens led their lives. He told his subjects, much as he would his sons, that a woman destined to share a realm had to be from a good family, should be nice-looking, have good habits, and possess money. Each of these qualities would assure the stability and success of a royal family. In the king's mind, the institution that grew around the royal court had to be protected from any attacks on its righteous standing. The most serious of these evils sprang from the "great sin and great error" of a queen's adultery. By such an act she betrayed the trust of her husband and committed treason against his entire realm.[12]

Even before Alfonso had laid out this short guide for the care and control of royal wives, a remarkable series of queens had begun their progress through Castile's royal court. From the early-twelfth into the thirteenth century, a good number of Castilian royal marriages turned out as less than successful, either due to lack of offspring or complete incompatibility between the marriage partners. When the great Castilian reconquest ruler, Alfonso VI (r. 1072–1109), also called the "Emperor of Spain," died in 1109, he had only one daughter, Urraca, to succeed to his expanding realm. Though a headstrong young woman, the new Castilian sovereign never seemed fully secure in her new position. Although already a survivor in a marriage which had produced a son, the new Castilian sovereign was forced to bow to her advisers and give into a marriage in 1109 with the remarkable reconquest hero, Alfonso I of Aragon (r. 1104–1134). This was clearly a marriage made anywhere but in heaven. The Aragonese king, who had spent most of his life on a campaign against Spanish Islam, preferred the company of muscular young men and was immediately put off by his overbearing new wife. After a year of mutual hatred, frustration, and unhappiness, the couple was broken apart, ironically not by any distaste for each other, but because of a papal charge in 1110 of their consanguinity, which made their marital union illegal and sinful. Though no longer bound by marital oaths, the two sovereigns could not abandon their hatred, and so continued to hurl troops against each other's territory until Urraca's death in 1126.[13]

In several subsequent Castilian reigns, princesses outnumbered their brothers and often outpaced them in administrative and political acumen. Two daughters of Alfonso VIII (r. 1158–1214), the illustrious victor at Las Navas in 1212, Berenguela and Blanca, were such over-mighty queen mothers who were important political figures in their perspective realms. The first married Alfonso IX of León (r. 1188–1230), a union that produced two sons and two daughters before the papacy declared it to be within prohibited degrees. Berenguela remained a staunch defender of her progeny, especially her son, Fernando III (r. 1217–1250), who continued Castile's military drive against the military and political forces of Islam in southern Spain. The queen also served Castile's political administration as a regent for her younger brother, Enrique I (r. 1214–1217), and as the manager of her vast dower holdings in León and Castile, from which she drew great profits, which she occasionally used to support the military campaign of her son, Fernando. Berenguela's sister, Blanca (Blanche), as the wife of the short-lived, French ruler, Charles VIII (r. 1223–1226), had a strong influence on her son, Louis IX (St. Louis) (1226–1270), one of France's greatest medieval king's.[14]

In the next reign, that of Alfonso X, several queens were very often important political figures, in spite of the actions of the king himself. As we have seen, Alfonso's first wife, Violante, Jaume I's daughter, interceded with her father to aid her husband complete the suppression of a bitter *mudejar* revolt and then conquer Murcia, one of the last independent, Muslim outposts between 1364 and 1366. After this triumph, the king's behavior seemed to change very much for the worse, and this thoroughly altered his relationships with his wife and children. This total alteration of his personality was attributed by contemporaries and modern scholars to an accident in 1269 in which the king was kicked in the head by one of his horses. His behavior toward his family so thoroughly changed that Violante left her husband on several occasions and stood against Alfonso when their son, Sancho IV (r. 1284–1298) rose in rebellion.

After her husband's death in 1282, the queen aided another rebellion, this time launched against Sancho by her younger son, Juan. This move set Violante in total opposition to Sancho's wife, María de Molina, who completely supported her son with the king, Fernando, who eventually became king in his own right in 1294.[15]

Much of the first half of the fourteenth century in Castile was dominated by Alfonso XI and his thoroughly unsettled son, Pedro I "the Cruel" (r. 1350–1366/1369). Finding little love with his father or mother, María of Portugal, the young prince was apparently under considerable danger from the Castilian king's "other woman," Leonor de Guzman, and her brood, led by her oldest son, Count Enrique de Trastámara. With his father's rapid demise from the Black Death in 1350 when Pedro was sixteen, he remained under the control of his mother's Portuguese advisers who eventually arranged for an advantageous marriage for the young man with the French princess, Blanche de Bourbon, the niece of the French king, Philippe VI (r. 1328–1350). Unfortunately for this diplomatically advantageous union, the new king some months before had fallen madly in love with a noblewoman, María de Padilla, who had supposedly bewitched the callow young sovereign to give all his love to her. No matter how this was brought about, María was successful in bringing Pedro under her spell, presenting him with a daughter in a little under a year.

Intimidated by his mother and her advisers, Pedro went through an elaborate wedding with Blanche at Valladolid in spring 1352. Still feeling the pressure of the royal establishment, he returned to the city in the summer to spend a few more days with his wife. Shortly after this Blanche was set up in the town of Arevalo in the province of Avila. At the height of the rebellion of his nobles in 1354–1355, Pedro had his queen moved to various Castilian towns until her death in 1361. Within two years of his meaningless wedding and formal acceptance of his mistress, Pedro fell in love—or at least in lust—with an aristocratic woman named Juana de Castro. Denying that his first nuptials had actually taken place, the king went through a form of marriage with Juana, but then immediately deserted her to return to María de Padilla. The king apparently went through his wedding-night duties, but after two days returned to his mistress. He saw neither of his deserted brides again, but eventually wed his mistress, and in December 1362, had their four children legitimized and his eldest daughter, Constanza, named as his heir and made a royal lieutenant. All these plans were overthrown with the king's death

30   D. J. KAGAY

at Montiel in 1369. In 1371, the Black Prince's brother, John of Gaunt, proposed marriage to Constanza, in hopes of gaining a title and a realm in Spain. Ultimately, nothing came of John's self-seeking venture, and he promptly deserted his gullible wife.[16]

3   NAVARRESE QUEENS

The small, landlocked kingdom of Navarre that stretched on both sides of the Pyrenees was the true origin of Aragon and Castile, the largest realms of the Peninsula which contested for power down to the fifteenth century. Ironically with the growth of these rivals and that of France on the other side of the mountains, the small middle kingdom had little room for expansion. From their kingdom's geographical position, Navarrese princesses were occasionally chosen to marry the crown princes or sovereigns of France, Aragon, or Castile. No Navarrese female rulers emerged until the end of the thirteenth century, and yet the realm passed no laws to prevent such an eventuality. As a matter of fact, several male contenders for the throne made their claims through their mothers.

In truth, the sex of the ruler was not as important as the stability of the dynasty itself. This practical proviso came into play when Enrique I of Navarre (r. 1270–1274) died leaving only a young princess, Juana I (r. 1274–1304) to succeed him. Fearful that her country might be swallowed whole by her ravenous, Iberian neighbors, the new queen presented her case to her French relative, Philippe III (r. 1270–1285), who solved Juana's quandary much to the benefit of his own realm by arranging for a marital union between her and his own son, soon to be Philippe IV (r. 1282–1314). This solution effectively removed Navarre's independence, making it little more than a French province, even though Juana retained her title as its sovereign. With the demise of the royal couple by 1314, Philippe's brothers successively held both realms until 1328, despite the survival of a princess, born from Juana's marriage to Philippe. With the death of the last of the royal brothers, Princess Juana II was finally accepted as Navarre's new ruler. With her husband, Philippe d'Evreux, she subdivided ruling responsibilities in Navarre. The couple left a male successor in 1343, but set an important precedent of female rulership for Navarre, whether the queen came under the ultimate control of her consort who ruled as king in his own land and in the Pyrenean realm, reigned as a partner with her husband who held no crown, or held complete power in her own realm, even if she was married. Each of these regnal solutions was employed in Navarre down into the fifteenth century.[17]

4   A REMARKABLE NEOPOLITAN QUEEN

One of the most famous—some would say infamous—rulers of the fourteenth century was Joanna I of Naples, a descendent of Charles I of Anjou (r. 1266–1285) who won southern Italy (the *Regno*) and Sicily and held it uncontested until the uprising of the Sicilian Vespers (1282), which unleashed over a decade of war between the Angevins and the rebels' supporter, Aragon, eventually splitting southern Italy from Sicily. The great-grandson of Charles of Anjou, Robert the Wise, who ruled Naples from 1309 to 1343, oversaw a court celebrated for its intelligence, culture, and dedication to a muscular Christianity, closely associated with the Spiritual Franciscans that had great influence in southern Italy and the western Mediterranean for over a century. Robert's second wife, Sancia of Mallorca, continued this support of the Spiritual Franciscans in Naples by engaging in several building projects, most especially the monastery church of Santa Chiara. With the death of Joanna's father, the duke of Calabria in 1328, Robert, considering the dangers besetting his Neopolitan realm, had no choice but to appoint his two-year-old granddaughter as his successor.

Shortly before her grandfather's death in 1343, the seventeen-year-old Joanna was proclaimed queen and shortly afterwards took a husband of the same age, Prince Andrew of Hungary. She quickly encountered problems with the prince's overbearing mother who insisted that her son be given a royal title equal to that of his wife. Joanna refused to comply with what she saw as a lessening of her sovereignty. This ran contrary to the demands of Pope Clement VI (r. 1342–1357) who claimed that Joanna's husband had to be given titles that equated his power with hers. Even when the queen was undergoing the throes of her first pregnancy in 1345, Andrew's request for increased political status had not yet been agreed to by his wife when on September 18 the royal couple was on a vacation at the crown's summer palace at Aversa, north of Naples. After Joanna had gone to bed early on that evening, Andrew was still awake in his bedroom when he was summoned outside to meet a royal courtier. When he entered the garden outside his quarters, he confronted a group of heavily-armed men who beat him to his knees and then strangled him.

32   D. J. KAGAY

Joanna insisted that she was innocent of any involvement with the heinous act, and yet within a few months she was actively occupied in seeking a new mate, the blond-haired and muscular Louis of Taranto, who lived with the queen for some four years until this union was formally approved by the papacy. With Louis's death ten years later and that of their two young daughters, the queen was still in the market for a husband, but hoped this time to find one that was not related to her within prohibited degrees as proclaimed by the papacy.

This was hardly to be the case since her third husband, Jaume IV of Mallorca, the son of Jaume III (r. 1324–1349), the ruler of the island kingdom and a good deal of territory in southern France, was the queen's cousin. His son was a tragic figure who had attempted to help his father win back his realm from another relative, Pere III of Aragon, who had toppled Jaume's hold on power in 1341, and resisted his attempts to regain his throne for the next eight years. Jaume IV, who maintained the title to his father realms, but never controlled them, was active in opposing the Aragonese king until 1349 when he served with his father in a campaign against the Balearic Islands which cost Jaume III his life and saw his son imprisoned in a cage for some fourteen years. Even after the prince escaped in 1362, he was afflicted with what today would be called Post-Traumatic Stress Disorder. Joanna had met Jaume when he was a twelve-year-old in 1348 and came upon him again shortly after he had regained his freedom. Joanna's third marriage took place in Naples in the spring of 1363. As with her other two marriages, the queen found the third even more impossible to maintain due to the prince's many dangerous outbursts and nightmares that sprang from a life dedicated to warfare and exacerbated by years of cruel imprisonment. Joanna was freed from this ordeal when the prince left her and their son for a series of military adventures that led to his death in 1375.

When Joanna took a fourth husband, Otto of Brunswick, in the next year, she gained a military insurance policy, but one she did not have to struggle with to maintain her throne. By the time of this last venture into matrimony, the queen was caught up in the opening intricacies of the Great Western Schism, which in some ways led to her demise in July 1382 when she was assassinated by Hungarian soldiers, probably paid by Andrew's relatives to avenge his death thirty-seven years previously. As an independent female ruler, the colorful queen of Naples greatly expanded her control in Southern Italy and Sicily. Most of these advances, however, did not survive her death. Though her realm was marked by both shameful and titillating sexual and political intrigues, she was often admired for her dogged defense of her ruling position. Joanna undeniably deserved Boccaccio's praise, which characterized her as a woman who governed a "mighty realm" and was renowned more than any other for her, "lineage, power, and character."[18]

5 QUEENS OF THE CROWN OF ARAGON

We have already met Petronilla in the first chapter, but only as a two-year infant who in 1136 was married to Count Ramon Berenguer IV, a ceremony that formalized the union of Aragon and Catalonia.[19] The elements of this agreement worked out between the Catalan count and Petronilla's father, Ramiro "the Monk," specified that Ramon Berenguer could not claim Aragon's royal title, but was called instead the "prince of Aragon," leaving the kingship for Petronilla to claim when she came of age. Until that time, the count and his Catalan government would administer Aragon, which formally owed Ramon Berenguer "feudal allegiance" (*fidelitas*).

This is how matters stood until the Barcelona ruler formally married the fifteen-year-old Aragonese queen in 1150. According to the binding agreement of 1136, Petronilla had full royal rights in Aragon and could use them in any she saw fit. How this power was to be utilized would remain unclear until April 4, 1152, when "lying and laboring in pregnancy at Barcelona" she dictated her wishes for her realm. In this first of two documents that functioned as wills, the queen proclaimed that if her baby was a boy, he would be the future, Aragonese king. If the infant proved to be a girl, her husband would see that she was honorably married. In this second eventuality, the Barcelona count would inherit full control of Aragon.

Petronilla's baby was a boy who was at first named Ramiro after his grandfather. With the death of her husband in 1162, the queen acted as a guardian for her son, eventually renaming him Alfonso after his Aragonese uncle, Alfonso I "the Battler." A year later, she resigned the crown to her ten-year-old boy, Alfons I (Alfonso II) (r. 1163–1196), but from the time she came of age until she stepped down, Petronilla may have been Aragon's only queen regnant. Because of the lack of surviving documentation, however, we know almost nothing about her ruling career or how it was understood.[20]

This complicated solution was by no means new in either Aragon or Catalonia. In the tenth-century county of Aragon, title to territory could be left to a noble family's sole surviving daughter, but she had no right to full "control" (*potestas*) which she held for her son. In contemporary Catalan law, especially the *Usatges of Barcelona*, *potestas* referred to the power to rule as well as the "public person" who did the ruling, a role specifically set aside for males. The twelfth-century agreement that built the Crown of Aragon allowed Petronilla to give her realm to a son but not a daughter. If the queen had no children or her offspring had died, Aragon would pass to the count of Barcelona and then to his son or nearest male relative. While female rulers did exist in some of the Catalan counties, such lordship was strictly forbidden by Jaume I and his grandson, Jaume II (r. 1291–1327). With the death of Martí I (r. 1395–1410) without a male heir, an official ruling, the *Campromis de Caspe* declared that, though Pere III's two sons had died and had no living male successors, his daughter Elionor, like Petronilla had the evident right to transfer royal control of the Crown of Aragon to her second son, Ferran I (Fernando II) (r. 1412–1416).[21]

As the Crown of Aragon proceeded into the second and third century of its existence, the twelfth-century blueprint for the unification of Catalonia and Aragon functioned extremely well, even expanding to include the new realms of Majorca, Valencia, and even new Mediterranean outposts such as Sicily and Athens. At the core of this vast expanse of territory were the itinerant courts and households in which royal business was conducted and the king, queen, their children, and officials were housed and fed. The formation of these royal families began with the king's choice of a suitable mate who was selected because of her beauty and her apparent readiness for the marriage, which was judged by her health, intelligence, and gentleness. Once the marriage ceremony had taken place, the ultimate test of the union was measured by how compatible the marriage partners were and how well they worked together.

Love was seldom considered overly important for the royal man and wife, but occasionally and quite surprisingly sprang from mutual respect in carrying out duties important for their growing family. The education and training of their children were some of the most important duties of Aragonese monarchs. These parenting obligations were clearly unequal between husbands and wives. Kings often only saw their offsprings on holidays such as Christmas and Easter. As their children grew toward adulthood which in the Middle Ages came in their early teens, they were gradually taken in hand by their parents with the princesses being readied for married life by their mothers and the princes receiving training in administrative and military life by their father and his officials. One thing these royal parents could not always do was to protect their children from the dangers often inherent in the lives in which the royal court engaged.[22]

In the reigns of the Aragonese king from the twelfth to the fourteenth century, sovereigns chose their consorts from a great number of regions, including Castile, Cyprus, France, Hungary, Navarre, Portugal, and Urgel. For the sake of this volume, an understanding of the relationships between Sicilian and Iberian royal courts is essential. The first of these connections that paired Iberian queens with Sicilian great nobles and kings began in earnest in the twelfth century. In 1117, while still a count, Roger II of Sicily (r. 1095–1154), married Elvira, the daughter of Alfonso VI of Castile, who remained with him after he had become king of Sicily on Christmas Day, 1130. She gave him three sons, but in 1135 died from a disease she likely contracted from her husband. Roger was so stricken by this loss that he shut up himself in his rooms for many days, refusing to see anyone except for a few servants. This "bitter grief" suggested a love between king and queen unusual in Sicilian royal annals.[23]

Near mid-century, another Spanish princess, Margaret, daughter of the Navarrese King García Ramírez (r. 1112–1150), married Roger's son, William I (r. 1154–1166). With her husband's death, the queen attempted to clean up the widespread corruption that had come to dominate the Sicilian court when she assumed the post of regent for her son, William. In this post, she maintained control over the royal government and all of Sicily. For the five years after her husband's death, Margaret proved to be a remarkable royal administrator who "conquered discontent through conciliation" while inculcating loyalty and love for her son.[24]

Aragonese and Sicilian royal marriages continued into the thirteenth century, when the young Sicilian king, who was soon to be the Holy Roman Emperor, Frederick II, arranged marriage with Pere I's daughter, Constanza, granting her great tracts of land around Palermo as her dower settlement. The bride-to-be was accompanied by a large retinue of Catalan and Southern French nobles. When three years later, Frederick left Constanza and her young son in Sicily while he crossed into Italy and went to Rome in search of supporters for his drive to attain the often-empty honor associated with the Holy Roman Empire. For the next four years, the queen, like Margaret in the previous century, functioned very much as a Sicilian ruler by carrying out the post of regent for her son. She clearly recognized, however, that she could not push her power too far, and so tried to keep her over-mighty subjects happy by granting them favors and territory across the island. Since Constanza was ten years older than Frederick and had been married before, her canny advise proved so invaluable to her husband that her sudden death affected him much as the rapid demise of Roger II's Iberian queen did.[25]

The most important of the Sicilian-Aragonese marriages of the thirteenth century was undoubtedly that of Pere II and another Constanza, the daughter of Manfred, the illegitimate son of Frederick II, who served as the last Hohenstaufen king of Sicily (r. 1258–1266). Manfred who died at the battle of Benevento (February 26, 1266), and was buried on the battlefield. Manfred's enemy, Charles I of Anjou, was to be Pere's foe for the rest of their lives. As a defender of his wife, the court of the young, Aragonese prince in Barcelona was to become a hotbed of Sicilian enemies of the new Angevin sovereign of Sicily, viewing Charles as a cruel interloper. This dangerous foreign policy direction was not opposed by Pere's father, Jaume I, who increasingly considered Sicily as an important target for his realm's military involvement in the Mediterranean.[26]

With the uprising of the Sicilian Vespers in the spring of 1282, Pere, who had been Aragonese king since Jaume I's death some six years before, brought a large fleet to Sicily in the early fall of the same year. When offered the Sicilian throne, he accepted but insisted that this honor should rightfully have been bestowed upon his wife, the granddaughter of Frederick the Great. In her first years as an Aragonese princess and queen, Constanza had repeatedly fulfilled her primal duty to Pere by giving him six children, three of whom would be kings. She also thoroughly remade the no-frills court of her husband into a glittering new institution famous for its luxury, culture, and improved administration that pointed back directly to the sparkling courtly world of her father, Manfred.[27]

While Pere II was accepted in 1282 as Sicily's monarch by the island's parliament, his wife's inheritance rights were not mentioned at this ceremony. From her position as Aragonese queen, she was eventually given the post of regent in Sicily along with her second son, Prince Jaume, when her husband decided to return to Spain to take charge once more of his Iberian realms. Like earlier Iberian queens, Constanza expanded a largely familial position into expansive control of her island homeland from 1283 to 1285 when Pere II died and was replaced in the Crown of Aragon by the crown prince, Alfons II (Alfonso III) (r. 1285–1291), and in Sicily by Jaume II (Jaime II) who ruled the island from 1285 to 1291. During the two-year period of her Sicilian rule, Queen Constanza appears to have been a careful manager of day-to-day administrative matters, and one who handled military emergencies effectively and without fear or indecision. As her first two sons stepped into the rule as Aragon and Sicily, the queen resigned from government service, leading a quiet life until her death in 1302.[28]

Most of the Iberian and Mediterranean queens discussed in this section were trained by their mothers as well as their tutors, ladies-in-waiting, and even the officials and servants assigned to them. This is largely true of Elionor of Sicily, whose immediate story we will now take up. She received much of this court training to ready her not for life in the bosom of her own family, but in the foreign environment in which she would live her adult life. The first part of this existence centered on her life as a wife and mother. This period was dominated by the birth of her children which occurred on an average of every 2½ years. After her children began to grow, they lived in their own households and saw their mother much less than during their first years. The queen, however, had control over their lives along with their courts until they came of age. By administering this myriad of household details and simultaneously caring for the more complex management of her dower lands, Elionor quickly showed herself to be a first-class administrator who soon won the respect and admiration of her husband and the many officials who served her. These two lives make Elionor a remarkable figure whose story we will endeavor to tell.

NOTES

1. Helen Castor, "Exception to the Rule," *History Today* 60, no. 10 (October, 2010): 37–43, esp. 38; Lois Honeycutt, "Medieval Queenship," 39, no. 6 (June, 1989): 16–22, esp. 20; Janet. L. Nelson, "Medieval Queenship," in *Women in Medieval Western European Culture*, ed. Linda E. Mitchell (New York: Garland Publishing, Inc., 1999), 179–207, esp. 204–5.
2. *The Black Death*, ed. and trans. Rosemary Horrox. (Manchester: Manchester University Press, 1994), 250 (doc. 77). Philip Ziegler, *The Black Death* (New York: Harper & Row, Publishers, 1969), 80, 113–14. For extent of the plague in France when the princess landed at Bordeaux, see John Aberth, *From the Brink of the Apocalypse: Confronting Famine, War, and Death in the Later Middle Ages* (New York: Routledge, 2001), map,

xiii. Ironically Joan's future father-in-law died about a year after she did of the same cause.

3. Nelson, "Medieval Queenship," 187–88, 204, John Carmi Parsons, "Mothers, Daughters, Marriage, Power: Some Plantagenet Evidence, 1150–1500," in *Medieval Queenship*, ed. John Carmi Parsons (New York: St. Martin's Press, 1998), 63–78, esp. 63; Ana Maria Seabra de Almeida Rodrigues, "Between Husband and Father: Queen Isabel of Lancaster's Crossed Loyalties," *Imago Temporis. Medium Aevum* 3 (2009): 205–18, esp. 206.

4. Parsons, "Mothers," 69, 71–72.

5. *BD*, 284–85, 287 (chaps. 379, 382); Joseph F. O'Callaghan, *The Learned King: The Reigh of Alfonso X of Castile* (Philadelphia: University of Pennsylvania Press, 1993), 185. Jaume seemed in quandary about how he should answer Violante's call for help. First of all, he did not want to abandon his daughter and grandchildren, and yet he knew how much his son-in-law resented his great military reputation and was afraid to ask him for help. If he did not come to Castile's aid, Alfonso would now be his open enemy and this would lead to trouble in the future.

6. Robert Fossier, *The Axe and the Oath: Ordinary Live in the Middle Ages*, trans. Lydia G. Cochrane (Princeton: Princeton University Press, 2007), 46–47; Nelson, "Medieval Queenship," 193–4. Since Elionor was not married until her twenty-fourth birthday, her pregnancies were limited and were not as regular as younger queens. Infant mortality touched the queen when her youngest son, Alfonso, died in 1362.

7. Parsons, "Medieval Queenship," 75. For the better intellectual training of royal children, see Lester Kruger Born, "The Perfect Prince: A Study in Thirteenth- and Fourteenth-Century Ideals," *Speculum* 3, no. 4 (October, 1928): 470–504, esp. 472–74, 492.

8. Anne Crawford, "The Queen Council in the Middle Ages," *English Historical Review*, [hereafter *EHR*], 116, no. 469 (Nov., 2001): 1193–1211, esp. 1193–94; Nelson, "Medieval Queenship," 184–91.

9. Lois Huneycutt, "Female Succession and the Language of Power in the Writings of Twelfth-Century Churchmen," in *Medieval Queenship*, 189–201, esp. 199; Nelson, "Medieval Queenship," 179–80, 182, 205; George Anthony, Thomas, "The Queen's Two Bodies: Sor Juana and New Spain's Vicereines," *Hispania*, 92, no. 3 (September, 2009): 417–29, esp. 419.

10. Nelson, "Medieval Queenship," 206.

11. Robert I. Burns, S.J., "*Stupor Mundi*," Alfonso X the Learned," in *Emperor of Culture: Alfonso X the Learned of Castile and his Thirteenth-Century Renaissance*, ed. Robert I. Burns, S.J. (Philadelphia: University of Pennsylvania Press, 1990), 1–13; Robert I MacDonald, "Law and Politics: Alfonso's Program of Political Reform," in *The World of Alfonso the Learned and James the Conqueror: Intellect and Force in the Middle Ages*,

ed. Robert I. Burns, S.J. (Princeton, NJ: Princeton University Press), 150–99, esp. 180–88. "The Many Roles of Medieval Queens: Some Examples from Castile," in *Queenship and Political Power*, 21–32.

12. *Siete Partidas*, ed. Burns, 2: 298–99 (Part. II, tit. vi., l. i, ii); Joseph F. O'Callaghan, "The Many Roles of Medieval Queens: Some examples from Castile," in *Queenship and Political Power in Medieval and Early Modern Spain*, ed. Theresa Earenfight (Aldershot, Hampshire: Ashgate, 2005), 21–32, esp. 21–24.

13. Therese Martin, "The Art of a Reigning Queen as Dynastic Propaganda in Twelfth-Century Spain," *Speculum* 80 (2005): 1134–71; Joseph F. O'Callaghan, *A History of Medieval Spain* (Ithaca, NY: Cornell University Press, 1975), 216–19.

14. O'Callaghan, "Many Roles," 29; Régine Pernoud, *Blanche of Castile*, trans. H. Noel (New York: Putnam, 1975); Miriam Shadis, *Berenguela of Castile (1180–1246) and Political Women in the High Middle Ages* (New York: Palgrave Macmillan, 2009), 81, 86–88); Theresa M. Vann, "The Theory and Practice of Medieval Castilian Queenship," in *Queen, Regents, and Potentates*, 125–47, esp. 137–38.

15. Mercedes Gaibrois del Ballesteros and Ana del Campo Gutiérrez, *María de Molina* (Pamplona: Urgoiti DL, 2011); Richard Kinkade, "Alfonso X, *Cantiga* 235 and the events of 1269-1278," *Speculum* 67 (1992): 284–323, esp. 290; idem, "Violante of Aragon (1236–1300): An Historical Overview," *Exemplaria Hispanica* 2 (1992–1993): 1–37; O'Callaghan, *Learned King*, 279–80.

16. Clara Estow, *Pedro the Cruel of Castile, 1350–1369* (Leiden: E.J. Brill, 1995), 131–34, 140–44, 149–50, 153, 210–12; Cristina Segura Graiño, "Las mujeres de la sucesión á la corona de Castilla en la Baja Edad Media," *Estudios de Edad Media* [hereafter *EEM*], 12 (1989): 205–14, esp. 207–8; María Tausiet, *Urban Magic in Early Modern Spain: Abracadabra Omnipotens*, trans. Susannah Howe (New York: Palgrave Macmillan, 2014), 87.

17. William Monter, *The Rise of Female Kings in Europe, 1300–1800* (New Haven, CT: Yale University Press, 2012), 56–62; Elena Woodacre, "Ruling and Relationships: The Fundamental Basis of the Exercise of Power? The Impact of Marital and Familial Relationships on the Reigns of the Queen's Regnant of Navarre (1274–1517)," *AEM* 46/1 (enero-junio de2016), 167–201, esp. 170–72, 175, 179–80, 195–96; idem, "The She Wolves of Navarre" (June, 2012) *History Today*, 48–51.

18. Caroline Bruzelius, "Queen Sancia of Majorca and the Convent Church of Sta. Chiara in Naples," *Memoirs of the American Academy of Rome* 40 (1995): 69–100; Goldstone, *Joanna*, 21–39, 133–34, 149–51, 204–16, 269–78, 303–4, 374–75, 379–80; Monter, *Rise of Female Kings*, 61–67.

19. See Chapter 1, p. 8.

20. Hirel Wouts, "Cuando abdicia," 2–3, 8–19; Stalls, "Queenship," 52–53, 60; Theresa Martin, "Fuentes de Potesdad para reinas e infantes. El infantazgo en los siglos centrales de la Edad Media," *AEM* 46/1 (enero-junio de, 2016): 97–136, esp. 121–22; José Ángel Sesma Muñoz, *La corona de Aragón. Una introcucción crítica* (Zaragoza: Caja de Ahorros de la Inmaculada de Aragón, 2000), 37–40.
21. Cristina Segura Graiño, "Derechos sucesorios al trono de las mujeres en la corona de Aragon," *Mayurga*, 22, no. 2 (1989): 591–99; *The Usatges of Barcelona: the Fundamental Law of Catalonia*, trans. Donald J. Kagay (Philadelphia: University of Pennsylvania Press, 1994), 34–38; Eulalia Rodon Binue, *El lenguaje técnico def Feudlism en el siglo XI en Cataluña: Contribución al este de latin medieval* (Barcelona: CSIC, 1957), 200–1; August 30, 2020.
22. Roger Sablonier, "The Aragonese Royal Family Around 1300," in *Interest and Emotion: Essays on the Study of Family and Kinship*, ed. Hans Medick and David Warrean (Cambridge: Cambridge University Press, 1984), 210–39, esp. 210–21.
23. Hubert Heuben, *Roger II of Sicily: A Ruler Between East and West*, trans. Graham A. Loud and Diane Milburn (Cambridge: Cambridge University Press, 2002), 64–65; Paul Oldfield, "The Imprint on Medieval Southern Italy," *History* 3, no. 3 (July, 2008): 312–27, esp. 316.
24. Heuben, "Roger II," 172–73; Olfield, "Iberian Imprint," 317–18.
25. David Abulafia, *Frederick II: A Medieval Emperor* (London: Allen Lane and The Penguin Press, 1988), 106; Oldfield, "Iberian Imprint," 321–22.
26. Steven Runciman, *The Sicilian Vespers: A History of the Mediterranean World in the Later Thirteenth Century* (London: Penguin Books, 1961), 222–35; Marta Van Landingham, "The Hohenstaufen Heritage of Costanza of Sicily and the Mediterranean Expansion of the Crown of Aragon in the Later Thirteenth Century," in *Across the Mediterranean Frontiers, Trade, Politics, and Religion,* ed. Dionisius A. Agius and Ian Richard Netton (Turnhout: Brepols, 1997), 87–104, esp. 89–92.
27. E.L. Miron, *The Queens of Aragon: Their Lives and Times* (London: Stanley Paul and Company, 1914), 114–15; Van Landingham, "Hohenstaufen Heritage," 92, 95–96; idem, *Transforming the State: King, Court, and Political Culture in the Realms of Aragon (1213–1287)* (Leiden: Brill, 2002), 190–93.
28. Van Landingham, "Hohenstaufen Heritage," 97–104.

CHAPTER 3

Two Realms and a Marriage

The state wedding of the thirty-year-old king of Aragon, Pere III, and his niece, twenty-four-year-old Sicilian princess, Elionor, in August, 1349 brought together two strong-minded and intelligent people who formed an effective yet complex personal and political relationship from a normal royal wedding, which would normally presage only a possibility of children and the hope of improved relations between kingdoms. The bride and groom represented. As we have seen, such nuptials often bound both people and regions with the very success of a united Christian army composed of Castilian, Aragonese, Navarrese, and French troops against a huge, Almohad army at Las Navas de Tolosa on July 16, 1212, the facade of Muslim power began to collapse both on the Iberian Peninsula and across the Mediterranean waters that surrounded it. Talented warrior kings from the major Christian states, such as Jaume I of Aragon and Fernando III of Castile (r. 1212–1250), rapidly established their control over at least two-thirds of Spain.[1]

While many royal couples had limited connections before the marriage this was hardly the case with Pere and Elionor since the Crown of Aragon, Sicily, and the central Mediterranean had a long mutual history even before Catalonia and Aragon were themselves bound together.

© The Author(s), under exclusive license to Springer Nature   41
Switzerland AG 2021
D. J. Kagay, *Elionor of Sicily, 1325–1375*, The New Middle Ages,
https://doi.org/10.1007/978-3-030-71028-6_3

1 Eastern Spain and the Mediterranean

For most of its early life as county and kingdom, Aragon, like Castile, launched military campaigns against the forces of the Caliphate of Córdoba and the *taifa*s that succeeded it. As a maritime state, Catalonia repeatedly sent its mariners and merchants across the Mediterranean in search of lucrative trade across the central Mediterranean into Italy but used the same type of ships to advance its military goals. During much of the early twelfth century, both Catalan counts and Muslim raiders attacked the Umayyad outpost of Balearic Islands. In 1114–1115, Count Ramon Berenguer III of Barcelona (r. 1097–1131) led a large army transported in ships rented from Pisa to attack Ibiza and Majorca, some of the chain's largest and wealthiest islands. Shortly before this Christian invasion, the Muslim governor had died, ostensibly leaving the island leaderless. The Christians were beaten off by Majorca's Muslim garrison, forcing the count to return to Barcelona, only to find his principal city under attack.[2]

This first intrusion of Catalan raiders into the Muslim lake that the western Mediterranean he long been was in the late twelfth century but could not be repeated for over a hundred years. With the stunning success of a united Christian army composed of Castilian, Aragonese, Navarrese, and French troops against a huge, Almohad army at Las Navas de Tolosa on July 16, 1212, the facade of Muslim power began to collapse both on the Iberian Peninsula and across the Mediterranean waters that surrounded it. Talented warrior kings from the major Christian states, such as Jaume I of Aragon and Fernando III of Castile (r. 1212–1250), rapidly established their control over at least two-thirds of Spain.[3]

After a troubled childhood caused by the death of his father, Pere I (Pedro II) (r. 1196–1213) at the battle of Muret in 1213, Jaume I did more than survive in a realm full of enemies until in 1228, he, as a strapping young man, was presented the tempting proposal of attacking Majorca. Fascinated by the plan and encouraged by the various estates of Catalonia's national assembly, the *corts*, the king led a massive expedition against the Muslim island stronghold in 1229, winning the major island, Majorca, after three years of hard fighting. Though the Majorca venture had attracted a large number of colonists from the Iberian mainland, the isolation and hard work island life entailed caused a steady decline in Majorca's population and eventually lead the Barcelona dynasty to release its only Mediterranean possession to a cadet house. Only in the 1340s

3 TWO REALMS AND A MARRIAGE   43

would Pere III reclaim Majorca from his cousin Jaume II "the Rash" (r. 1243–1311) who had long ruled the Balearics and part of southern France. With its slow advance toward prosperity, Majorca pointed the way for an era of Aragon's extended, Mediterranean conquest.[4]

As Castile was inexorably moving across Andalucia toward Granada, and Aragon was consuming great swaths of Valencian and Murcian territory, Catalonia won repeated Mediterranean conquests, but with a difference. Unlike other Peninsular campaigns, which required a great number of men with requisite provisions and equipment,[5] the Catalan advances into the Mediterranean of the thirteenth and fourteenth centuries were not royal ventures but were carried out by individual captains and companies. Like the *conquistadores* in the New World, the conquest of the Balearics had little to do with government of any sort. A representative of the Gerona bishopric, Guillem de Mongrí, led a small force in 1234–1235 against Ibiza and Formentera, conquering these Balearic islands closes to the Iberian mainland, with little bloodshed. Though barely qualifying for Catalan noble privileges, Montgrí and his most important colleagues held a great amount of territory and served as administrators for the small islands.[6]

The fluctuation between royal and private conquests across the Mediterranean continued into the fourteenth century with Sicily the prime target of this activity. Catalan military endeavors in the region intensified in the later thirteenth century, when fortunes were to be made in the transport of grain, an important Sicilian commodity since ancient times. The ready money to be earned in ventures of this kind led many Catalan merchants and sailors to establish their trading headquarters in Sicily in order to facilitate business between their old and new residences.[7]

These individual actions were eventually intensified by the influence of Queen Constanza and her husband, Pere II, who looked to the middle sea as a likely place for establishing a military record similar to that of his father, Jaume I. As we have seen, the period between 1260 and 1280 was a time of conspiracy against Charles I of Anjou by Sicilian supporters of the Hohenstaufens who had to flee their homeland after the disastrous defeat of Benevento in 1266. They found a warm welcome in the court of the Aragonese prince, who had completely taken up the cause of his wife, the Sicilian princess, Constanza. By the early 1280s, Pere II, now the Aragonese king, began to solidify support for a Sicilian invasion. He attempted to disguise the formation of an army and fleet by letting it be

44   D. J. KAGAY

known that he was planning to use his forces against the Muslim dynasty of Tunis, which was conveniently close to Sicily.[8]

While Pere was docked near Tunis, supposedly ready to take on his Muslim enemy, the townspeople of Palermo rose against their hated French enemies during Holy Week of 1282 and proceeded to kill as many of Charles I's troops as they could before opening the island to the Aragonese king who became their sovereign later in that same summer. Interestingly, this offer was made by Sicilian leaders only after they had petitioned the French pope, Martin IV (r. 1281–1285) to grant independence to the island. This humbly phrased request gained nothing for the Sicilian cause. Instead, Pope Martin immediately ruled in favor of King Charles and against his Sicilian enemies by issuing a sentence of excommunication against them.[9]

Events in Sicily hardly broke the Angevin king's power which remained virtually untouched in Provence and the Regno because of the unfaltering support of the Papacy. What eventually brought down Angevin rule in the central Mediterranean was the decade of war after the Vespers in which the great southern Italian naval hero, Roger de Lauria, never lost a battle against the Provencal fleets, that Charles I sent against him. In 1283 at Malta, though outnumbered, Lauria demolished the enemy squadron, inflicting some 4,000 casualties on Charles's seamen. In the summer of the following year, an Aragonese task force blockaded Naples, causing such damage to the city and its economy that Anjou's son, Charles of Salerno, led out a large fleet which Lauria thoroughly demolished. Lack of trained seamen was not the only reason for the continual Angevin defeats; a growing lessening of allegiance to Charles I and his family soon became apparent and would increase after his death in 1285. The Aragonese naval wing was such a formidable force that the deceased king's son, now Charles II (r. 1285–1309), sued for peace in 1302 at Caltabellota. He attained his wish after paying a large indemnity to the Aragonese and pledging to accept Pere II's third son, Federico III as the Sicilian king for as long as he lived.[10]

After twenty years of war which even included a French invasion of Catalonia in 1285 in support of Charles I, many of the residents of the Western Mediterranean and many popes were dead set on getting the Aragonese king, Jaume II out of Mediterranean affairs and protecting the Angevin rulers and people of Naples. To undermine Aragonese ambitions concerning Sicily and its neighbors, the papally brokered Treaty of Anagni

(1295) forced the Aragonese king to keep out of Sicilian affairs, but Boniface VIII (r. 1294–1303) tried to make Jaume's defeat more acceptable by giving the king title to the islands of Sardinia and Corsica.[11]

Despite these actions to bring about peace in the Mediterranean by largely keeping the Aragonese and Catalans out of it, the diplomats forgot about the great number of troops that were released on civilian societies without putting measures in place to deal with the out-of-work warriors. With the end of the long, destructive, and even profitable War of the Sicilian Vespers, the discharged troops did little to find a new profession but established themselves as mercenaries, a profession which many of them had never left. With few opportunities for their talents in the central Mediterranean, a large corps of men who had fought for the Aragonese and Sicilians, now formed themselves into the Catalan Company under the command of the talented and mercurial Roger de Flor.[12]

The core of this small group of under 1,500 men were the *almogaveres*, poor rural residents who lived on the frontiers with Muslim territory in the Iberian realms of Castile, Murcia, and Valencia. Living in rural districts, they led dangerous lives by raiding into enemy territory. Like many Iberian raiding parties, they were commanded by an *adalid*, who led their lightning raids across Muslim borders, and divided all captured booty. The thirteenth-century, Bernal Desclot, describes their clothing as a simple tunic, rough breeches, and leather sandals. Their only weapons were a long knife, a lance, and two spears. With a reputation for savagery, these troops set a ruthless standard for the entire Catalan Company when it was employed against the Ottoman Turks by the Byzantine emperor, Michael IX (r. 1295–1320). The company was so dangerous that after being dismissed by the emperor in 1305, it terrorized Greece for the next six years before killing their last employer, Duke William of Athens, and establishing a ring of territory around the ancient city that would eventually remain under the control of the Sicilian kings until 1390.[13]

The Aragonese monarchy did not involve itself in Mediterranean affairs until 1323, fully thirty-two years after Jaume II had returned to assume his Iberian crown. In these troubled decades, domestic problems, most especially the threats posed by the Aragonese and Valencian *Unión*, captured most of his attention. It was obvious that he had never forgotten the Catalan soldiers, sailors, and administrators involved in the continuing war against Islam when in 1311 he wrote to Pope Clement V (r. 1305–1314). To him, these faraway endeavors were linked in Christianity's continuing struggle to tear Jerusalem away from the infidel.[14] To the

46   D. J. KAGAY

string of Iberian islands pointing toward the Holy Land, Jaume would eventually add the name of Sardinia, although he had done nothing about taking any sort of control of the island during the two decades after it had been granted him by the papacy. In reality, the king may have hesitated about the small island since, though it was a ready source of wheat, salt, and other agricultural products, it was largely undeveloped, and covered with a sullen population that seemed ready to fight rather than accept the king's domination, no matter how uplifting he promised it might be. They had already suffered the riotous presence of the Genoese and Pisans who had fought each other for over a century to make Sardinia theirs. There would be no possibility for the establishment of a cadet royal house for the island as had happened in Sicily and Majorca. Instead, Sardinia would be incorporated directly into the Crown and Aragon and would be ruled by royal administrative representatives rather than junior kings. The same fate would soon await the other islands. Looking on the Sards as barely human, Jaume and his advisers thought that the islanders could be "governed without divisions and quarrels," a view they would soon think better of. Indeed, Alfonso's son, Pere III would spend an immense amount of money trying to subordinate the Sardinians, all to no effect.[15]

If the Aragonese "empire" in the Mediterranean was worthy of the name, it was the result of a preconceived plan or series of plans. These, however, were not always carried out. Even if this had been the case, the energy and adaptability of individuals often counted for more than the assumptions and orders of government agents. The last phase of the Aragonese and Catalan experience in the Mediterranean bears this out well. By the end of the fourteenth century, many of the individuals who had won and ruled over the Aragonese off-shore holdings became so self-centered in the pursuit of power that sovereigns like Pere III eventually had to step in and reestablish power over these outposts.

In Sicily, bad luck seemed to take over when its young ruling couple, María (1363–1401), the daughter of Federico IV and Constanza, the oldest daughter of Pere III, and Martí the Younger (r. 1379–1410), son of the Aragonese king, Martí I, took over the island in 1292. Infant deaths, however, had a drastic effect on the Sicilian succession. The young king of Sicily saw his son, Pere, die in 1400 and his queen pass away a year later. In 1402, he married Blanche of Navarre the younger sister of Pere III first wife. They had a son, Martí, who died in 1404. At the end of this string of ill fortune, Martí died in 1409, fighting in Sardinia. The Aragonese king, Martí I, now became sovereign of Sicily for one year before he himself died without a legitimate heir. The ultimate change for the Crown of Aragon and its Mediterranean holdings then came when the Compromise of Caspe chose the Castilian prince, Ferran I as the new ruler of eastern Spain. Within a century, Castile ruled all sides of Spain as well as the offshore conquests of Aragon.[16]

2   Pere's First Marriages

Pere III, the king with the longest reign in the history of the Barcelona dynasty, was born to Teresa de Entenca, the first wife of the future Aragonese king, Alfons III, on September 5, 1319, at the Catalan town of Balaguer. The small prince's older brother, Alfons, was a sickly infant who died within two years of his birth. Pere himself was such an underweight and feverish infant that his mother feared for his life, but more importantly his soul. She thus had him baptized in the very room in which he was born. This "feeble and rickety" baby wore out seven wet nurses in his first year, giving pensions to three of them after he had become king.[17] In his first eight years, the small prince grew to respect his father, who was one of the great heroes of the conquest of Sardinia in 1223. He clearly loved his mother, whom he said with some melancholy was good to him. Besides her maternal qualities, Pere appreciated the queen for her spirited defense of his position as crown prince once her husband became king in 1327. Her son, Teresa insisted, formally had to be declared Alfons's successor. Pere's uncle (also of the same name), the count of Roussillon and Empuries, hoped to have himself named as the crown prince and then follow his brother, Alfons III, to the throne. He was, after all, the last of Jaume II's legitimate sons. Queen Teresa courageously fought off this drive for royal power, and so it was with some irony that when Pere became king, Prince Pere would stand as his most important adviser.[18]

After his eighth birthday, the crown prince's happy life largely disappeared with the death of his mother during childbirth on October 27, 1327. King Alfons was quickly in the market for a new bride and did not have far to look. His older brother, Jaume, who had served as a crown prince before Alfons and was being trained to follow his father, Jaume II, to the throne, had in 1319 already married Leonor (1307–1359), daughter of the Castilian king, Fernando IV (r. 1295–1312). After the ceremony he had fled from his new bride to a Hospitaller convent in Tarragona. After joining the order, he renounced his royal office as well as his wife. The jilted Castilian princess, compensated with some castles on

Aragon's border with Castile, was sent home, presumably still a virgin.[19] Leonor was back in Aragon's public life within a decade when Alfons took the princess as his bride. They married in February 1329 at Tarazona before a large crowd of Aragonese and Castilian great nobles and knights, including the new queen's father, Alfonso XI. One of the few unhappy members at the wedding party was the crown prince, Pere, who had immediate suspicions about his new stepmother and her advisers. This new Castilian faction quickly bore out his fears with the "many and divers persecutions" they launched against him.[20]

For most of the next ten years, Pere and Leonor conducted such a bitter and open feud that Alfons III could hardly avoid picking sides. With the birth of the queen's first son, Ferran (Fernando), in 1329 and her second, Juan, in 1331, Alfons came to treat the new princes with a generosity that infuriated Pere. Ferran, especially, profited from the increasing hold that Leonor had over her husband. Honored when very young with the title marquis of Tortosa along with the grant of vast tracts of surrounding land, Ferran was also made the lord of Alicante, Játiva, Algiceras, Murviedro, Burriana, and Castellón. By these grants and others to Juan, Alfons had clearly weakened Prince Pere's position and, even if indirectly, had divided his nobles between Leonor and her stepson.[21] Even the Aragonese king had to suffer through his wife's repeated outbursts when she angrily told her husband that no Castilian king would put up what she had to from her stepson. Past the point of prudence, Alfons told his wife that the Aragonese were not slaves to their sovereign as the Castilians were, but were instead "good vassals and companions."[22] One could imagine how Leonor, a good Castilian, took this observation.

With Alfons's death in 1336, Leonor and her sons rapidly left Aragon, fearing the support Pere had gained with his nobles. As a widow with two adolescent sons, she had little option but to seek the hospitality and protection of her brother, Alfonso XI (r. 1312–1350) at the Castile court. Though basically penniless because of Pere's diversion of all the revenues from her dower properties, Leonor was able to prosper in her brother's court, and from this safe haven plotted revenge on the new Aragonese king. The opportunity for this would come in 1346 when she aided her sons in attaining command posts in the Valencian *Unión*. Within two years, the Aragonese king decided to make peace with his troublesome relatives, if only to remove them from his concerns. The scheming Leonor met a very different fate at the hands of her nephew, Pedro I who had her killed in 1359 by his Muslim troops.[23]

With this stormy parade through Pere's adolescence toward his early adulthood, we see in great detail how his wives were chosen and his marriage ceremonies carried out, but almost nothing of the women with whom he lived in supposed connubial bliss. Two years a king and entering his adulthood at age nineteen, Pere agreed to take as his first wife, the second daughter of Philippe III "the Wise" of France and Navarre. The marriage negotiations had begun in 1332, and centered on Philippe's oldest daughter, the eight-year-old Princess Joanna, who eventually eschewed marriage to become a nun, and then settled on the five-year-old María. This change in proposed bride required a new marriage contract to replace the one drawn up for the elder princess. This was brought to Navarre by an Aragonese delegation headed by Archbishop Lope de Luna. Pere's ambassadors began negotiations with the Navarrese delegation headed by Enrique de Sulli, governor of the Pyrenean realm. After extended discussions, the two delegations finally came to an agreement in 1337 with a document tailored for the younger princess, María. She was to receive from her parents a dowry of 100,000 *libras* of Barcelona to be paid in full or in two installments. If this proved impossible, the Navarrese royal couple would raise the money by taking a specified percentage from the annual tax revenues that supported them. Pere agreed to the marriage contract and had it witnessed by two royal delegates in 1338. With these formalities in place, the king expected to see his bride in the near future.[24]

Even before the Navarrese wedding party crossed from Tudela where the princess had been lodged, the Aragonese king had made elaborate plans for his upcoming nuptials. In spring, 1338, he demanded from all his realms, the financial support traditional when a royal wedding was in the offing. Even before there was sufficient money in his coffers, the king arranged for the purchase of the" pearls and precious stones that would be needed for the making of two gold crowns" and six fine rings for his intended. As María, now ten years old, was on the point of beginning her journey into Aragon, her older sister, Joanna, renounced all inheritance rights that could have possibly come to her from the earlier marriage agreement. With these last legal matters attended to, the Navarrese wedding party left Tudela and moved down south bank of the Ebro River. When the group reached the small town of Alagón, some sixteen miles from the Aragonese capital, it halted since the little princess had become ill. After a few days, however, Pere along with his court traveled the short distance to Alagón, where on July 23, 1338, the wedding took place. Shortly after the service, the entire throng of well-wishers went back to Zaragoza, where several days of celebration took place across the city, all in honor of the young king and his even younger queen.

Some weeks later, the same process was repeated at Barcelona with the nuptials being sanctified again, and María, like any modern bride, was loaded down with all kind of domestic treasures. Many of the determined well-wishers even followed the king and his bride north to Gerona and then across the foothills of the Pyrenees to Perpignan There, after yet another wedding ceremony took place, the queen, at least, attained the possibility of enjoying a well-deserved rest in the expansive royal palace and its surrounding well-tended grounds that were dotted with fruit trees and other plants.[25]

After this whirlwind of ceremony and earnest celebration, the king was pulled back into the thousand details connected with his office, and we hear almost nothing else of the queen, who was clearly still a young girl, for months to come. All we know of her is from the blanket statement in the king's *Crónica* that she was a "lady of saintly life and great modesty."[26] Though María and Pere were married for nine years and had four children together, very little else besides this personally tied them together except for the fact that the king tried to communicate to his wife in French, perhaps danced with her at least once, and had with her four children.[27]

The first of these offspring, Constanza, was born in 1343, and was long considered the king's only viable successor. She married her cousin, Kind Federico IV of Sicily and bore his successor, María. Pere's second daughter, Joanna, also married a cousin, Count Joan of Empuries. María's third child was a girl named after her mother who died before her third birthday. From the fourth pregnancy came a boy named Pere after his father. This blessed birth which took place on April 9, 1347, at Valencia led the southern capital into an outburst of "great joy and contentment," but plunged the well-wishers into bitter disappointment and anger when the little prince died on the very day he was born. The queen passed away five days after her son's birth on April 14. Though she had wished to be buried in the royal pantheon at the monastery of Poblet, she was laid to rest at the monastery of Sant Vincent in Valencia.[28]

With a dead wife and two minor children to raise, the Aragonese king very quickly grew desperate about the succession to the Aragonese throne. With the death of his little son, the survival of the Barcelona dynasty seemed less and less certain. Reports of Castilian interference in the worsening *Unión* situation in the realm of Valencia deepened his fears concerning the continuance of his family's rule in eastern Spain. It seems that at this point, Alfonso XI, his sister, Leonor, and her sons still roundly hated the Aragonese king.[29] Under this darkening situation, Pere turned to immediate action. By the beginning of the summer, he had sent two of his most trusted administrators, Lop de Gurrea and Pere Guillem, to the court of the Portuguese king, Afonso IV (r. 1325–1357), to ask for the hand of his third daughter, Leonor, for their royal master. This was not an easy decision for the Portuguese monarch who was being simultaneously pressured by Alfonso XI who wanted the princess as a wife for Prince Ferran, his nephew, and Pere III's hated half-brother. While this delegation was taking place in Portugal, the Aragonese king had sent letters to the French, Norman, and Sicilian courts with similar royal requests concerning the availability of suitable princesses to serve as his wife. Ironically, in the light of later events, the request to King Ludovico of Sicily concerned his "sister, the most distinguished princess, Elionor," Pere's interest in marriage prospects in the other courts faded, however, when the king received a report from his ambassadors concerning the Portuguese princess, Leonor, whom they considered "very beautiful... [endowed with] a gentle disposition,... greatness of person... and very excellent virtues."[30]

Both the Portuguese royal family and nobility were in favor of the marriage, signifying, as it did, an Aragonese alliance against the Castilians. Afonso thus provided a dowry for his daughter of 50,000 *libras* of Barcelona which was to be matched by Pere with dower revenues of the same amount. Once the marriage terms were agreed upon, Afonso immediately began laying out how his daughter would be conveyed to her new husband. Considering the enmity of his Castilian neighbor, the Portuguese king was not willing to subject his daughter to a land journey across Castile, thus making arrangements for a small flotilla of ships to bring Leonor, her ladies-in-waiting, and a great number of Portuguese clerics and nobles to Barcelona where the wedding would take place.

In early August, 1347, Pere and the members of his court journeyed west from Lerida to the Aragonese town of Tamarite de Litera, to the northwest of Barcelona, where he met Portuguese envoys who had traveled overland across Castile to communicate Afonso's final plans. At the same time, the Aragonese king began issuing invitations for the wedding to his uncles, Pere and Ramon Berenguer, as well as important members of his great nobility, many of whom also served as his officials. Representatives of the major cities of Catalonia and Majorca were also invited to attend the nuptials.[31]

Delayed by another uprising of the Aragonese and Valencian *Unión*, the king postponed his journey to the marriage site, Barcelona, for over three months. When he finally made it through his rebellious realms and was in sight of Catalonia, he supposedly exclaimed: "Thank God for delivering Us from a rebellious and wicked country."[32] Leonor's small fleet arrived at Barcelona in the late fall after a largely uneventful journey down the Atlantic coast, passing through the Strait of Gibraltar, and into the Mediterranean where her captains successfully avoided corsairs all along the Valencian and Catalan coasts.

While celebrations that broke out in Barcelona with the arrival of the princess, family troubles drew away her future husband's immediate attention. The king's younger brother, Jaume of Urgel, who had aligned himself with the cause of the *Unión*, caused his older sibling no end of trouble for all of 1347. As a guest at the king's second wedding, his sudden death, whether from natural causes or poison, cast a pall over Pere and his nineteen-year old queen that would never lift. After celebrating Christmas at the Catalan capital, the king and Leonor left Barcelona in late-December bound for Valencia. Arriving in Murviedro (Sagunto) north of Valencia city in late-January 1348, the royal couple encountered there angry members of the Valencian *Unión* who kept the king and his bride there as virtual prisoners for over two months. Pere especially would never forget this dangerous and embarrassing affront.[33]

After escaping the insults and threats they had suffered in Muviedro, the royal couple experienced terrors of a completely different order when the Black Death spread across most of the Crown of Aragon in the late spring of 1348 and remained virulent in the region until the following winter. The royal family suffered their first loss in June when the king's youngest daughter, the "little princess María," then three years old died the terrible death of the plague.[34] Fear tied up with superstition overwhelmed the royal family and their subjects as the raging pandemic claimed 300 persons a day in Valencia. "Signs and wonders" purportedly occurred every day in a natural environment which had begun to act very unnaturally. The Ter River at Gerona flowed darkly "like a river of death."[35] Becoming increasingly disturbed by each day's events, Pere

and his court fled from Valencia, a place in which life seemed danger-
ously under siege. Fleeing northwest toward Zaragoza, the royal family
entered Teruel in the second week of October. Pere then led his people
back across the Aragonese border to the Valencian town of Jérica, but this
could not help the queen who had possibly been infected on the last leg
of this journey.

On October 29, 1348. Pere ordered his seal-bearer, Francisco de
Prohom, to produce a new will for the queen from a list of notes Pere
had given him. On the next day, the king sent messages to four of his
physicians in Valencia to come to Jérica to attend his rapidly worsening
wife On November 1, Pere informed his Portuguese in-laws "of the
sorrowful death of Lady Leonor...,[their] very dear daughter and [his]
very dear wife." The symptoms of the illness that claimed her young
life was "great pain from a constant fever," which rapidly removed her
to "God's glory from the misery of the world."[36] On the next day, the
king informed Pope Clement VI (r. 1342–1352) of the twenty-year-old
queen's demise, praising her as one who gained her high office from the
honesty and maturity of her life. He also assured the pontiff that Leonor
had received great consolation from "the ecclesiastical sacraments as a
true Christian."[37] Some months later on March 15, 1350, the Aragonese
monarch had his wife transferred to the royal pantheon in the monastery
of Poblet.[38]

Having buried two wives in a little over six months, Pere III, a cautious
man and a survivor on many levels, grew increasingly worried about
who would follow him to the Aragonese throne. Even before his second
wife had died, the king had conceived the idea of having his first child,
Constanza, accepted as his successor. Consulting several educated clerics
and laymen, he discovered that legally he could leave his realms to his
daughter if he had no sons. A conclave of twenty-two such experts, gathered from his major realms in 1347, officially responded to this crucial
question by declaring that the king had the right to leave the Crown
of Aragon to either his oldest legitimate child—even if a daughter—or to
his brother, Jaume de Urgel. When Jaume hear of Pere's official query, he
was furious, and from that time began to plot against the king. Ill-feeling
about Pere's attempt to guarantee a legal succession grew throughout his
realms down until the time of his second marriage.[39] As the king had
pointed out to his brother, his concerns about the succession constituted
a prudent act that reflected the deep fear he might not father a male heir.
With his third marriage, the fear would quickly prove unfounded.

54   D. J. KAGAY

3   THE THIRD BRIDE: ELIONOR OF SICILY

Pere's third wife came to him from a Sicilian cadet dynasty that actually owed its existence to Pere II and Queen Constanza. Created from the bitter rivalry between Aragonese and Angevin sovereigns that was legislated into peace with the Treaty of Caltabellotta in 1302, the second phase of Sicily's Iberian dynasty began with Jaume II's third son, Federico III (r. 1295–1337). Surrounded by Mediterranean enemies such as Naples, Genoa, and Venice, the Sicilian king also had to pay close attention to his Aragonese relatives and the military and naval forces they employed around Sicily. Though the longest-lived of the Sicilian kings who ruled during the so-called "ninety-year war" that swirled around the central Mediterranean from the 1280s to the 1390s, Federico's powers were continually reduced by the low-level, but seemingly continuous baronial conflicts that gradually weakened Sicily and made it increasingly susceptible to foreign attacks. Even the Sicilian king's longevity guaranteed no real permanence for his dynasty, since by the 1302 agreement, after Federico's death Sicily would fall to Joanna I of Naples or her successors. This built-in impotence of his dynasty apparently had little effect on the king's production of heirs with his queen, Eleanor of Anjou—five sons and four daughters—or with his principal mistress—three sons and two daughters.[40] When Federico turned fifty in 1322, he appointed his crown prince as his co-ruler, Pietro II (r. 1322–1342) but little is known concerning his duties when he became co-ruler at age eighteen. It is clear, however, that the bloody rivalries among Sicily's chief baronial clans intensified during the last years of Federico's life. The same was true of the political and economic disputes between the islands greatest cities, Palermo and Messina. All of these struggles allowed both nobles and churchmen to establish great estates that Sicily's royal power had very little control over. The greatest political cloud to hang over Pietro II and his sons was the institutional hatred of the first Avignon popes who repeatedly attacked the ruling titles of the Aragonese rulers of Sicily and supported as consistently the efforts of the Angevin kings of Naples to win back the island.[41]

Like his father, Pietro II had a large family of nine children, all born within wedlock. With his wife, Elizabeth of Carinthia, he had three sons, the first two, Lodovico and Federico, followed him to the throne, but at young ages and in ill health, conditions which made their ruling success virtually impossible.[42] The third son, Giovanni, died as an infant. Pietro's daughters far outclassed his sons in numbers and ability. The oldest princess, Constanza, served as regent for Lodovico from 1352 to 1354 and lived into her thirties without submitting to marriage. Elionor, the second daughter lived to the ripe old age of fifty as queen of Aragon. Beatrice married Elector Rupert II of the Palatinate and bore him a son who eventually assumed his father's office. Euphemia did not marry and served as regent for her brother Federico until he took the throne in 1355. Violante, like her brother Giovanni, was a child of her mother's last child-bearing years and died young. Blanche, the last princess, was captured with Violante and held prisoner during a Neopolitan attack on Sicily and for some six years afterward. She became a ward of Elionor, and through the Aragonese queen's effort, was married to Count Joan I of Empuries.

We know little of the workings of the court in which Elionor grew up except to say it was dominated by strong-willed women whose energy occasionally directed the weak and ill members of the Sicilian court. The head of this remarkable sorority was Federico III's wife, Eleanor of Anjou, whose robust religious sense touched the family and realm she helped rule. From early in her career as wife and mother, she showed her devotion to the church by unstintingly supporting the construction and repair projects of holy sites which she often paid for by selling or pawning her jewels. Other contemporary, European queens engaged in such good works, but were perhaps not as motivated as Eleanor was by a messianic Christianity influenced by the teaching of Joachim of Fiore and Arnau de Vilanova, both of whom proclaimed that the end of the world was at hand. Though this belief was a common one at the time, Eleanor used it as a basic tenet for the rule of her dower lands in Sicily and the Regno, which routinely castigated her officials and tenants guilty of blasphemy and the popular activity of gambling.[43]

Eleanor influenced all of her children with the assurance of a millennial future and the duties the awful reality imposed on them. This clearly entered Pietro II's family and was especially apparent in the characters of his three oldest daughters who showed themselves to be remarkably strong-willed and fully dedicated to the preservation of the Sicilian dynasty and the service of their siblings. Constanza and Euphemia never accepted the duties of marriage or escaped them by entering a religious order. Instead, they spent a good part of their lives overseeing the education and political training of their younger brothers who would accede to the throne. Elionor would emulate her grandmother's and mother's

56   D. J. KAGAY

examples as a wife who attempted to inculcate in her life a sense of duty to the realm and to the family that ruled it. She also followed the path of religious activism in the support of clerical institutions and in the advancement of the royal government of which she became a crucial part.

There is little indication of the Sicilian reaction in 1348 to Pere's interest in marriage with Princess Elionor except for her mother's joyful response to the possibility that her daughter could now herself become a royal wife. After the Aragonese king had settled on the Portuguese candidate for his new queen, Elionor would have to wait for another marriage proposal. What she thought of this turn-of-events we are not sure, but certainly, her mother must have been disappointed. Incredibly, such an offer came in the spring of 1349 and from the selfsame party who had evinced interest in Elionor months before.

Still concerned about the crucial matter of succession, Pere III rushed his marriage agents, Lord Galceran de Anglesola of Bellpuig, the royal *mayordomo*, and Lop de Guerrea, the king's chamberlain, to the Sicilian royal court which was then established in their palace at Messina. The ambassadors carried a set of instructions for the wedding negotiations. To begin with, Pere promised that he would "honor the goods, friends, and debts" that Princess Elionor had in Sicily. The ambassadors would arrange with the Sicilian king a dowry of 150,000 *libras* of Barcelona or 300 marks of gold or silver. The new queen's household would be supported by the rents of castles and towns in the king's realms, which would come to an initial grant of 10,000 *libras* of Barcelona. All these matters would be arranged by the time of the princess's arrival in the Crown of Aragon and could not be changed. The terms of the wedding treaty had to be acceptable to the Sicilian king, Ludovico, his mother, the queen, and the Aragonese and Catalans living in Sicily. The ambassadors also had to engage in discussions concerning "peace and concord" on the island with the Sicilian "prelates, counts, nobles, barons, and others."[44]

Coming before Queen Elizabeth, Elionor's mother, shortly after completing the journey to Sicily, Pere's envoys announced their master's desire to wed the "little princess," which could be completed with some straightforward negotiation concerning Elionor's dowry and dower rights. Shortly after this, the envoys consulted with Lodovico, who had been Sicilian king from his father's death in 1342, concerning a series of other matters that also had to be agreed upon. When the negotiated terms were accepted by both sides, they were sworn to as part of a general "peace and accord" between Aragon and Sicily, which was sworn to by the ambassadors and Sicilian "prelates, counts, nobles, barons, and others." The credentials that Pere's envoys carried contained a number of articles that their king would fulfill before the marriage could proceed. Pere swore he would fulfill all the stipulations of the dowry as well as the contents of the other articles. If the Sicilian authorities, including the princess, agreed to the marriage, the envoys would immediately arrange for the princess to travel "safely and honorably" to the Crown of Aragon. If the queen refused to accept Pere's wedding proposal, the ambassadors were to have the right to bargain for any other of Elionor's sisters as their king's wife. Fortunately, all of them were unmarried at the time. If no decision could be agreed to, the king would not be bound to supply a dowry. If Elionor, the "older princess," accepted the king's marriage proposal, the promise to wed by the king would remain in effect. The envoys were in charge of the ships and the 100,000 *libras* promised King Ludovico as his sister's dowry. Pere III's representatives then swore to the Sicilian queen mother that the children born to the king and Princess Elionor would be "profitably and honorably raised." The wedding would take place in Valencia "where the lord king wished it and would take care to have it there." The ambassadors then immediately engaged with no delay, bringing about "peace and concord," in having the marriage concluded. The princess and her entourage would have to immediately set out in a small fleet for eastern Spain. Her husband-to-be would use the intervening time to arrange all the details of the wedding.[45]

The diplomatic mission of 1349 went as smoothly as it did because Pere's ambassadors already had considerable previous knowledge about the Sicilian princess which they received after Leonor of Portugal had been chosen by their master in the previous year. Pere, a well-known employer of spies, had written his envoys to inform them that a "credible person" who knew the Sicilian court had provided a description of Elionor as "twenty-one or twenty-two -year-old, with a white [complection] but with red blemishes....and very long and thin black hair." This agent had also proved a description of Elionor's younger sister, Euphemia, who was a blond teenager who was "very graceful," but was not greatly accustomed to adult company. The "height and build" of the two princesses were similar to the princess he would marry shortly after this communique, Leonor of Portugal.[46]

Elionor had over a year to consider at least the possibility of being the wife of her uncle, the young and powerful king of Aragon, but did not have to face some of the unpleasant realities of the institution of marriage itself until the wedding agreement was signed in the summer of 1349. Provided a papal dispensation was arranged with the papacy, the Sicilian princess was willing to enter a matrimony with a close relative, and so quickly accepted Pere's long-distance proposal. Almost as quickly as Elionor made her decision, Mateo de Palici, a leader of one of Sicily's great baronial families, spoke for his aristocratic fellows, demanding that the princess renounce all rights to the Sicilian throne. Her perspective power to rule the island in her own name was only one of the problems. What gave the barons pause was the possibility that the Aragonese king or his children with the princess might eventually try to take back a throne that his grandfather, Jaume II, had formally abandoned a half-century before. For her part, Elionor had no intention of giving up a royal dream, which she confidently believed she could accomplish at some time in the future.

For her mother, Elizabeth of Carinthia, this attitude was the result of unforgivable stubbornness that could cost her family an even steeper and more rapid descent into poverty and political weakness than it had suffered in the past decades. Unwilling to humor her daughter's unrealistic ambitions, Elizabeth, as both the Sicilian queen and Elionor's mother, would now subject her to intra-family pressure to make her see sense. The queen mother thus surrendered the twenty-four-year- old princess to the control of her aunt, Lady Catalina, the abbess of the monastery of the St. Clares in Messina. After a very short confinement in this austere environment, the princess made a formal renunciation of all royal rights in Sicily and signed a document to that effect. Four years later, on June 18, 1352, she swore that this declaration "was neither witnessed nor signed and was carried out against the princesses's will."[47] Furious at her treatment, Elionor, called for the Aragonese ambassadors and quickly agreed to the marriage terms that had already been accepted by her family and the other Sicilian great men. Still angry at the mere thought of her imprisonment, no matter how brief, the princess expedited her preparations and on July 13, 1349, left Messina for a new life in eastern Spain. She would never again see her immediate family, except for her sisters, Violante and Blanca as well as Lodovico's two illegitimate sons.[48]

The small fleet of Aragonese and Sicilian vessels docked at the El Grao, the port of Valencia, in the first week of August where her husband and many of his courtiers were waiting. The marriage took place a few days later. Writing back to her brother, Ludovico, the new queen of Aragon described the vast crowds that had awaited her in Valencia and the great "hustle and applause" they gave to the passing of her carriage. The great cathedral *(Seu)* of Valencia hosted the wedding and was filled with many joyful barons and nobles who were residents of the city. Bishop Ugo of Valencia oversaw the nuptials. The king solemnly took Elioner as his wife., and the couple experienced an "intimate exchange of ...[their] bodies... and blood." Afterward, the community of Valencia, still reeling from the effects of the Black Death, hailed their king's third wife "with great solemnity and celebration." From the queen's point-of-view, this entire chapter of her life was covered with "joy of exultation."[49] Within a year, the king would lead the merrymaking when Elionor gave him a healthy son.

NOTES

1. For Las Navas de Tolosa, see Martín Alvira Cabrer, "De Alarcos á las Navas de Tolosa: Idea y realidad de la batalla de 1212," in *Alarcos 1195: Actas de Congreso Internacional Comemeraticva de VIII Centenario de Batalla de Alarcos*, ed. Ricardo Izquierdo Benito and Francisco Ruiz Gómez (Ciudad Real:Universidad de Castilla-La Mancha, 1996), 254–64; Miguel Gómez, "Alfonso III and the Battle of Las Navas de Tolosa," in *King Alfonso VIII of Castile: Government, Family and War*, ed. Miguel Gómez, Damian Smith, and Kyle C. Lincoln (New York:: Fordham University Press, 2019), 143–71.
2. Felipe Fernández Armesto, *Before Columbus: Exploration and Colonization from the Mediterranean to the Atlantic, 1229–1492* (Philadelphia: University of Pennsylvania Press, 1987), 12; Anwar G. Chejne, *Muslim Spain: Its History and Culture* (Minneapolis: University of Minnesota Press, 1974), 93; Hugh Kennedy, *Muslim Spain and Portugal: A Political History of al-Andalus* (London: Longman, 1996), 174; Lomax, *Reconquest*, 83.
3. For Las Navas de Tolosa, see Martín Alvira Cabrer, "De Alarcos á las Navas de Tolosa: Idea y realidad de la batalla de 1212," in *Alarcos 1195: Actas de Congreso Internacional Comemeraticva de VIII Centenario de Batalla de Alarcos*, ed. Ricardo Izquierdo Benito and Francisco Ruiz Gómez (Ciudad Real:Universidad de Castilla-La Mancha, 1996), 254-64; Miguel Gómez, "Alfonso III and the Battle of Las Navas de Tolosa," in *King Alfonso VIII of Castile: Government, Family and War*, ed. Miguel Gómez, Damian Smith, and Kyle C. Lincoln (New York:: Fordham University Press, 2019), 143–71.
4. *BD*, 69–135 (chaps. 47–126; Fernández Armesto, *Before Columbus*, 25–27; Alvaro Santamaria, "La expansion político-militar de la corona ad Aragón bajo la dirección de Jaime I: Baleares," in *Jaime I y su época, X congreso de história de la Corona de Aragón* [hereafter *X CHCA*], 3

vols. (Zaragoza: "Institución Fernando el Católico," 1979). Ponencias, 93–149.

5. Donald J. Kagay, "Army Mobilization, Royal Administration and the Realm in the Thirteenth-Century Crown of Aragon," in *Iberia and the Mediterranean World*, ed. Paul E. Chevedden, Donald J. Kagay, Paul G. Padilla, and Larry E. Simon, 2 vols. (Leiden, 1996) 2:95–115; Antonio Palomeque Torres, "Contribución al estudio del ajercito en los estados de la reconquista," *Anuario de História del Derecho Español* [[hereafter *AHDE*], 15 (1944): 205–551.

6. Fernández-Armesto, *Before Columbus*, 31–33; Lomax, *Reconquest*, 142.

7. David Abulafia, "Catalan Merchants and the Western Mediterranean, 1236–1300: Studies in the Notarial Acts of Barcelona and Sicily," in *Italy, Sicily, and the Mediterranean 1100–1400* (Aldershot, Hampshire: Variorum, 1997), Study VIII, pp. 409–42; Hiroshi Takayama, "Central Power and Multi-Cultural Elements of the Norman Court of Sicily," *Mediterranean Studies* 12 (2003): 1–15; Mario del Treppo, "The Crown of Aragon and the Mediterranean," *Journal of European Economic History* 2 (1973): 161–85, esp. 167.

8. Michele Amari, *History of the War of the Sicilian Vespers*, 3 vols., ed. Earl of Ellesmere (London: Dalton House, 2015), 1:138–46; Vicente Salver y Roca, "La expansión catalano-aragonesa por el Mediterraneo en el siglo XIV," *AEM* 7 (1970–1971): 17–38, esp. 23–24; J. Lee Sheidman, "Aragon and the War of the Sicilian Vespers," *The Historian* 22, no. 2 (February 1960): 250–63.

9. Amari, *War*, 1:177–83, 288–89; Hiroshi Takayama, Sicily and the Mediterranean in the Middle Ages," in *The Middle Ages in Sicily and the Mediterranean* (London: Routledge, 2019), Study IX, pp. 147–66, esp. 162.

10. Jean H. Dunbabin, "The Household and Entourage of Charles I of Anjou, King of the Regno, 1266–1285," *Historical Research*, 77, no. 1977 (August, 2004), 313–336, esp. 336; Lawrence V. Mott, *Sea Power in the Medieval Mediterranean: The Catalan-Aragonese Fleet in the War of the Sicilian Vespers* (Gainesvill, FL: University Press of Florida, 2003), 31–50; Kenneth Setton, *The Papacy and the Levant (1204–1571)*, 4 vols. (Philadelphia: American Philosophical Society, 1976); Takayama, "Sicily," 160–61.

11. Vicente Salvert y Roca, *El tratado de Anagni y la expansion de la Corona de Aragón* (Zaragoza: CSIC, 1952), 44; J. R. Strayer, "The Crusade Against Aragon," *Speculum*, 28, no. 1 (Jan. 1953): 102–13. David Abulafia, *The Western Mediterranean Kingdoms: The Struggle for Dominion* (London: Lnngman, 1997), 115.

12. Fernádez Armesto, *Before Columbus*, 34–35; Alfonso Lowe, *The Catalan Vengeance* (London: Routledge & Kegan Paul Books, 1992), 34–38.

3 TWO REALMS AND A MARRIAGE   61

13. *The Chronicle of Muntaner*, 2 vols, trans. Lafy Goodenough (London: Hakluyt Society 1909, 1921), 2: 480–527; Francisco Montcada, *Expediciones de Catalanes y Aragoneses al Oriente* (Np., 2013); Kenneth Setton, *Catalan Domination of Athens* (Cambridge, MA: Harvard University Press, 1948).
14. David Abulafia, *A Mediterranean Emporium: the Catalan Kingdom of Majorca* (Cambridge: Cambridge University Press, 2005), 236.
15. Adulafia, *Western Mediterranean Kingdoms*, 125–26; Antonio Arribas Palau, *La Conquista de Cerdeña por Jaime II de Aragón* (Barcelona: Instituto Español Mediterráneos, Publicaciones, sobre historia, 1952), 54–55, 64, 133–38, 154; Cécile Crabot, "I problemi dell'espansione territoriale Catalana nel Mediterraneo: Conquistare unfeudo in Sardegne, un bene o un male? L'esempio dei Sentmenat, signori di Orosei (sec XIV)," *AEM* 33/2 (2003): 816–48, esp, 822–23, 830–31
16. Abulafia, "Italian South," 506–7, idem, *Western Mediterranean Kingdoms*, 160, 172, 181; Lalinde Abadía, *Corona*, 21–22.
17. Pere III, *Chronicle*, 1:137, 170 (1: 1, 40).
18. Ibid., I:173 (I, chap. 42); Kagay, "War and Government," 68–69; María Pou y Martí, *Visionarios beguinos, fratrecelos atalans* (Vich: Editorial Serífica, 1930), 308–96; Ferran Valls i Taberner, *El Tractat "De Regimine Principum" de infant Fra Pere d'Aragó* (Barcelona: Editorial Franciscana, 1927), 5–19.
19. Pere I, *Chronicle*, 1:173–74 (I, chap. 42); Jeronimo Zurita y Castro, *Anales de Aragon*, ed. Angel López Canellas, 9 vols. (Zaragoza: "Institución Fernando el Católico," 1969–1985), 3:117–22 (VI:xxxi); Alejandro Recuro Lista, "Doña Leonor: infanta castellana, reina aragonesa y elemento de discordia en las relaciones castellano-aragonesas en la primera mitad del siglo XIV," *Estudios Medievales Hispánicas* 2 (2013): 221–49, esp. 226–27.
20. Pere III, *Chronicle*, !:174–75 (1: chap. 43].
21. Ibid., 1:175 (1: chaps. 44–47); Recurdo Lista, "Doña Leonor", 228–29.
22. Pere III, *Chronicle*, I:177–79 (I: chap. 38); Recurdo Lista, "Doña Leonor", 229–30.
23. ACA, CR, R. 1138, ff. 66v-67; Pere III, *Chronicle*, 2:493–94 (VI: chap. 2); María Ferrer i Mallol, *Entre la paz y la guerra. La corona catalano-aragonesa y Castille en la baja Edad Media* (Barcelona: "Institució Milá Fontanals, 2005), 338–40, 550–52; Donald J. Kagay, "The Dynastic Dimension of International Conflict in Fourteenth-Century Iberia," *Mediterranean Studies* 17 (2008): 77–96, esp 86–87; Recurdo Lista, "Doña Leonor", 234–37.
24. Castro, "Matrimonia," 57–58, 61, 64; Rafael Olivar Betran, *Bodas reales de Aragón con Castilla, Navarra y Portugal* (Barcelona: Alberto Martin, 1949), 136–37; Miron, *Queens of Aragon*, 179–81.

62   D. J. KAGAY

25. Castro, "Matrimonio," 73; Miron, *Queens of Aragon*, 178–79; Olivar Betrand, *Bodas*, 114–16, 119, 121. Rafael Tasis i Marca, *La vida dei Rei En Pere III* (Barcelona: Editorial Aedos, 1949), 53
26. Pere III, *Chronicle*, 2:213 (II, chap. 31).
27. Ibi.d., 38, ftn. 118, 1:380 (III, chap. 199).
28. Pere III, *Chronicle*, 2:395-96 (IV, chap. 7; Prospero Bofarull y Moscaro, *Los condes de Barcelona vindicados*, 2 vols. (Barcelona: Imprenta de J. Oliveres y Monmany, 1936), 2:273; Castro, "Matrimonio," 63–64; Miron, *Queen of Aragon*, 179–81.
29. Pere III, *Chronicle*, 2:396, fnt. 10; A. López de Meneses, "El canciller Pero López de Ayala y los reyes de Aragón," *EEMCA* 8 (1967): 189–264, esp. 232–34.
30. Pere III, *Chronicle*, 2:396 (IV, chap. 7); Olivar Bertrand, *Bodas*, 137, 147–48.
31. Miron, *Queens of Aragon*, 182–83; Olivar Bertrand, *Bodas*, 140–41.
32. Pere III, *Chronicle*, 2:418–19 (IV, chap. 33).
33. Ibid., 2: 420–44 (IV, chaps. 34–38); Miron, *Queens of Aragon*, 183–85; Olivar Bertrand, *Bodas*, 140–41.
34. ACA, CR,, R. 1562, f. 15; Amada López de Meneses, *Documentos acerca de la Peste Negra en la dominion de la Corona de Aragón* (Zaragoza: Escuela de Estudios Medievales, 1956), 301 (doc. 111).
35. Miron, *Queens of Aragon*, 187.
36. ACA, CR, R. 1063, f. 61v; R. 1131, f. 107v; López de Meneses, "Documentos," 323–24 (docs. 37–38).
37. ACA, CR, R. 1131, f. 108v.; López de Meneses, "Documentos," 324–25 (doc. 40).
38. ACA, CR, R. 1134, f. 32v; López de Meneses, "Documentos," 377, doc. 94).
39. Pere III, *Chronicle*, 2: 392–94 (IV, chaps. 4–5, 11); Alfonso García Gallo de Diego, "La sucesión al trono de Aragón," *Anuario de Historia del Derecho Español* [hearafter *AHDE*] 36 (1966), 5–188, esp. 33–34.
40. Bachman, *Decline and Fall*, 29–67.
41. Abulafia, *Western Mediterranean Kingdoms*, 158–59; G. Mollat, *The "Babylonian Captivity" of the Medieval Church*, trans. Janet Love (New York: Harper & Row Publishers, 1963), 174; Giuseppe Quatriglio, *A Thosand Years in Sicily: From the Arabs to the Bourbons*, trans. Justin Vitiello (Mineola, NY: Legas, 2005), 60–62.
42. Lodovico was five when he ascended to the throne and Federico, 13.
43. Bachman, *Decline and Fall*, 288-89.
44. ACA, CR, R. 1534, ff. 1–4v.
45. ACA, CR, R. 1534, ff. 8–9v.
46. ACA, CR, R. 1131, f. 127; *Epistolari de Pere III*, ed. Ramon Gubern (Barcelona: Editorial Barchino, 1955),101–2 (doc. 11).

47. ACA, CR, R. 1534, ff. 89v–90.
48. Pere III, *Chronicle*, 2:449 (IV, chap. 64); Miron, *Queens of Aragon*, 187–88; Zurita, *Anales*, 4:181 (VIII:xxxvi).
49. ACA, CR, R. 1537, ff. 13v-14; Pere III, *Chronicle*, 2:449 (IV, chap. 64); Zurita, *Anales*, 4:181 (VIII:xxxvi); Fancisco Martínez, "El tercer casmiento de Pedro el Cerimanioso," in *III Congreso de história de la Corona de Aragón dedicado al periodo comprendido entre la muerte de Jaime I y la proclamación del rey don Fernanso de Antequera*, 3 vols. (Valencia: Imprenta del hijo de F. Vives, 1923–1928), 1:542–77.

CHAPTER 4

Elionor and Her Departed Homeland

1 ELIONOR'S CONNECTIONS TO HER ORIGINAL FAMILY

After Elionor left her island homeland in 1349, Sicily followed a course of decline that had already begun in the last years of her grandfather's reign and greatly intensified during the loose rule of her father Pietro II. In the simplistic chronicle view of the era, Federico III was a "thoroughly good man, who completely loved the Sicilian and considered all of them as sons and daughters."[1] In reality, through most of his reign, the great number of the Aragonese and Catalan population that flooded into Sicily during the reigns of Pere II and Jaume II and stood as favored vassals of these kings brought a rapid and deeply felt backlash among the island's more ancient nobilities which owed their existence to the Hohenstaufen and Angevin reigns of the past century. With Pietro II's rule, even the claim that Sicily only had one nobility was clearly untrue and was rapidly abandoned by the crown.[2] With Pietro's death in 1242, the broad agricultural zones of the island spawned a series of mini-wars between the old and new nobilities. These struggles were only temporarily held in check by Pietro's brother, Duke Giovanni of Athens and Neopatria, who acted as regent for his five-year-old nephew, Ludovico, whose kingship in the months after his father's demise could barely qualify for the name. To pay and feed troops needed to control civil war, the duke established an emergency tax that applied even to Sicily's clergy and nobility of all ranks. In the midst of Europe's first experience with the Black Death which

© The Author(s), under exclusive license to Springer Nature
Switzerland AG 2021
D. J. Kagay, *Elionor of Sicily, 1325–1375*, The New Middle Ages,
https://doi.org/10.1007/978-3-030-71028-6_4

65

swept across the island in the fall of 1347, Sicily suffered another great loss in the following year with the duke's death which quickly intensified scattered but bitter conflicts between baronial factions.[3]

As a sickly and undersized ten-year-old, Ludovico I "the Child" lost his only chance at becoming an effective, or, in fact, any kind of ruler with his uncle's death. Not yet attaining the age of manhood, which in the Middle Ages normally came at age fourteen for males, the king fell under the dominant and effective control of his sister, Constanza, who served as his regent until he came of age in 1352. Hoping to find some money to tamp out the many small fires of civil war in his realm, Ludovico, in one of his first acts as king attempted to impose his will on his warring nobles. To the rebels on both sides of the proliferating conflicts, Ludovico, though he hardly looked the part, was a tyrant. In the minds of those who considered themselves real Sicilians, he threatened to unleash the forces of Aragon on the island a fate that Sicily had only just evaded since the Treaty of Anagni in 1295. In reality, the Aragonese kings were thoroughly occupied with domestic matters such as the rebirth of the Aragonese and Valencian *Unión* in the 1340s. Yet after Elionor's marriage to Pere, the protection of Ludovico, which also could bring peace to his realm, eventually convinced her husband, Pere III, that playing peacemaker in Sicily could be good for the renewal of his dynasty's power in the region. Thus, only months after Elionor's marriage, a small Aragonese naval squadron under the command of Pedro de Montcada made its appearance in Sicilian waters, but did nothing to increase Ludovico's power over his largely uncontrollable barons.[4]

Ludovico's death at age thirteen on October 16, 1355 cast his younger brother, Duke Federico of Athens, and Neopatria into the royal spotlight. When he came to the throne as Federico IV some months later, he remained under the regency of his older sister, Euphemia, for another year. Undersized from various illnesses, the new king tried to model himself on that "glorious prince... and eminent sovereign," his grandfather, Federico III, but thoroughly failed to live up to this official image. Instead, early in 1356, Messina fell to Neopolitan troops which saw two of his younger sisters, Violante and Blanca, captured and held hostage for years in Joanna I's court at Naples. Despite his shortcomings, the young Sicilian monarch yet again attempted to break the baronial stranglehold on his realm once the Neopolitans were driven from the island in 1372. In the same period, he made peace with his over-mighty subjects, but had to admit that from doing so he was weaker than ever. He appreciated the help offered from his most powerful sister, the Aragonese queen, but could never fully understand exactly why she offered it. He must have had some suspicion about Elionor's motives since she had never abandoned her claims to the Sicilian crown. Nevertheless, Federico died on January 27, 1377, still a puppet of his feuding nobles and of the increasing and perhaps self-seeking aid to the Aragonese monarch. Federico "the Simple," however, was successful in one important matter, the leaving of a successor for the Sicilian realm, his daughter María, whose unfortunate lack of surviving heirs once more put Sicily firmly in the Aragonese orbit.[5]

The disintegration of Sicily's political institutions in the period between Ludovico and María was equally obvious in economic and urban terms. The disastrous initial appearance of the Black Death and its several periods of rebirth led to an unbelievable population decline of up to seventy percent both in the island's agricultural provinces and in those regions dominated by major cities, such as Palermo and Messina. Palermo, clearly the largest of the island's cities, saw the number of its households (the most accurate measure of city size and tax assessment in the medieval centuries) drop from 100,000 to 50,000 inhabitants during the years of the plague. A similar decline affected Messina in the late decades of the fourteenth century and explains in some ways the violent relationship of the two population centers. Their competition also sprang from the fact that neither controlled a large hinterland like other European cities and thus could not control agriculture and industry as they did. The violent interaction between Sicilian city and countryside made urban citizenship a dangerous business that both upper and lower classes went to some lengths to avoid. In many ways, then, the reality of power in large Sicilian cities was determined by the much greater economic control that the island's heavily populated agricultural districts enjoyed. Indeed, all these factors encouraged a low-level but constant climate of dissatisfaction and fear that could erupt into violence at any moment.[6]

Like the realities of any royal life in the Middle Ages, those that surrounded Elionor had gradually altered her goals to the dictates of her Sicilian family which was assuredly passing from one crisis to another during her formative years. Though sacrifice for the greater familial good was one of the aims of her upbringing, this sacrifice caused deep anger in the Sicilian princess which she directed toward her mother and aunt who had attempted by force to make her resign her claims to the throne which was reserved for her inept brothers. The pall of her familial relations could

68   D. J. KAGAY

not be avoided for long, even after the new life laid out by her marriage had begun.

Within a few months of landing at Valencia, she began a singular correspondence with her family members in Sicily as well as with many of her servants and officials she had known since childhood. All these remnants of her earlier life helped the Aragonese queen to keep alive in her mind a family group most of whom she would never again see. This activity would also advance the political goals she had set for herself in her adult life.

In the first months as Pere III's wife, Elionor repeatedly expressed how happy she was with the new life she had found on the other side of the Mediterranean as the queen of an important sovereign and an important figure in a glittering court that very often made the important city of Barcelona her home. She happily told her Sicilian relatives about the court life she soon had adapted to. As the years passed, the notes she sent to her old home often expressed a homesickness that would remain with the queen through her child-bearing years and into what the Middle Ages saw as the unfortunate beginning of a sad old age.

Elionor's attempt to help herself by helping her family continued throughout her career as a royal wife and administrator. She used the excellent notarial and archive system of her new realm to send letter after letter ostensibly in aid of her failing homeland. During the reigns of her weak and greatly manipulated brothers, Ludovico and Federico, the Aragonese queen tried to form a group of supporters for the Sicilian crown whose allegiance was not weakened by their connections to either Sicilian or Iberian baronial circles. What she thus repeatedly requested during these years was the protection of the Sicilian king and the viability of his crown.[7]

These matters that the queen claimed to have undertaken only to aid her family were also marked by her self-interest and desire to advance her new realm. She thus sent a stream of ambassadors, whose missions extended well into the 1360s. Though they often carried instructions about the improvement of the Sicilian royal family, they also acted to advance the international position of the Aragonese king and his wife who employed them. As with the envoy of Berenguer Carbonell in 1358, Elionor's ambassadors occasionally tended to family matters like weddings and travel arrangements for her relatives whom she longed to see once more. They also brought up in quasi-official ways the possibility of alliances between Aragon and Sicily against the Genoese and the

Angevins of Naples.[8] These diplomatic missions could be so complicated and dangerous for her envoys that the queen occasionally felt bound to reward them with monetary or territorial gifts expressing her gratitude.[9]

Elionor's carefully crafted image as defender of her family and former realm was accompanied by a desire she had long harbored for increased power in ruling decisions concerning the island she left in 1349. As we have seen, she formally claimed that her dowry was unpaid even months after her marriage. Four years later, she made an agreement with her mother to have the dowry funds which had still not been paid turned over to her.[10] As the years went by, this money was not forthcoming. As her brothers died off, the Aragonese queen continued to make claims on the island kingdom. With Ludovico's death in 1356, she claimed half of his possessions and the ruling rights over Sicily if its barons would help her. In April of the same year, she opposed an assembly of nobles and townsmen who hailed her second brother, Federico, as Sicily's next king. Elionor angrily denied that this action was valid since by the political doctrine of primogeniture she had to be the island's next ruler. Clearly, with the death of her sister, Constanza, in 1355, Elionor was the oldest surviving heir. By her reasoning, Federico, sixteen years her junior, had no right to the Sicilian crown, which should belong directly to her.[11]

Even after his sickly brother was ushered on to the throne, Elionor, though a queen of another realm, continued demanding her rights to the Sicilian throne. Between 1356 and 1358, she took another tack claiming, it was only prudent for her to be hailed as Federico's successor since he had no successors, and was not likely to have any. During these years, several diplomatic missions attempted to entice Federico to acknowledge her sister or one of her sons as his successor on the Sicilian throne. The Aragonese queen's drive to be accepted as the sovereign of her homeland continued into the early 1360s when she continued to point out how dangerous it would be for Sicily if her weak brother neither produced a successor nor named one, the most prominent of whom had to be Elionor herself.[12] Most of the letters the queen received from the Sicilian court in the early years were written by noble men and women inquiring after "her new and happy arrival" in eastern Spain. Elionor's correspondence in those first years began extending invitations to important figures of her homeland to visit her court in Barcelona. In the late summer of 1350 during her first pregnancy, she requested the company and support of Sicilian noblewomen, whom she hoped would see her through the birth of her first child. At approximately the same time, the queen requested one of her Sicilian officials the grant of "a beautiful palfrey, gentle and fit for traveling" to make the long distance of the new realm less of an obstacle.[13]

In these missives, we see a young woman who has just emigrated from her original family home to a new courtly environment. Though a new life stretched before her, presaging at least the possibility of increased power, the old influence with her surviving parent and siblings remained and could not be left behind. As if she had moved to a higher elevation, Elionor could now see both family circles and how she was connected to them. On the surface, the inquiries about the "bodily health" of the figures she grew up with,[14] while heartfelt, often formed a mere prelude to discussions of family business which she hoped to influence in a positive way from her new position in the Aragonese court. In very short order, at least in her own mind, the new queen had established in December 1350 an important role within her new courtly environment by giving her husband a healthy male heir, Joan. Even before her son's birth, however, she hoped to continue with the advancement of her own importance in the political milieu of the Crown of Aragon which she was certain would prove crucial for the survival of the Sicilian dynasty from which she had sprung.

In the first few years of Elionor's life as Aragonese queen, we witness her attempting to solve problems with and for her Sicilian family by using practical economic resources which she could access through her new position. Some of these problems she solved without reference to Sicily. Thus after her mother, Elizabeth of Carinthia, had traveled to Valencia for her daughter's wedding and had stayed with her well into 1350, Elionor took it on herself to have Elizabeth's expenses paid through financial mechanisms of the Aragonese government.[15]

The queen showed the same administrative skill and determination that would mark her later royal career when she attempted to recover a great deal of money owed her, not by hectoring her husband with sorrowful complaints, but by skillful use of the various laws of her new realms. In a formal meeting in Valencia a few days before Christmas in 1349, the queen, in the company of her husband, formally demanded her dowry which had not been given to her by King Ludovico. Quoting the wills of her grandfather, Federico III, her father, Pietro II, and her uncle, Duke Giovanni, she demanded the 10,000 *onzas* of gold these documents promised her. From this sum, she specified that her debtors would be paid, and the remainder would immediately be turned over to her by the leader of Sicily's Catalan faction, Blasco de Alagon. Because of "certain arduous and necessary issues," the noblemen were duty-bound to dispatch as quickly as possible her dowry as well as all her "jewels and goods."[16] Shortly after this proclamation, the royal couple sent a copy of it to Alagon warning him that failure to act expeditiously would cause him and his supporters "very great peril." If the Aragonese king had to make Alagon do his duty by attacking Sicily, the nobleman's position of power, fragile as it was, would collapse.[17]

Later in Christmas week, Elionor wrote to her sister, Euphemia, and brother, Federico, for their help in the dowry problem. On the next day, December 19, she sent two further letters to Duke Federico, all but demanding his help with Alagon and the other barons who controlled much of Sicily's government, such as it was. At the same time she fired off another stern message to Alagon threatening him with the news that her husband was about to send a number of galleys to bring some semblance of peace and order to the island and return to Valencia with the queen's money and possessions.[18] Unfortunately, threats had little effect on men who had long held the Sicilian king and his brother under their control.

Many of Elionor's long-range plans for Sicily could not be discussed from an Aragonese point-of-view alone, but always needed the cooperation of her less-than-forceful brothers, who as kings had to support the projects she wanted to see carried out. Acting like her mother, the Aragonese queen turned to the complicated problem of getting her younger sisters, Euphemia, Violante, and Blanca married. This desire to contribute to the "honor of the lady princesses" motivated the efforts of the Aragonese queen throughout 1351 to get Euphemia married to a Navarrese prince.[19] When this project fell through, Elionor formed an even more complicated plan whereby her sisters would be wed at the same time to several of their Pyrenean cousins, including Count Pedro of Ribagorza.[20] She had even engaged a German servant to act as ambassadors in these marriage matters, but he attained little success, since Ludovico had no money to spare for dowries, even for Elionor herself.[21] Despite the queen's increasing displeasure with "the Child," her self-appointed role as news agent between Sicily and Aragon led her to formally announce Ludovico's death and Federico's ascent to the throne in the last months of 1355.

To maintain the lifeline between her old and new homes, the Aragonese queen utilized both Sicilian and Aragonese officials to carry out her orders and function as her "eyes on the ground" in both realms

72 D. J. KAGAY

and in between. Many of her officials had begun their careers within the Sicilian court. In 1351, the queen received a request from one of her father's old officials, Guillem Arnaldun, a native of Palermo, who was seeking a new administrative post. After being threatened "during the disturbances of the civil war" that marked the last years of Ludovico's reign," the Aragonese queen felt it her duty to accept him into her household on the same conditions of service and salary as her Iberian officials.[22] This marked the first of a number of Sicilian émigrés who took service with the queen and often acted as messengers and envoys to her homeland. Elionor's acceptance of Sicilians into her courts and households was repeated with some frequency between 1351 and 1370. Each of these new officials was accepted on the same terms as her other servitors.[23] Since some of these men also entered the ranks of the queen's advisers and were occasionally given missions of trust which took them back across the Mediterranean to their former homeland, they also had to carry tasks of less importance such as the delivery of fine cloth to major Sicilian barons to have liveries made for their own servants. In all likelihood, spying on the courtiers of her royal brothers may not have been outside the realm of their duties.[24] As was normal with most royal agents, ranging from messengers to ambassadors, the men serving on a mission to Sicily all carried letters dictated by the queen which identified the bearer, and commanded the addressee to consider carefully what her representative had to say to them and then to apply "credible faith" to their words.[25] Since Elionor's Sicilian officials had to make at least a two-week voyage, to get to Sicily, depending on the winds, and then spend some days in carrying out their mission, they could easily spend up to a month to fulfill their duties and get back to eastern Spain. With a per-diem rate of up to 4 Barcelona *sous* a day, these officials had to be paid a sizeable sum once they returned to Elionor's court and submitted a suitable expense report. Other officials like the Aragonese king's secretary who spent long weeks in Sicily as an ambassador could receive a single payment of up to 2,000 Barcelona *sous*.[26]

The Sicilian members of Elionor's court personnel whom she sent to her homeland to carry out her wishes there ranged from merchants and notaries up to secretaries and lawyers. Their duties could range from the delivery of green cloth to King Federico's court or four braids of fringe to decorate his dagger. These missions, however, also involved the queen's men in important state business such as sending envoys to the Papal Curia in Avigion or dispatching a troop of soldiers to protect such representatives. These agents also delivered important messages originating with Pere III and then forwarded by his wife. They occasionally contained royal instructions to increase Sicily's grain quote for the eastern Spanish grain market, which was often prone to seasonal shortages. They also carried important instructions to Federico's royal sister such as that of 1356 concerning his upcoming marriage to Pere III's first-born daughter, Constanza. In her first years as queen, Elionor was not above deputizing citizens of Palermo to "defend in person... and protect... [her] family from the disturbance of the [civil] war." She also asked her officials, whether permanent or not, to keep their eyes peeled for all political and military events that she had to know about.[27]

The diplomatic and administrative means that quickly gave Elionor a simple and fairly effective means of communication with her home island quickly convinced her how terrible things had become for Ludovico, who though hailed as king had no means of enforcing his will, even if he knew what it was. Subject to several regencies which concluded with that of his older sister, Constanza, in 1353, the king did little to improve the steadily worsening situation. Watching from afar but well informed of how her land was falling to pieces, Elionor now was determined to become more deeply involved in Sicilian affairs.

By September 1349, though her little brother had been crowned, but was under the close control of Blasco de Alagon and his associates, the view the Aragonese queen saw from Spain was of a kingdom oppressed by ever-darkening "rumors of war." Moved to help Ludovico if possible, Elionor fired off letters to her younger sister, Euphemia, the urban council of the Sicilian city of Catania, and several supporters in Messina. By these missives, the queen called for a public response to the widening danger to which Sicily was daily falling into. Royal officials of the island had to enforce the fealty to its ultimate lord, King Ludovico. The various classes now had to defend themselves courageously and with a "similar zeal for honor."[28]

As the years passed and the violence never abated, Elionor's calls for peace and mutual respect for Sicily's royal institutions widened to include aid from power brokers of her new kingdom. Her language during these hard times was not always hopeful, but she did mention her brother's few supporters with honest praise. In August 1351, she wrote to the town council of Perpignan, asking for what help it could give for the "defense of our faithful Catania" against Sicilian rebels by helping convince them

74   D. J. KAGAY

to lay down their arms. What Pere III's northernmost city thought of the queen's simplistic appeal is not known. What can be said of her general appeals for Sicily, however, are that she believed in the righteousness of the seemingly hopeless cause she had espoused. At the beginning of 1352, the queen made another appeal to her urban citizens, this time to the "fortunate men of Panormia (Palermo)." She called on them to reject "perfidious sedition with its various crises and... many dangers." There was no solution save the avoidance of "pestiferous war.... calamities of battle... and the destruction of all types of goods." She begged Palermo's citizens to take the right road to peace by making earnest appeals to St. Luke and the Blessed Virgin Mary.[29]

Through the first years of her queenship, Elionor's drumbeat in support of the Sicilian sovereign was initially accompanied by naval and military aid from her husband. In October 1349, only some two months after her wedding, the queen arranged to send one of her officials on a secret mission to Sicily. Within a month, she wrote Blasco de Heredía, an Aragonese official serving in Sicily, to have him take on the enemies of her brother by raising companies of horse and foot and coordinating attacks with her other brother, Giovanni.[30] In another letter dated November 9 in which she included a description of her "tranquil voyage" to Valencia in some ten days and her arrival "safe and sound... to meet her beloved husband and lord," she also mentioned that Sicilian ambassadors accompanied her. Shortly after this the new queen wrote to Ludovico's first regent, Mateo de Plizzi. She told him of the meeting with the Sicilian envoys "in her chamber," and how she had informed them that Pere would aid, the "illustrious king of Sicily" with a fleet of galleys (*stolium gallearum*) that would hopefully bring about a "peaceful and tranquil state" across the island.[31]

In the following spring of 1350, when the Aragonese king had begun fitting out galleys and gathering troops and sailors for the "Sicilian enterprise," Elionor sent letters to a long list of Sicilian nobles of the Catalan faction assuring them that they would receive 40 Barcelona *sous* for each man recruited, who themselves would receive a daily wage of six *sous* for a guaranteed two-months service. During the same period, she continued her correspondence with Heredía begging him to use the Iberian nobles in Sicily to protect Ludovico who would soon be in great danger. Any horsemen the official recruited would have to swear their allegiance to the Aragonese queen "in a public letter." The proposed payment for these fighting men jumped—probably from Elionor's desperation—to 20

Barcelona *libras*. At approximately the same time, the queen sent a similar request to the men of Palermo.[32] As we have seen, an "invasion" of Sicily had taken place in late 1349 when Pedro de Montcada led a fleet of galleys into Sicilian waters, but accomplished little either on land or sea.[33] Certainly, none of these actions calmed Elionor's fears; over two years later, she swore that she had no evidence that her brother had ever renounced his royal office, nor would she accept such a surrender of power, even if it were made.[34]

Even though Elionor's message was hopeful during the first days of Ludovico's reign, she occasionally singled out for criticism enemies of the king who utilized for their own benefit the anarchy that was becoming commonplace in Sicily. In this vein, she wrote in the summer of 1350 a scathing attack on a knight called Jaume Mostaça who in the command of some horsemen of Messina ravaged Catania's agricultural environs. Despite this thorough dressing down, the queen left room for reconciliation by observing that despite his evil actions against Ludovico, he might still be remembered positively for the honest "service and [good] deeds he had once carried out for her."[35]

Elionor sent the same kind of mixed political message in August of the same year to her other brother, Duke Federico of Athens and Neopatria, not about the commission of evil deeds, but concerning the neglect of doing his duty. Though younger than Ludovico, his sister had asked the prince time and again to take a more meaningful part in "improving the condition of the reduced realm" by helping with the arming of a Sicilian fleet that could support the Aragonese naval unit. Such determined and unified action would demonstrate "the solidarity of ... [Federico's] allegiance." Despite the fact that the duke had nothing to support his brother, Elionor and her husband had fully supported the younger prince after his brother's death on October 16, 1355, with the fond though, thoroughly unrealistic hope that the new ruler would act successfully for the "repair of [Sicily's] good estate."[36]

Elionor's support of the new king, like that of his sibling, was connected more with royal than family preservation. Over a month after Ludovico's demise, Elionor learned of the unhappy fact from the governor of Sardinia, but heard nothing of Ludovico's death and the crisis that it caused from her brother but rather from her many personal and political contacts in Sicily. If Federico did not rapidly claim the "diadem of the realm" and become the king of the island, his sister was afraid that a repeat of the "irreparable damage" of the past two decades could not

76   D. J. KAGAY

be prevented. She counseled her brother to send a "special ambassador" to the Aragonese king in order to work out a suitable treaty with him and then have it validated by Pope Innocent VI.[37]

Only after her brother was crowned in the fall of 1355 did she write to the new king and his great nobles to offer her advice. On January 23, 1356, Elionor sent the same letter to Sicily's barons, and, in it, characterized Ludovico's death and his brother's advancement to the throne as a godsend. The kingdom was at peace, and by acting in unison they could all keep it in that happy state. They would ultimately require the help of the Aragonese king and the pope, however, to finalize such a viable solution for the island.[38] In a second communique, she finally dealt directly with her royal brother and expressed great joy at his advance to the throne. Though she assured Frederico that he could depend on the help of the great nobles, she repeated a sentiment she had expressed to Ludovico; namely, that the royal court was surrounded by dangers which the king had to protect against. She was thus sending him her invaluable secretary Berenguer Carbonell to help put out the political "fires" that surrounded him. In a poignant postscript, she wished him "happiness and health," and sent the same wishes from her husband, and three-year-old son, Joan.[39]

In the next few months, Elionor moved to strengthen Federico's political position as king. In February 1356, she informed the pope of Ludovico's death and asked for help in setting up a proper ruler for the island insisting this had to be her brother Federico. By May, she told Innocent VI that she was sending ambassadors to him to see if together they could work out a proper settlement for the island.[40] At the same time, the queen, sent the Sicilian "master of accounts" (*magister racional*) in the Aragonese court to her brother to help him improve the primitive state of his finances. In her way of asking for many things in a few words, Elionor instructed this expert accountant to be "sufficiently attentive, diligent, and anxious" with the decrepit state of Sicily's finances.[41]

Even before Federico IV had been unenthusiastically hailed as king, he faced a crisis which in many ways had led his older brother to the grave and which still had to be addressed. In the spring of 1354 after Joanna I of Naples had conspired with several barons of Sicily's Latin faction, she unleashed a small invasion that caused yet another civil war on the island. By summer 1356 after a year-and-a-half of military strife across the island, the Aragonese queen once more thought it was time to get involved in calling yet again for the possibility of Sicilian peace.

On July 22, she dispatched her secretaries, Francesch de Bellcastell and Berenguer de Carbonell, to aid in the peace negotiations at the Papal Curia in Avignon, which she and her husband had long urged Federico to engage in.[42] When the peace efforts of Aragon's royal couple failed to bring about meaningful change—very much through Federico's obstinate inaction, Elionor became increasingly angry with her brother. On October 24, she wrote him proclaiming that the "operations of the Devil" held her homeland under their control. The perennial episodes of scattered warfare were now transforming into the "greatest of calamities." Despite this, the Aragonese queen was confident that God would arrange a tenable peace for Federico if he would work to see it carried out. Yet, as she had sarcastically pointed out to the Sicilian king on many occasions, he now had to "[actually] make peace rather than pretending to." He had to give up his efforts at conquest, ineffective as they had been, and turn resolutely toward peace. This would largely depend on negotiations with his baronial enemies, a task he was not often willing to engage in Though his sister would declare "her appreciation and sincere love [for the king]," Federico had long distrusted her as a rival for his very throne.[43]

This change in the Sicilian king was caused by what the preeminent Sicilian historian, Francesco Giunta, called Elionor's "iron will" in putting her stamp on Sicilian political affairs. As 1356 passed, she openly began to engage in behavior which revealed her growing frustration with her brother. On May 23, she temporarily recalled the Sicilian baron and royal adviser, Orlando of Aragon, and specifically instructed him to stay away from Federico. With this order, she ended his previous role as a kind of super-adviser for the Sicilian sovereign. Her distaste for the laziness and stupidity of Federico "the Simple" became more obvious in the next few months. In the late fall, Elionor exceeded the limits of her publicly expressed patience. In very specific terms normally used by a superior person to one in an inferior position, she ordered her brother to pay traditional imposts to the papacy, and make good a longstanding debt to a Sicilian baronial family which he had incurred with the purchase of one of their castles. On December 13, she again complained to the king that his ambassador at Avignon had done little to represent Siciliy's national rights in a conference with Joanna I's representatives and would accept her as Sicily's ruler after Federico's death.[44]

In spite of the differences between the Aragonese and Sicilian kings, they were able to collaborate on many important issues. In Pere III's opinion, the most important of these for the security of Federico's reign

78   D. J. KAGAY

was his marriage to Constanza, Pere III's oldest daughter from his first marriage. As the original guarantor of his own succession, the Aragonese sovereign had long considered this union a largely painless way of reestablishing closer ruling ties for his dynasty with Sicily. In 1355, Pere began making this long-held plan a reality by sending envoys to Avignon to arrange for a papal dispensation for the cousin's marriage. In a few months, the proper paperwork had been requested, approved, and issued; now the husband-to-be became a full partner in the legal process which had now openly begun.

All of this complicated activity had gone on in the Aragonese court, and it was not until 1356 that Aragon's royal couple took it on themselves to officially inform the Sicilian king and his barons concerning the wedding arrangements. In a long letter sent to his brother and future son-in-law on October 26, Elionor announced that she and her husband had moved to successfully complete these "Sicilian matters" by bringing Federico's marriage to completion. To clear the royal schedule for this momentous event, she instructed her fifteen-year-old brother to immediately make peace with the queen of Naples and settle other disputes with Innocent VI which had lingered far too long. When his diplomats had accomplished these matters, Federico formally learned that his bride was to be the thirteen-year-old princess, Constanza, whom her father, Pere III "loved very much." The Aragonese king considered their nuptials so important that, even though Pedro I of Castile had recently declared war on him, he would not postpone the wedding because he assumed, quite wrongly, that the conflict, which ultimately lasted ten years, "would not have a great duration."[45]

After a four-year delay for the final completion of the wedding plans, due principally to Pere's lingering war with Pedro I of Castile, Constanza and her sister, Joanna, were informed in March 1360 that the wedding was again to go forward. In early summer, Pere wrote to his oldest daughter—"as dear to him as a daughter can be"—that several galleys were being readied for her trip to Sicily. She was to have 3,000 gold florins for travel expenses, but mirroring his desperate need for money, the king instructed her to return all her jewels as well as the gold and silver vessels she had long used to her father's officials or the monastery of the Saint Clares in Barcelona., where they would supposedly be kept for her if she ever returned to eastern Spain. This extraordinary action was finally explained when a public proclamation, signed by Pere, Elionor, Constanza, and her sister, Joanna, was issued on September 28, 1360. In this public document, Pere formally admitted that he had pawned the silken clothes, ermine furs, "jewels and brilliant gems" that he had given to his daughters."

With these precious symbols of royal wealth temporarily turned into ready cash, the king paid for her trip to Sicily. Elionor borrowed 26,000 Barcelona *sous* from a banker of the Catalan capital, Guillem Terri, and promised its repayment in less than a year. Constanza then swore she would repay all the money raised for her nuptials once she became the Sicilian queen. Fortunately, this sum was reduced because of urban revenues in Roussillon which all Pere's daughters would receive in the next year. Elionor took the responsibility for having this money collected and applied to her stepdaughter's travel debts.[46] This remarkable monetary exchange between Pere III and his family shows how expensive five years of war had become for the Aragonese monarch.

The bride-to-be, her sister, and ladies-in-waiting left Barcelona on November 9, 1360 and crossed to Sardinia where the bridal party spent Christmas. Their vessel then passed across the Tyrhhian Sea, landing at Trapani on January 10, 1361. While the actual bills for the wedding continued to surface for months after Constanza had left her family, the Aragonese money-raising activities also continued. In December 1360 when Pere and his daughter sold off a castle for ready cash, Federico disregarded how expensive his new family ties were for his in-laws and happily took command of the two hundred horsemen who were to receive salaries from his father-in-law for some months.[47] Constanza showed that she was her father's daughter by the way she took charge of her court responsibilities. Perhaps the most important of her duties was giving birth to her daughter, María, on July 3, 1363, which led to her own death a few days later.

After Constanza's death and her daughter's removal from the Aragonese court, Elionor relations with Sicily slowly changed. In the previous years, she was interested in her brother's military achievements against Neopolitan raiders and Sicilian barons, as limited as they were. Even before his marriage to Constanza, Federico could happily report that he was temporarily supported by Aragonese ships and troops. These Sicilian clashes also caught the interest of Pere III and the Aragonese court. As she often did, the queen attempted to gain information about her brother's military ventures and negotiations with the pope. Writing to her sister, Euphemia, and other important allies of the Sicilian king on the

80   D. J. KAGAY

same day (July 12, 1357), Elionor inquired again about a minor victory won by royal forces in which her brother received a minor wound.[48]

Sicily's low-level fighting continued between Federico and a number of opportunist foreign enemies including Neopolitan battalions, and forces paid by the Visconti dukes of Milan, Barnabò (r. 1354–1385) and Galeazzo (r.1354–1385). We have little record of Elionor's interest in her brother's gormless doings through the late 1360s and down to 1370 when the Sicilian monarch entered into negotiations with Joanna I about settling their long dispute. Elionor had already begged her brother in mid-May 1370 to involve her husband in these negotiations, Federico, as always, gave into his dominant sister and accepted the involvement of an Aragonese adviser in these talks in June. While these diplomatic meetings were in session for well into the fall, Pere sent another envoy to take part in the decisions that were finally announced in late October 1372.[49] Perhaps under the influence of the ambassadors, Federico agreed to the settlement of the past century that his title would remain until his death, but the Neopolitan ruler could immediately claim the title of Sicilian queen. Though this settlement hardly pleased the Aragonese royal couple, they had no need for worry since Federico had no intention of living up to the agreement.

Even after his sickly brother was ushered on to the throne, Elionor, though a queen of another realm, continued demanding her rights to the Sicilian throne. Between 1356 and 1358, she took up another tack, claiming it was only prudent for her to be hailed as Federico's successor, since he had no successors and was not likely to have any. During these years, several diplomatic missions attempted to entice Federico to name her sister or one of her sons as the successor to Sicily. Elionor's drive to be accepted as the sovereign of her homeland continued into the early 1360s when she continued to emphasize the danger that would come to Sicily if her weak brother produced no successors and named none, the most prominent of which was to be Elionor herself.[50]

2   ELIONOR'S DIPLOMACY

Most of Elionor's letters to her homeland after she left it for good in 1349 were directed to her brothers and sisters and concerned private and public matters, all of which she considered the personal matters of their family. Because she often stood between her old home and her new one, she was occasionally engaged in communications with Mediterranean powers that often interacted with her old and new realms.

The Aragonese queen never set aside her concern for Sicily and her brothers who ruled it. This was not simply due to the absence of any effective central power on the island but also evolved from the constant splintering of baronial groups who fought to control the occupant of the Sicilian throne, no matter who he or she might be. Elionor and her husband were deeply worried about the Mediterranean powers, both Christian and Muslim, that hoped to gain political and economic power political and economic advantages from a weakened Sicily. In 1359, the Aragonese queen took on these problems one by one. In September, she opened negotiations with the sultan of Morocco, Abu-al-Husan [Bonnen], and was successful in gaining a ten-year truce with Federico's Sicily and the sultan's promise that he would supply his new ally with the use of ten to fifteen galleys or five-hundred horsemen whenever they were needed. Elionor also arranged that the Aragonese commander of the Castle of Caller in Sardinia would supply the Sicilian ruler transport ships for his military operations.

Affair of the Princesses

In the midst of the queen's general concerns for her departed homeland, the Aragonese queen had to take up the mantle of protection for her family by repeating to all her diplomatic partners an identical call for help for her two sisters, Violante and Blanca, who had been in Neopolitan "courteous custody" for months.[51] These younger siblings had been captured during the daring raid launched by Joanna I on the day before Christmas in 1356. The queen apparently only heard of this family disaster in the first part of 1357, and after making her anger clear to the new Sicilian king, Federico, she sent her secretary, Berenguer Carbonell, to attempt some way of having the princesses freed. A full year later, the matter remained unchanged, despite Pope Innocent VI's attempts to have Elionor's sisters released from their imprisonment and transferred to the Aragonese castle of Caller in Sardinia. A year later, in 1359, the pontiff made another attempt to move the princesses to Avignon, but this effort also failed.[52]

At the same period, Elionor also turned to direct negotiations, sending an envoy, Laurenç Texon, to Naples where he was to engage in talks concerning the release of the princesses, their transfer to Sardinia, and how much money the Aragonese queen would pay to see this justice done. In June 1359, Elionor started making long-term plans by alerting her relative, the Marquess of Montestrat, to be ready to receive the queen's relatives when they were finally released from their Neopolitan captivity. No real movement took place, however, and after some months had passed, Elionor began to beat the diplomatic drums once more asking the pope and a number of Sicilian and Catalan clergy for help. Not until 1362 did Joanna I and her current husband, Louis of Taranto, agree to the release of Violante and Blanca. They left the transfer expenses to their rival, the Aragonese queen, who had to scrounge money from her own revenues to bring her sisters to Barcelona and conclude this family disaster, but only after six years had passed.[53]

Further Attempts at Negotiation with Naples

With matters on the periphery of her main concern in the Mediterranean settled or at least addressed, Elionor in March 1357 turned to her fear for her brother's shaky control of Sicily by providing a list of detailed instructions to her envoys to the island, Berenguer de Carbonell and Nolfo de Procida. This list would comprise the subjects to be discussed with King Federico. In this directive to her trusted officials, the queen declared that her husband was willing to financially support any legitimate military operation the Sicilian king was planning to undertake in the next year. This would largely be carried out by supplying and funding a "good company of horse and foot" for the agreed-upon period. Of course, this would depend on Pere III's own financial needs in his long-running conflict with Pedro I of Castile. If this proved the case, the Aragonese king's use of administrative and diplomatic means to attend to his brother-in-law's needs would also serve his own.[54]

In other clauses of the 1357 list, Elionor expressed her anger and that of her husband at the shocking fact that a formal coronation had not been immediately carried out for Federico after Ludovico's death. Instead, her brother had been acting as king for two years without such a ceremony to make his rule legitimate. One of the queen's greatest concerns was an immediate diplomatic settlement was the Neopolitan capture of Messina in the previous year, and with it the imprisonment of her younger sisters, Violante and Blanca. As on many other occasions, Elionor demanded that Naples' queen should free the princesses who ranged from thirteen to twenty-three years old. She warned Joanna I that Pope Innocent VI had already been notified of the shocking and illegal act of holding royal women hostage and Naples' ruler would suffer serious consequences if she did not comply. Though the royal couple had already set the deadline for such compliance, it had already passed and so they set a new one, an act which did not promise any hope for immediate success.[55]

While the conference which Elionor laid out in 1357 did take place in the next year, very few of the issues she listed for consideration were taken up in any meaningful way. A year after this meeting, the queen still complaining concerning the illegal imprisonment of her sisters wrote the pope who forced Joanna to free the princesses and turn them over to Elionor in 1363, seven years after they had been captured in Messina. Blanca, the queen's youngest sister, was now twenty-one years old. In the next year, she married Count Joan of Empuries dying nine years later without children.[56] The Aragonese queen continued to address the threat of Sicily's Mediterranean enemies in the summer of 1359 when she warned off the Marquis of Montferrat as well as the doge and Commune of Genoa from helping Pere's principal enemy, Pedro I of Castile, who shortly before this had attempted to negotiate an alliance with Joanna I of Naples.[57]

Sardinia

While the Mediterranean islands of Corsica and Sardinia came into the hands of Jaume II of Aragon in 1296, nothing was done about them besides inserting their names in the king's regnal list until 1323. In that year, Jaume unleashed a naval invasion of Sardinia and, in alliance with the strongest baronial leaders of the island, the judges of Arborea quickly accepted the concept of Aragonese rule over the Sardinians. This persisted despite scattered rumbles of indigenous rebellion and persistent Genoese interference. The inhumane Aragonese treatment of the Sards over the next decade shattered Jaume II's alliance with the current judge of Arborea who found enthusiastic support in the Commune of Genoa. If this was not bad enough, the Sards in the early 1350s began attacking Aragonese and Catalan settlers on the island who were guilty of enslaving sizeable sections of the island's native population.[58]

As Sardinian instability increased, Pere III in 1354 emulated his father, Alfons III, when he brought a moderately sized fleet against the Mediterranean outpost offloading an army at least as large as the force that won Sardinia twenty years before in an attempt to establish fuller control over the Arboreans and their Sard allies. After superficially putting out the flames of revolt on the island, the Aragonese king returned to Spain leaving garrisons in important castles to monitor any future Sardinian resistance.[59]

On January 1, 1354, standing on a scaffolding set up in front of Santa María de la Mar in Barcelona, Pere III announced his intention to act as a "good shepherd" in pacifying the ungrateful and violent island of Sardinia. Though the king did not mention his wife among the "other officials of... [his] household" who were at this public meeting, it was highly unlikely that she was not there, because of the reputation she had gained as somewhat of a Mediterranean expert since her appearance on the Crown of Aragon's courtly scene six years before.[60] Within three weeks of her husband's speech, Elionor wrote to Blasco de Alagon, King Ludovico's principal adviser, asking that he try to convince his young master to engage in a "league or agreement" that would add Sicilian troops to the Aragonese invasion force. According to the queen, this mere promise of aid would lead directly to the "repair of the kingdom of Sicily."[61]

After remaining for a full year in Sardinia, the royal couple returned from Cagliari to Alghero and due west across the Mediterranean to Barcelona where they arrived in the second week of September 1355.[62] Some months later, Elionor was asking for help from the monastery of Santa María Poblet to attain a suitable horse or mule for her own travel needs. While journeying with her husband to the "parts of Sardinia," the queen explained that both the Aragonese army and court suffered from a "great scarcity of horses" through the effects of battle and rustling.[63] At the same time, the queen began to raise money from her own urban revenues to help provide general funds for the continuing Sardinian conflict and smaller grants to individuals who were still fighting for her husband's cause on the island. She also set about collecting from her Aragonese cities sufficient funds to pay off the debts incurred from the Sardinian trip which still remained unpaid.[64]

In the years after Sardinia came off the boil, Pere III paid less attention to the island because of the ever-expanding war with Castile. Even before she first became her husband's lieutenant in 1362, Elionor spent a good deal of time gathering intelligence about the fluid Sardinian situation from the island's townsmen and nobles. She also occasionally sent along the king's orders about preventing "danger, damage, and scandal" in Sardinian main urban sites of Sassari, and Alghero as well as the royal castle of the Cape of Lugidor. This was to be accomplished by denying "foreigners" access to these places. This category of unwelcome intruders included Genoese and Pisan traders and even the native Sard population.[65]

Elionor's support of her husband's attempts to suppress the episodes of low-level opposition in Sardinia continued into the last years of her life. She very publicly heaped her praise on the count of Arborea who had left his rebellious relatives to join the Aragonese side. The queen also took it on herself to have large supplies of biscuit and bread made transported to Pere's troops on the island. She also appointed some of the officials who readied galleys for Sardinian service. In all these matters, she helped her homeland by arranging for the export of Sicilian food across the Tyrrhenian Sea to Aragonese bases on Sardinia. She continued gathering money to help maintain her husband's continuing efforts in the western Mediterranean, but at times had to divert these funds to repair the galleys that linked eastern Spain to Sardinia. By 1374, she tried to insure an Aragonese presence on the island—something her husband had largely despaired of—by granting preferment to those who would maintain the fight to guarantee a continuing Aragonese presence on the island.[66]

Iberian and Mediterranean Rivals

While the Aragonese queen continued to keep Pope Innocent VI informed of Sicilian affairs in her first decade of rule, she also used this diplomatic pipeline to settle disputes with her own clergy, but also to keep before the Papal Curia Aragon's long-term and temporary disputes with its principal Iberian enemies, Castile and Granada, and its continental opponents, France and Genoa.[67]

The Castilian threat to the Crown of Aragon was well-known in the Mediterranean thanks to the Aragonese queen's regular correspondence to her Sicilian relatives on the War of the Two Pedros after it began in 1356. During the first phase of the conflict, Elionor informed Artal de Alagon, the justiciar of Sicily, that her husband was advancing on the evil Castilian king, who now had no chance to avoid battle as he had managed to do before. The Sicilians were to be ready to help their good Aragonese friend if needs be.[68] The queen routinely volunteered such war news to her new subjects and those of her homeland during the next years. In July 1359 Pedro I commanded a fleet consisting of 127 vessels that sailed from Seville into the Mediterranean and then along the Valencian and

86   D. J. KAGAY

Catalan coasts attacking Guardamar, Ibiza, and Alicante, before returning to Seville.

The Aragonese queen notified the residents of the affected coastal areas telling them of the great danger Pedro I of Castile (the king's and queen's enemy) posed to them and how they as good vassals could help the royal couple. At the same time, Elionor spread the news that the Castilian king was forced to lift his siege of Ibiza by her husband's fleet. Yet, she and her officials had no idea of the fate of Pere's fleet. Calmly but with obvious concern, the queen asked her clergy, nobles, and townsmen to get word to her of her husband's fate. Her worry quickly lifted, however, when Pere, after dividing his fleet at Majorca, quickly returned to Barcelona.[69] In the last years of the conflict with Castile, the queen drew from funds pledged by the Aragonese *cortes* to pay some of the expenses of privateers who were to attack all Castilian vessels they encountered. Despite her clear dislike of the Castilian king, Elionor did not pass up the temporary descent of peace on the Peninsula to improve her own relations with her erstwhile enemy. By 1368, however, she was aiding the passage of mercenaries into Castile to aid in the final victory against Pedro I.[70]

While Elionor maintained at least some general correspondence with the French monarchy as well as with her German relatives, the duke of Bavaria and the count palatinate, her more memorable letters were those sent in defense of her subjects against the depredations of French mercenaries across Roussillon and Granada's capture and imprisonment of Valencian citizens.[71]

Due to its clear danger to her Sicilian homeland, Elionor had long viewed the Commune of Genoa as an enemy. After her marriage she understood that the Genoese cast a long economic and naval shadow over her new home. As Aragon became more embroiled in Sardinia, her husband found the Genoese such a potential threat that he eventually joined with the Serene Republic of Venice in a naval conflict that spanned most of the later 1360s.[72] The Genoese merchant marine continued as a dangerous threat in the central Mediterranean and along the Catalan and Valencian coasts, but the Commune's merchant/settlers in Sardinia, Sicily, and Catalonia itself caused even greater alarm to Queen Elionor who viewed these unofficial Genoese colonists as a kind of "fifth column" in a war-torn land which had been repeatedly overrun by Castilian attacks.

During the summer of 1359, when Pedro I brought his large fleet up the Valencian/Catalan littoral and against the Balearics, the Aragonese queen viewed the control of the Genoese in Catalonia as essential for the region's safety. She thus sternly instructed the Duke and Commune of Genoa to aid in removing all Genoese citizens away from the Catalan coast. If this middling population failed to fulfill these orders they would soon find themselves guilty of *lèse-majesté* against the Aragonese king. All Genoese settlers in Catalonia had to be formally listed as aliens before they were moved inland. The forced march, led by Bernat de Cabrera to Barcelona, was to begin on August 11, 1359. The queen granted all the Genoese a safe conduct for their journey to the Catalan capital. Once there, they were permitted to board Genoese ships and depart for their original homes. Those that remained were to swear to uphold the agreement recently made between the Aragonese king and the Commune which forced the Genoese who intended to stay in Catalonia to confirm their allegiance to Pere III. Similar meetings were to take place in the Catalan town of Manresa. Queen Elionor was given the responsibility of seeing that the targeted Genoese carried out these orders to the letter.[73]

Despite this attempt to declare the Genoese under her control as foreign nationals who could be trusted to honor their word, Elionor, at almost the same time, warned her own people that Pedro I of Castile had himself equipped four Genoese galleys to fill out his great armada. According to the queen, this was another reason to keep a close eye on the Genoese under her control.[74]

Queen Elionor's remarkable career as an unofficial representative and spokesperson for Sicily and her family, especially her sickly and thoroughly inept brothers who served as kings, leaves a picture of a truly singular woman. As Francesco Giunta observes about the queen: "this woman…demonstrates an iron will in the fulfillment of her goals."[75] Her adaptability in the face of the defeat of her long-held plans could, according to the same author, "only be explained by a very strong-willed character."[76] Such an assessment can only fully be borne out by a careful study of Elionor's administrative and political career in the Crown of Aragon.

NOTES

1. *Cronache Siciliane Inedite*, 107–8.
2. Giunta, *Aragoneses*, 130.
3. Ibid., 131–34; Zurita, *Anales*, 4:180 (VIII:xxxvi).
4. Giunta, *Aragoneses*, 135–36; Zurita, *Anales*, 4:180–83 (VIII:xxxvi); 252 (VIII:lv; Goldstone, *Joanna I*, 235–37.
5. Giunta, *Aragoneses*, 158–77; Lalinde Abadía, *Corona*, 20–21; Zurita, *Anales*, 4:277–78 (VIII:lx).

88   D. J. KAGAY

6. Henri, Bresc, "Palermo in the 14th-15th Centuy: Urban Economy and Trade," in *A Companion to Medieval Palermo: The History of a Mediterranean City from 600 to 1500*, ed. Annliese Nef (Leiden: Brill, 2013), 235–67, esp. 236, 240, 246, 251; Epstein, "Cities," 17–22, 26, 29–30, 35, 47; E Igor Mineo, "Palermo in the 14th-15th Century: The Urban Society," in *Companion*, 269–96, esp. 273–74, 283–84.
7. ACA, CR, R. 1537, ff. 6v, 28v–29; R. 1582, f. 9v; Deibel, "Reyna Elionor," 358–59.
8. ACA, CR, R. 1565, f. 143v; R. 1567, ff. 56v–58; R. 1576, f. 32v.
9. ACA, CR, R. 1582, f. 53.
10. ACA, CR, R. 1534, ff. 90r–v.
11. ACA, CR, R. 1566, ff. 31r–v, 52.
12. ACA, CR, R. 1566, ff. 170v–171; R. 1567, f. 55; R. 1570, ff. 51–52; Giunta, *Aragoneses*, ff. 174–76.
13. ACA, CR, R. 1563, ff. 4, 21r–v, 30 r–v, 104, r–v; R. 1566, f. 169.
14. This kind of concerns were common in the queen's early communications. The following letters are typical: ACA, CR, R. 1562, ff. 66, 106, 108v, 109, 144; R. 1567, f. 54v.
15. ACA, CR, R. 1563, ff. 100–101. The final total for Elizabeth's junket was 561 Barcelona libras and ten sous.
16. ACA, CR, R. 1563, ff. 36–38.
17. ACA, CR, R. 1563, ff. 38v–39v.
18. ACA, CR, R. 1563, 29–30.
19. ACA, CR, R. 1563, ff. 179–80, 181–82.
20. ACA, CR, R. 1565, ff. 177–78v, 187; Giunta, *Aragoneses*, 155.
21. ACA, CR, R. 1563, f. 180v; R. 1565, ff. 187–88.
22. ACA, R. 1563, f. 164.
23. ACA, R. 1563, f. 197v; R. 1565, f/74v; R. 1566, f. 94v; R. 1567, f. 93.
24. ACA, R. 1565, f. 167; R. 1567, f. 154v; R. 177, ff. 26, 676; R. 1579, f. 42.
25. ACA, Cr, R. 1565, ff. 106–8, 144v; R. 1567, f. 91v.
26. ACA, CR, R. 1563, ff. 178r–v; R. 1565, f. 110v; R. 1566, f. 113v; R. 1570, f. 121.
27. ACA, CR, R. 1563, ff. 142v–43; R. 1565, v. 10v, 28v–29, 109 r–v; R. 1566, f. 114r–v; R. 1567, f. 153; R. 1570, f. 153.
28. ACA, CR, R. 1563, ff. 32–33v, 34v.
29. ACA, CR, R. 1565, ff. 2v–4v.
30. ACA, CR, R. 1563, ff. 6, 12v–13.
31. ACA, CR, R. 1563, ff. 10v–11v, 30.
32. ACA, CR, R. 1563, ff. 66–67, 89r–v, 98.
33. Zurita, *Anales*, 4:181 (VIII:xxxvi).
34. ACA, CR, R. 1534, ff. 89v–90.
35. ACA, CR, R. 1563, 104v.

4 ELIONOR AND HER DEPARTED HOMELAND 89

36. ACA, CR, R1563, ff. 102v–103; R. 1566, ff. 33r–v; Zurita, *Anales*, 4:276–77 (VIII:lx).
37. ACA, CR, R. 1566, ff. 102v–103; R. 1566, ff. 17v, 18v. Copies of this letter was sent to Pere, Federico, Artal de Alagon, and Count Francisco de Urbent.
38. ACA, CR, R. 1566, ff. 30–31v. This letter was sent to the Sicilian barons, the town councils of Messina Trapani, Mazara, and several regional administrative units.
39. ACA, CR, R. 1566, f. 30.
40. ACA, CR, R. 1566, ff. 39v–58. Federico's ambassadors to the Papal Curia were Batolomé de Altavella, Juan de Calvells, a knight, and Manfred de Miles.
41. ACA, CR, R. 1566, f. 52v.
42. ACA, CR, R. 1566, ff. 93r–v; Goldstone, *Joanna I*, 224–37; Giunta, *Aragoneses*, 175.
43. AVA, CR, R. 1566, ff. 86r–v.
44. ACA, CR, R. 1566, ff. 60v, 93v, 96; Giunta, *Aragoneses*, 175.
45. ACA, CR, R. 1566, ff. 87–89. For this ten-year war between Castile and the Crown of Aran, see: Chapter 7, Sect. 1.
46. ACA, CR, R. 1534, ff. 126r–v; R. 1570, ff. 18v–19, 43–46, 49–50v.
47. ACA, CR, R. 1570, f. 66; Giunta, *Aragoneses*, 180.
48. ACA, CR, R. 1566, ff. 116v, 132, 151r–v; Goldstone, *Joanna I*, 242–43; Guinta, *Aragoneses*, 177.
49. ACA, CR, R. 1579, ff. 34v, 91v, 165v; R. 1581, f. 118; Goldstone, *Joanna I*, 286–87; Giunta, *Aragoneses*, 191–93.
50. ACA, CR, R. 1566, ff. 170v–171; R. 1567, f. 55; R. 1570, ff. 51–52; Giunta, *Aragoneses*, ff. 174–76.
51. ACA, CR, R. 1566, ff. 140v–141v; Goldstone, *Joanna I*, 236; Giunta, *Aragoneses*, 177.
52. ACA, CR, R. 1566, f. 116v; R. 1567, ff. 65r–v, 77r–v.
53. ACA, CR, R. 1567, ff. 90–92, 93r–94v, 152–53; R. 1570, ff. 17v–18, 115v.
54. ACA, CR, R. 1566, ft. 33r–v; Giunta, *Aragoneses*, 174–75.
55. ACA, CR, R. 1566, ff. 118–19; Giunta, *Aragoneses*, 178.
56. ACA, CR, R. 1567, f. 74; Zurita, *Anales*, 4:530 (IX:lix).
57. ACA, CR, R. 1568, ff. 13r–v; Giunta, *Aragoneses*, 178.
58. Pere III, *Chronicle*, 1:144–67 (I:9–35); Abulafia, *Western Mediterranean Kingdoms*, 123–28, 179.
59. Pere III, *Chronicle*, 2:479–91 (V:31–43); Abulafia, *Western Mediterranean Kingdoms*, 179–80. For a description of the 1354–1355 campaign, see: Mario Orsi Lázero, "Estrategia, operaciones y logística wn un conflicto mediterráneo. La revuelta del juez de Arborea y la "Armada y Viatge" de Pedro el Ceremonioso a Cerdeña (1353-1354)," *AEM*

38/2 (julio–diciembre, 2008), 921–68, esp. 941–52; María Teresa Ferrer i Mallol, "La organización militar en Cataluña en la Edad Media," *Revista de Historia Militar*, Special Issue (2001): 119–222, esp. 171–73; Tasis i Marca, *Pere el Cerimoniós*, 88.

60. Pere III, *Chronicle*, 2:481 (V:33).
61. ACA, CR, R. 1565, ff. 143v–44.
62. Pere III, *Chronicle*, 2:490 (V:42); Zurita, *Anales*, 4:275 (VIII:lix).
63. ACA, CR, R. 1398, f. 19v; R. 1566, f. 40v; Orsi Lázaro, "Estrategia," 962.
64. ACA, CR, R. 1534, f. 108v; R. 1566, ff. 37v, 46.
65. ACA, CR, R. 1566, f. 117; R. 1568, f. 59.
66. ACA, CR, R. 1580, ff. 110, 130v, 133v–134, 137, 146v; R. 1581, f. 10; R. 1583, f. 99.
67. ACA, CR, R. 1568, ff. 38, 58v, 83r–v, 85; R. 1579, ff. 65v–66.
68. ACA, CR, R. 1566, f. 87v. Both of the queen's assertions in this letter were unfounded. Her husban would not engage Castile in offensive campaigns against Castile until late 1363, and though there were naval actions in the conflict, they extended no farther east than the Balearic Islands. See: Donald J. Kagay, "Battle-Seeking Commanders in the later Middle Ages: Phases of Generalship in the War of the Two Pedros," in *The Hundred Year War (Part III): Further Consequences*, ed. L.J. Andrew Villalon and Donald J. Kagay (Leiden, 2013), 63–83. Villalon and Kagay, *To Win and Lose a Medieval Battle*, 100.
69. ACA, CR, R. 1566, f. 87v; R. 1568, ff. 16v, 28v. For Pedro I' sea campaign of 1359, see Pero López de Avala, "La Crónica del Don Pedro," in *Cronicas de los reyes de Castilla*, ed. Cayetano Rosell, 3 vols., Biblioteca de Autores Españoles, 66 (Madrid, 1875), 1:401–593, esp. 494–93 (1359, chaps. xi–lxix); Pere III, *Chronicle*, 2:523–25 (VI, chaps. 23–26).
70. ACA, CR, R. 1567, f. 84; R. 1568, ff. 66r–v; R. 1570, ff. 169v–170; R. 1576. f. 2 v.
71. ACA, CR, R. 1568, ff. 15, 63–64v; R. 1583, ff. 155r–v; R. 1585, f. 11v.
72. Pere III, *Chronicle*, 2:469–71, 483–844 (V:20, 36); Chaytor, *History*, 169, 181; Tasis i Marca, *Pere el Cerimoniós*, 53–56.
73. ACA, CR, R, 1568, ff. 13r–v, 49–50, 66r–v, 71, 77v–78, 85v–86.
74. ACA, CR, R. 1568, ff. 66r–v.
75. Giunta, *Aragoneses*, 175.
76. Ibid.

CHAPTER 5

The Fiscal Support of Queen Elionor

1   Medieval Marriage's Support Structure

The full-scale financial backing and sustenance of Pere III's wife, the women who by the legitimate children she gave birth to helped guarantee the survival of the dynasty, seemed not only a husband's duty but a king's crucial obligation. With all noble and non-noble marriage partners, this concern for each other manifested itself with the donations of money or property they exchanged with each other. In the *Siete Partidas*, Alfonso X spelled out in great detail how such unions were to be tied together by a wedding gift (*sponsalaticum*) that could consist of money, jewels, or other property. If the groom died before the wedding took place, the bride-to-be had to return all the gifts that had bound together the union. If they had already engaged in sexual relations, she could keep half of these donations. These grants signified the bride's affection that could possibly bloom into love for her mate. With the husband, this initial gift often reflected how he planned to take care of his wife in the future years of the marriage.

Even before the nuptials had taken place, the bride's father showed his concern for his daughter's successful marriage by promising her a dowry (*dos, dotalicum*) which became the wife's property, and often remained separate from the joint possessions of the couple. This grant could include jewels, a complete wedding trousseau, and rents from various lands. The property, however, normally remained with the father. With royal

© The Author(s), under exclusive license to Springer Nature
Switzerland AG 2021
D. J. Kagay, *Elionor of Sicily, 1325–1375*, The New Middle Ages,
https://doi.org/10.1007/978-3-030-71028-6_5

92   D. J. KAGAY

marriage partners, these grants could include extremely large sums of money that often had to be paid off in a number of installments.

The husband's contribution to his wife's security and that of his children after his death was the dower right (*arras, dos propter nuptias*). Often made before marriage and sealed with an exchange of rings, this promise for the security of a man's wife and children normally consisted of the tax revenues or profits to be drawn from land, urban sites, or other commodities that would support a husband's widow and minor children after he had died. Though in many cases the division of the dowers favored the children, their mother normally received one-third of the pledged possessions. This tidy solution, however, could break down if the children sought to gain control of property put aside for their mother. Such a shameful free-for-all was not rare, even occurring with Pere's fourth wife, Sibilla de Fortia and Joan I's second queen, Violante de Bar.[1]

The weakness of the medieval dower system for a wife and widow was the relationship that the adult children occasionally had with their mother who had become a widow. Women from the "poor and miserable people" in large cities such as Barcelona routinely suffered from the lack of enough funds or money-producing property to avoid a disastrously underfunded old age.[2] In royal circles, a queen supported by the promise of dower rights could attain economic security or fall into a disastrously under-funded old age, even if monetary basis of her landed insurance policy was sufficiently financed. Pernicious and greedy mothers or offspring could consume such protected rights in a surprisingly short time. Talented, strong-willed queens like Berenguela of Castile (1179–1246), Blanche of Castile (1188–1252), and Eleanor of Provence (1223–1291) in the thirteenth century as well as Philippa of Lancaster (1360–1415) in the fourteenth often utilized the economic advantages of their royal position along with their God-given talent to not only survive but thrive in courtly settings that were often so unkind to those who came to their married life from another realm speaking another language.[3]

Of all these rulers, the most similar to Elionor of Sicily was the queen of Henry III of England (r. 1216–1272), Eleanor of Province, who came to her husband's realm after the disastrous rule of John I (r 1199–1216), during which "Lackland" lost a good portion of his crown's French lands only to be humiliated by a group of his barons who forced on him a galling political surrender connected with the acceptance of *Magna Carta*.[4] The daughter of Count Ramon Berenguer IV of

Province, Eleanor of Provence was a princess without a dowry when she married Henry at age twelve. With no money of her own to count on, Eleanor had to rely on a percentage of funds drawn from a certain class of royal fines, dower rights to revenues from certain royal lands, and the occasional grants Henry bestowed on his young wife.

The annual sum drawn for the queen's income drawn from the top class of royal fines fluctuated in Eleanor's first years as queen, but eventually saw a steady increase from the steady mulcts on Jewish individuals and communities throughout England. In the late 1230s, the queen took a great step in the control of her finances by appointing her own collector of royal fines and expanded the revenue from this source by offering to cancel such fines if the guilty party would pay in lieu a sizeable fee into the queen's treasury. Henry III had agreed with Eleanor's father that the queen would ultimately receive the revenues from her dower properties. In reality, this money came into Henry's hands and was never turned over to his wife. In the last decades of Henry's reign, a growing number of these lucrative properties came into Eleanor's temporary control from the estates of underage heirs and deceased nobles without heirs. These irregular funding sources were eventually made in a permanent font of revenues for the queen through the funding pathway of her wardrobe. With more money coming into her hands from these fluctuating funds, Eleanor invested wisely except in regard to Savoyard relatives who became an unfortunate fixture in her court. Despite the backlash this brought down on the queen by Henry's court, Eleanor stands as one of the more skillful money managers among European queens during the later Middle Ages. According to Margaret Howell: "very large sums passed through her hands and she administered them responsibly."[5]

This profile of Eleanor, a princess from a dynasty with a glorious past that had fallen on hard times who had no dowry but made up for it by utilizing all the economic opportunities that came her way, but who never fully left behind her original family unit is reminiscent of a Sicilian princess who married her uncle, only six years her senior, gave him healthy children, oversaw and expanded the economic support system initially supplied by the king, and eventually became a true ruling partner with her husband who recognized her administrative talent by making her a governor of one of his realms and a lieutenant who spoke directly for him, after he had done the unthinkable by having her formally crowned as his consort. In all these ways, Elionor of Sicily proved herself as a fitting member of the Aragonese court and representative of the Sicilian royal

94   D. J. KAGAY

household in which she was born and raised. She also stands as one of the memorable members of the sorority of royal women who graced the thirteenth century.

2   First Years of Elionor's Fiscal Support

When Elionor came to Valencia in 1349, her financial state was hardly looking up. Though her grandfather, father, and uncle swore that she was owed a dowry of 10,000 *onzas* and her brother, King Ludovico, had agreed in the presence of Pere's ambassadors that the princess was owed the same sum, which could serve as a dowry, the king, in his youth and unhealthy condition, hardly had the power to guarantee such a grant would take place. When the princess started a new life in Spain, she would have to completely rely on her husband for financial support, whether she had children or not.

Unlike her husband's earlier wives, the Sicilian princess, at age twenty-four, was hardly a young woman by medieval standards when she stood at her wedding in August 1349. As we have seen, shortly after becoming Pere III's queen, she took on herself the unofficial post of adviser for her royal younger brothers and spokesman for the Sicilian dynasty to other Mediterranean rulers. With this confident view of herself, Elionor would soon see that her fate rested in many ways in her own hands due to the reliable funding that supported her court and the many other enterprises for which she was responsible. Like all residents of the medieval centuries, she knew "land equaled wealth... and anyone who controlled land held power in the family and larger world."[6] Power, however, was not Elionor's only aim. Rule and the administration that made it work had long been her wish in her old homeland and now seemed at least possible in her new realms.

Elionor's financial support system had begun to function even before she had landed in Valencia. After the marriage, in late September and early October 1349, Elionor received control of a number of towns in Catalonia, Aragon, and in the Pyrenean region of Roussillon. They had been held by Pere III's earlier wives and Elionor held them according to the same terms. The Aragonese town of Tarazona came under the queen's control on September 27, 1349, when Pere notified the judge (*justicia*) and town council of the site that he was transferring control of it to his new bride. On the same date, he dispatched all but identical communiques to Teruel and Collioure, a Mediterranean port on the French side of the Pyrenees. For the queen, the critical part of this grant was the transfer of a list of taxes which included all sale taxes, general revenues, tolls, fines for holding another person for ransom, fees paid in lieu of extending hospitality to the king and his court as well as all other fiscal rights not specifically mentioned. These administrative and legal contributions constituted the basic revenues that supported the queen and all her administrative activities. The inhabitants of these communities would be called upon to take a feudal oath to their new lady promising service in whatever way she chose. This new formal relationship was hardly a personal one, since the queen seldom if ever saw these vassals. The reception of the oath, the delivery of her orders, and any other matters were carried out by Elionor's representatives or, in the following years, were increasingly communicated by written documents. This does not mean that Tarazonna and the queen's other rate-paying sites were ever far from Elionor's mind since the administration of these towns, cities, hamlets, and villages meant that decisions about issues of all kinds had to be made with some regularity.[7]

Like the document issued on September 27, 1349, the standard contract for the queen's fiscal support normally contained the same elements. The sites in Aragon, besides Tarazona, were the city of Teruel, on the Turia River due south of Zaragoza, Jaca north of the Aragonese capital on the Aragón River, the villages of Biescas and Candanchú near Jaca and another Pyreanean village, Thuir, southwest of Perpignan. The total yearly amount of the revenues these sites produced was 10,000 libras of Barcelona, which came to the queen in several installments each year. Since Elionor had assumed the title of queen in late summer of 1349, Pere had the payment of this entire sum given to his wife in the late fall of that year.[8] Again, Elionor's revenue contracts for these locations closely resembled those held by Pere's earlier wives, María of Navarre and Leonor of Portugal. Thus, the king assured his third mate:

> you shall hold, have, and possess these places just as well and profitably as your predecessors customarily did, and just as fully and completely, the past queens were accustomed to hold the said cities, castles, and villages which were assigned to them for a royal treasure or dowry.[9]

Since the Crown of Aragon was still feeling the dilatory effects of the Black Death, Pere III's confidence that his new queen would be drawing an amount really equal to her predecessors was completely unrealistic due to the "great mortality" that had swept over the land in the year since his second wife had died. As often happened with medieval rulers trying to make up shortfalls in tax receipts, the Aragonese king, attempting to temporarily offset the decline of the population that the pandemic had caused within the sites designated for Elionor's support, turned to a source of money that often bailed out Iberian rulers in such emergencies. In mid-1349, the king tried to fill in these funding holes by temporarily giving his wife control of the financially dependable Jewish and Muslim *aljamas* of Barcelona, Borja, Cervera, Gerona, Lerida, Valencia, and Vilafranca. Some of these communities had already suffered serious losses during the uprising of the Valencian *Unión* and during the first phase of the pandemic's passage. Despite these linked disasters, the Aragonese, Catalan, and Valencian non-Christian settlements served the queen well until the constant pressure of the War of the Two Pedros drove many of their inhabitants to desert the Crown of Aragon for Castile and Granada.[10]

With a basic core of Elionor's revenues in place within a few months, Pere III continued to reward his new wife with more and more grants of revenue-bearing sites to solidify her security and also to reward her for the birth of their first son, Joan, in the winter of 1350. Thus, during her second year as queen, two days before Christmas, Elionor, received the first of a pair of Aragonese castles, Birta and El Bayo. These would be the first of a string of fortresses that she would eventually have across the Crown of Aragon. A month before this on November 18, 1350, the king continued to shower his wife with more revenues when he turned over to her Minorca and Ibiza, the second and third largest islands of the Balearic chain. In this grant, the king reinforced the right of these islands to issue licenses for ship captains or owners to act as corsairs in the waters around these islands. It was unclear, however, if the queen would profit from such activity.[11] On January 11, 1351, Elionor received the promise of revenues from two other villages in the high country of Roussillon, Volono and Montesquieu.[12]

3   Elionor's Revenues During the War Years

As Elionor and her husband entered the second half of the 1350s, the Crown of Aragon suffered through a tumultuous period of war first with Sardinian and then with Castile. Each of these conflicts reduced the amount of the queen's revenue-producing properties because they were either captured by Castile or had their overall worth reduced because of extensive damage to their hinterlands due to Castilian attacks. The reduction of the funds she depended on to meet all her living expenses came as a shock to the queen whose income had been in such a positive state and continued to grow in 1353 with the royal grant of the Valencian towns of Puig de Santa María and Peñaguila as well as several other villages of the same realm.[13] In 1354 the queen felt secure enough to buy with her own funds the Valencian city of Lliria northeast of the capital. The community had been held by Pere III's cousin, Count Ramon Berenguer of Empuries, since 1340 when he purchased the town. On May 7, 1354, Elionor, who greatly wished t have it, bought the site at a much higher price than the count had paid; namely, 407000 sous of Barcelona. Though Elionor may have assumed that this transaction was a successful one since it was put in effect by a "letter of favor" (*carta gratie*), in which the king was not bound to restore the original purchase price if he reclaimed the property. Since this is ultimately what the king did, Pere directed his relative to return his purchase price and the profit he had turned on the resale to the queen. In effect, this constituted a sizeable loss for Elionor, who began to complain shortly afterward about how far she had fallen into the red.[14]

With the beginning of Pere III's conflict with Pedro I of Castile in 1356, Elionor saw her living funds steadily decreasing. The drop in the purchasing power in at least one of Aragon's principal coinage types, the *sou* of Jaca, caused the steady decrease of the real value of the taxes paid off in this type of money. Along with her disappearing purchasing power, the queen saw one of her principal cities, Tarazona, disappear from her account books when the settlement fell to the troops of Pedro I on March 9, 1357.[15] As a result of the steady decline in her operating funds, the queen had to find other ways to support her own court, as well as those of her children and Princess Constanza. She soon made it clear to her many vassals that she was in desperate need of their help during this deepening emergency.

In the fall of 1356 when the Aragonese military cause went from bad to worse, the queen unrealistically attempted to bolster her failing finances by calling for a small percentage of any plunder won from Castilian citizens in the Crown of Aragon, and petulantly demanded from her husband revenues which in reality could no longer be fully paid due to war damage. By December, she had to publicly admit that her funds were running out and that her husband could no longer help her. Unwilling to see before her a possible financial collapse, she ruthlessly pressured officials of her town of Lliria to give her all the money that they had, no matter the consequences.[16] In May 1357, the queen had already negotiated letters of credit from two citizens of Lerida, and was thus able to borrow enough to maintain sufficient funds to support the several courts she was responsible for. Shortly after this, on May 10, she set the taxation levels for her Jewish and Muslim ratepayers in Teruel, Vilafranca, Gerona, Barcelona, and Cervera. Despite the financial downturn because of the war, there would be no reduction of tax rates which had to be paid as always during May and September of the current year.[17] A few days later, she informed her treasurer, Berenguer de Relat, that she was in need of 220 *sous* of Jaca for the necessities of her court.[18]

At the end of the summer of 1357 when Elionor was staying at the castle of Montblanc, she wrote on September 11 and 18 in a spirit of clear gratitude to the town council of Montpellier which from "pure generosity" had sent her enough food and other supplies so her depleted court could subsist for weeks. Knowing how dangerous such charitable actions could be in judicial terms, the grateful queen swore that such unselfishness would never become a legal precedent that could be used against them in the future.[19] At the beginning of the winter, the queen, now in Teruel, begged the Aragonese city to give her its normal yearly subsidy of 1,000 *sous* of Jaca immediately, even though it was normally paid out in several installments, and the first of these was not due for some months. She had to admit to her vassals in Teruel that she was once again in financial trouble because of the loss of her revenues from Sardinia due to its uprising against the crown and for "various other causes."[20] Her gratitude for her vassals' help is again palpable.

Elionor was forced to tell the same sad story on several occasions well into the next year, especially after the fall of another one of her Aragonese cities, Tarazona, in March 1358. In her days of mounting financial distress, her messages could hardly hide a truth that her vassals had themselves experienced. Instead, she frankly admitted that she was in great need because of her steadily escalating expenses and declining revenues caused by a long string of Castilian victories. Pere had already informed his Aragonese subjects of the queen's financial woes. They were, he insisted, not her fault, but were caused by the steady attacks many of his wife's ratepayers had repeatedly suffered from Castilian invaders.

Despite their losses, however, it was their sworn duty to support their lady in every way possible during the hard times they themselves faced.[21]

Shortly before Tarazona was conquered, the queen demanded that Teruel and its organization of hamlets make up with a grant of 18,000 *sous* of Jaca her court's serious shortfalls. This deficit was largely caused because of expenses for her trip to Sardinia (1354–1356) which still remained unpaid. She included in the reasons for her fiscal crisis the fall of many of her Aragonese revenue-producing holdings, most especially the Castilian threat to the city of Tarazona. In July of this hard year, she continued her hard line and now demanded a subsidy from her major Aragonese cities "to pay for necessary expenses."[22] While the Aragonese king openly called for help in better funding his wife, he fully intended for her to continue doing her part in supporting the courtly responsibilities, despite the war raging around her. On September 13, 1358, then, he gave her the right to export from Aragon three thousand wagon loads of wheat or any other grain to Navarre or Catalonia. This transaction could only be carried out by Elionor's agents and the proceeds would not pay any royal tax but would be used only for the financial support of the queen. Elionor used this expedient under the same terms several more times during the War of the Two Pedros. Pere's only restriction on such trading was that his wife could not export grain to his Castilian enemy.[23]

Pere tried to help his wife a few weeks earlier when on July 28, 1358, he turned over to Elionor's control Alcoy, Gorga, the Valley of Seta, and a number of smaller villages, all of which were in Southern Valencia across the Segura River from the former Muslim kingdom of Murcia. Though these towns and small valleys were at the center of major Castilian military operations during the last years of the conflict, Pere was happy for his wife to hold these communities, not for the revenues they might earn her, but rather as a guarantee that this region would not slip from royal control.[24] Shortly after this on September 23, he gave his wife more help when he put the storied castle of Montcada near Barcelona on the list of her revenue-bearing sites.[25] In all of these grants of 1358, the king explained to his wife that "just as the Most High wanted we and you to be one flesh," they were meant to hold these properties, "so we may preserve then for our heirs."[26] Despite this familial view behind the more practical understanding of royal finances, the queen's fiscal report of her operating expenses in 1360 painted a picture of an efficient administrative operation controlling cities, towns, hamlets, villages, and castles bound by feudal ties

100   D. J. KAGAY

to Elionor and contributed to her operating funds amounting to 305,000 sous of Barcelona.[27]

4   HIGHS AND LOWS OF ELIONOR'S REVENUES

The expansion of Elionor's revenues to this great financial plateau was principally the doing of her husband, but in a strange way could also be attributed to the seemingly never-ending war with Castile. Compensation for the queen's revenue losses was clearly in the king's mind in February 1360 when he gave to his wife the use of the moderately sized Catalan towns of Montblanc, Tarrega, and Vilagrassa. Since Catalonia had little connection to the war against Pedro I which was still raging, the Catalan grant was clearly a replacement for war losses, but also compensated the queen for the temporary transfer of several of the Jewish *aljamas* on her revenue list to the ten-year-old crown prince. The Catalan towns would not stay under the queen for very long for the king almost immediately returned them to the count of Trastámara who had held them for some years before this.[28] Despite this disappointment for Elionor, the king was preparing to bestow on Elionor his wife the Valencian holdings of Queen Leonor, his hated mother-in-law who had been brutally murdered by Pedro I in 1359. This would soon be followed in 1363 by a transfer of the lands of Prince Ferran after his murder at Pere's own court.[29]

Further compensation for properties in Catalonia by the king's constant land trading in Aragon and Valencia where Elionor had lost great swaths of frontier land during the war was obviously on the king's mind at Christmas time in 1362 when he gave his wife the Albufera, a large saltwater lagoon south of Valencia that ran parallel to the Mediterranean. This remarkable water feature brought a considerable annual income from the sale of fishing rights, many types of sea food, and sea birds. Shortly before New Years Day of that year, Pere added to the queen's revenue list the large salt pans that bordered the Albufera which annually produced a large supply of the commodity.[30]

As the War of the Two Pedros continued into the early 1360s, the financial status of the Aragonese queen was never far from the hard times of the past decade, not from her direct losses of towns, villages, and castles, but rather from the large amount of money she plowed back into her husband's military campaigns, especially those in Valencia.[31] For his part, Pere III seemed always on the hunt for new opportunities to keep Elionor's revenues in a healthy state. One of these new chances for advancement came about either by careful planning or blind luck when a solution for the king's troublesome half-brother presented itself. Indeed, Ferran had been Pere's proven enemy even before he became king. Under the unforgiving and determined tutelage of his mother, Queen Leonor, Ferran stood against his half-brother in 1348 and 1356 saw the sense in deserting deep-seated enmity for a more comfortable peace. On the second occasion, the prince had served Pedro I, but soon found him too unpredictable to continue under his cousin's banner, and in the winter of 1357, he joined the Aragonese side. Never much of soldier, he relations with his half-brother soon soured. Pere, like Pedro, looked on Ferran as a mediocre and cowardly soldier, who might even have been guilty of "disservice" to the Aragonese crown.[32] Besides his half-brother, Ferran had made several powerful enemies in the Aragonese court, the strongest of whom was one of Pere's principal advisers, Bernat de Cabrera, and the king's most reliable captain, Enrique de Trastamara. When in July 1363 the king was spending a summer vacation at the northern Valencian coastal town, Castellon de la Plana, he invited his half-brother to join him. There, however, Ferran's many enemies caught up with him on July 16 when he was ambushed, and, though fighting bravely, was finally caught down.[33]

Whether the hands of the Aragonese king were bloody from this horrific event, he and his wife would soon profit from it. On the same day that the prince died, Pere notified the citizens of the Aragonese, Catalan, and Valencian cities, towns, villages, and castles of their lord's death and claimed them as royal vassals once more.[34] Like the feudal holdings of Ferran's mother, those of the prince (who also held the titles marquis of Tortosa and viscount of Albarracín) were soon transferred to Elionor, both because of her lingering financial need and since she had little obvious hatred for her cousin. Thus a little under two weeks after Ferran's death on July 28, the queen became the beneficiary of his demise and the feudal lord of Tortosa, Albarracín, Fraga, Igualada, Novelda, and a number of other villages and castles scattered across Pere's realms. Ironically, many of these sites had been under the prince's control since he was a little boy.[35]

The transfer of these properties, including several other important Valencian and Catalan towns controlled by Jaume II's widow, María of Portugal, continued the increase of Elionor's revenues, but this mountain of potential money was often eroded by her husband's need for immediate funds. The royal grant of Ferran's massive list of property brought with it legal complications that took over a decade to settle in court. This judicial marathon ultimately cost the Aragonese queen 10,000 florins to help compensate the prince's wife at the time of his death. Besides these legal battles and settlements, the queen was occasionally hit with demands for emergency funding to support the serious "matters of war" that Pere III faced in Valencia. The king attempted to return these funds to Elionor's coffers in July 1363, but could not maintain the stability of his wife's finances when Castilian forces had simultaneously captured Calatayud, Murviedro, and Puig de Santa María. In the following year on July 31, the Aragonese ruler issued a list of how much income the queen had lost due to Castilian attacks and victories.[36]

The royal revenue compensations the queen received in the last years of the Castilian war would continue until a period of undeclared peace in 1366. On July 28, 1363, Pere again recognized the great amount of annual money payments Elionor had lost with the Castilian conquest of the cities of Berga, Lliria, Murviedro, and Puig de Santa María as well as all the agricultural land and villages that surrounded them. In the next year, the king made a similar admission when he attempted yet again to compensate his wife for all property she had lost during the war, including "meadows, pastures… trees, mills, aqueducts, and olive groves." This list also referred to all "Muslim and Jewish men and women [on these lands]."[37]

Elionor's fiscal situation began to improve in 1366 when Count Enrique de Trastámara took advantage of promises of Pere III to pay the salaries of his most successful captain and 3,000 troops for an invasion of Castile. Though the king had made this offer in 1363, the count could not take advantage of it until March when he drove into his homeland once more and was promptly hailed as king and drove the one-time sovereign, Pedro I, into exile.[38] Up to this point, when Count Trastámara became King Enrique II of Castile, he and his troops were supported by revenues from the Catalan towns of Montblanc, Tarrega, and Vilagrassa; the Aragonese cities of Tamarite de Litera, Ricla, and Epila; and the Valencian settlements of Castellón de la Plana and Vila-Real. On May 8, 1366, the new Castilian sovereign formally returned the Catalan towns of Montblanc and Tarrega to Elionor and the queen accepted them with equal formality. On the same day, the king added to the queen's now burgeoning revenue list all the other Aragonese, Catalan, and Valencian settlements that had supported Trastámara when he served as Pere's captain.[39]

5 THE FISCAL SUPPORT OF QUEEN ELIONOR   103

During the last days of the War of the Two Pedros, Pere III was informed by his accountants and treasurers that Elionor's yearly income stood at 305,000 sous of Barcelona. The king also recognized that she had several built-in expenses that came off the top of her annual income. These had to do with family responsibilities including yearly grants to Juana, Pere's second daughter by his first wife, and to María de Luna, his second son's fiancé, as well as the support of her own twelve-year-old son Martí and ten-year-old daughter Elionor in their own courts. Pere also realized that his wife had a "royal standing (*status reginalis*)", which included her burdens as a wife as well as "the other... extraordinary and ordinary burdens" that she had to take upon herself."[40] For this reason and "because of the bad weather and great lack of commodities and food," the king decided to upgrade Elionor's annual level of expenses by 32, 800 sous, making her average income 333,800 sous.[41]

The queen's confidence was greatly increased by her husband's fiscal action, but also by the extraordinary grant he bestowed on her in the last months of his war with Castile. To provide her with more revenues, many of which she had held before, but had with the victories of the Castilian enemy, Pere surrendered to his queen, the Aragonese cities of Calatayud, Tarazona, and Teruel and the Valencian towns of Aqualata, Lliria, Murviedro, and Puig de Santa María. In these cases, her officials were responsible for the return of property to the members of these communities who had lost their possession to the Castilian occupiers or the homegrown traitors who had profited from supporting the enemy.[42]

5   ELIONOR'S LAST YEARS

Within the last decade of Elionor's life, we have a very accurate picture of the total amount of revenues that supported her and those she was responsible for, as well as her administrative activities in regard to these funds. In 1368, the worth of her revenue list was accurately estimated for the four realms of the Crown of Aragon, and the accuracy of these figures was sworn to by Prince Joan and his mother. The grand total of 337,800 sous of Barcelona was an addition of the following sums: Aragon: 97,000 *sous* of Jaca, Valencia: 150,500 *sous* of Barcelona, Catalonia: 77,800 *sous* of Barcelona, and Majorca: 21,000 *sous* of Barcelona.[43]

With the Aragonese queen's situation stabilized in her last years, she turned in the summer of 1366 to a kind of property speculation along with her husband. After the purchase of Vilagrassa, due east of Lerida, the

104   D. J. KAGAY

royal couple were forced to engage in a lawsuit against the noble couple, Felipe de Castro and Juana, Enrique de Trastámara's sister, over the final ownership of the town. Though it seems that Pere's most important captain was given control of the revenues of this community to support him and his troops, the court ruled in favor of the royal couple because Trastámara had no right to sell the town and thus his sister and brother-in-law had no real title to it. After winning this suit, the queen became involved in a complex land deal of her own. She sold at a profit the small town of Molins del Rei just south of Barcelona on the Llobregat River to her faithful treasurer and adviser, Berenguer de Relat. With this money, the queen purchased the Castle of Arraona and the city of Sabadell, both due north of the capital. Providing Relat's money as a down payment, she added it to a sizeable amount drawn from the inhabitants of the two sites, the queen bought the two properties agreeing to recognize the new privilege the townsmen thought they had just purchased. Even though she had not paid the agreed-upon full price for castle and city, the townsmen in short order would soon be presented with a tax bill payable to the queen. This piece of shady dealing was never given enough time to become legend for in four years, the royal couple traded the two sites for another castle.[44]

In the last six years of Elionor's life, when, by medieval standards, her children were grown and ready to be married, the need for further infusions of money to guarantee Elionor's financial security seemed to be replaced by a kind of horse trading apparent in the Sabadell affair. The last of the large royal grants to come her way was that of the Valencian town of Cocentaina which had been held as a fief by the wife of one of Pere's nobles who had passed away in August 1373 and was now bestowed on Elionor.[45] With the last of these kinds of donations, Pere seemed to view Elionor's treasury as a source of steady fiscal support for royal projects that he considered essential. Thus from 1369 to 1375, Pere expected a grant of 30,000 *sous* of Barcelona from his wife on January 1 on every one of these years. These funds were then immediately transferred to his treasury. These regular payments were supposedly not forced on the queen but were only accepted by Pere if his wife agreed to them. Though her finances were stable at this time, such a regular outflow of money could occasionally cause her financial embarrassment, which required that he beg for help from her urban vassals.[46] In 1369, especially, she was forced to ask for an extraordinary grant of 8,000 *sous* of Barcelona from the Muslim community of Játiva "because we cannot pay our creditors the great amount of money... [owed] nor... use our jewels which we have pawned."[47]

As Roebert correctly points out, Queen Elionor during her twenty-six years of administrative service for her own holdings and as a royal administrator of the highest order, often acted as an independent agent who made decisions without consulting any other member of the royal government, even the king. This trust in her own decision-making abilities never turned the queen into a rogue element among Pere III's corps of officials. Instead, she worked as a full-fledged partner with her husband, who increasingly relied on her good ideas and courage in carrying them out. Her stalwart support during the war with Castile made her indispensable to the king.[48]

In the last years of her queenship after Pedro I had initially been defeated and then returned to power after the battle of Nájera (April 3, 1367), when the royal government had recovered all territory, urban sites, and castles lost to Castile during the war, the queen's role as a team player slowly begin to fade before the ambitions of her son, Crown Prince Joan, and even the desires of her husband.

Joan was twenty in 1370, and within three years would take as his first wife the French princess, Matha de Armagnac. As governor of Valencia, he had worked with his mother, who held the governorship of Catalonia, even acting as a witness for her list of revenues in 1368. The queen grew to dearly love his first daughter-in-law, but had increasing trouble with her ambitious first-born, especially about property and the power that sprang from it.[49] Their arguments became public in 1370 when a boundary dispute erupted between Tarrega, the capital of the province of Urgel, which the queen held, and Granyena de Segarra in the old county of Cervera, which the crown prince controlled. As the authorities of record for the two sites, the queen and her son both entered into litigation, not about the boundary and authority questions of the two towns, but rather about a large fine that was part of an earlier verdict which bound both territorial units. The dispute was adjudicated by Pere III himself as the head of the Crown of Aragon's royal administration and the count of Barcelona. The king ruled in favor of his wife against his son.[50] This hardly endeared the crown prince to either of his parents and administrative disputes would soon entangle the parents and son in 1372 when officials of Joan and his wife overrode Eleanor's orders over the Jewish *aljamas* which she had controlled for decades. The prince's officials collected extraordinary taxes from these two Jewish communities, which was, in effect, taking money from the queen's coffers. Pere, as supreme judge, again agreed to his wife's legal argument and ordered Joan to pay his mother over 3,000 florins.[51] Furious at this obvious affront, Joan ordered his officials to collect this fine from yet another Jewish community, that of Murviedro in Valencia, or any other of the *aljamas* that his mother happened to control.[52] Behind these political disputes was Elionor's fear for her son's overweening ambition, a desire that was not always well-served by his weakness of character. Over her decades of government service, she had come to realize that the "commonwealth" (*cosa publica*) of the realms that made up the Crown of Aragon was far more important than personal advancement. As she wrote to her son in the year before her death, "the *cosa publica*, of which the Lord King and you are its heads, must be protected from iniquitous men and those wishing evil."[53]

Through most of their married life, Pere III openly supported his third wife in personal, economic, and political terms. She had early on become crucially important to his reign as the mother of three healthy children. He maintained herself and the many officials and servants she controlled by carefully maintaining sites of all kinds that provided revenues every year, and then patiently adapted her annual income when the war with Castile removed a great many of the communities she depended on for financial support. The queen became a talented administrator taking care of her own holdings as well as issues that touched many of Pere III's various realms. This was especially obvious during the War of the Two Pedros, when she pawned many of her own valuables, helped raise troops, equipped at least ten galleys to supplement the king's fleet, and publicly acted as supporter of the war effort both within the Crown of Aragon and in other European and Mediterranean courts. If deep dissatisfaction with her husband lurked in her heart, it was not apparent until the last decade of her marriage, and had little to do money, property, or power. Instead, it was something that Elionor could only describe as a personal betrayal by her husband, who in his sixties all but deserted his wife and entered into a very public affair with a young widow, Sibilla de Fortia.[54]

As Queen Elionor lived much of her life in seeing to the smooth functioning of her administrative responsibilities, she in some ways was served by that very administration. From the governmental point-of-view, her life as wife and mother was segmented into time periods at the end of which reports outlined how much money she spent for the completion of her enterprises, private and public, and how great were the revenues that supported her. Like tree rings counting off the years, these reports full of statistics at least for the royal government stood for the queen. We thus witness Elionor's death on April 20, 1375, as a ledger of the queen's profits and debits kept, as in so many other years, by her indispensable secretary, Berenguer de Relat. This record, which cut off with such shocking finality, was, in line with governmental protocol, audited "justly and correctly" by the king's accountant and entered into the books of the *magister racional*. Only after this process was completed on May 8, 1375, was the record of his most important wife handed back to the king.[55]

NOTES

1. ACA, CR, R. 1971, ff. 484r–v; *Siete Partidas*, 4:930–45 (Part. IV, Tit, XI, ll. i–xxxii); Heath Dillard, *Daughters of the Reconquest: Women in Castilian Town Society 1100-1300* (Cambridge, 1984), 25–48, 58–59; Fossier, *Axe and Oath*, 100–1; Maria Luisa Ledesma Rubio, "El Patrimonio real en Aragón a fines del siglo XIV: Los dominos y rentas de Violante de Bar," *Aragon in la Edad Media* [Ejemplar dedicado á estudios de economía y sociedad (siglos XII a XVI] 2 (1979): 135–70, esp. 141–43.
2. Mireia Comas-Via, "Widowhood and Economic Difficulties in Medieval Barcelona," *Historical Reflections/Réflexions Historiques* 43, no. 1 (Spring, 2017): 93–103.
3. Jennifer R. Goodman, "The Lady with the Sword: Philippa of Lancaster and the Chivalry of the Infante Dom Henrique (Prince Henry the Navigator," in *Queens, Regents, and Potentates*, 149–65; Lindy Grant, *Blanche of Castile* (New Haven, CT: 2016; Vann, "Theory and Practice," 125–47.
4. David Starkey, *Magna Carta: The Medieval Roots of Modern Politics* (New York, 2015); W.L. Warren, *King John* (Berkeley, 1978).
5. Margaret Howell, "The Resources of Eleanor of Provence as Queen Consort," *EHR*, 102, no. 403 (April, 1987): 372–93, esp. 293. See also: Nancy Goldstone, *Four Queens: The Pronvençal Sisters who Ruled Europe* (London, 2007), 60–70.
6. Linda E. Mitchell, "The Lady as Lord in Thirteenth-Century Britain," *Historical Reflections/Réflexions Historiques* 18, no. 1 (Winter, 1992): 71–97, esp. 87.
7. ACA, R. 1535, ff. 12r–v, R. 1536, ff. 1r–v; Roebert, "Que nos tenemus," 235. Collioure was an important seaport for Queen Elionor which he used to have galleys fitted out in 1359 to reinforce her husband's fleet.

108   D. J. KAGAY

She bought the bailliwick of Collioure six years after she was given rights to town's revenues.

8. ACA, CR, R. 1534, ff. 12r–v, 30v; R. 1535, ff. 12r–v; R. 1536, ff. 1r–v; Deibel, "Reyna Elionor," 431–32.
9. ACA, CR, R. 1536, f. 1v; Roebert, "Que nos tenemus," 235.
10. ACA, CR, R. 1534, ff..16r–v; R. 1535, ff. 16v–17. For the weakening of eastern Spanish *aljamas*, during the early 1350, see: López de Meneses, *Documentos*, 335–35 (doc. 54); 342–43 (doc. 61), 394–95 (doc. 116), and 426 (doc. 150); M. Rodrigo Lizondo, "La Unión valenciana y sus protaginistas," *Liganzas* 7 (1975): 133–66, esp. 161–66.
11. ACA, CR, R. 1534, ff. 33–36v, 41r–v; R. 1535, ff. 27r–v; R. 1536, ff. 11–13v. This subject had already been broached in a document issued almost a year before on December 13, 1349 then on August 15, 1350 in a chamber of the royal palace at Barcelona, and finally on April 6, 1351. For fate of Aragonese and Valencian Jews during the War of the Two Pedros, see: ACA, CR, R. 697, ff. 117, 120v–121; R. 699, ff. 230r–v; R. 700, ff. 22v–23, 74v–75; Máximo Diago Hernando, "La movilidad a ambos lados de la Frontera entre las Coronas de Castilla y Aragón durante el siglo XIV," *Sefarad* 63 (2003): 237–82, esp. 280.
12. ACA, CR, R. 1534, ff. 45v–46; R. 1535, ff. 29r–v; R. 1536, ff. 68r–v; Roebert, "Que nos tenemus," 236. Roussillon remained under control of Catalonia and then Spain until 1659 when by the Treaty of the Pyrenees it came under the France of Louis XIV.
13. ACA, CR, R. 1534, ff. 82v–82; R. 1535, ff. 33r–v; R. 1536, ff. 19–21v, 41bis.; Roebert, "Que nos tenemus," 236.
14. ACA, CR, R. 1536, ff. 23–36v; María Teresa Ferrer i Mallol, "El patrimoni i la recuperacio del senyorius jurisdiccionls en els estats catalano-aragoneses a la fi de segle XIV," *AEM* 7 (1970–1971): 351–491, esp. 367–70; Roebert, "Que nos tenemus," 237.
15. ACA, CR, R. 1149, f. 96v; R. 1151, r. 65v; R. 1379, ff. 147–48v; Ayala, *Pedro I* (1357, chap. III); Mario Lafuente Gómez, *Dos Coronas en Guerra. Aragón y Castilla (1356-1366)* (Zaragoza, 2012), 67–68.
16. ACA, CR, R. 1366, ff. 81v, 89v, 97.
17. ACA, CR, R. 1566, ff. 122v, 128 r–v.
18. ACA. CR, R. 1566, f. 147v.
19. ACA, CR, R. 1566, f. 147v.
20. ACA, CR, R. 1566, ff. 164r–v.
21. ACA, CR, R. 1534, ff. 117v, 121v.
22. ACA, CR, R. 1566, ff. 45v–46; R. 1567, ff. 25v, 43.
23. ACA, CR, R. 1534, ff. 120r–v; R. 1537, f. 128v; R. 1580, f. 184v.
24. ACA, CR, R. 1534, ff. 118v–119; R. 1535, ff. 47r–v; Deibel, "Reyna Elionor," 430–31; Roebert, "Que nos tenemus," 238. The Valley of Seta contained important sites of anti-Morisco conflict in the sixteenth

5 THE FISCAL SUPPORT OF QUEEN ELIONOR   109

and seventeenth centuries. See Bryon Ellsworth Hamann, *Bad Christians, New Spains, Catholics and Native Americans in a Mediterranean World* (London, 2020), 18–19.

25. ACA, CR, R. 1534, ff. 122v–123; R. 1535, ff. 494–v; R. 1536, ff. 38–40; Roebert, "Que nos tenemus," 238.
26. ACA, CR, R. 1534, f. 119v; R. 1536, f. 29v.
27. ACA, CR, ff. 81v–86, 884r–v.
28. ACA, CR, R. 1534, ff. 142v–41; R. 1536, ff. 45–46; R. 1567, f. 182v; Deibel, "Reyna Elionor," 432, 438; Roebert, "Que nos tenemus," 239.
29. Roebert, "Que nos tenemus," 238–39; Recuerdo Lista, "Doña Leonor," 228–29.
30. ACA, CR, R. 1536, ff. 50v–51, 54r–v; R. 1537, ff. 49–50v; Roebert, "Que nos tenemus," 239–40. All Aragonese kings from the time of Jaume I claimed a tenth of all profit made from the Albufera, which was principally drawn from the extensive fishing trade, the netting of sea birds, and the sale of districts around and across the lagoon to tax farmers. A great amount of tax revenues came from the salt works near the Albufera. See Robert Ignatius Burns, S.J., *The Crusader Kingdom of Valencia: Teconstruction of a Thirteenth-Century Frontier*, 2 vols. (Cambridge, MA, 1967), I: 152–58, 185, 289; idem, *Medieval Colonialism: Postcrusade Exploitation of Islamic Valencia* (Princeton, NJ, 1975), 46, 146–50.
31. ACA, CR, R. 1537, ff. 58v–59.
32. Kagay, "Dynastic Dimension," 86–95.
33. Ibid., 94–95.
34. ACA, CR, R. 1188, f. 40; R. 1189, ff. 206v, 215; Kagay, "Dynastic Dimension," 95.
35. ACA, CR, R. 1536, ff. 71v–74; R. 1537, ff. 58v–59, 72v–73; Roebert, "Que nos tenemus, 240.
36. ACA, R. 1197, ff. 60, 68; Josep Maria Madurell Marimón, "Una Concordia entre Pedro el Cerimonioso y María de Portugal, Infanta de Aragón," *AHDE* 41 (1971): 425–38, esp. 428–38; Roebert, "Qus nos tenemus," 240. The new settlements that Elionor received from Jaume II's widow consisted of the Catalan towns and villages of Berga, Burriana, Pals, and Torroella de Montgrí.
37. ACA, CR, R. 1537, ff. 74–77v, 78v–80v.
38. ACA, CR, R. 1543, ff. 66v, 70; Pere III, *Chronicle*, 2:578–79 (VI:61); Kagay, "Dynastic Dimension," 84–85; Zurita, *Anales* 4:457 (IX:xliv).
39. ACA, R. 1537, ff. 86–88; R. 1563, ff. 78v–79; Kagay, "Dnynastic Dimension," 84–85.
40. Roebert, "Que nos tenemus," 243; Dawn Bratsch-Prince, "The Politics of Self Representation in the Letters of Violant de Bar (1365-1431)," *Medieval Encounters* 12/1 (2006): 2–25, esp. 18–19.
41. ACA, CR, R. 1536, ff. 57v, 32v–84v, Roebert, "Que nos tenemus," 243.

42. ACA, R. 1535, ff. 51–55; R. 1536, ff. 60v–61, 67r–v; R. 1537, ff. 90v. 91.
43. ACA, CR, R. 135, ff. 55v–57; R. 1536, ff. 81–86v; Roebert, "Que nos tenemos," 267.
44. ACA, R. 1537, ff. 83–85, 86r–v, 91v; Roebert, "Que nos tenemus," 243–45; Zurita, *Anales*, 4:540 (IX:lxii).
45. ACA, CR, R. 1537, ff. 126r–v; Roebert, "Que nos tenemus," 246.
46. ACA, CR, !574, f. 188; R. 1577, ff. 69v–70; Roebert, "Que nod tenemos," 246–47.
47. ACA, CR, R. 1577, ff. 110v–11.
48. Roebert, "Que nos tenemus," 247–48. See also Chapter 7.
49. Miron, *Queens of Aragon*, 209–12.
50. ACA, CR, R. 1537, ff. 108v–109; Roebert, "Que nos tenemos," 249–50.
51. ACA, CR, R. 1537, ff. 38r–v; Roegbert, "Que nos tenemus," 250.
52. ACA, CR, R. 1209, ff. 58r–v; R. 1574, ff. 11–23; R. 1577, ff. 33r–v; R. 1582, ff. 106r–v; Mark Meyerson, *Jews on the Iberian Frontier Kingdom: Society, Economy, and Politics in Morvedre, 1248-1391* (Leiden, 2004), 241, 251–57; Roebert, "Que nos tenemus," 250.
53. ACA, R. 1582, ff. 85r–v; Roebert, "Que nos tenemus," 251. For the political concept of *cosa publica*, see José Antonio Maravall, *Estudios de historia de pensamiento español* (New York, 1970); Joseph F. O'Callaghan, "The Ideology of Government in the Reign of Alfonso X of Castile," *Exemplaria Alfonsina* I (1991–1992): 1–17; esp. 4–5; Donald J. Kagay, "Rule and Mis-rule in Medieval Iberia," in *War, Government, and Society in the Medieval Crown of Aragon* (Aldershot, Hampshire, 2007), Study IV, pp. 48–66, esp. 50.
54. Miron, *Queens of Aragon*, 196.
55. ACA, CR, R. 1534, ff. 170r–v.

CHAPTER 6

Elionor of Sicily as Courtier and Administrator

1   THE ESTABLISHMENT OF THE ROYAL COURT

While, as we have seen, Elionor of Sicily served as a successful wife to Pere III for twenty-six years, but was also an important member of his court during the same period, neither she nor any other Aragonese queen was seen as important in the crucial business of ruling. According to the written history of administrative institutions in Aragon and Catalonia, and finally in the linked realms that constituted the Crown of Aragon, women and government structures had very little to do with each other. To test this theory, I will follow the accepted history of courtly structures in eastern Spain between the twelfth and fourteenth centuries and then will demonstrate in very specific detail how Elionor became a cog in this ever-turning administrative wheel.

For all the Iberian realms and dominions of the Middle Ages, the royal court originated from the Visigothic "senate" (*senatus*), the meeting in which the king sought the advice of his most important "noblemen" (*seniores*), and the "chamber of the king" (*aula regis*), the assembly of the king and his great officials that met in the royal palace to adjudicate legal differences and promulgate new laws. The corps of officials included the treasurer, head of the chancery, administrator of the royal patrimony, the chief chamberlain, and a number of military leaders.[1] Much the same kind of ad hoc situation remained in effect in royal households across Europe until the twelfth century. One modern historian characterized the king's

© The Author(s), under exclusive license to Springer Nature   111
Switzerland AG 2021
D. J. Kagay, *Elionor of Sicily, 1325–1375*, The New Middle Ages,
https://doi.org/10.1007/978-3-030-71028-6_6

court until that time as "both the household of the extended royal family, and the central organ of the entire state administration, the government."[2] This partial home, partial government seemed to expand it power in exact proportion to the control the monarch exercised over his court.[3] In these changes wrought in the twelfth century, the often bitter rivals, England and France, seemed to take the next step to a much more organized and we can even say modern type of governmental structure. Both Henry I of England (r. 1100–1135) and Philippe III Augustus of France pointed the way to the new style of royal court (*curia regis*). Each of these personal governments were still served by the same style of on-site officials, the chancellor, steward, butler, chamberlain, and constable. From this court structure that seemed to never change as the centuries passed, the English and French monarchs did make organizational and economic changes that moved their governments toward modernity. They did so by dividing their growing realms among regents who freed their royal masters of the ruling minutiae of an entire kingdom, establishing efficient accounting systems, improving the issuance and storage of records, and dispatching circuit judges that expanded the reach of royal justice.[4]

In eastern Spain, the royal court in Aragon and that of the count of Barcelona went through similar changes in the twelfth century. In many ways, such eastern Spanish, proto institutions were still clearly the children of their Visigothic parent until changes began to follow the education of the kings of Aragon and counts of Barcelona. This alteration followed the employment of one important band of political advisers after another that came to be identified as a "grammarian" (*grammaticus*) or a "professor" (*doctor*).[5] All of these men had been university trained in the study of Roman or canon law. With this kind of academic preparation, they made distinct changes to legal structures and the role of the sovereign as a legislator. His primary role was to "look after the temporal goods which Divine Clemency temporarily conceded to him."[6]

This was an apt description of warrior/rulers such as Ramon Berenguer III of Catalonia and Alfonso I of Aragon, but cannot fully describe the work of the new monarchs of the unified realms, Ramón Berenguer IV and Alfons II who spent most of their time in overseeing the establishment of general laws such as the *Usatges of Barcelona* and the *Fueros of Aragon* for their combined lands and the increased use of written documents, which as we have seen were stored in depositories across the Crown of Aragon. The Peace and Truce movement as well as the production and protection of new royal coinage expanded the power of the hybrid king across his realms.[7]

These trends extended the ruling powers of the king of Aragon and gave rise to a much more complicated royal court and one that worked hand-in-hand with the new evolving national assembly called the *corts* in Catalonia and *cortes* in Aragon and Valencia. Like the Visogothic *aula regia*, the *curia regia* or royal court was still a collection of servants, courtiers, and advisers who aided their royal master in making important decisions, even as he and a hundred or so members of the court traveled from realm to realm, often depending on the help of their clergy, nobles, and townsmen for aid of all kinds. The principal officials of the emerging institution remained the chancellor, several mayordomos who managed the physical needs of the court, and the admiral, who tended to all naval concerns. Each lent his expertise to various subjects about which the king asked their advice. These subjects, which were well on their way to becoming departments, regularly focused on general advisory matters, justice, the treasury, and the production and storage of documents. The last two had by the end of Jaume I's reign established permanent offices at Barcelona and in other urban and monastic sites throughout the Crown of Aragon. Each of these last two were in constant communication with the king's itinerant court through permanent officials and the constant flow of messengers. The chancery especially grew increasingly complex with scribes and notaries who concentrated on the production of documents in Latin and several other languages, including Aragonese, Catalan, Castilian, Arabic, and Hebrew. The storage of these official writings in all these languages forced broader governmental activity which led to the maintenance of a steadily increasing number of manuscripts outside of the royal court. This desire for the preservation of official papers did not prevent Jaume's court from taking critical documents with it while engaged in journeys.[8]

The victory of the Sicilian Vespers in 1282 eventually installed Pere II and his son Jaume II as kings of the island and thoroughly familiarized them with the Angevin ruling methods which they maintained in many ways. Especially after the disastrous War of the Sicilian Vespers, central government began to disintagrate and the kings operated in some ways along with the courtly guidelines of Jaume I. The kings worked with both their appointed officials of the central government and the elected bailiffs, judges, and secretaries who had more power in the countryside. The crown, desperate to gain fuller control over the island, was much

114   D. J. KAGAY

more willing to use these outsiders than in the Iberian realms. One of the solutions that came from this diffuse government was the *maestre racional* that ultimately established more efficient control over royal funds.[9]

With the return of Jaume II to the Crown of Aragon in 1291, the new king attempted to expand his power over his own subjects and his neighbors. He met with failure on both fronts.

With his own people, Jaume, like his older brother, Alfons II, ran afoul of the powerful *Unión* in both Aragon and Valencia. With Aragon's age-old enemy, Castile, he became mired in a decade-long conflict that, while giving him certain parts of Murcia and recapturing southern Valencia, virtually guaranteed that Murcia would remain Castilian. This steady attempt at the hemming in of royal power was underpinned by a cluster of economic forces that reconfigured the structure of the Crown of Aragon through a steady weakening of Catalonia and advancement of Valencia. Jaume II's success rested in the promotion of an image of Aragonese kingship that he wished his subjects would look on as true. This royal image was manufactured through the architecture of newly constructed and expanded royal palaces, as well as the promotion of royal ceremonies such as coronations and formal entrances of royal courts into cities such as Barcelona. These structured celebrations embodied in colorful form the king's formal concept of royalty.[10]

The ceremony that reinforced royal power was nowhere more evident than in the formal description of the royal court's structure made by Pere II and his sons, Alfons II and Jaume II. For the first time in the history of the royal court, Pere the Great's ordinances which were issued in late 1276 or earlier 1277 and then on April 22, 1277, listed the important officials of the royal household and of the *curia regis*. They also specified the salaries and expenses officials could collect for carrying out their duties. The orders of these "high officials," which included the mayordomo, head cook, quarter master, baggage master, scribe of accounts, messenger, and a number of other servants, had to be obeyed. Pere wanted a peaceful courtly environment and so forbade games of chance, only allowing backgammon of chess within the courtly environment. All officials were given a portion of food for the meals they ate at count. If they happened to be ill or were Jewish or Muslim, they were given food to eat at home.[11]

In the second of his ordinances, the king laid out general rules for the travel of his court. To limit the size and expenses of his itinerant court, Pere ordered that only the nobles of the kingdom in which the royal court was traveling would be able to accompany the monarch. To prevent misunderstanding about this, Pere declared that he would be in Valencia and Murcia between November and February; in Aragon between March and June; and in Catalonia between July and October. The king also warned irregular members of the court not to present themselves there unless formally summoned and warned that if they did, they would not be paid.[12]

The court ordinances of Alfons II were promulgated on February 28, 1287, March 11, 1288, and May 1, 1291. In the first, the king established his general schedule for the week, saying he would hear all public petitions on Monday, and meet officially with his advisers on Tuesday and Friday, although they had to be in constant contact with him. His judges would hear cases in the king's household. Court accounts were to be compiled daily and regularly checked and corrected by a committee of three officials not involved in such accounting. All members of the court could claim reimbursement on the last day of the month.[13] In the second ordinance, the king attempted to halt the fiscal oversight of the crown's finances which had begun when Pere II returned from Sicily. Alfons did so by abrogating the offices of the *maestre racional* and the bailiff general. The treasurer was now responsible for all money owed to the king and had authority overall officials who collected this money. To hold down expenses, there would be no more than one official for each office of the household.[14] Alfons's last ordinance attempts to define the extent of royal finances and how this money would be administered. He lists all the taxes his government could collect and how these funds would be transported to the Aragonese court. Two court officials would transport the tax money in a chest which for security had two locks and could only be opened with the keys which the king's men carried separately. The records of these collections were entered into three books, each kept by a separate official. The overall finances of the crown would be accounted for to the king three times a year and the record of all payments would be entered in an official register.[15]

Jaume II issued his court practices on August 23, 1308, and largely emulated his father's description of the duties of the major court officials and how they should deport themselves. He even laid out a seating order for those who dined at court, with major officials, important members of the nobility, urban leaders, and royal physicians eating at one table, sons of knights and lesser townsmen at another, and falconers at yet another. He also applies the same kind of rules to his chamberlain who could eat

116   D. J. KAGAY

alone, and to the wives, widows, and daughters of his officials who would eat at one table. The rest of Jaume II's court regulations specify the cuts of meat that the head cook could claim from the left-overs of royal meals and lists the amount of wax granted every month to each major member of the court.[16]

Jaume II's grandson, Pere III, continued this definition of court operations, but on a much greater scale when he had translated from Latin to Catalan Jaume III of Majorca's brilliant *Leges Palitinae* to a work entitled *Ordinacions fets sobre lo regiment de tots los officials de la sua cort*. This thorough review of how Pere's court functioned, discusses the duties of Pere's major officials, reviews in detail how his chancellery worked, how his revenues were collected and audited, how his household operated, how the religious needs of the court were handled, and how the king maintained the working of his government when he went to war.[17]

Echoing the sentiments of his hated cousin, Jaume III, Pere III apparently attempted to understand how his court and household should be governed, so he could better explain his wishes to his people. He thus could not be a good ruler without the aid of a "council of wise men, experienced and disposed to act in all loyalty."[18] To make this hopeful theory a reality, he couched his expectations of the major officials who served him and his realms in practical terms.

The leading official of the king's council was the chancellor. He regulated who could approach the king, and who should stand or sit in his presence. He was the chair of all official meetings and decided who could present their opinions. He also determined in what order they would speak, normally allowing the less important to air their opinions first and preserving the last word for the more important men. Mirroring an emerging view that secular authority should regulate that of clerics in all secular matters, the chancellor controlled all churchmen in the royal court, no matter what their position. This became extremely dicey given the long tradition that a chancellor of the Aragonese court should be at least a bishop who possessed a doctorate in the "two laws."[19] Below the chancellor, stood the protonotary, who maintained all of Pere's official records and secret seals, and the vice-chancellor, who assured that each letter leaving the court was written in "good Latin" and marked with an "order" (*iusssio*) at the bottom of the last page stating who had authorized the missive and who had written it.[20]

One of the most significant changes to the Aragonese court resulted from Pere II's rule in Sicily in the years after he became ruler of the island.

Despite the rapid disintegration of the Sicilian government after Pere the Great and Jaime II, it still maintained the most forward-looking institutional element that owed its existence to the Hohenstaufen rulers from the era before the Vespers, the "auditor of accounts" (*maestre racional*). Sicilian royal finances were divided between three of these officials who were responsible for the yearly auditing of all royal accounts. Though Jaume I had used a similar centralization of finances by appointing Jewish general bailiffs, such fiscal control of the *maestre racional* remained a fixture of Aragonese royal government until the fall of the Barcelona dynasty in 1410 and into the Trastámara royal family two years later.

With large departments of subordinate officials, this chief accountant was charged with "going over the books" every six months and issuing financial reports of the king, queen, and major officials of the court.[21]

For Elionor of Sicily's political career, the most important change to the governmental structure of the Crown of Aragon was the development of the procurator or lieutenant general. Those who bore this title were not royal officials in the accepted sense but were royal appointees who were normally chosen during times of national emergence when the king's presence was needed on several fronts. In real terms, the procurator, normally a member of the royal family or the upper nobility, carried credentials that described them as the king's "alter-ego" (*alter nos*) who represented his person in all the actions he or she might undertake during their term of appointment. Acting as the sovereign, the procurator could engage in adjudication, oversee legal inquisitions, prepare for war by staffing and provisioning castles, and doing everything else needed to protect "the good estate and the preservation of the realm."[22]

These largely unprecedented actions were first taken by the wildly successful reconquest warrior king, Jaume I, who doubled the land he controlled with the conquests of Majorca and Valencia. In 1270 when he was already in his sixties, he appointed control of the older reigns, Aragon and Catalonia to his son, Prince Pere. Jaume's son, Pere II, did much the same for the same reason when in 1284 he left his new kingdom of Sicily to return to his Iberian realms and left his queen, Constanza, and second son, Jaume, in charge of the island. In the same year, he established a ruling precedent by appointing his first son, Prince Alfons (soon to be Alfons II) as a general procurator for Aragon, Catalonia, and Valencia. Jaume II gave the same type of appointment to one of his nobles, Pedro de Queralt, who would rule Sicily in the king's absence. In 1361, Pere III endowed his first son, Joan, with the titles, duke of Gerona and count of

118   D. J. KAGAY

Cervera and four years later named the fifteen-year-old prince a general procurater for all his Iberian realms. For our purposes, the most important of these grants was to Elionor of Castile in 1359 when the war with Castile was in its full fury. It will be more discussed in Chapter 7.

In the topsy-turvy years after the conflict ended in 1366, the lieutenant had become such a usual political feature in realms of the Crown of Aragon that in 1367 the Aragonese *cortes* at Tamarite de Litera recognized formally that the king could appoint a lieutenant in the realm and no matter the title the king gave him or her, all of the king's subjects would accept this official's authority and jurisdiction. One modern scholar typifies the spread of the use of the procurator as Aragon's most important administrative development of the fourteenth century and one that served as a handy instrument for the strengthening of royal power throughout Spain, the Mediterranean, and into the New World.[23]

2   ELIONOR'S COURT MANAGEMENT

The queen's court, like that of her husband, was filled with over 150 officials and servants who worked under three major divisions. Surely the largest of these was headed by the majordomos, the most important of whom during her reign was Ramón de Pagara and Joan Berenguer de Rajadell. They commanded a large cook staff, butlers, bakers, cooks, launderers, all of whom attended to the daily needs of the queen, all of the administrators and servants in the court, and Elionor's visitors.[24] Chamberlains, such as Ramon de Castelló, Ramóa de Copons, and Beremguer Ripoll, shared physical control of Elionr's court with the mayordomos, commanding a large number of skilled servants, ranging from hairdressers, dressmakers, furriers up to doctors and surgeons and down to palace guards.[25] The chancellor had autonomy over many intellectual and professional aspects to the queen's court. For most of Elionor's career, the duties of the chancellor was carried out by Bishop Romeus de Cescomes of Lerida. Since he commanded the royal chancellery, many familiar names for modern scholars who have worked through Elionor's documents served under the chancellor. These included the secretary Berenguer Carbonell, and the royal scribes, Bernat de Puig and Guillem d'Oliver, royal adviser and famous legist, Jaume de Vallseca, and Guillem de Serra, the director of the queen's archive in the "New Palace" (Nova Palau).[26] The office of the *maestre racional* handled all the money the queen received from all sources and spent for every possible reason. This crucially important and often unpopular post in Elionor's court was filled by Blasco Fernández de Heredia and Jaume de Sos. They commanded the important treasurer, Berenguer de Relat, notary and commissioner, Ferrer Sayoll, and scribes, Geralt Spelunca and Bernat Conill.[27]

Served by so many well-educated and -experienced functionaries and officials, one wonders what kind of specific activities Elionor was routinely involved in within her court. They were both personal and professional and sometimes a mixture of the two. Though her court was not as itinerant as her husband's, she did move a goodly amount of her possessions from one site to another. On one occasion, in late-winter of 1358, she was forced to beg the city council of Zaragoza to provide a mule train for one of her servants to bring her best frocks to Teruel where she was planning to celebrate the New Year.[28] Whether the Zaragozans complied with this request or not, it shows the queen at her most charming as a women who loved beautiful things and knew how to ask for them from her subjects. Besides beautiful clothes, the queen was drawn to jewels. Throughout her reign, she had come to know the individual components of complex pieces of jewelry and eventually found it cheaper and less complicated to buy the raw materials wholesale and then have them assembled into a finished piece by a jeweler closer to home. She also collected books and furniture. In addition to a love for these beautiful things, things she may not have had in her youth, Elionor was savvy enough to know that they were easily transported and could be pawned for ready money to be redeemed at a later date. She also used these items to attain loans from Barcelona bankers and once sold much of her collection in Avignon, perhaps so her husband would not find out. Even with the love of precious items, she never refused to turn her gems into money when her husband needed it.[29]

While the queen took seriously the administrative duties that the court imposed on her, her greatest obligations were those to her family. We have already seen how much care she took with the nuptials of her stepdaughter Joanna, by using all of her persuasiveness to convince many of her Valencian cities and towns to put up extra funds to make the ceremony a success. This included forcing 200 florins out of her husband's notoriously tight fists to give his own daughter a dowry, a boon that the queen herself had never received from her father or brother.[30] In her later years, the queen was called upon less to manage upcoming royal marriages in this way, but never let down her Aragonese family in welcoming new brides. In spring, 1363, she sent a letter to Princess

120   D. J. KAGAY

Matha de Armignac, soon to be Crown Prince Joan's first wife, to express her "supreme pleasure" with the upcoming wedding. A decade later in winter, 1374, she again did her duty in regard to another royal wedding, that of her daughter, Elionor, and Prince Juan, the son of Enrique II of Castile. Though the queen did not approve of this union, she did what was expected of her by acting as an intermediary between her husband and the Castilian ambassadors. On December 19, 1374, she received the marriage terms that had just been agreed upon and forwarded them to her husband.[31] On January 1, 1375, only some three months before her death, she again expressed her stern disapproval of the Castilian match, not because of any ill feelings about Prince Juan, but because of long history of distrust for his father, King Enrique II. In the next few days, she sent other letters, repeating her concerns to the king of Navarre, Carles II "the Bad" (r. 1349–1387) and more to the Aragonese marriage negotiators, but all to no avail. She opposed the match but did not have to undergo the shame of attending the wedding which took place on June 18, 1375. Fortunately for the queen, she had died some months before.[32]

Much of Elionor's courtly work had to do with the support of her children, especially after they were old enough to have their own households, but before they had come of age. In 1357, we witness the queen demanding funds to provision the new domestic establishment of Prince Martí, who was still an infant. Many of the expenses associated with her children were handled by the purchasing agents of their courts who routinely had to be reimbursed by the queen out of her own funds. By the end of the 1350s, Elionor's support of three small children put her own finances in jeopardy. In 1359, she was thus forced to call for a general subsidy from all of her revenue-producing sites since the money she used to provide for her own domestic establishment and that of her children was rapidly running out.[33]

From Elionor's communications to her children's officials and to her own functionaries, we can get some idea of their relationships. As we have seen, the queen's exchanges with her first born after he came of age in 1366 were not always happy ones On November 9 of that year, she continued support of the crown prince as she had for every year of his life by having barley confiscated from Teruel, which had spent much of the last three years under Castilian control. She then sent a large shipment of the grain sent to Joan's court, also supplying him with a mule for the long trips he made across his lands. She also reached into her own funds to pay her son's confessor 200 *sous* of Barcelona.[34] In these years after her young son had established some distance from his mother, Elionor constantly demanded that Joan's officials keep her informed of his health and generally what he was up too. When Joan suffered an accident in December 1367 which she only found out about several days after it had happened, she wrote in high dudgeon to officials of the prince's court, demanding that they inform her of Joan's condition "with all speed." Clearly distraught about the crown prince, she was also adamant that no suspicions or scandal would seep out about his accident.[35]

Unlike his older brother who had caused his mother many heartaches, Martí seemed to be the apple of her eye. In 1359, when he was three years old, she began the process of setting up his court by having the revenues of southern Valencian castles and villages established as his principal financial support. When her second child was thirteen, she provided sage advice about how to extricate himself honorably from a dispute with the abbot of Ripoll over control of the village of Olot. Since the prince's cause had been taken up by the residents of the nearby village of Camprodón, she advised her son to now stay out of the matter which threatened litigation which could have caused great damage to his good name and that of his parents. As was usual in many of these cases, we know very little about how they turned out, but we do know that her love for Martí never cooled, and she left him in her will a remarkable cross constructed of "nine sapphires, nine rubies, a middling-sized emerald, four large pearls, and as many small ones."[36]

The references to Elionor's third child and namesake are not numerous, but the ones that survive show that the younger Elionor led an exciting life as a young girl. Again, though her mother opposed the betrothal of her daughter to Enrique's son, Juan, she, had long been sick with worry, when wrote her "little heir" in late June, 1366 to express her relief when, although young Elionor was scheduled to go to the Castilian court as Prince Juan's intended, she eventually came under the protection of the bailiff of Murviedro and other royal officials when war loomed against the half-brothers, Pedro I and Enrique II, who both claimed to be the one-and-only Castilian king. Finally finding safety in the Castilian court, the Aragonese princess was eventually taken under the protection of Enrique II until his defeat at the battle of Nájera on April 3, 1367. With this critical defeat, the young Elionor could have been delivered into Pedro I's clutches, but was brought back unscathed to her mother and father by Prince Juan, her future husband, who at the time was some six months younger than his intended.[37]

122   D. J. KAGAY

As compensation for the lack of power they had compared to their husbands, many queens attempted to compensate by acting as dictators to their children and especially to their officials and servants. This was hardly the case with Elionor. She fought to have her representatives, especially those sent on missions across the Mediterranean to Sicily, reimbursed with royal funds as quickly as possible. From her own funds, she replaced their mounts, whether mules or palfreys. She also paid in full the sizeable fees charged by her doctors and surgeons.[38] These actions, however, could be understood as a matter of duty rather than sentiment; such a characterization of the queen, though, could hardly stand up in light of her many kindnesses to the members of her court. A good number of her faithful minions were rewarded with up to 5,000 *sous* of Barcelona to help pay for weddings of their daughters or even granddaughters. For one official, Berenguer de Palacia, who had served the queen since she landed at Valencia in 1349, but who left court service with a beautiful black palfrey he used on many of his missions, she waived any charge for the use of the animal, but instead gave him an honorarium of 150 *sous* of Barcelona.[39]

3   Elionor as General Administrator

In effect, Elionor was an administer in two fields. She managed the affairs of her court and those of her children. This normally involved the purchase of food and a great number of other items that these self-contained little worlds often needed. Her officials and servants took care of the royal family's needs, protected them, attempted to maintain their good health, entertained them, stored and audited money owed to the queen, and finally used this money to make purchases of items that the queen needed and wanted for herself and her children. The second phase of Elionor's administrative career was the price she paid for the yearly support from the residents of so many cities, town, villages, and castles who underwrote the life that she and her children led. Since she was feudally tied to these people, their support demanded the return of hers. In many ways, she acted exactly as her husband did by solving complicated urban problems, keeping fortresses in condition for war, protecting and maintaining discipline over the "king's treasure," the Jewish and Muslim communities whose residents were also her vassals, adjudicating legal cases that involved all of her "supporters," and finally to living up to her marriage agreement to love, protect, and honor her mate. In all these duties, except for the last, she utilized the same functionaries that inhabited her court environment, but over a much larger sphere of operations.

The queen's officials occasionally carried out their duties away from the court and its immediate needs. They maintained communications between their lady and the king about any number of subjects. In some ways, they served as secure messengers who shared information of all kinds between the rulers. They also served as ersatz paymasters who helped transfer money from the queen to other officials who spent most of their time away from Elionor's court on foreign missions. At times, they acted to maintain a line of communications between the courts of the queen and that of her husband. The most important of these royal agents working away from the court were commissioners who bore specific credentials to handle a set of large-scale problems in one urban community or in a several such neighboring sites. Though with a fairly long history in the first decades of the fourteenth century, they were used increasingly by Pere and Elionor to investigate cities and town such as Lliria, Murviedro, Teruel, and Tarazona which Pedro's forces had captured which had attracted a great number of Castilians who viewed them as sites where one could get rich quick. The commissioner was tasked with finding property which had been sold or granted to Castilian newcomers or those members of the original population who had treasonably worked with the enemy to get rich. The commissioner's final task was to return all stolen houses, land, and anything else to the original owners.[40]

The queen's men also occasionally acted as diplomats on both the local and international levels. They were very often utilized as messengers between the queen and such important figures as the chief Hospitaller official in the Crown of Aragon, Juan Fernández de Heredía, the castellan of Amposta, when Elionor attempted to turn over this crucially important clerical site to a secular lord.[41] Some of the queen's functionaries served as agents of the royal government when, during periods of hostility with one of Aragon's principal Mediterranean enemies, Genoa, they were ordered to confiscate the goods of Genoese merchants in Barcelona.[42] They also facilitated communications between royal families caught in the middle of complex preparations for a royal wedding, such as that of the Castilian prince, Juan, and "that very beautiful creature," Princess Elionor in 1375.[43] They could also be called on to raise troops in case of surprise attacks, such as that of Jaume IV, Joanna I's third husband, into Roussillon in 1373–1374.[44] Because of the ongoing connection to her inept

Sicilian relatives, the queen was in all but constant contact with the Papal Curia at Avignon that she frequently sent her court officials to supply money to her diplomats who maintained a veritable fleet of galleys to facilitate negotiations between Elionor and Urban V (r. 1362–1370).[45]

Within the Crown of Aragon, the queen's officials spent a great amount of time in solidifying all aspects of Elionor's control over her urban sites and castles. From the first year of her reign to the last, Elionor acted as a guardian for many of the urban sites entrusted to the king by God. She stood as a feudal lord in the places granted to her as the sources of her financial support and from this position, there were few limits to her action.[46] She occasionally engaged in a kind of urban planning in the Catalan town of Tamarit de Litera by allowing the citizens to build onto their surrounding lands while increasing their security with the extension of the town's fortifications.[47] The Aragonese city of Teruel had undergone great damage for the three years after 1363 when it was held by the Castilians. To head off widespread hunger among her vassals there, the queen appointed commissioners whose only job was to import large supplies of wheat and barley to prevent starvation among the citizenry. Even before this, the queen had licensed certain of her subjects to engage in grain transport across the Crown of Aragon.[48]

To reduce expenses, the queen was not above getting double service for her *sou* by paying one salary to a castellan and expecting him to administer both his fortress and the village that neighbored it.[49] The official accounts of every one of Elionor's men were audited by the *maestre racional* and those whose books did not balance were quickly removed from their posts of trust and then required to answer to the royal law.[50] Besides avoiding these fiscal temptations, Elionor's representatives had to bring "unity, love, and charity" to urban environments scarred by all but perennial feuds. She also demanded "peace and concord" between major cities and their ring of hamlets which had erupted into open conflict during the thirteenth century.[51] Several of the queen's functionaries, especially her "doorman" (*porter*), numbered as one of his many duties the arrest of urban trouble-makers and their incarceration in municipal jails where they might long await a verdict from the municipal *justicia*.[52]

The principal duty of the queen's representatives in her urban sites was the recovery of money owed, but not paid to their lady. Though, as with her Jewish and Muslim ratepayers, this could happen because of a general decline in urban fiscal health due to plague or prolonged war, Elionor's men often faced more unexpected difficulties. In 1357, a townsman and his wife from Teruel committed "enormous crimes," by borrowing money and not repaying it. Instead, they used what amounted free cash to buy goods and make an expected profit on their resale. The queen would forgive them if they repaid the loan and then gave to her officials a "free will gift" of 1200 *sous* of Jaca which ultimately had to be returned to the queen. A year later, Elionor was shocked to find out that a shipment of money from the Aragonese town of Tarazona had been stolen "after some murders had been perpetrated."[53] As with so many crimes described in the queen's documents, it is not known if this heinous offense was punished. Toward the end of the Castilian war in 1365, the queen found that the Catalan village of Raviolos had kept back property found near the site, which had been won in military skirmishes. When Elionor found this out, she demanded that the villagers return one-fifth of it to comply with the rules of the royal fifth.[54]

Since all of her urban sites were crucial to the Aragonese queen since they guaranteed her financial security and that of her children until they came of age, many of her communication with her townsmen concerned taxation. To avoid factors like weather and illness that could reduce tax yields from year to year, the queen was not above selling off some of her tax revenues. In 1359, she did this very thing by selling toll revenues (*pedagium*) in the Aragonese village of Campfranch for 90,000 *sous* of Jaca. In other places, she continued to have the same impost collected even as the Castilian war continued.[55] The message that the queen wanted her officials to deliver to the sites she drew revenue from was that the money her vassals owed her had to be paid and on time. After so many collection cycles, it is hardly surprising that this was the message delivered to the queen's rent payers in May 1375, even though their lady had already been dead for some weeks.[56]

Despite this hard-headed approach to taxes, Elionor would not always place stubbornness over reality and was known to reduce tax obligations under extraordinary circumstances. When in 1357 the queen heard that many houses had fallen into disrepair in Lliria, a Valencian town she had bought three years before, she thought it would be a "helpful remedy" for the townsmen to utilize the taxes they owed her to repair the structures and, in so doing, increase the total value of the site. In Teruel's hamlets, a year later, after she had heard that these small communities had been infected with plague, she ordered that their taxes should be collected in June and August, but then returned to them, to help with the care of her ill vassals. In 1360, she did much the same thing for Huesca, but this

126   D. J. KAGAY

time to help repair its grain market. In 1366, the queen made a similar reduction in the tax bill of the Valencian town of Morella, not from any emergency, but since she had recently received the community from her husband and hoped that the lessened tax bill would instill the townsmen's good will for her. From the steady flow of money from her coffers to her husband during her last years, it is unlikely that such reductions would increase during this period. The final reduction among her urban vassals had nothing to do with building decay, plague, or good will, but occurred in Calatayud in 1370 because many of the city's important citizens would not pay their taxes, and her officials were too afraid of them to press the issue.[57]

From the first to the last of the communities and properties the queen took charge of during her long administrative career, she sworn or it was sworn for her that she would settle disputes in civil law justly, with no prejudice for either side, and punish crimes with ruthless efficiency, but also with fairness for the accused. She was also responsible for the investigation and punishment of her officials who had violated their service oaths by absconding with royal funds, maltreating civilian populations under their official control, or committing treason by revealing official secrets to the enemy.

Since Elionor had so many fiefs to defend as a feudal lady because of the continuing grants her husband had bestowed on her during every decade of their married life, the queen took it as her duty to adjudicate legal battles that involved real estate with two or more litigants claiming to be the undisputed owner. In 1359, she directed her procurator, Domenic Lull, to influence the vicar of the Valencian town of Elche to render a decision between the current holder of the village and its rents, on one hand, and another noble of the region who also claimed full rights to the site. The final verdict in this case is unknown, but, considering Elionor's generally conservative views on landholding, it probably trended toward the litigant who held the village when the case had begun.[58] This same respect for a record of original property ownership is hardly apparent in a suit of 1374 over unnamed goods that was brought in the town of Sant Esteve de Litera between residents of the villages of Torrico and Arcadells. Since an original settlement of the case had been "nullified," Elionor was adamant that the matter be tried again, this time "according to the *fuero* and the law."[59]

6 ELIONOR OF SICILY AS COURTIER AND ADMINISTRATOR   127

In the last decade of her life, the Aragonese queen fought several suits, all connected with the sites that provided funding for herself or her children. In 1369, she wrote one of her officials about settling a legal claim concerning her rights to the castle of Montcada which her husband had granted her nine years before. To bring some pressure on the other litigant, she ordered him to come before her or her secretary, Berenguer de Relat, in ten days at Barcelona, and bring with him the evidence on which he based his case. In 1370 and 1371, King Pere recognized the justice of his wife's earlier claims concerning Huesca and had them certified before his principal bailiff of Barcelona.[60]

Compared with the civil actions she fought, Elionor found herself much more involved in the litigation of a remarkable variety of crimes committed on the streets of her towns and villages. The queen and her officials adjudicated an astounding number of misdeeds that involved both stealth and violence. Between 1364 and 1370, she sentenced individuals and groups that today we might call gangs who were guilty of stealing money and a great deal of property. She even charged and sentenced wealthier townsmen who colluded to gain profit from such illegal enterprises.[61]

By far the greatest number of legal decisions Elionor had to make as the lady of such a long list of urban holdings dealt with violence which was often accompanied by crime. One of the most disturbing offenses that the queen or any of her fellow administrators had to face was the crime of murder. As is often the case today, homicide very often took place between spouses within the home. Such was the case of Berenguer de Gerona, a townsman of Sabadell, who in 1369 killed his wife, Francisca. Though proved guilty before the town bailiff, the accused produced a number friends and associates who swore to his innocence and thus seemed to escape punishment.[62]

Group violence, especially in an urban setting, was something Elionor could not abide. In 1356, she wrote Martín de Turibas, a Valencian lawyer, to accomplish a "suitable correction" for a "disreputable matter" which had taken place in the village of Luera near Lliria. A veritable rampage had taken place in the small community when three brothers "under the pretext of the Castilian war" had gone on a violent spree which seemed to include house breaking. This criminal family eventually paid for their crimes with a large fine of 100 *morabatins*.[63] In 1372, Elionor presided as a judge in two cases of what can only be called urban riots. On January 26, she reviewed a series of bloody disputes between

128   D. J. KAGAY

citizens of Teruel and the Community of Teruel's hamlets which centered on Castile's destruction and plunder of the region during the recent war which led to the loss of a great amount of property. To render as just a verdict as possible, the queen declared that the former owners would be restored their property as quickly and simply as possible. On April 4, she called for the rendering of a verdict against Christian citizens of the Aragonese city of Huesca who had murdered and terrorized the local Muslim *aljama*, even raping some of the community's women. If the local officials did not render justice for the oppressed infidels, Elionor promised they would soon experience her justifiably famous "ire and indignation."[64]

The Aragonese queen also reviewed a great number of cases of group violence that gave shelter and opportunity to criminals. In 1370, a citizen of the Catalan town of Tàrrega was badly beaten and robbed by other townsmen. According to the queen, the culprits deserved to be "bitterly distrained" and have judicial vengeance taken on them by her officials. Another case of profitable violence took place in 1373 when a group of robbers disrupted a fair at Tamarit de Litera by engaging in a riot during which they made off with a great amount of merchandise. Elionor also reviewed a much more open and formalized criminal groups when she asked the lieutenant of Ibiza to investigate the increased piracy around the island to see if it was being supported by Ibizan residents.[65]

The Aragonese queen also ruled on crimes, which though not involving violence were crimes, nonetheless. In 1372, she sternly ordered the bailiff of Sabadell to arrest a woman of Barcelona, known variously as Alagorça and Valeco, who had been accused of adultery by her husband, Palan Burgo. Though this kind of wrongdoing might seem strange to appear before a criminal court, it was most definitely considered a serious crime. The queen obviously agreed with this feeling that Burgo deserved justice, even if this brought shame to his wife.[66] Another non-violent crime that both the king and queen ruled on during this period involved the stockpiling of counterfeit gold coinage discovered in Teruel by officials of Elionor's household. This came about when they were investigating this bogus specie, some of which was used in paying the queen's tax bill. Pere III could hardly be shocked by such an illegal development since he himself had overseen a counterfeiting operation against Castile during the War of the Two Pedros.[67]

Though the queen was adamant in seeing crimes, whether violent or non-violent, properly punished, she became convinced, as her administrative tenure continued from year to year, that much of this litigation was "running up immoderate expenses and costs." She did not abandon the punishment of the guilty, but increasingly sought extreme verdicts in hopes that she could dissuade her possibly guilty vassals from taking the dangerous road of crime.[68]

The accusations the queen brought against members of her on-court attempted to prevent malfeasance against the communities or the individuals that they served. In 1369, she instructed her lawyer, Berenguer Miron, to investigate charges of crimes committed by one of her officials, Guillem Bernat de Podiolo, within the bailiwick of her castle of Montcada outside of Barcelona. This offense was rendered more serious by a bloody attack Podiocolo carried out on a villager within the boundary of the castle itself. The queen was supposedly content with whatever decision her lawyer came to, but reminded him the "law and reason have to be fulfilled in order to stop the crimes committed against the goods of others."[69] As usual in many of these cases, we have no final verdict, but in most accusations of malfeasance, the officials were either disciplined within the court structure or turned over to direct royal justice for adjudication.

Since Elionor exercised feudal control over so many urban sites, she also had legal jurisdiction over the officials of these communities, no matter the size of the community. In 1370, in one of the most distant places that supplied fiscal support for the queen, the Balearic island of Minorca, one of her officials, Ferrer Gilabert, was accused of official misconduct, and his record would be suitably investigate before a final verdict was rendered. At first, the queen insisted that these legal proceedings were to be brought to her court at Barcelona by a "trustworthy person." She eventually had the accused transferred to the mainland, where he would undergo her personal investigation.[70] In late January 1375, a few months before her death, the queen received a report of illegal administrative practices in Gerona. As governor of Catalonia, she immediately sent one of her officials and a Barcelona lawyer to initiate a formal investigation which quickly came to the king for his inspection, and was almost as quickly was forgotten by history.[71] Some two weeks later on January 29, Elionor commenced a similar investigation of Guisbert Roig, a scribe of the small Mediterranean coastal town of San Feliu de Quíxols, who presented a public letter at Barcelona which substituted

130   D. J. KAGAY

the names of men from the vicarates of Gerona for the rightful officials who held office in Sant Feliu. To determine if this was done with criminal intent or from sheer ineptitude, Elionor had Roig submit to yet another royal investigation.[72]

From these proceedings, the queen clearly insisted on abiding by the legal procedure of the realm in which the supposed misdeed took place. In all these cases, the Aragonese queen insisted on a thorough and unbiased investigation. Unfortunately, for Elionor's reputation as the purveyor of royal justice, her most important case, that of one of her husband's principal advisers, Bernat de Cabrera, showed her in much less than a positive light.

4   THE INVESTIGATION AND EXECUTION OF BERNAT DE CABRERA

Bernat Cabrera, the viscount of Cabrera, came from an important family of Ausona, one of the original possessions of the count of Barcelona before he held Old and New Catalonia. His predecessors were important advisers to the family of the count and claimed the county of Urgel. One of his ancestors, Ponc III, "the Troubadour," was a friend of the southern French poet, Bertran de Born, who characterized him as the "richest and most cultured man in Catalonia."[73]

This worldly man enjoyed an extensive political career and his son, Guerau IV, was even more important in this regard, serving as an important adviser for Pere I and Jaume I.[74] Guerau's grandson, Bernat II, was born in Calatayud in 1298. When a young man of twenty-four and still known by the diminutive title of Bernardi since his father was also called Bernat, he took part in the invasion of Sardinia in the early 1320s with King Alfons III. He survived the campaign and returned to Catalonia to assume his deceased father's title of viscount.[75]

After becoming a close adviser of Pere III in the same year as he became king, Cabrera served with few gaps in this position until 1344 when he resigned to take up a life of resignation and meditation at the Benedictine monastery of Breda, an institution that had long been supported by the Cabrera family. He remained away from the world until 1347 when, Pere called him back at age fifty to help deal with the widespread revolt of the *Unión*. Because of his age which was considered quite advanced in the medieval centuries, Bernat was considered a weakling whom the leaders of the *Unión* thoroughly underestimated. Using this to his advantage, Cabrera apparently helped to remove Pere and his first queen from virtual unionist imprisonment at the Valencian town of Murviedro. Whether this is true or not, he did help break up the solidarity of the rebels according to Pere by offering them everything they wanted without any intention of giving it to them. His role in the military actions against the Sardinians and the Genoese in the 1350s solidified his military reputation, but also began to enflame Pere III's mounting jealousy of his most important adviser.[76]

Cabrera, who only years before had deserted public life for religious meditation, again emerged as a great man with a great reputation for "valor and prudence," in the late 1340s. This led the king in 1351 to appoint the viscount as the guardian of the crown prince. We are not sure when he first met Queen Elionor, but Cabrera soon discovered that his royal master's new wife had no love for him or the clique of royal officials he headed, who like him came from the Pyrenean region of Roussillon. The queen, who viewed the new guardian as a dangerous influence on her son, soon found supporters among such members of the royal family as the king's uncles Pere and Ramon Berenguer and most of the Aragonese and Valencian upper nobility.[77] None of this would ever have been more than an example of courtly jealousy and backbiting had the king not gotten involved.

The two men who had once stood together as a team now began to fall out over the "very dangerous matter" posed by the great influx of mercenaries over the Pyrenees seeking employment after a peace accord between France and England was negotiated at Bretigny in 1361. The Aragonese king wanted to call out all of Catalonia's adult male population under the article of the *Usatges*, *Princeps namque*. Cabera opposed this solution as a kind of overkill. Not surprisingly, the already shamed adviser lost this fight and his sad fate was becoming ever clearer to everyone in Pere's court, including Queen Elionor who for the last decade of her court life had kept up a campaign of "vindictive and relentless persecution" against her only true enemy in the ranks of her husband's court.[78]

Cabrera's official downfall commenced in the royal palace at Barcelona in December 1361 when the courtier's refusal to support his royal master on the matter of *Princeps namque* brought a royal lawsuit alleging Cabrera's treasonous activities As a member of the administration, the queen was undoubtedly at this meeting. Her husband was eventually swayed by his adviser's powerful associates, but the old official now seemed to be living on borrowed time.[79] Despite his fear of the king's unpredictable

132   D. J. KAGAY

temper and the queen's open hatred, the rapidly aging adviser found few opportunities to escape the Aragonese court, especially after his son and namesake, the count of Osona was captured when Calatayud fell in 1362.[80] Pere's confidence reached its low in 1363 when Cabrera served as a peace negotiator with the unscrupulous and even more untrustworthy, Charles II of Navarre, who insisted on a secret clause concerning the assassination of Count Enrique de Trastámara in the treaty that followed. Even though this scurrilous article was never put into effect, the king surely heard of it, and as a result Pere displayed lessening confidence in his adviser by removing from him royal offices he had long held and cast blame on the aging counselor for military and diplomatic mistakes that the king himself had made.[81]

In February 1364 when the Navarrese negotiations and the Castilian war were both going badly, the Aragonese king demanded that his sixty-six-year-old adviser appear at the continuing talks at the Aragonese frontier town of Almudevar. Though traveling with the court, he was suffering from a lingering illness. Pere thus visited Cabrera in his sickroom on March 22, hoping he could convince the official to return to the last phase of the negotiations with Navarre, by emphasizing how important he was to all of the king's foreign affairs. Pere also tried to calm Bernat's fears about Queen Elionor and her supporters, even though he knew them to be completely true.[82] Afraid of what might happen to him if he came under the tender mercies of the queen, the old and sick administrator made for the Navarrese border, probably hoping to cross into France. He then wrote his royal master, saying he would answer any and all accusations in writing. Eventually, encountering a Navarrese official, he asked for asylum, but was immediately arrested and returned to Aragon.[83]

By April 1, 1364, the Aragonese king had written his wife about the Cabrera case, venting to her his disgust at the "evil and detestable" actions of both Bernat and his son. In the king's mind, there now seemed little room for judicial fairness; instead, the queen's duty as his lieutenant was to "diligently get at the truth," that is, to document the obvious guilt of the wrongdoers, both of whom had betrayed the king and his people.[84] By mid-April, 1364, the charges against Cabera and the absent count of Osona were largely drawn up and Cabrera was rapidly charged as a contumacious rebel who [repeatedly committed] nefarious treasons and shameful crimes of *lèse majesté*. From this legal declaration, Bernat and his namesake were branded as outcasts, and any who helped them would suffer a large fine.[85]

On June 10, Cabrera came before a legal conclave headed by Queen Elionor in the royal palace at Barcelona. The other judges were Elionor's supporters and so disputes about a just verdict were all but non-existent. Since Cabrera was still held under Navarrese arrest, and his son was in Castilian custody, they did not appear before the tribunal. Some days into that proceeding Cabrera's legal representative, the abbot of Breda and a townsman from Gerona appeared before the queen and, with few signs of respect for Pere's representative, complained that the Cabreras had been denied their rights in several ways. They had not been given the opportunity to appoint champions for trial by battle, and by the obvious prejudiced nature of the case caused by the queen and her mignons. The judges had clearly violated natural law, a right that all living things, even "the devils of the Inferno" were entitled to.[86] None of these arguments were accepted in any way since Cabrera's advocates had not been properly appointed and thus were not recognized by the tribunal. Even before they had appeared, on the first day of the trial, the queen instructed one of her officials to publicly summon the two Cabreras by name on three different occasions. When they obviously did not answer, being hundreds of miles away in Navarre or Castile, the queen declared them guilty of all charges.[87]

All the work for the Cabreras' condemnation was long finished before the first day of the trial. It consisted of a series of interviews conducted by royal and municipal officials about the actions of the Cabreras in undermining Pere's realms "in a diabolical manner."[88] The vast amount of information the queen's tribunal plowed through came to it from one "sworn inquest" (*inquisitio*) after another that produced mounds of "evidence" that amounted to little more than hearsay. Even at that, none of this manufactured proof contained a "smoking gun" which actually proved the Caberas guilty of treason. The testimony that purported to show these cowardly acts could do little more than demonstrate that Cabrera senior talked or shook hands with Pedro I. From one point-of-view, it showed him as a proven traitor; form the other, it portrayed the actions of a skilled diplomat.[89]

Despite the weaknesses of the case Elionor and the "judges" put together against the two Cabreras, it was successful because it gave the king exactly what he wanted with the complete destruction of Bernat Cabrera's reputation as one of Crown of Aragon's great men. On July 26, 1364, at nine in the morning, after being hectored by his mother, the queen, to do so for weeks, Crown Prince Joan had his guardian–a man

134   D. J. KAGAY

he was clearly very close to–executed by "having his head cut off from his shoulders" in the marketplace of Zaragoza near the Toledo gate.[90] The count of Ososa evaded this shameful end, but his last day was little better. After years of Castilian imprisonment, he died in 1368 again fighting in a lost cause, that of Pedro I against the new Castilian king, Enrique II.[91] Pere III maintained his hard line against the Cabrera until Elionor's death in 1375. Five years after that, freed of his wife's unbending hatred of Bernat and his son, the king finally came to publicly admit that the elder Cabrera was a man of "elevated courage and great counsel" and he had used him badly because of a "suspicion... provoked by anger and indignation."[92]

What remains is to try to understand what drove Queen Elionor to declare war on an official as high-placed as Bernat de Cabrera before she had fully become a power in her husband's administration. Her distaste for the "Great Favorite," as Cabrera was called at the height of his power, probably began not from politics, but from jealousy. He was, after all, in a position that in most cases was bestowed on the mother. As a result of what the queen viewed as a sleight, she was separated from her first born, and this feeling of distrust and disappointment is apparent through the remaining lives of the mother and son. In a broader sense, the queen fell into a feud with the Cabreras by following her husband's often-distrustful view of his underlings and extending this era of bad feelings by applying the often-vicious standards of politics she had learned in Sicily to that of Aragon. In the end there was no separate opinion for the Aragonese king and queen in the matter of Bernat Cabrera. As with so many other things in their marriage, they acted as a unit to weaken, hamstring, and finally execute the greatest official of Pedro's reign.

5   Elionor's Jewish and Muslim *Aljamas* in Peace and War

By the reign of Jaume I, the long history of the Jewish presence in Spain was well over a millennium old. During the reign of the "Conqueror," the Jewish population in the Crown of Aragon reached an approximate total of 15,000. Many of these new settlers sought new homes in Christian land recently won from Muslim rulers, viewing these less populated territories as lands teaming with "new opportunities."[93] Sizeable Jewish communities (*aljamas*) appeared in the major cities of eastern Spain, Barcelona, Valencia, and Zaragoza as well as smaller settlements such as

6 ELIONOR OF SICILY AS COURTIER AND ADMINISTRATOR   135

Calatayud, Elche, Jaca, Játiva, Murviedro, Orihuela, Tarazona, Tarragona, and Teruel.[94] With the death of Jaume I in 1276, the advanced status they had gained under his rule quickly disappeared, and to compensate for the loss of salaries they had drawn as skilled treasury officials, they extended their money-lending activities, which brought deepening resentment with their Christian debtors.[95] With the steady passage of the Black Death across the Crown of Aragon in the spring of 1348 worsened Christian-Jewish relations even further, causing numerous attacks of *aljamas* and a steady abrogation of Jewish debts.[96]

For decades after the appearance of the pandemic, Jewish communities underwent one disaster after another. We can follow this sad road through the documents of Queen Elionor who controlled one of the largest blocs of Jewish *aljamas* in the Crown of Aragon down to her death in 1375. From the first years of her queenship, she received the financial support of the *aljamas* of Barcelona Valencia, Lerida, Gerona, Besalú, Vilafranca de Penerdes, and Berga. In 1359, she received the town and Jewish community of Murviedro, which she would lose to Pedro I in 1363, only to regain it two years later after the town was recaptured by her husband's army.[97]

As the immediate authority over these communities, each of which survived as a much smaller and segregated unit of Christian cities and towns, the queen dealt with small ruling councils in a straightforward, businesslike manner. Their relationship centered on the yearly tribute, which came into the queen's treasury twice a year, in May and September. There normally was an argument about this and how it was to be carried out. The only real differences the two parties normally had was exactly which imposts would be tapped to provide the annual sum owed the queen. This was determined by the bailiff of the urban site in which the *aljama* was located or by the queen's direct representative there. From most of the messages the Jewish communities received from the queen, there seemed few questions about tax issues. An amount was set at the beginning of the year and her officials were to compel its collection "strongly and directly."[98]

The tribute that came into Elionor's coffers from the Jewish communities was an extremely regular one. It was normally paid at the same time of the year and consisted of a similar sum. When the queen needed extra money because of events beyond her control, such as the uprising in Sardinia in 1354 which moved Pere's court to that island for over two years or the "war between the most illustrious king (my dear husband

136   D. J. KAGAY

and lord) and his public enemy, the king of Castile," she called for an extraordinary subsidy from her *aljamas* which had to be paid at a set time, normally a few months after its announcement, and a specified amount which greatly exceeded the annual tribute. Though these general events explained the need for extra money, it was the overall lack of funds to meet her normal expenses that the queen emphasized to her Jewish ratepayers.[99]

Like any good debt collector, Elionor used both the authority of her name and the personal threat of her officials to induce recalcitrant ratepayers to pony up the money in question which was due to the queen as their lady to whom they had sworn feudal allegiance. She emphasized time and again that the funds demanded from her Jewish communities was clearly not for her own pleasure, but because of the many duties it would allow her to effectively carry out. Her normal means of squeezing out unpaid taxes was to send a series of letters, each of which became more harsh in its verbiage and the last normally suggesting that, more than deadbeats, the stubborn *aljamas* were getting very close to being traitors. By the time the queen's men visited the targeted communities, the Jews were normally more than willing to pay their proper share.[100]

As the War of the Two Pedros wore on, Pere III himself began to realize the crisis that the conflict posed for Jewish communities, one of his realms' most important funding sources. *Aljama* society was in the process of a political disintegration, marked by a crisis among its local leaders who could no longer carry out the orders of the Aragonese crown as efficiently as they had done in the past. Even before the conflict with Castile had begun, Jewish communities, such as that of Murviedo, was beginning to bleed population. Many of the families that took to the road completely deserted Aragon for safer spots in Castile or Granada that presented greater opportunities.[101] A good example of the dysfunctional direction that Jewish communities followed in the 1350s and 1360s is provided with the Aragonese town of Tarazona where a Jewish boy was sold into slavery by the Castilians who had overrun the place in 1357. When the conquerors left in 1366, the boy's father left to see if he could find his child. Returning after some months of a fruitless search, the disconsolate father found that his Jewish neighbors had ransacked his house.[102] Despite the largely ineffectual efforts of the Aragonese king to lessen their burdens, then, both Jewish and Muslim societies in the Crown of Aragon had entered a desperate state that prevented them from supporting Christian demands as efficiently they had earlier in the fourteenth century.[103]

After the undeclared end of the war in 1366, Pere attempted to rebuild the Jewish and Muslim communities by remitting taxation for up to five years while at the same time informing Jews who had fled their homes in Aragon that they had committed a crime and anyone helping them were equally guilty. All the fugitives and their abettors were thus guilty of acts that could cost him their lives and property.[104]

Elionor engaged in many of the same types of measures to help the Jewish families she ruled over. In the first years of the war, she returned tax money to some of her *aljamas* that either had been severely damaged during Castilian attacks or purposely demolished by the residents of the very cities and towns in which the Jewish communities existed. With it, she instructed their remaining leaders to rebuild the parts of the Jewish quarters that had suffered the greatest amount of damage.[105] As the conflict moved slowly toward its inglorious end in 1366, the Aragonese queen had no choice but to continue the policy of either taking less tax funds from her Jewish subjects or returning to the Jewish ratepayers a portion of the collected taxes. In either way, the money returned amounted to between forty and fifty percent of the original tax bill.[106]

In spite of the Queen Elionor's tendency toward leniency for her oppressed *aljamas* in the last years of the conflict with Castile, she was still a strict task master especially in the enforcement of law and order in her Jewish and Muslim *aljamas*. In 1357, she punished "different frauds" in her city of Lliria concerning a tax sold on meat prepared in butcher shop according to standard practices of Judaism. Since there was even a Christian tax on this commodity, the Aragonese queen insisted that it be collected by Jewish butchers under pain of heavy fines.[107] As in the Christian neighborhoods of her cities and towns, the queen insisted on the maintenance of public peace, even if it involved an internecine struggle which involved only Jews and took place repeatedly throughout the 1360s inside a Jewish homes or synagogues.[108]

Elionor also issued harsh warnings against Christians who threatened their Jewish neighbors. Thus within a few days in 1371, she forbade Christians in Huesca from making loans with interest to the city's Jews. In this directive, she was not particularly taking the side of her Jewish subjects, but rather threatening to punish Christian moneylenders for the heinous sin of usury. Within a day, she gave a tongue-lashing to the lieutenant of the Aragonese governor for forcing Jews of the city to give up

138   D. J. KAGAY

to him and members of his family the use of their bedrooms. Though not illegal, it infuriated the queen who saw the practice as the worst kind of dictatorship of office. In all disagreements that pitted one Jew against another, she urged the peaceful give-and-take rather than real or threatened violence.[109]

The message of royal control also radiated to the Muslim communities that helped provide financial support for the Aragonese queen. Despite the bad times all of Aragon's Muslims had gone through during the war with Castile, the Muslim *aljama* of Huesca was expected in 1367 to commence again a long tradition of annually presenting the queen with two rams. Despite the hardship this might have caused Huesca's Muslims, it demonstrated that the queen would not allow her officials to bypass an age-old privileges within their communities, even during the uncertain time of war.[110] Elionor also ajudicated various cases involving Muslim women by attempting to impose an unbiased application of the law. Thus in 1369, she prevented Muslim wives from seeking new and presumably wealthier husbands, by advertising their female charms in the bustling grain exchange at Játiva, but defended the legal rights of Muslim women who had been raped in the small Aragonese village of María.[111]

6   CONCLUSION

Even before she had become queen, Elionor of Sicily's never flagging belief in her own abilities made her an extremely effective administrator. With her father's death and her brothers' youth, she took on herself many political functions for the Sicilian royal family. As soon as she wore the Aragonese crown, she served as a spokesman for King Ludovico in the Aragonese court, attempting to have her husband, Pere III, take up the Sicilian cause. In this way, she hoped to ward off her homeland's present and potential enemies. She served as a go-between with other royal families of fourteenth-century Europe for the purpose of arranging important marriage agreements for her younger sisters.

In her new land, she quickly exceeded her husband's expectations by rendering moot his real fears about succession with the delivery of three healthy children, two of whom would serve as Aragonese kings after their father's death in 1387. In charge of her own court, those of her children, Pere's daughter by his first wife, Joanna, and her second son's intended, María de Luna, the queen showed herself to be a no-nonsense executive who acted wisely for her offspring and other charges, while establishing a reputation of fearless defense for her own political position. Though clearly capable of instilling fear among her underlings in this courtly environment, she also took great care in protecting and rewarding officials and servants who had served her faithfully and with efficient care.

As a member of Aragon's general administration and a manager of all the urban sites, *aljamas*, and castles feudally bound to her, the queen soon gained a reputation of fearsome determination in defense of her husband's position and long-range projects as well as her own importance in the government of the Crown of Aragon. Once she was formally crowned and then made Governor of Catalonia and royal lieutenant, she acted in many ways as if she were the king of the Crown of Aragon.

NOTES

1. Alfonso Garcia Gallo, *Manual de historia del derecho español*, 2 vols. (Madrid, 1967), I:98–99; P.D. King, *Law and Society in the Visigothic Kingdom* (Cambridge, 1972), 16–17; O'Callaghan, *History*, 60–61; Claudio Sánchez Albornoz, "El aula regia y las asambleas políticas de los godos," *Cuadernos de la Historia de Españ* 5 (1945): 5–110.
2. Norbert Elias, *The Court Society*, trans. Edmund Jephcott (New York, 1983), 1.
3. Ibid., 42.
4. C. Warren Hollister and John W. Baldwin, "The Rise of Administrative Kingship and Philip Augustus," *AHR* 83, no. 4 (October, 1978): 867–905, esp. 868.
5. ACA, Pergaminos de Ramón Berenguer III, nos. 50, 69, 132–33, 173; Kagay, *Usatges*, 17–18; Josep, Trencs Odena, "La escribanía de Ramón Berenguer III (1097-1131): Datos para su estudio," *Saitabi* 31 (1984): 11–36, esp. 17.
6. ACA, Pergaminos de Ramón Berenguer IV, no. 241; Kagay, *Usatges*, 21–22.
7. Bisson, "Organized Peace," 223–26; idem, "The Problem of Feudal Monarchy: Aragon, Catalonia, and France," in *Medieval France*, 237–55, esp. 243–45.
8. Burns, *Society*, 28–29; A.M. Aragó Cabañas and Josep Tenchs Òdena, "Las escribanías reales catalanoaragonesas de Ramón Berenguer IV a la minoría de Jaime I," *Revista de archivos, bibliotecas y museos* 80 (1977): 421–42, esp. 239–42; Josep Tenchs Òdena, "Los escribanos de Ramón Berenguer: Nuevos datos," *Saitabi* 29 (1979): 5–20.
9. Fabrizio Titone, *Governments of the Universitates. Urban Communities of Sicily in the Fourteenth and Fifteenth Centuries* (Turnhout, 2009), 22–25, 37.

140 D. J. KAGAY

10. Titone, esp. 44–46, 48.
11. ACA, R. 1529, CR ff. 1–5; 6:5–16, VanLandingham, *Transforming the State*, 201–11.
12. ACA, R. 1529, CR, ff. 5r-v; *CDACA*, 6:15–16; VanLandingham, *Transforming the State*, 212–13.
13. ACA, CR, R. 64, last folio, Vanlandingham, *Transforming the State*, 214–15.
14. ACA, CR, R. 74, f. 93, Vanlandingham, *Transforming the State*, 216–17.
15. ACA, CR, R. 73, f. 102; Vanlandingham, *Transforming the State*, 218–20.
16. ACA, CR, R. 1529, ff. 5v–6v; *CDACA*, 6:17–19; Vanlandingham, *Transforming the State*, 221–23.
17. "Ordinacions fetes por lo molt alt senyor en Pere terç, rey d'Aragó sobre lo regiment de tots officials de su cort," *CDACA* 5: 9–296, esp. 8–9, 65–67, 78–84, 96–97, 109, 126–27, 134–43, 149–56, 161–66, 281; Kagay, "War and Government," 73–75; Vanlandingham, *Transforming the State*, 33–38, 106–14, 144–54, 169–72.
18. Vanlandingham, *Transforming the State*, 30.
19. Ibid., 34.
20. Ibid.
21. Yitzhak Baer, *A History of the Jews in Christian Spain,* trans Louis Schoffman, 2 vols. (Philadelphia, 1992), 1: 144–45; Vanlandingham, *Transforming the State*, 144–45.
22. Aneas Hontangas, "Reines lloctinents,", 10; Ladero Quesada, "Ejercicio de poder," 51; Lalinde Abadía, *Gobernación*, 23; O'Callaghan, *History*, 445–46. For fuller discussion, see Chapter 8.
23. Teresa Canet Aparisi, "La aministración real y los antecedentes históricos de la audencia moderna," *Estudis: Revista de Historia Moderna* 32 (2006): 7–40, esp. 21–23; Luís González, "Primeras resistencias contra el lugarteniente general-virrey en Aragón," *AEM* 8 (1989): 303–14; José Antonio Lalinde Abadía, "Vivveys y lugartientes medievales en la Corona de Aragón," *CHE* 31–32 (1960): 98–172, esp. 105–6, 108–10.
24. Deibel, "Reyna Elionor," 401–2.
25. Ibid., 408–10.
26. Ibid., 417–22.
27. Ibid., 425–30.
28. ACA, CR, R. 1567, f. 66v.
29. ACA, CR, R. 1566, f. 81; R. 1567, ff. 53v, 87r-v, 112v–15v, 187r–v; R. 1574, 192v, 195; R. 1575, f. 126; R. 1579, f. 19v; Roebert, "Que nos tenemos," 251 Dr. Roebert suggests that the process of turning the queen's valuables to ready cast for the king eventually caused hard feelings with the queen.
30. ACA, CR, R. 1581, ff. 103, 178.

6 ELIONOR OF SICILY AS COURTIER AND ADMINISTRATOR 141

31. ACA, CR, R. 1582, f. 113.
32. ACA, CR, R. 1582, ff. 116v, 121; Pere III, *Chronicle*, 2: 588–89 (Appendix 2).
33. ACA, CR, R. 1566, f. 113; R. 1567, ff. 101–2v, 69v, 75v, 139v.
34. ACA, CR, R. 1573, ff. 102, 117; R. 1574, f. 192.
35. ACA, CR, R. 1575, f. 79.
36. ACA, CR, R. 1537, ff. 138r–v; R. 1569, ff. 8v–9; R. 1578, ff. 118v, 132r–v, 137.
37. ACA, CR, R. 912, ff. 165v–166; R. 913, ff. 222–23; R. 914, f. 166; R. 1574, ff. 77v.
38. ACA, CR, R. 1567, ff. 53v; 181v–82; R. 1577, f. 165v.
39. ACA, CR, R. 1567, ff. 131r–v; R. 1573, f. 137v; R. 1574, f. 175v.
40. ACA, CR, R. 1568, ff. 10, 29v, 51v–52; R. 1574, ff. 102r–v; 134; R. 1577, f. 45v.
41. ACA, CR, R. 1582, ff. 30v, 60.
42. ACA, CR, R. 1580, f. 164v.
43. ACA, CR, R. 1582, f. 120; Pere III, *Chronicle*, (Appendix 2).
44. ACA, CR, R. 1582, f. 98v–99; Goldstonr, *Joanna I*, 317.
45. ACA, CR, R. 157, f. 106v.
46. ACA, CR, R. 1584, f. 70v.
47. ACA, CR, R. 1576, ff. 20r–v.
48. ACA, CR, R. 1574, f. 19.
49. ACA, CR, R. 1566, ff. 158r–v.
50. ACA, CR, R. 1536, f. 15; R. 1577, f. 15.
51. ACA, CR, R. 1184, f. 1; R. 1566, f. 46v; *Documents Historichs Catalans del Sigle XIV: Colleció de cartas familiars Corresponents als regnats de Pere del Punyalet y Johan I* [hereafter *DHC*] (Barcelona, 1889), 19–20. For the disputes between Aragonese cities and hamlets, see Donald J. Kagay, "Two Towns Where There Once Was One: The *Aldea* and Its Place in Urban Development of the Aragonese Middle Ages," *The Journal of the Rocky Mountain Medieval and Renaissance Association* 14 (1995): 33–43.
52. ACA, CR, R. 1568, f. 67; R. 1581, f. 97.
53. ACA, CR, R. 1566, f. 166; R. 1567, f. 67.
54. ACA, CR, R. 1573, f. 108.
55. ACA, CR, R. 1566, f. 100; R. 1567, f. 122.
56. ACA, CR, R. 1537, f. 179; R. 1667, f. 154.
57. ACA, CR, R. 1566, ff. 131r–v; R. 1567, ff. 13v, 176; R. 1574, v. 182v; R. 1579, f. 151.
58. ACA, CR, R. 1577, f. 103.
59. ACA, CR, R. 1583, f. 92v.
60. ACA, CR, R. 1537, f. 123; R. 1579, f. 91.
61. ACA, CR, R. 1573, ff. 61v, 104v; R. 1577, ff. 157v–58.

142   D. J. KAGAY

62. ACA, CR, R. 1577, f. 62.
63. ACA, CR, R. 1566, ff. 90r–v.
64. ACA, CR, R. 1537, ff. 121–22; 123v.
65. ACA, CR, R. 1577, f. 169; R. 1580, f. 37v; R. 1582, f. 68v.
66. ACA, CR, R. 1581, f. 50. For adultery in the Middle ages, see Paulette L'Hermite-Leclercq, "The Feudal Order," in *Silences of the Middle Ages*, vol. 2 of *A History of the Women in the West*, ed. Christiane Klapisch-Zuber (Cambridge, MA, 1992), 202–66, esp. 237; Claudia Opitz, "The Late Middle Ages," 267–317, es. 279; Emmanuel Le Roy Ladurie, *Montaillou: The Promised Land of Error*, trans. Barbara Bray (New York, 1978), 161.
67. ACA, CR, R. 1574, f. 68v; Villalon and Kagay, *To Win and Lose a Medieval Battle*, 166; Joaquin Miret y Sans, "Negociations de Pierre IV d'Aragon avec la cour de France (1366-1367)," *Revue Hispanique* 13, no. 43 (1905): 76–135, esp. 80-102-3.
68. ACA, CR, R. 1583, ff. 139r–v.
69. ACA, CR, R. 1577, ff. 71–72.
70. ACA, CR, R. 1577, f. 188.
71. ACA, CR, R. 1584, f. 54v.
72. ACA, CR, R. 1584, f. 65v.
73. Santiago Sobrequés i Vidal, *Els barons de Catalunya* (Barcelona, 1980), 37–38; Shneidman, *Rise*, 1: 166
74. Sobreques i Vidal, *Barons*, 38.
75. Pere III, *Chronicle*, 1: 316 (III:99); 418 (IV:32); 412–14 (IV:29–30); 422–26 (IV:38–40); 473–74 (V:24); Zurita, *Anales*, IV: 234 (VIII:lii).
76. Pere III, *Chonicle*, 1:204–205 (II:26); Sobrequés i Vidal, *Barons* Sobreques i Vidal, *Barons*, 150–52.
77. Ramón D'Abadal y de Vinyals, *Pere el Ceremoniós i els inicis de la decadència political de Catalunya* (Barcelona, 1972), 84–85; Donald J. Kagay, "The "Treasons" of Bernat de Cabrera: Government, Law, and the Individual in the Late-Medieval Crown of Aragon," *Mediaevistik* 13 (2000): 39–54, esp. 40–41; J.B Sitges, *la muerte de D. Bernardo de Cabrera* (Madrid, 1911), 5; Sobrequés I Vidal, *Barons*, 154–55.
78. Manuel de Bofarull y de Sartorio, "Proceso contra Bernardo de Cabrera, Mandado formar por el rey don Pedro IV," 3 vols. in *CDACA*, 34: 31–51, 56–67; Kagay, "Treasons," 44–45; Miron, *Queens of Aragon*, 193.
79. *CDACA*, 34: 37–39, 50, 56–57; Sitges, *Muerte*, 1–5.
80. ACA, Cartas Reales [Pedro IV], caja 52, no. 6241; Antonio Gutiérrez de Velasco, "Las fortalezas aragonesas ante la gran ofensiva castellana en la guerrs de los dos Pedros," *Cuadernos de Histori "Jerónimo Zurita"* 12–13 (1961): 9–15, esp. 12–13; Lafuente Gómez, *Dos coronas en guerras*,

96–98; Donald J. Kagay, "A Shattered Circle: Eastern Spanish Fortifications and Their Repair During the 'Calamitous Fourteenth Century'," in *War*, Study III. 11–35, esp. 32; Sitges, *Muerte*, 5.

81. *CDACA*, 34: 430–35, 465–66, docs. 7, 10; Pere III, *Chronicle*, 2: 473–75 (V:24); Estow, *Pedro*, 217–18.
82. *CDACA*, 32: 142; 33: 364; 373–74; Pere III, *Chronicle*, 2: 607, doc. 4; Kagay, "Trasons," 46; Sitges, *Muerte*, 19–23.
83. *CDACA*, 32:142, 306; 33: 364, 373–74: Pere III, *Chronicle*, 2: 543, 607 (VI:39); Sitges, *Muerte*, 22–23.
84. *CDACA*, 33:98; Kagay, "Treasons," 46–47; Sitges, "Muerte," 34–36.
85. *CDACA*, 32: 1–9, 31–34; Sitges, *Muerte*, 36–38, 41–42.
86. *CDACA*, 32: 14–21; Kagay, "Treasons," 46–47; Sitges, *Muerte*, 40–41.
87. *CDACA*, 32: 10–12, 28–36; 34: 105–8; Sitges, *Muerte*, 41.
88. *CDACA*, 32: 136–38; 149–50, 158–61, 165–67, 176–78, 288; 33:160, 330–31; Kagay, "Treasons," 50–51.
89. *CDACA*, 32: 204–6; 33: 200; Kagay, "Treasons," 51–52; Sitges, *Muerte*, 24.
90. *CDACA*, 34: 275–76; Sitges, *Muerte*, 68–69.
91. *CDACA*, 33: 167–68; Sobrequès, *Barons*, 160–61.
92. *CDACA*, 34: 480; Miron, *Queens of Aragon*, 194–95.
93. Baer, *Historia*, 1:138; Diego Hernando, "Movilidad," 237; José Luis Lacave Riaño, "Los judíos en España medieval," *Historia* 16, no. 58 (1981): 49–61; Shneidman, *Rise*, I:416.
94. Baer, *History*, 1:79–80; Lacave Riaño, 104–6; César Tcach, "Las aljamas de la Corona de Aragón u su organización interna (siglo XIV)," *El Olivo: Documentación y estudios para el diálogo entre Judíos y Cristianos* 13, no. 29–30 (1981): 245–70.
95. Mark D. Meyerson, *Jews in an Iberian Frontier Kingdom: Society, Economy, and Politics in Morvedre, 1248-1391* (Leiden, 2004), 176–209; Jonathan Ray, *The Sephardic Frontier: The "Reconquista" and the Jewish Community in Medieval Iberia* (Ithaca, NY: Cornell University Press, 2006), 56–60; Joseph Shatmiller, *Shyllock Reconsidered; Jews, Moneylending and Medieval Society* (Los Angeles, 1983), 144–47, 189–90; Maya Soifer Irish, *Jews and Christians in Medieval Castile: Tradition in Medieval Castile: Tradition, Coexistence, and Change* (Washington, DC, 2016), 221–37.
96. ACA, CR, R. 654, ff. 4, 129r–v; R. 708, ff. 155r–v; R. 887, f. 145v; R. 1062, f. 83v; R. 1134, ff. 361r–v; Meyerson, *Jews*, 211–12.
97. ACA, CR, R. 1537, ff. 5–7v; Meyerson, *Jews*, 56–58; Roebert, "Que nos tenemus," 262, 264; Zurita, *Anales*, 4: 533–36 (IX:lxi).
98. ACA, CR, R. 1566, ff. 47, 103, 145r–v, 160–61, 184v–85; R. 67, f. 18; R. 1574, ff. 34, 102, 183.

144 D. J. KAGAY

99. ACA, CR, R. 1566, f. 46; R. 1566, ff. 46, 104–5, 110; R. 1573, f. 92v; R. 1574, f. 182.
100. ACA, CR, R. 1566, ff. 107, 110, 115v, 161.
101. Meyerson, *Jews*, 231–33.
102. ACA, CR, R. 728, f. 68; Diago Hernando, "Movilidad," 280.
103. For Pere's attempts to help his *aljamas*, see ACA, CR, R. 697, ff. 117, 120v–21; R. 700, ff. 74v–75. The Muslim *aljamas* underwent the same problems as did their Jewish counterparts during the War of the Two Pedros, see Julia Campón Gonsalvo, "Consequencias de la guerr ad los Dos Pedros en el condado," *Anales de Uneiversidad. de Alicante* 8 (1990–1991): 57–68, esp. 61–62; Cabezuelo Pliego, *Guerra*, 149–51. Many of them were thoroughly destroyed and those that remained soon saw severe depopulation of long-time residents who took as many possessions as they could carry and fled to Granada. Descriptions of these places were always the same: "totally shattered and demolished." Many of the Muslim population that remained in southern Valencia faced the same harsh reality of capture and being sold into slavery.
104. ACA, CR, R. 1379, ff. 161r–v; Cartas reales [Pedro IV], no. 6100; José Vicente Cabazuelo Pliego, "Las communidades judías del mediodía valenciana, De la vitalidad á la supervivencia," *Miscelánea medieval murciana* 29–30 (2005–2006): 75–104, esp. 89–91.
105. ACA, CR, R. 1566, ff. 98v–99; R. 1567, ff. 154r–v.
106. ACA, CR, R. 1566, f. 115v; R. 1567, f. 60v; R. 1574, ff. 109, 116v.
107. ACA, CR, R. 1566, ff. 167r–v.
108. ACA, CR, R. 1567, f. 156; R. 1574, f. 148v.
109. ACA, CR, R. 1577, f. 85v; R. 1580, ff. 64v, 66.
110. ACA, CR, R. 1567, ff. 173v–74; R. 1576, ff. 27v–28.
111. ACA, CR, R. 1537, ff. 100v–101, 124v.

CHAPTER 7

Elionor of Sicily as a Wartime Leader

1 The War of the Two Pedros

Open Frontiers

As a landscape of high peaks, deep valleys and rapidly flowing rivers, the four principal kingdoms of the Iberian Peninsula in the Middle Ages, the Crown of Aragon, Castille, Navarre, and Portugal were separated by frontiers that were fought over from the beginning of the *reconquista*. After the rapid victory of the Muslim invaders in the early eighth century when most of Spain fell under their control, small pockets of Christian control established a form of minuscule war marked by the *cabalgada* or lightning raid in which the forces of a town would raid across the poorly defined frontiers and ravage an enemy's crops and livestock. In most cases, this asymmetrical warfare pitted Christian against Muslim forces, but conflict between Christians was not unusual.[1] As a result of limited fighting, certain frontier zones became "hot spots" for raid and counter-raid throughout much of the high and later Middle Ages. By the mid-fourteenth century, these favored war zones were: (1) Aragon's eastern border with Castile between the border cities of Catlayud and Tarazona, and (2) the southern border of Valencia with Murcia, the Segura River.[2]

The only Iberian territories that were guarded, thus distinguishing the territory of one kingdom from another were the Pyrenees passes. Many other such dividing lines existed on maps, but in many instances were

© The Author(s), under exclusive license to Springer Nature Switzerland AG 2021
D. J. Kagay, *Elionor of Sicily, 1325–1375*, The New Middle Ages, https://doi.org/10.1007/978-3-030-71028-6_7

145

146   D. J. KAGAY

totally unprotected. As a result, kingdoms approached each other along a wide swath of territory which seemed to have a national life of its own. The border populations on either side made their living by smuggling and trading in extensive black markets that had existed on both sides of the frontier for decades. These open borders also proved tempting for the launching of frequent *cabalgadas* which proved a ready source of profit from the rustling of livestock and the taking of Muslim and Christian prisoners who were after sold into slavery. The respective kings who both claimed parts of this territory were fully aware of the situation and of the identities of the "robbers...and plunders" who made a handsome living from such attacks. They attempted to stop this illegal activity by drawing up treaties by which plundered property would be returned to its rightful owners on the other side of the frontier. This occasionally proved impossible since the stolen goods were traded out of the region almost immediately. The ultimate result of these events was a violent and independent way of life that no one could control. It is hardly surprising, then, that these "open spots" on the map constituted as sites of major campaigns in the war between Castile and Aragon that began in 1356.[3]

War's Beginnings

As we have seen, Aragon and Castile were ruled by two extremely different types of sovereigns at the beginning of the war. The former possessed as its ruler the canny and scheming thirty-seven-year old Pere III and the latter by the valiant but mentally disturbed Pedro I who at the beginning of the war was twenty-two-years-old. Though the two monarchs had shown themselves to be accomplished military leaders in the years before the Iberian war came into being, they had never fought against each other before 1356. In the 1340s and 1350s, Pere engaged in successful conflicts against his cousin, Jaume III of Barcelona, the Aragonese and Valencian uprisings of the *Unión*, and in largely unsuccessful conflicts against Genoa and Sardinia.[4] After becoming seriously ill after taking the Castilian crown in 1350 and deserting his French wife for his Castilian mistress three years later, Pedro had successfully defeated a baronial uprising in 1356.[5]

Few wars commenced in such an offhanded way as did this conflict which pitted the most important, Christian rulers of Spain and their realms to a full decade of warfare. After beating back a full-fledged baronial rebellion in the first years of his reign, Pedro I in the late summer sought some rest and recreation by taking a royal ship down the

Guadalquivir River, anchoring at the small Atlantic port of San Lucár de Barrameda from where he prepared to try his luck at deep-sea fishing in Atlantic waters teaming with tuna. Back in port and engaging in less energetic pastimes, the king witnessed the capture of two Pacenzan galleys by a privateer commissioned by France but commanded by one of Pere's most important officials, Francesch de Perellós. Since the two merchantmen were from an Italian city allied to Genoa and the Castilian king was bound by treaty of friendship to the same Italian city-state, he looked on this attack as both a great "dishonor and insult" (*deshonor, gran baldón*) to himself and a blatant attack on his realm.[6] Pedro followed this somewhat overblown declaration by attempting to run down Perellós in a chase that followed him all the way into Portuguese waters without every catching up with him. The king's strangest reaction to the San Lucár events was not to blame the young French king, Charles V (r. 1364–1380) who employed the privateer, but to lay this treacherous act at the feet of his "good friend," Pere III of Aragon.[7]

The Aragonese king presumably knew nothing of the sea action until August 18, 1356 when a Castilian courier delivered him a remarkable letter from a still-furious Pedro I. This missive commenced a series of an increasingly bitter exchange between the two monarchs down until December 6 of the same year. In his first letter, the Castilian king clearly revealed that he held much more against the Aragonese king than merely the San Lucár affair. Pere had been a "dear and true friend" for the past few years, but now he had sent his men "into our ports to make war on us."[8] In Pedro's mind, the Aragonese king had crossed the line just one time too often. Though not an announcement of hostilities, Pedro's words sounded very much like a *diffidamentum*, a formal breaking of feudal ties, which stood as a "virtual declaration of war."[9] From the Aragonese king's point-of-view, Pedro's complaints had nothing to do with him. He had not appointed Perellós as a privateer. This had been done by the French government; so why had Pedro not taken this up with them. Still if the young Castilian ruler would suggest an acceptable punishment for the elusive official who was now making extra money as a corsair, Pere would be glad to carry it out, when it became possible. The Aragonese king did make, however, the insulting assertion that the Castilian king had broken political ties with Aragon "without just cause."[10]

Though these accusations and justifications went on for several more months, the war between Castile and Aragon now seemed to have a life of its own. In the first months of the fall, Pedro fought very much like the leader of a *cabalgada* by dividing his troops and unleashing these smaller units in rapid raids that did maximum damage while paying off his troops with the great amount of booty they had captured. Pere was immediately thrown on the defensive and could never break away from this conservative strategy for many years to come. The difference between the two strategies had very much to do with the expenditure of money. At first, this was not a problem for the Castilian king, for his first raids largely paid for themselves. By contrast, the Aragonese monarch from the very beginning realized that neither the use of feudal troops nor money supplied to the crown by regular taxes were sufficient to defend the wide circle of war he now faced.[11] New funds which could be continually renewed had to be found.

After a few months of this kind of Castilian military pressure which led to the conquest of several Aragonese villages and an ever-increasing expenditure of money, Pere III grew even more desperate. In the Aragonese king's mind, his "principal enemy" was a "young fellow whose character was very much in doubt."[12]

As the defeats of his forces continued, the Aragonese king turned more directly to God for help, since he was fighting a "good and just (albeit inefficient) war."[13] In order to strengthen his confidence in divine aid, he turned to the church. On November 5, 1356, he sent a set of prayers to his archbishops and most important bishops that were to be inserted after the Eucharist ceremonies at every mass celebrated in the Crown of Aragon on the following Sunday. In these appeals to "Blessed George" the archangel, the harried king hoped that by divine help he could "gain victory over our enemies."[14]

Middle Years: Land Battles

As the war spilled into its second year, Castilian attacks became more persistent with sieges beginning to replace widespread raiding. In spring, 1357, Pedro's attacks centered on the large cities and towns that stretched along Aragon's eastern frontier. With Castilian territory so close to this theater of operations, larger attacks and easier provisioning led Pedro to attack Tarazona, on the edge of the Sierra del Moncayo, where Aragonese, Castilian, and Navarrese frontiers came together. Despite its dangerous location, "the city was considered "better defended than any other place in Aragón."[15] This soon proved to be unfounded over-confidence when in early March Castilian troops easily crossed the mountainous districts above Calatayud and besieged Tarazona, overrunning the city on March 9. Though Pere attributed this shameful defeat to "great treason and wickedness" among Tarazona's defenders, it was due far more to Aragon's weak military leadership.[16]

The Aragonese monarch devised a response to the Tarazona disaster by hiring Castilian mercenaries that fought under popular commanders like Count Enrique de Trastámara and the king's own half-brother, Prince Ferran. Each of these mercenary captains had good military reputations, but Enrique showed himself to be the better of the two. Using these paid troops, Pere was better able to hold off Castilian attacks by choosing the count as his chief captain and encouraging him to directly take on his hated half-brother, King Pedro, within Castile itself. In September 1359, Trastámara took up this challenge by leading a fast-moving force of 800 horsemen and an unspecified number of infantry across the Jalon River into the Sierra del Moncayo which stretched across the Aragonese and Castilian borders. On September 22 at the headwaters of the Araviana River, Enrique led his band of Castilians against another force of his countrymen. This small army, consisting of Castilians who, for whatever reason, had remained loyal to Pedro, was commanded by his principal adviser, Juan Ferrández de Henestrosa. At the end of the day, 300 of Pedro's soldier, including Henestrosa, lay dead on the field and many others were captured by Trastámara's army.[17]

Humiliated by this remarkable triumph, Pedro was seething for vengeance especially since the disaster of Araviana was inflicted on his men by his hated half-brother. Shortly after this, he had an opportunity to vent his anger when Enrique in the spring of 1360 led a force of 1,500 horse and 3,000 foot into Castile along the Pilgrim's Road to Nájera. Hearing of this affront, an infuriated Pedro led a much larger army out in pursuit, making a permanent camp north of the city. Assembling his army on the last Friday of April 1360, there quickly followed the so-called first battle of Nájera which took place outside the city. The king's larger army quickly broke through the count's lines and drove him back toward the city. After having to scale the walls to get back inside the city, Enrique, with almost no provisions, seemed at the mercy of his half-brother. On the next morning, when Pedro readied his forces to commence a siege of the city, he encountered one of his young horsemen weeping uncontrollably over his father who had been captured and executed by Enrique's men.

150 D. J. KAGAY

This tangential encounter seemed to break the king's resolve who abandoned the siege on that very day. This remarkable turn-of-events allowed Enrique and his men to slip back into Aragon and wait for another day to take on his half-brother. This opportunity, however, would only come to the count some seven years at the battle of Nájera (April 3, 1367).[18]

Middle Years: Sea Battles

In the midst of these military actions between the Castilian half-brothers, Pedro I attempted to hamstring Pere III by sea. In May 1359, he fitted out a formidable fleet of 127 ships, including Genoese, Granadan, and Portuguese vessels. While this armada was being equipped, he sent a small force against Guardamar, a Valencian port on the banks of the Segura River where it emptied into the Mediterranean.[19] Having readied his fleet by the first week of May, Pedro led his ships down the Guadalquivir River and into the Atlantic. After waiting at Algeciras for the arrival of the last Portuguese vessels, he slowly passed into the Mediterranean at Cartagena. During this period, Pere informed all of his coastal urban centers of the approaching Castilian danger, commanding them to help with the arming of merchant ships to hold off the enemy. He also put into effect *Princeps namque*, the article of Catalonia's traditional law, the *Usatges*, that demanded the help of all Catalan men against any foreign invader against the count of Barcelona.[20]

When the Castilian fleet reached Valencian waters in the third week of May, Pedro was able to resupply and make necessary repairs to his vessels in the newly-conquered port of Guardamar. He then headed directly for Barcelona, anchoring outside the city on June 10 where he faced for the first time Pere's own naval force. Before he could undertake a landing, much of the city's beaches were covered with Catalan troops, mostly drawn from the capital's guilds. On the next day, the Aragonese and Castilian fleets circled each other with few results except for the firing of a bombard from one of the Aragonese ships.[21] There then followed some two weeks during which the Castilian fleet slowly coasted southward toward the Llobregat River. After a few days, however, Pedro's fleet turned eastward toward Ibiza. Reacting to the Castilian's new course, Pere took the Aragonese fleet (now numbering between forty and fifty vessels) from Barcelona, quickly sailing toward Majorca.

In the meantime, the Castilians carried out a successful amphibious landing at Ibiza. After ravaging the small island, they put its principal city under siege. The Aragonese king then launched a surprise attack against the Castilian siege forces. This minor action did little to dislodge Pedro's forces, but, as at first battle of Nájera in the next year, seemed to dissipate his drive for a great victory. Almost immediately, then, he broke off the Ibizan siege and sailed back to the mainland.[22]

Pere III crowed that his enemy was guilty of a blatant act of cowardice, brought about from his fear of the Almighty for the "unjust war he was waging."[23] Having assumed the moral high ground, the Aragonese leader took a number of his galleys and triumphantly sailed back to Barcelona. As we will see, the uncertainty of her husband's fate during this period, caused Elionor a great deal of concern. The rest of the Aragonese ships under the command of Bernat de Cabrera shadowed Pedro's fleet as it approached Valencia. Aware of the proximity of the enemy vessels, Pedro asked his advisers how he should proceed. Some argued that since Pere had left the Aragonese fleet, it would be shameful to attack a reduced Aragonese naval force; others declared that if Pedro attacked the Aragonese fleet, they would do everything in their power to assure him a glorious victory. He weighed the two positions until he brought his fleet into Alicante for reprovisioning and then decided to completely break off the naval campaign and take all of his ships back to Seville.[24] Again the Castilian king had faced a major battle and turned away from it.

Valencian Campaigns (1363–1365)

In December 1363, the Castilian king turned his efforts against Valencia by leading a large army out of Murcia and across the Segura River into southern Valencia. The Aragonese troops led by the thirteen-year-old crown prince, Joan, did almost nothing to hold back this large raid. Some days later, a resident of Valencia city came before Pere III in his court at Sesa in northern Aragon, warning that the Valencian capital might not be able to hold out against a Castilian siege because of a "dangerous scarcity of food" within its walls. Pedro I, in fact, had set up his camp with 6,000 horsemen in the dockyard district (*grau*) which stretched along both banks of the Guadalquivir River and along the Mediterranean coast just to the south of the capital.[25] Rushing to save one of his largest cities from being overrun by the troops of his bitterest enemy, the Aragonese monarch led a large army of 1,722 horse and 16,000 foot into Valencia. Besides its size, Pere had a marked advantage with his command staff,

152   D. J. KAGAY

which included his talented relatives, the counts of Denia, Prades, and Empuries, and the important captains, the viscount of Cardon and the count of Trastámara.[26]

The Aragonese army reached Valencia in late April after a remarkable march from southern Aragon into northern Valencia mostly made at night to hide its position. Pere also did the unthinkable for any commander, medieval or modern, by dividing his troops, and only bringing them together when deep in Valencian territory on the outskirts of Burriana up the coast from the capital where the Aragonese attacked a Castilian encampment. Its commander warned Pedro of the surprise attack by smoke signals, driving him into a rage because none of his well-paid spies knew anything of the Aragonese approach. Stirring his troops from sleep, Pedro quickly led them up the coast road toward Murviedro, hoping to surprise his opponents who were driving directly toward his army on the same road. On April 24 at dawn, the forces could see each other. Pere drew up his troops "in good order" on a sloping beach which faced southward toward the Castilian troops. For the first time in his life, he gave a battle harangue which tried to convince his men that the next few hours would settle the conflict which the last eight years of fighting had been unable to. By the clear "judgement of God," they would be able to avenge Pedro the Cruel's evil deeds. Those of his troops who were Castilian already knew what a "great traitor" their king was and how he had decimated their families and "dishonored [their] wives, daughters, and sisters." If these foreign troops, however, did not fell able to fight against their former king, Pere gave them permission to cross the field and join him. These men who had served as mercenaries in the Aragonese war effort for so long emotionally cried out that Pere was their lord now and they would fight for none other.[27]

Over the next few hours, fighting would take place across the beach the Aragonese held, but none of it involved Pedro I or his Castilian troops. Instead the king sent a small unit of Muslim light cavalry (*jinetes*), presumably to soften up his enemy, who now had stood in formation for some hours. A larger, Castilian attack, however, did not come. Instead, Pedro led his men to the safety of Murviedro, where a large Castilian contingent was based. The coast road was now open to the Aragonese king who led his men to Valencia city, where they received a riotous welcome from the capital's citizens who only hour before had faced Pedro I's cruel wrath.[28]

Pere III's way of war which kept all of his troops hidden until they made their first attack severely angered his Castilian opponent who claimed that Pere acted like an *almogavèr*, a frontier trooper who lived off the land while fighting an un-chivalric guerrilla war. Furious at this affront, the Aragonese king took his army out of Valencia on May 2, 1364, and, after traveling up the coastal road for two days, pitched camp outside of Murviedro. He then sent a messenger to the Castilian king, saying that he was in the neighborhood and had every intention of fighting the cowardly, Castilian ruler and his men. After standing ready for some hours with no Castilian reaction, Pere returned to Valencia still a battle virgin.[29]

While the two kings were not fighting on the Valencian mainland, their reconstituted fleets came back into action. In June, 1364, the much smaller Catalan force, after sighting Pedro's fleet which was just as large as the armada he brought into Valencian waters the year before, the Catalan admirals attempted to avoid battle by sailing up the Júcar River at Cullera. Jumping at the chance to bottle up his enemy away from the Mediterranean, Pedro had three of his own ships sunk at the river mouth. Hearing that his ships were in danger, Pere took a portion of his army from Valencia down to Cullera. Posting his men on the northern bank of the Júcar, they were able to hold off the Castilians while helping their colleagues escape the river.[30]

While these complicated maneuvers were taking place on both sides of the Júcar, the unpredictable Mediterranean had its say. The trade winds of the summer which normally blew to the north and west changed to a stiff gale to the east called a *solonot* that threatened to drive the Castilian ships on to the shore where Pere army would cut the crews to pieces. The disaster was diverted when the east wind's fury dropped off and the mariners regained control of their vessels. The normally irreligious Castilian sovereign was so touched by the event that he attributed to the Almighty the "lessening of the force of the wind." The king was still so moved by this miraculous event that when his ship docked at Murviedro, he immediately went to the church of Santa María, wearing only a shirt and breeches with a halter draped around his neck so all would know he was fulfilling a solemn vow in return for his remarkable escape.[31]

Minor Aragonese campaigns kept both kings away from their protracted duel on Valencian battlefields and seaways until the fall of 1364 when the Aragonese king established a new headquarters northwest of Valencia at Mora de Rubielon. Before he was even fully established there,

154   D. J. KAGAY

Pere received reports of Pedro's bloody treatment of the small Aragonese village of Castelhabib which had risen in rebellion against its Castilian military governor. Incensed at such disrespect for his authority, Pedro ringed the village with siege engines and bombarded it for almost two days. With almost every house destroyed and many of the townsmen dead or wounded, surrender to their oppressor became the only possible thing the villagers could do.[32]

With Pedro still a threat to Valencia, Pere readied his army for the next year's campaigning by quickly moving out of Aragon to Valencia's Mediterranean coast. By December 1, 1364, the Aragonese and Castilian armies again seemed to be moving toward a long-awaited conclusion. Pere's force was smaller than that of his Castilian enemy but he still slowly made his way down the coast road and then turned inland toward Orihuela, one of his most important castles in southern Valencia that was now endangered by advancing Castilian troops. In this region described as "waste and desert," Pere's scouts sighted a forward party of the Castilian army headed by his old enemy. As they advanced on this smaller contingent, Pere was quickly informed that Pedro's main army was nearby. As he had done the year before, the Aragonese king drew up his men for battle, waiting for his adversary's logical next move which never came.[33] Then entering Orihuela, the king's army received a hero's welcome and, in turn, he characterized the citizens of the fortress-town as "good people...whose valor and courage...safeguarded our affairs... for which they have gained great fame."[34]

The next year brought the largest fighting to date in Valencia. In the first months of 1365, the Aragonese king gathered another sizeable force, not this time to fight the "wicked and false traitor" who still ruled Castile, but to start the process of winning back the Valencian towns and castles that had been under foreign control for almost three years.[35] He rapidly captured a number of castles above the Valencian capital, but his principal target was Murviedro, a town he had hated since 1348 when it was dominated by the Valencian *Unión*. His enemy had used it as a headquarters in the previous years' fighting, and now Pere was ready to reconquer it. This took a full six months and was not accomplished until the king had engaged in long negotiations with Pedro's commander in the town. On September 14, the Aragonese king and most of his besieging force entered the battered town. With its capture, the whole length of Valencia's coast road was in his hands, a fact that marked Pere's final victory in his southern kingdom. His vengeance on the nondescript site was both swift and long lasting, taking some years to complete. Shortly after its conquest, the king attacked Murviedro's very existence by declaring that because of its "wickedness and rebellion" it would lose all of its privileges and be ruled by the Valencian city council. At least in the beginning, then, he made good on his promise of making the town little more than a "street of Valencia."[36]

A Largely Unnoticed Conclusion

This war between imperfect rulers and severely tested realms would last for ten years before the fighting simply seemed to die away in the first months of 1366. During the course of the conflict, two popes, Innocent VI and Urban V (r. 1362–1370), attempted to impose peace on the warring Iberian realms through two papal legates, Cardinal Guillaume de la Jugie and Bishop Gui de Boulogne of Porto. The first arranged a year-long truce in June, 1357, which the Castilian king rapidly violated.[37] The second negotiated a full-fledged treaty, the Peace of Terrer, in 1361 (which fell apart in only about a year),[38] and another, the Peace of Murviedro, in 1363, which also was very short-lived.[39]

In the first months of 1366, the war which always seemed to move at its own pace now rolled to a halt. By the end of the year, the ten-year conflict was no longer living, but had become a historical event which the Aragonese king said had occurred in "past times" (*temporibus praeteritis*) or "not long ago" (*dudum*).[40] With no declared end of the war, this language was surely a kind of wishful thinking with Pere and his wife, who both wanted the ordeal of a decade-ling conflict to be over. Since Castile had lurched into civil war from March, 1366 when Enrique de Trastámara took up his employer's support and invaded his homeland, Pere and his wife had survived the ordeal. As the Castilian conflict led directly to the Battle of Nájera in 1367 and then to Enrique's murder of his half-brother in 1369, Elionor and her husband held their breaths and hoped to "conserve the tranquil state" of their own lands.[41]

2   ELIONOR AS WAR ADMINISTRATOR

The Queen as Lieutenant

As we have seen, the rapid expansion of the Crown of Aragon under Jaume I made personal government an increasingly complicated matter

156   D. J. KAGAY

for the king. Though his four realms would in many ways be ruled by an increasingly complicated governmental system, the Conqueror was adamant at keeping his ruling name in front of a quickly growing body of scattered subjects. To do so and give his sons crucial ruling experience, he established the post of general procurator for his two oldest offspring, Jaume and Pedro, to whom he assigned his newly-won kingdoms, Majorca and Valencia, while he retained governing control of the original realms, Aragon and Catalonia.[42] These delegated offices eventually acquired the name "governor' (*gubernador, governador*) and "lieutenancy" (*lugarteniente, lutenant*). From the last decades of Jaume's reign, his sons and other appointees had been given "absolute power to rule as he did" in the realms under their control.[43] As the Crown of Aragon spread its power into the Mediterranean, the course of the offices began to diverge with governors controlling islands such as the smaller Balearics and Sardinia. That of the lieutenant, and especially the lieutenant general, was reserved for members of the royal family. From the fourteenth century, this most important royal posts would become open to queens. With this guaranty of defined royal power, they could finally stand as true consorts of their husbands.

There is some disagreement about which Aragonese queen first served as a royal lieutenant. One school, surely the largest, attributes this honor to Jaume II's first wife, Blanca of Anjou (1283–1310), who accompanied her husband when he took part in a joint attack with Castile on Almería, an Andalusian city on the Mediterranean coast. Blanca traveled with Jaume II on this campaign but was left in charge of the Crown of Aragon in late spring, 1310. She died in October of the same year.[44] Another of these supposed original queenly lieutenants, Teresa d'Entenza, was said to have been in charge of Jaume II's realms in 1327 when he himself lay dying. This seems unlikely since Teresa, the first wife of Crown Prince Alfons, would not be the normal family member to attend to the realms administrative affairs since the king's third wife Elisenda de Montcada was still living and Alfons would be in the Aragonese court before his father's demise on November 2, 1327.[45]

The principal reason for rejecting the first two candidates was that neither of them were formally declared to be lieutenants by a proper royal document that specified exactly what their duties were and what kind of powers they had to carry them out. This same amorphous situation applied to Queen Elionor from the time of her marriage in 1349 for almost a decade. Her powers were connected to her courts, households, as well as the cities, towns, villages, *aljamas*, and castles she controlled, and whose revenues supported her. Her power in this first decade resided in her hard-headed determination, to successfully fulfill her duties, but also to instill trust in the people that worked for her. None of this was bestowed by the crown; instead, it came from her own efforts. In a sense, her decade of successfully doing her administrative job pointed directly to the post of lieutenancy general that would be conferred on her six times from 1359 to 1374.

We must consider how this momentous change came about and what drove Pere III to make it. It is clear that before his Sicilian wife came along, his experience with marriage had been a failure, not in regard to love, but in the crucial issue of producing a male heir, which would save the Barcelona dynasty, a line which had never failed in this regard since the ninth century. His first wife had left him two daughters, the oldest of which would have to stand in for a male heir, if one did not appear. With Elionor, not one but two male heirs eventually appeared. With this all-but miraculous event, the king grew to deeply trust his third wife. Within two years of his first son's birth, he moved to honor her in a way he never considered for his first two mates: formal coronation. By this step, he transformed their marriage into a true political union, in which the queen became a true consort who acted for the king as if she herself was the king. As a lover of political philosophy and history, the king knew this kind of language by heart. He engaged in it, however, not only to honor a faithful and accomplished wife, but for even more personal reasons: the fulfillment of a long smouldering desire for vengeance.

As we have seen, Pere III's youth was shaped by the hatred of his mother-in-law and her first son, Prince Ferran. When the two siblings finally reached a settlement in 1357 after Ferran had betrayed his half-brother by fighting with Pedro I against Aragon and then deceiving his cousin by defecting from Castile to Aragon, Pere eventually established his half-brother as his captain general and procurator general.[46] Since this set of agreements gave the prince at least the possibility of acceding to the throne if his nephews, Joan and Martí, could be removed. Even the possibility of such a take-over gnawed at Pere and very well may have led him to bestow on his wife a political position that could offset his half-brother's power. As we have seen, these concerns became moot in 1363 with Ferran's violent death.

Besides the fear of even the possibility of his half-brother advancing to the throne, Pere, after years of war with Pedro I of Castile, a person

158   D. J. KAGAY

he seemed to hate as much as his half-brother seemed increasingly over-whelmed by the protection of the "commonwealth of his realms" from the dangers of any advancing Castilian threat, he felt impelled to share some of his administrative obligations by bestowing on his wife the title of "lieutenant general" (*locumtenens generale*), Since he was hopeful that the end of the Castilian conflict might be in sight, he limited his wife's new post to two years. Her catalogue of extended powers sounded some-what like those of Catalan bailiffs, commissioners, and vicars, but were much greater in scope. As lieutenant, then, the queen could hold offi-cial meeting in which she had the right to settle "all arduous matters and questions." She could investigate and punish "all crimes and offenses," carry out everything else connected to royal government "just as if… [the king] had done so."[47]

Though this grant of advanced power extended until November 8, 1360, Pere felt it prudent to renew Elionor's lieutenancy on June 19, 1359, right at the point of joining his fleet and seeking out his Castilian enemy in the waters that surrounded the Balearics. Once more Pere extended to his wife the right to rule "in all… [his] realms on this side of the sea." He again expressed why he had endowed his "most dear consort" with this great power.[48] In the 1358 document, he claimed that he had done so because of her "intelligent caution, prudent foresight, mature and discrete advice, and… other virtues."[49] In that of the next year, he made the grant, "justifiably trusting in… [her] distinguished and prudent foresight."[50]

In summer, 1359 when attending to coastal defense and seeing to the formation of the fleet that would oppose his "principal enemy," the Aragonese king had taken time to assure his realms that he had yet again endowed his wife with the post of lieutenant general. On July 8 when the queen wrote members of the Catalan clergy to ask their advice about helping her husband take on the Castilian king who "had increased his fleet and was waiting every day to fight," Elionor, in her own name and "on the part of the king whose place she was taking," commanded the great clergy to appear before her at Barcelona, five days after they received her letter.[51] This order, written in the matter-of-fact language of many of the queen's written communications, announces yet again to its recipi-ents that she had taken a step-up in official authority; for at least the time being what she said is exactly what the king would have said, and what she did was exactly what the king would have done. This kind of wording was normal in Elionor's correspondence when her husband was fighting off Castilian naval threats in 1359–1360.[52]

In the next four years, Pere renewed his wife's lieutenancy powers twice, in 1362 and 1364. In the first two grants, the king had justified the awarding of such power to Elionor from his crucial need to give his sole attention to the Castilian conflict. With these, the queen was to be used as a ready substitute in government matters that he did not have time or did not wish to attend to. On September 12, 1362, Pere declared that he absolutely had to be in Perpignan to engage in "some arduous negotiations." He thus left his wife, as "lieutenant and procuratrix" to handle in his place the normal workload, the "free and general administration" of royal government. In this position, she could sell royal property, transfer its ownership, mortgage it, establish title to it, release title to it, and issue every possible kind of contract. The king promised that he would never revoke any official or legal action she took.[53]

On January 22, 1364, Elionor was again issued lieutenancy power in the midst of a worsening military situation, in which the Castilian monarch increasingly attacked "by sea and land." "For the utility of... [his] commonwealth," the king, following the path of Almighty God who had given Adam a "helper and consort," turned for help to his queen. She would hold extended power for the crown prince who had just come of age when he turned fourteen. In this post, the queen's power equaled that of the king's in issuing laws, statutes, privileges, and grants, minting coins, investigating and punishing crimes, and issuing and sealing official documents for herself and that of Prince Joan.[54] On the same day of January 22, the king specified the powers his wife would exercise over the crown prince and assured his other procurators—all important royal officials—that her power would not override theirs.[55]

These grants of extended authority which allowed the queen to act for the king were temporary, often brought about by a crisis demanding the king's full attention elsewhere and allowing his wife to function in the normal realm of government. A good example of such a period occurred between 1363 and 1365 when Pere was away from Barcelona for long periods commanding troops in Valencia. Once the period of emergency had passed, the queen stopped bolstering her official actions by referring to her great, though transitory powers until the next time her husband awarded them to her. She thus called herself "the king's consort and lieutenant" (*consors et locumtenens*) For his part, Pere seemed to show his trust in his queen by increasingly referring her his "comrade or consort" (*companyona*).[56] The announcement of the renewal of these powers were special grants of extensive power that Queen Elionor seemed to exercise more and more frequently.

The standardization of the queen's power becomes obvious on August 12, 1364 when Queen Elionor declared that because of the increasing attacks of Pedro I's "armies and forces" on the frontiers of her husband's realms of Aragon and Valencia, she had to accompany him to these hot spots. This meant that she could not be in Catalonia to carry out her duties as "*procuratrix and lieutenant*." She thus needed "some suitable and excellent person" to carry out these duties until she could return to assume them once more. She turned to a family member who had long acted as an adviser, the king's uncle, Count Ramon Berenguer of Empúries. By this grant which was issued in the royal palace at Zaragoza, she transferred her powers over Catalonia, Sicily, Sardinia, and Corsica to the count and formally allowed him to exercise them as the queen and king did. To support him in carrying out his duties, Elionor arranged to have Ramon Berenguer paid 2,000 *sous* of Barcelona a month until she returned to resume her duties. With this grant, the queen extended the powers of the lieutenancy by having them transferred to a substitute who could presumably extend them in the same way.[57]

On February 3, 1372, Pere III announced to his Catalan subjects that for the time being he would not be in their land due to "arduous negotiations" to be carried out with the Aragonese *cortes*. He therefore instructed his queen, acting as "royal lieutenant," to remain in Barcelona, taking charge of negotiations about Sardinia from her position of "pure and mixed power." She was also to be responsible for collecting money from the realm's "Christians, Jews, and Saracens" and rendering "public justice" to them. She also could sell off her rights to any revenues or holdings within Catalonia. She was also empowered to pay salaries, make grants and concessions, and issue contracts within the borders of Catalonia.[58] Two years later, on November 17, 1374, the king again announced expanded powers for his wife. No specific crisis spurred this action. The king was at Cervera near Lerida and could not immediately reach the Catalan capital, where he was scheduled to "carry out different matters." He thus assigned to his "dear consort…the great power which was equal to that which was entrusted to us by the Lord." The Catalans thus had to obey Elionor as the king's lieutenant general… in all things in the same way they would obey…[him].[59]

In many ways, such grants of expanded power from the king recognized the efficiency his wife had long shown in fulfilling her administrative duties. From Elionor's point-of-view, the power attributed to her from her role as queen was often sufficient to perform exceptional acts of royal government without having to depend on the goodwill of her husband for declarations of expanded power. From 1349 to 1359, she had done quite well without them.

The Queen as Raiser of Money and Secondary Commander

With the sudden beginning of the war with Castile in fall, 1356, Elionor was caught between a royal government that suddenly had to divert much of its working capital to the support of troops posted to the Aragonese frontier. The queen quickly sensed the importance of the new conflict when her husband had to divert a good portion of the funds earmarked for her defense to the general war effort. She also suffered further financial losses as the Castilians began to capture many of the cities, towns, and castles on which her financial support depended. Rather than complaining to her husband, she explained the desperate situation to her vassals, and called for their help. With the stunning defeat of Tarazona in 1357, she explained in some detail her financial needs and hoped to get direct donations from the members of every estate who had sworn their allegiance to her. This type of financial help was often slow in coming, but often brought great sums when not expected. Thus in 1357 and 1358 she received bulk payments from one Saracen *aljama*, her Sardinian holdings, and other Catalan villages whose tax payments had long been in arrears.[60]

In 1358 and 1359, she started looking for other ways to defray her expenses. A particularly effective way of putting money in her hands was the sale of wheat and barley from Aragon and Majorca. These transactions were carried out by the delivery of this crucial commodity into the Castilian province of Vizcaya or by the sale of the grain supplies within the Balearic Islands.[61] At times, Elionor was rescued from her fiscal "danger" by monetary grants given by individuals as well as clerical and urban organizations that bestowed on her provisions and money out of "sheer generosity."[62] Since numerous Castilians, acting as merchants, tradesmen, and shepherds were in the lands and urban sites that the queen held, she began to confiscate a portion of their property. In line with the "royal fifth," she also took some of the booty won from Castilian troops.[63] As in peaceful periods, Elionor often used her money to buy "golden

162   D. J. KAGAY

crowns…, silver, gold, and other kinds of jewelry." Some of these expensive purchases were made for her children, but with the coming of war, these goods were either sold or pawned.[64]

Though something the royal couple tried to stay away from, borrowing money to maintain government operations and support the war effort could not be avoided during the decade of the Castilian conflict. While the queen borrowed "with a free spirit" from the wealthiest of her subjects who gave her generous terms, she was also responsible to a whole generation of bankers and moneylenders, some of whom parleyed their positions of pressure to enter into queen's circle of trusted officials.[65] Although Pere tried to avoid the weak-money policies of his Castilian adversary, he occasionally had to make ends meet by having new coinage produced with a standard "design and weight." The queen thus profited from grants of these new coins to maintain the fiscal stability of her court and other enterprises.[66]

Even while struggling to reestablish the fiscal stability of the administrative units she managed, the Aragonese queen saw that her main duty was to contribute as much money as possible to the royal war effort. In the first months of the conflict, the king had issued her a "letter of indebtedness" for the sum of 47,000 *sous* of Jaca for the revenues she had already lost and would lose in the future due to Castilian military successes. The queen put this donation on hold and made a loan of the same amount to support her husband and his troops. She also began laying aside funds to purchase functioning crossbows of various types, many quarrels, "lances, shields, armor, arrows, helmets, and many other weapons." A good meny of these were to be stored in her castles. She also appointed urban commissions to deal with the rounding up and maintenance of war horses[67] We can get some idea of Elionor's financial condition from a fiscal account issued on July 9, 1359, which demonstrated how much she had borrowed from a Barcelona banker, Jaume de Vilar, and how much she had begun to pay back. As with her husband, the queen hoped to establish financial stability by taking out and reservicing loans while making sufficient repayments to maintain her credit reputation.[68]

As the war heated up in the chaotic summer of 1359 when the Castilian king took his huge fleet up the Mediterranean coast with the hope of delivering a knock-out blow to Pere's fleet, Elionor freely dispensed advice and warnings to all of the military leaders including her husband. On July 13, 1359, she warned Pere about diverting tax money from

7 ELIONOR OF SICILY AS A WARTIME LEADER   163

Majorca to fully pay off all the back pay owed his best captain, Enrique de Trastámara. Even though the queen cared little for the Castilian captain, her advice was not directed against the Castilian military leader, but a call for fiscal sanity, by using the money to partially repay their Barcelona banker, to whom the royal couple owed a considerable sum of money.[69] Elionor, speaking with the directness that was natural to her character and intensified by her appointments as lieutenant general, pulled no punches in a remarkable series of letters she sent to a number of her husband's captains shortly after she had given such unheeded advice to her husband.

On July 13, she wrote a scathing letter to one of Pere's most important captains, Juan Fernández de Heredía, the castellan of Amposta, who had been called by Innocent VI to immediately return to the Roman Curia. If he gave into this order from his religious superior, the queen was certain that he would commit treason in regard to her husband who was now risking his life on the Mediterranean fighting his "principal enemy." The castellan thus could not obey the pope's directions and if he did leave his military post in a time of "such great peril," he would bear a burden of "perpetual confusion" for the rest of his life.[70] Shortly after this, she also instructed Prince Ferran, Count Enrique de Trastámara, and Arnau de Eril that, even though her husband was not there to discipline them, she would assume the responsibility if they left their frontier posts without permission and some "scandal or damage" occurred because of their actions. Even if the salaries for their troops were in arrears, this did not give them the right to ignore their duty. They should trust her to make up the demanded salary payment, and in the meantime, return to their posts, and stay there until formally relieved by the king. This was surely not the first time they had experienced Elionor's strength of character, but the male tenor her words must have infuriated them.[71]

The Aragonese queen's tone was no less forceful and direct during the same summer when she attempted to raise funds in support of the crown from the clergy, nobility, and townsmen of Catalonia. Throughout July, 1359, she sent her officials and lawyers through the land she was the Governor of to demand financial aid while at the same time writing letter after letter to the targeted Catalans to break down their resistance. Although she assured them that she would be glad to accept whatever they could afford to contribute, this was not the story her agents told, carrying as they did a list of specific sums that each of the targeted Catalans had to contribute in order to support the king's fleet that was simultaneously fighting the Castilian enemy.

Elionor suggested that the great clerics and nobles could relieve themselves of the pressure and bother of the demanded sums by having their villagers pay the same sum as they had for parliamentary subsidies by the use of the *fogatge*, a set payment for each "household" (*foch*). The fee that each of these homes owed was attained by dividing the traditional sum the national assembly owed by the amount the queen demanded from each Catalan prelate, great noble or town. Since she was reacting to an emergency, none of the exempted classes could claim they did not have to pay–at least in the queen's mind. Since the sums owed and the names of those who owed them were the same as those set out in the *corts*, the lists of those Catalans who had to contribute to the queen's emergency fund, which her agents used in doing their work, were extremely complete. Elionor would eventually use these funds to expand and refit the king's fleet and pay for companies of horsemen to patrol the Catalan coast and sound the alarm in case of a Castilian attack.[72]

The queen's forthright and sometimes threatening manner was reserved for those who absolutely refused to pay into the emergency fund. The most blatant of these were the great clerics and their immediate vassals. In her sometimes emotional letters of the time, Elionor begged these prelates to consider their unspotted record for helping all Aragonese kings when they were in danger. According to the queen, this accurately described the dangerous situation her husband was in: Pere's fleet was in sore need of being reprovisioned while the king of Castile's armada was fully rearmed.[73] She would no longer tolerate their "delays and postponements" in refusing to do their "duty for the good of the commonwealth … and the lord king."[74] Since their contributions would go directly to their royal lord who at that very moment was risking his life in the defense of his realms and the Balearic Islands their further delay could only be interpreted as treason. From her direct and unswerving words, the queen made it clear that those who did not pay into this critical subsidy of their own free will would be forced to do so.[75]

The Queen's Towns

When the Castilian war began in 1356, her principal connection with all her cities, towns, villages, and hamlets was to draw from them as much extra money as she could. She utilized her regular officials to collect these funds and transfer them to the king's court where these fresh resources would replenish her husband's war chest. In the first three years of the conflict, the queen demanded from her townsmen large sums "in defense of … [the king's] honor and of his crown." Royal bailiffs or members of her court often served as the collectors of this money which the queen admitted was beyond the funds pledged in the parliamentary assemblies of the three realms of the Crown of Aragon. Elionor also demanded the surrender to her agents or all Castilian money that was hoarded in her cities and towns.[76] The explanation for these requests was logical enough, even though the sums requested grew ever more shocking. No matter how they were accepted, the queen's townsmen had to raise the money as vassals of the king and queen. In defending his realms, their lord had run up such a "great debt" that he had been forced to sell off castles and villages, while pawning his own jewels and that of the Lady Queen.[77] She seemed much less concerned with explanations while imposing subsidies on her Jewish and Muslim *aljamas*, communities that had long before grown used to suffer financial pain in silence.[78]

As the years of war passed, Elionor's concern for her urban sites increased with the Castilian capture of Tarazona, Calatuyud, and Teruel between 1357 and 1363. During this same period, she became even more concerned for the lives and economic health of her urban societies. After the amazingly expensive year of 1359, she made a habit of meeting with urban representatives and occasionally started to reduce their normal tax quotas by up to thirty percent. The queen sometimes directed how this money was to be spent, but often left it to the town council.[79] Elionor also had to make provisions for the domesticated animals of her townsmen by ruling that their sheep and cattle had to be pastured near the homes of their owner and as far away from the Castilian border as possible. The queen, however, disallowed "foreigners" (whether Castilians or residents of Aragon or Catalonia) from entering the Valencian town of Lliria without the town council's permission. She also forbade any royal or local taxes from being exacted against her urban vassals engaged in round-ups and pasturing of horses to be used in the king's military.[80] At times, she was also called upon to have her legal professionals render verdicts concerning violent arguments that occurred within her towns while Castilian attacks took place outside the walls.[81]

Hoping to maintain the defenses of her urban sites, Elionor may have reminisced about a letter she sent to her bailiff of Tarazona on March 3, 1357, warning him to increase the defenses of the town because of the presence of Pedro I and his army in the neighborhood. When the town fell to enemy forces a week later, she must surely have felt deep regret

166   D. J. KAGAY

about this turn-of-events.[82] In the next two years when time and again she saw her richest towns threatened with Castilian attacks, she attempted to provide them some kind of protection. She first tried to form local militias from townsmen who had horses and weapons and at least some experience in the use of them. These forces were often assigned as guards in small villages and hamlets that had no fortifications. With large military dangers, such as the passage of Free Companies through Roussillon and northern Catalonia in 1368, the queen instructed some of the region's towns to carry out all measures possible to protect the more exposed villages from the dreaded mercenaries.[83]

Elionor's main concern for the defense of her urban holdings was the decrepit state of their walls and other outer defenses due to the hot and humid climate which made urban fortifications brittle and apt to crack, especially when struck by artillery shot. To make her cities and villages more war-ready, she had their walls patched and sometimes made higher. She also ordered their moats dug out to make them deeper and wider. Perhaps remembering that the Castilian king won Tarazona by an attack through its lightly defended, Muslim quarter, the queen either ordered these largely forgotten sites fortified or had their population evacuated.[84] In the cities and larger towns, the money for these expensive construction projects normally came from the royal diversion of urban taxes. In the case of villages and hamlets, the queen often assumed these construction costs herself. If any of her urban holdings resisted the queen's command to rebuild or improve their fortifications, she threatened them with a large fine and an even more open-ended warning of directly experiencing her "ire and indignation."

Besides repairing fortifications that had fallen into disrepair, the queen occasionally had her exposed urban sites supplied with many different types of weapons.[85] Since a surprising number of the queen's towns were attacked by Castilian counterweight artillery, whole rows of houses had been badly damaged. If money was left over from the improvement of fortifications, Elionor allowed the repair of such residences and bridges that had become impassable due to enemy attacks.[86] To render newly repaired fortifications more effective, Elionor often issued unpopular orders directing her officials to tear down badly damaged structures of all sorts, especially those that stood outside the walls and could give cover to an invading enemy. Dove cotes, gardens, and stables were among the many structures flattened to give defenders an unimpeded view of the land stretching away from their walls.[87]

The Queen's Castles

As with her cities, towns, and settlements, Queen Elionor was gradually given several fortresses during the twenty-six years she wore the Aragonese crown. As most of them stood near urban environments, they supplied a steady income. Some were much more rural and provided a smaller amount of revenue which was largely came from small villages that grew up around them. The list of the queen's castles, though often changing, was a large one and supplied her a steady income. Her largest fortresses were associated with the Aragonese cities of Tarazona, and Teruel as well as the Valencian towns of Lliria and Peñaguila. One of the oldest, most important, and largest castles she held was Montcada. Among the large number of middling-sized towns that the queen received from the estate of Prince Ferran shortly after his death in 1363, she received seven Catalan castles, the most important of which were Camarasa and Cubells. At the end of the Castilian war she gained control of the Catalan castles of St Pol and Marmillar.[88] As with some of her other holdings, the queen gained control of fortresses for a very short time and then exchanged them for other property. Her husband occasionally set up such deals, but always left her with land or urban sites that were equal to the value of the fortress she surrendered. Her control of castles and the villages, farmland, and vineyards that surrounded them occasionally involved her in litigation with other individuals and institutions.[89] Since castles were occasionally granted to her children for their fiscal upkeep, the queen had to manage them until her offspring came of age. At the height of the Castilian war, the queen and her husband had to sell off castles in their Pyrenean lands to make ends meet.[90]

While Elionor visited few of the castle complexes assigned to her except for Montcada which she occasionaly lived in, she held them as she would any feudal lord in the Crown of Arargon, who was subject to castle rules contained in codes such as the *Costum de Espanya* and the *Commeracions de Pere Albert*. With each site she took control of, her representative witnessed the surrender of "control" (*potestas*) by the previous lord and then would formally claim everything associated with the property by sending three vassals to the highest point of the structure to call out their lord's name. The representative then placed a stake or lance on the structure to show that it had been transferred to a new lord, along with everything inside. When a new castellan and garrison were installed in the fortress, the queen was ultimately responsible for all salaries and provisioning costs. If any of the castle personnel disobeyed Elionor's order, they were considered traitors and would be treated as such.[91]

The first decision the queen had to make about castles that came under her control was the appointment of the castellan who was in charge of recruiting a garrison and administering most matters connected with the fortress complex. Though many of these men sprang from royal and urban officialdom, in one emergency the queen appointed her baker to temporarily act as a castellan. He received a yearly salary, with which he paid the garrison and attended to meet normal expenses. He then billed the queen for all other costs.[92] Elionor normally chose castellans from the corps of local officials and knights who had property connections in the area, and urban leaders who occasionally took control of fortresses within or near town centers.[93] In the midst of the Castilian war, however, the queen was asked to turn over some of her castles to captains her husband had appointed. She affirmed these appointments were temporary but assumed that they would clearly cease at the end of hostilities. The allegiance of these military appointees was divided between their commanding officer and the queen. Since they had swear fealty to Elionor, she was never afraid to assert her ultimate control. This was clear in 1363 when she declared to one of her military appointees: "this power which we give to you by the present letter [will last] as long as it pleases us and no longer." With the uncertainties of the war years, she moved castellans from one of her fortresses to the other, often inserting more trustworthy men in regions that were rendered more dangerous because of the current flow of the conflict.[94]

As we have pointed out, Elionor's castellans received varying yearly salaries depending on how large the castle in which they served was, and how dangerous its location was during the war. With this money, they had to support themselves and the garrison they recruited, which could range from forty to a hundred men. While Castilians or foreign mercenaries launched dangerous incursions, the queen occasionally took it on herself to hire important auxiliaries such as the Christian and Muslim crossbowmen whom she directly paid up to 18 *dinars* a day. She was also known to have sent contingents of Muslim light cavalry to threatened castles such as Crevillente in southern Valencia.[95] To avoid such dangerous situations which had already caused a great deal of "damage and dishonor" by 1359, the queen instructed her castellans to use the high towers of their castles to maintain constant surveillance on enemy troop movements. They were to use smoke and fire signals to spread this intelligence to other units of the king's army. To protect civilians from lightly defended villages, Elionor had the residents and animals moved to the nearest castle until the military crisis passed.[96]

According to the *Costum de Espanya* and other Catalan castle customs, a lord could remove a castle from his castellan if he refused to surrender control of the fortress when required to, if he deserted his lord on the battlefield, or if for no reason he broke his feudal connections to the lord.[97] Few of these conditions applied to royal castellans bound to the king or his wife. Men who held their fortresses were most often accused of "villainous… and evil treason" for one simple reason–the surrender of a royal castle to the Castilian enemy. This could lead to the loss of their titles, fiefs, and chattels or even more serious royal actions.[98] The cases of "castle treason" that came before the queen, however, often had less to do with the unfortunate conclusion of sieges and more with the stealing or selling of goods stores in the castle and other specified crimes. None of the accused officials were dealt harshly provided they handed over the stolen goods or the profit derived from them and formally surrendered the castle they commanded.[99]

As with her urban holdings, one of the greatest concerns Elionor had about her castles were their condition for holding off enemy attacks. As the conflict with Castile began to take its toll on her fortresses, she began to look for means of keeping them in fighting trim. She sold the goods confiscated from her dishonest castellans and used the money to have her largest and most strategic castles inspected and repaired before enemy attacks made this impossible.[100] During the war years, she often paid annual upkeep fees to castellans to see that fortress repair was an ongoing project.[101] The castellan was often aided in these projects by the queen's special agents who routed the funds to the castle and inspected the repair work that it supported. In all the aspects of wall and moat repair, the castellan was to use "supreme diligence." Urban castles could petition funds from ruling councils to have such work carried out. In any of these cases when nonroyal money was used the queen was responsible to reimburse either the castellan or the town council. If the castellan had anyone on his staff who could serve as an engineer, he was to report to the queen about structural problems in the building and then report back to her about how they were attended to. In none of these repair projects did Elionor spend as much as on the castle of Montcada which served as one of her residences. The repairs were overseen by a Barcelona townsman and the individual expenses were sent for approval to the royal treasurer, Berenguer de Relat.[102]

The reasons for the queen's steady expenditures were explained time and again in her letters. In the first years of the war, money was spent so castles, which were liable to be attacked by the enemy, would be "well-fortified and guarded." In the period after the war, which witnessed very different dangers, castles which had avoided attack in the Castilian war, now experienced such threats, but from different enemies; namely, from forces attacking across the Pyrenees.[103] Though many of the repair projects for Elionor's castles were carried on by experienced foremen and work gangs, smaller fortresses did not rate such expensive labor forces and utilized men of the garrison or the neighboring villages to do the work. When builders were used ostensibly to make repairs, some of the construction rendered the castle more comfortable for the castellan and his family. The first and last decision for many of the queen's fortresses, especially those in rural areas, concerned their condition. If they had not been occupied for a long time and required considerable work to make them viable structures, the queen ordered her castellans to destroy them, using as much of the salvaged materials as possible.[104]

One of the castellan's principal and most constant duties was the provisioning of their castles with food and drink. If the fortress was near a city, these items were much easier to acquire, though much more expensive. If located in a rural area, provisioning was intimately connected with transport costs for the use of mule trains. The castellans normally bore the cost for the provisions and transport expenses to the castle, but during the war with Pedro I, the queen often supplemented their salaries to offset these expenses which normally increased in a war environment. A large portion of these costs went to the purchase or replenishment of weapons of all sorts. The castellan normally bought such items directly with a special fund provided him by the queen. Royal agents also delivered to the queen's fortresses "weapons, food, and other things necessary in the time of war," and yet if they did not carry out these missions with "great diligence," any damage that came to the castle would be considered their fault. These deliveries included "very many weapons," among which were grappling hooks, lances, crossbows and quarrels, bows and arrows as well as coats of mail, armor breast plates, and helmets. Occasionally, these weapon stockpiles included disassembled artillery pieces. As Elionor saw it, an under-supplied castle "could easily be defeated by the king's enemies"[105]

Elionor and Her Soldiers

Because of Elionor's status as queen, administrator, governor, and lieutenant general, her role in the War of the Two Pedros was very much that of her husband's partner, in explaining his military goals, informing his subjects of the latest military news, issuing general orders, recruiting and paying troops, interacting–sometimes brusquely–with royal captains, and attempting to maintain as much as possible the legal boundaries between soldiers and civilians.

When war broke out across Pere's realms, his wife showed herself to be an energetic and forceful military administrator who often acted independently, but ultimately for the good of the king's general war effort. In her mind, the dissemination of accurate war news was essential for a general strategy of undermining Pedro I's way of combat. To spread such information, Elionor utilized the notarial service that worked under her to produce letters, and then to have them delivered and returned as quickly as possible. She sought this information across the war fronts with all kinds of people and groups, but especially sought accurate intelligence from her husband's captains who occupied frontier positions which normally served as the front lines between the Crown of Aragon and Castile. From the often disconnected bits of information she discovered in this way, Elionor could occasionally predict the movement of Pedro I's forces and suggest how they could be best anticipated by her husband's troops or by soldiers she herself had recruited.[106]

With this general understanding of the major theaters of combat in the War of the Two Pedros, Elionor occasionally called for the movement of troops to strengthen soft spots and turn back Castilian advances while carrying out valuable service to the king. Her actions of this type were greatly accelerated during Pedro I's naval offensive of 1359. With her husband and the Castilian king occupied in Ibiza, Elionor rightly surmised that Pedro would attack Valencia before he took his fleet back into Castilian waters. To anticipate such an attack, she asked her uncle, Ramon Berenguer, and other, Pyrenean barons to meet her at Tortosa on July 10 with a full five companies ready to serve for the next two months. Even though this meeting never took place, the queen was right about the Castilian danger to Valencia, which eventually took place down the coast at Alicante.[107]

Hearing from a member of her husband's court about this attack, the queen contacted two of her husband's faithful advisers, imploring them

172   D. J. KAGAY

to confront the Castilians and to relieve their royal master of taking on his adversary after he had just confronted him elsewhere. She also hinted that the royal coffers were close to empty and so the king's vassals now had to fight for him, while paying for the privilege. At the same time, she instructed Aragonese officials to confiscate that year's tax receipts to pay military salaries and drive off the Castilians. A short time after this, Elionor, now getting bad information, again wrote to the Aragonese claiming that their realm was about to be attacked by a large contingent of Castilian cavalry. Within a day, she wrote to Jordan Perez de Urries, the lieutenant of the Aragonese governor, insisting that he raise 6,000 troops, many under the command of the military orders, and then station them along the king's western border. This would also require a large war fund for their support.

While her plans for the defense of Aragon were going forward, the queen began to consider how she could help her husband's naval campaign. On July 30, she forgave the noble, Arnau de Eril, from frontier service because of "some malady" he had contracted. She asked him, however, to aid her in raising men to be used as crews in the galleys she was planning to provision and turn over to the king. This drive to keep men with special skills out of service with front line troops had once influenced the queen to exempt blacksmiths from military service.[108] Since there was little indication that Aragon was under any real danger at this time, the kingdom's governor and his officials did very little in preparing troops to meet a Castilian threat. This lack of action brought a caustic missive from the queen on the very next day, July 31. In it, she claimed that the Aragonese officials did not deserve their "privileges and liberties" since they had done nothing to fend off with all their might the threat of Castilian attack. These frantic communiques warning of the mounting danger to Aragon's western frontiers continued to arrive for the next few days until on August 14, 1359, Elionor sent to the Aragonese governor twenty-three identical letters calling for immediate help for the king and then dispatched to the realm's greatest nobles. Two similar emotional calls for help were sent two days later to Aragon's great nobles.[109] Their queen ended the second message with phrases that can stand as her philosophy of war:

> We well know that victory in battle comes neither from the encounters nor the conflicts; nor does it rest in the multitude and great numbers of men, but rather in the hands of Our Lord God and in the hearts of the warriors and in the good justice and truth which the Lord King and we maintain for Him.[110]

Not sure of her husband's fate until August 29, 1359 when he brought back half of his fleet to Barcelona, the normally hard-headed queen seemed to have lost control of her emotions. Without any knowledge of where the king was, she seemed to fear the worst and immediately took the war effort completely on herself. Certain that Pedro would continue his attacks since he had already besieged Ibiza and Almería, she frantically moved to ready Aragon for an attack she firmly believed to be in the offing. Her outbursts of temper showed how concerned she had become day by day with no news of her husband. Her detailed plans for the defense of Aragon, although ultimately unneeded, showed what a remarkable administrator she had become.[111]

Elionor's frantic calls for the immediate defense of Aragon in the late summer, 1359 were surely influenced by her mounting fear for her husband, who for the first time in their marriage had actually gone to war. It also shows how confident she was in issuing such orders during the same year. In February, she began sending another series of letters dealing with the army Pere III was raising to defend against his Castilian enemy. In February, she countermanded part of her husband's army decree by ordering, "for the greater usefulness of the commonwealth," that an engineer, a citizen of Elche should not be drafted into the army, but left in his community to see that the great damage it had suffered in the war would be immediately repaired. In the queen's opinion, his services as an engineer far outweighed the contributions he might make as a soldier.[112]

From late July of the same year, however, her attention was fully on the recruiting of soldiers for the protection of the realms of Valencia and Aragon. For this reason, she arranged for 150 troops to help with the defense of the Valencian capital, hired Muslim crossbowmen to aid in the defense of Prince Martí's castles of Elche, and Crevillente, diverted money from these Valencian towns to the king's military coffers, saw to the destruction of several decrepit castles on the Aragonese frontier with Castile, and help bolster the defenses of the Aragonese capital and its massive Aljafería castle complex.[113]

174   D. J. KAGAY

Though Elionor seemed willing to use some of the funds she relied on for her own support and that of her children to bolster her husband's war effort, she often served as a transfer agent for royal money intended for the payment of the king's captains and their troops. She perfected this activity by entrusting the funds to one of her court officials and then having them transferred to other agents who worked nearer the troops scheduled to be paid. These transactions were documented by receipts which eventually ended up in the office of the *maestre racional*. The queen was scrupulous about the transfer of this money and the accounting procedures designed to totally chronicle its official journey. When she discovered sloppiness or dishonesty, Elionor immediately registered her disapproval, saying that the officials' actions might lead to "damage to the commonwealth." In the naval crisis of 1359, she attempted to rapidly link funds with the troops that needed this money, but was not always successful in such enterprises, especially when she undertook to both station and pay troops.[114]

Even before Pere III had left Aragon and Catalonia to engage during 1363–1365 in Valencian military operations, Elionor, as Governor of Catalonia and the Lieutenant General, often acted as paymaster and royal representative with the increasing number of captains who served the king. For this reason, Elionor was in fairly constant contact with the king's most important commanders, Count Enrique de Trastámara and Prince Ferran. Her relationships were never overly friendly and, as we have seen, she had no reluctance in dressing them down when she thought it necessary. On July 15, 1359, she forbade these principal commanders and their subalterns from abandoning their posts on the Aragonese frontier to seek rest and recreation in Zaragoza. Even if they claimed they were in the Aragonese capital in pursuit of money with which to pay their troops, the queen would not accept such a flimsy excuse.[115]

With Trastámara, her discussions always seemed to be about money. She complained that he was clearly the highest paid of all of king's commanders and had received this money on a regular basis. With the "great danger to the realm" that her husband was now fighting to defeat, the count had to be patient and remain at his post. She was careful to see that money flowed to the count from the large war chests that Pere was increasingly using to fund his fleet, but it is clear that she kept the fiscal pipeline flowing "more from necessity than kindness."[116] She did realize, however, how important the count was to her husband's war effort and carefully followed the royal line that Trastámara was the "greatest captain of the kingdom of Aragon." During her fear of Castilin attack in summer, 1359, she begged both the count and his brother, Tello, to resist fighting the Navarrese and to stand up for the Aragonese citizens who were in danger of having "their throats cut and killed," and to do this "in service and for the honor of the lord kind...especially since he was absent from the land."[117]

Prince Ferran, who as Elionor's cousin, was "as dear to ... [her] as a brother," did not always escape her wrath for things he had done and other things he had failed to do. On August 7, 1359, she informed her relative that one of the important Valencian captains had "wrongfully surrendered" the castle of Olamo to the Castilians, and it was the prince's duty to put that fortress under a "good guard." He was also to formally investigate this matter for the queen. A few days later she complained that he had not transferred one hundred horsemen to Elche which was threatened by an immanent Castilian attack. From her reports, the prince was still thirty men short from filling her order, and she was clearly unhappy about it. In early September, she informed him that one of his Valencian villages, Alcoy, had engaged in numerous lawsuits against the crown, and had not paid into the Valencian war fund or the smaller collection designed to compensate the region's muleteers for the long hauls they engaged in for the king's army.[118]

The two military men the queen most relied on was the king's uncle, Count Ramon Berenguer of Empuries and Archbishop Lope of Zaragoza. The count served as Elionor's counselor and seemed the first person she passed news on to. He also extended the reach of her letters by passing them on to Catalonia's Pyrenean cities. Like so many others, however, he did not comply with the queen's desperate call for help against the putative Castilian attack on Aragon in 1359.[119] Lope Ferrández de Luna, who served as archbishop of Zaragoza from 1351 to 1384 and, as the leader of the important Luna clan, stood as one of Pere III's most important military advisers. By the time the Castilian war broke, the prelate was getting up in age, but sill commanded a company of horsemen, the funding of which the queen was responsible for.[120]

In spite of the differences Elionor had with the royal captains who served against Castile, she supported them economically and was extremely careful to protect their professional reputations, no matter what she privately might have thought of them for. When they violated their feudal allegiance to the king by defecting to the Castilian cause or simply trying to leave their post, the queen used all means at hand to capture

176   D. J. KAGAY

them and arrange for their punishment. Ever cognizant of the crown's reputation, however, she used all means available to hide their treason. Her actions in matters of this sort were clear in the case of Ferran Gomez de Albornoz, a Hospitaller commander of Montalbán, a man important to the Luna family and to the king before and after the war, who seemed to have deserted his post near Albarracin in summer, 1359. For an unknown reason, Ferran and his brother, Alvar García de Albornoz were called to Avignon by Innocent VI. As with López de Heredía, Elionor would not allow such a mission to serve as an excuse to leave an Aragonese military post devoid of its commander. When Gómez de Albornoz thus deserted the castle of Huelamo, the queen moved into action, having the fortresses reoccupied and making every effort to see the nobleman and his brother taken into custody. As is so often the case with stories that spring from archival sources, the end of this story is not left to us. Since the commander of Montalbán was in Pere III's good graces after the war, we must assume that this military peccadillo was forgiven.[121]

Elionor's Ships

Elionor's most remarkable feats of wartime administration occurred in response to Pedro I's naval offensive of summer, 1359. Since the fleet that Pere III took out to meet his enemy in the waters between Barcelona and the Balearic Islands was much smaller than the Castilian armada, the Aragonese king, the king had put out a general call for help in refitting his naval force after he had taken on the Castilians. Pere's queen took very seriously this call for refitting her husband's ships should they need it. She assumed the force would need her help, and began to consider the best way to deliver it. Though the queen was sufficiently acquainted with Mediterranean seafaring from her Sicilian upbringing, she needed some advice about how this help could best be given. To assure herself and to inform her wealthy, Catalan clerics of her remarkable plans, she started calling meetings with them at Barcelona throughout June and July of 1359. Every few days, the queen convened these meeting that were supposed to include the archbishop of Tarragona, and the bishops of Barcelona, Tortosa, Lerida, Vich, Urgel, and Elna. Though her calls for attendance largely went unanswered, Elionor repeatedly asked them by letter what they were prepared to do to aid the king, and then proceeded to spell out very clearly what they would have to do to protect their king. By July 13, she had sent one of her officials to Ibiza to consult with the king and estimate his needs. At the same time, she was trying to put her plans for the defense of Aragon and Valencia into operation. Within a week, she had received a report that two Catalan ships had defeated three Castilian vessels, killing all their crewmen except for forty survivors. By her view of recent history, this action had forced Pedro I to break off the Ibiza siege and sail southward down the Catalan coast. At this crucial point of the war, she began to demand ever more forcefully for Catalan help for the support of her husband's fleet.[122]

The queen's first step in her plan to keep Pere's fleet seaworthy and ready to take on Pedro's larger force was her stunning donation on May 30, 1359 of 14,000 *sous* of Barcelona to outfit one of the king's galleys that would be at sea in some three weeks.[123] She wrote her husband two weeks later to assure him she was not spending money already pledged to important accounts such as that assigned to the salaries of Trastámara or other captains. Elionor was also blocked from utilizing tax money due from Minorca until its date for payment. She also wrote a public letter to demonstrate how 16,000 *libras* could effectively be used to refit a good number of the king's ships.[124] With her rough plans laid out for the establishment of a new squadron, Elionor began to utilize the pressure she was so good at applying on many different kinds of people. Since Pere's fleet was at the point of leaving Barcelona, the queen latched on the plan of refitting other galleys and providing a captain, helmsman, and crew for each vessel. These freshly provisioned vessels would eventually join the king's fleet and serve to make up for the losses of any vessels he might suffer.[125]

As always, money was the principal drawback for attaining success in such schemes. Besides the considerable refitting expenses, the queen had taken it on herself to buy galleys that could then be armed and provisioned.[126] To attain funds to make these plans a reality, Elionor involved her officials, servants, as well as her oldest son in a money-raising scheme which required contributions from all of Catalonia's major clergy. Her agents were to use "good persuasion" to help the king in his time of "great need." They were also to give colorful descriptions of the successes the king's fleet had enjoyed against the Castilians. Rather than undermining her appeals for money with these celebrations of happy victories, she emphasized that even if the Castilian navy was defeated, the land war also had to receive monetary support.[127]

In the beginning, Elionor's naval money-raising campaign attained little success due to the cool reception with which many of the Catalan

178   D. J. KAGAY

prelates greeted the plan. The bishops of Barcelona and Gerona largely saw through Elionor's call for their presence at court, knowing full well that it was their money rather than their advice that they wanted. To hold off her "great insistence," the Catalan prelates put forth a number of written excuses, and then sent their canons to explain why the bishop could not possibly confer with the queen at the present time. Elionor quickly lost her temper, and all but branded her great churchmen as traitors to the "loyalty and allegiance they owed the king and queen."[128]

The queen's campaign for naval and military funds continued well in August, 1359. In July, she sent her oldest son to convince the bishop of Urgel that it was his duty to provide forty rowers and thirty cross-bowmen for service on the royal fleet. At the same time, she sent letter after letter to Pyrenean villages reinforcing the need for their support of the king in a time of such great danger. She wrote again to the bishop of Barcelona reinforcing royal military need and assuring the prelate that Pere was winning great victories on the sea. In many of the directives she sent out, Elionor was clearly past the stage of asking for individual contributions, but now turned to the "household tax" (*fogatge*) as a way of gaining "aid and help for the defense of the commonwealth."[129]

The Aragonese queen now sent out her protonotary, Matheu Adrian, to the bishoprics of Vich and Urgel where he instructed the royal officials working in the area to start the collections the queen had ordered. The queen also gained help in this enterprise from Count Pere I of Urgel. (r. 1347–1408) and extended the collection of subsidies across the kingdom of Aragon, and the Catalan cities of Barcelona, and Tarragona. She sent another agent, the lawyer, Bertrand de Vall, to the Pyrenean regions of Roussillon and Cerdanya to lay out the format of the subsidy for the region.[130] Other agents of the queen helped establish the subsidy format in the bishopric of Lerida and Gerons.[131] She again wrote the archbishop of Tarragona, the Catalan bishops and abbots, and the Principate's major monasteries, warning them all to "leave off all excuses and delays...[and now think only of] the honor and good of the Lord King."[132]

As this money-raising campaign went on, the queen began the process of finding suitable ships that could be refitted and sent to serve in the royal fleet. Her officials found likely vessels in the Mediterranean ports of Collioure, Narbonne, and Sant Feliu de Guixols and then the queen turned to her uncle, Count Ramón Berenguer, for help and advice. She was sure that the towns would help and asked the count to line up nobles along the Mediterranean coast who would provide other vessels. From early June 1359, she started sending trusted agents into the Pyrenean lands to bring her plans to fruition. Throughout July she wrote all the towns in Roussillon and Cerdanya explaining her plans and calling for their help. At the same time, she made similar calls for help to Gerona and Valencia cit.[133] By July 29, the Aragonese queen declared that she had identified ten galleys to be repaired and provisioned for fleet service. She then named trustworthy citizens in the Mediterranean ports who were given "full power" in refitting the vessels with "supreme care and diligence." This new activity among Catalonia's Mediterranean ports was of crucial importance for towns like Collioure which had suffered such significant depopulation that Pere III was afraid it could easily be overrun by the mercenaries that currently swarmed across France at the time.[134]

Refitting of galleys was only the first step in getting them ready as an efficient addition to the king's fleet. Each vessel needed a certain sized crew depending on how large the ship was. The men recruited had to have some experience as sailors and so Elionor sought crews in the same ports that provided the galleys and the villages around them. Along with these seamen who numbered up to two hundred per-ship, each vessel would have up to fifty crossbowmen, who would unleash a cloud of quarrels against any approaching enemy ship.[135] Each region through its cities, towns, and villages supplied from three to ten seamen and up to twenty-five crossbowmen. All in all, the areas around large cities could supply up to 200 men.[136] If any of the towns or villages scheduled to provide crewmen of any type failed in this task, they would quickly experience the dangerous side of the queen's temper.[137]

When Elionor's ten galleys were fully fitted out for fleet service, the officials who had the repairs and provisioning began to provision them with equipment such as an extra mast, sails, anchors, and cables. They also carefully stowed below decks freshwater, wine, vinegar, olive oil, meat, and wheat. The most important prepared product on board was the sea biscuit which was made from barley. As a kind of hard tack, it remained eatable for well over a year.[138] Once the galleys were loaded with provisions and their crews were settled on board, the ten vessels were sailed from the Mediterranean ports down the coast to Barcelona. The captains were the queen's agents who had carried out the refitting operations. The real seamanship was trusted to the helmsmen who brought the galleys across the gulfs of Lion and Rosas into the greatest port of Catalonia. The vessels were handed over to the queen's representatives as soon as they beached at the capital.[139] Since Pere III only remained with his

180   D. J. KAGAY

full fleet for a little over a month and Pedro I left Valencian waters a month after that, it is not clear that Elionor's galleys caught up with either division of the Aragonese fleet in the summer of 1359. What is crystal clear, however, is the administrative skill and personal determination Queen Elionor displayed in carrying out all phases of her land and maritime operations in the summer of 1359 and in later years when she had vessels fitted out for various missions.[140]

The Queen and the War Parliaments

As a member of the royal administration, Elionor was not expected to attend the Aragonese or Valencia *cortes* meetings. As the Governor of Catalonia and Lieutenant General, she was extremely important in the Catalan *corts* of the war years. In the assembly of Barcelona in 1358, she was the subject of discussions on military finances. After the meeting, the queen directed that the procurator for "our most dear child," the two-year-old Prince Martí, was to pay into the parliamentary fund designed to pay soldiers for the next two years. Some two years later in 1360, the queen herself was caught up in military funding when the emerging political arm of the Valencian *coetes*, the *Generalitat*, declared her responsible for the payment of some Valencian troops because of the large amount of money she drew from Valencian revenues.[141]

The Aragonese king, while hating the monotonous drone of parliamentary procedure, had been careful to meet with the public assemblies of his three peninsular realms between 1357 and 1363. After that, his presence at such assemblies was severely hampered by the crucial military campaigns in Valencia. In Catalonia, one of his richest realms which had suffered the least from the Castilian conflict, he found a trustworthy representative, his wife, Elionor. Summoning the *corts* at Tortosa for February, 1364, the king soon changed the meeting place at Barcelona in next month. He was now needed in Valencia, however, and so sent the queen in his place, despite the drum-roll of Catalan legal opposition which asserted that only the king of Aragon/count of Barcelona could oversee the Catalan *corts*.

Since, as usual, the king was in desperate need of money, he did not dare postpone the meeting again, and so, on March 10, Queen Elionor sat on her throne before the assembly. The reason for the change was well-known to the members of the assembly for the king had written them to say that the Castilian king had again unleashed his troops on Aragon and

Valencian, and so it was now incumbent on the Catalans to now stand for the "good estate, protection, and defense" of their homeland.[142] In her opening speech, delivered perfectly in Catalan, the queen reinforced why her husband was not standing before them. He was leading an army into Valencia to stop the Castilian "path of perdition" which the Catalans were all too familiar with. It was now the duty of her husband's oldest realm to raise money for its own defense and that of the king's other subjects. The 120,000 libras she called for would pay the wages of Catalan soldiers and sailors and provide meaningful help to Pere's other lands which were coming very close to their breaking point. Even if the Catalans did not want to pledge their money in this way, Elionor reminded them if Aragon or Valencia fell to the Castilians, a similar fate would soon await them.[143]

In principle, the Catalans accepted the queen's arguments, but this did not stop them from grumbling about Pere's "great and intolerable expenses incurred on both land and sea." After months of haggling and finger-pointing, the Catalans finally established another *fogatge* to collect the required funds. Six months later, not a *sou* had come to the king who was still fighting in Valencia. Even more desperate for money than he had been, the king nagged his wife to go before the *corts*, and ask the members for 20,000 libras to tide him over.[144] To carry out her husband's wishes, she had to reassemble the Barcelona meeting, establishing its new meeting date as All Saints Day (November 1). She first scheduled this reconvened *corts* at Barcelona and then farther south at Tortosa with the hope that the king could break away from the Valencian fighting long enough to make an appearance before the *corts*. This proved impossible, leaving Elionor in the unhappy conundrum of trying to balance the schedules of the distant parties, all to no avail.[145]

When the Aragonese king made it back to Barcelona for the Christmas holidays to find that his wife had not forced the Catalans to meet, he angrily got them in his presence and by April 7, 1365 had forced them to agree to yet another tax scheme; namely, 350,000 *libras* over the next two years, to be raised like all the others through a hearth tax.[146] Although the Catalans grew increasingly furious about this settlement forced on them by the king, they could not openly show their dissatisfaction with Pere, but vented it repeatedly on his long-suffering wife.

Still short of cash since none of the Catalan hearth taxes agreed to since 1363 had been fully collected, the king, now close to what he thought was an ultimate battle with his "principal adversary," demanded that his wife and administrator summon another Barcelona assembly, which ultimately

182   D. J. KAGAY

convened on July 17, 1365. At the opening session in one of the large chambers of the royal palace, Elionor, "sitting on a throne wearing royal garb," watched the members of the assembly slowly parade to their places. She then solemnly announced that her husband was again fighting for his and their lives outside of the Valencian capital. Because their promised subsidies had brought almost no money, they had to vote another subsidy, and, this time, effectively collect it. Shortly after she had dropped this unhappy news on them, she brought before them news that was even more shocking; the king needed an immediate infusion of cash–65,000 libras–to keep his troops in the field. The anger of the Barcelona assembly now spilled out repeatedly on to the queen.[147]

Following the lead of the urban estate which saw the crown's call for repeated taxes as increasingly detrimental to the Catalan economy, the clergy and nobility refused to give into yet another round of taxes. Instead, the assembly at large offered to grant the king one-tenth of the income of all three estates for the next three years provided all the earlier parliamentary taxes between 1363 and 1365 were declared null and void. All money that was collected would be used only to pay Catalan troops and crews.[148] Nonplussed by the assembly's failure to vote for another subsidy, Elionor prorogued the meeting until late August, 1365 when she reconvened it in Barcelona's largest Franciscan monastery. Near tears, she told the members that she had endured a "month of fifty days" waiting for them to do their duties and aid their king and lord. She gave them two days and when they met again, she expected them to do their duty as good vassals.[149]

Unfortunately for her position as head of the *corts*, Elionor was caught in the middle of a power struggle between Pere and the members of the assembly. He had written his wife on August 11, answering her recent note which described her problems with the unruly members of the *corts*. In line with his character, Pere begged her not to lose her temper, but if they remained adamant about not paying taxes, she should threaten them with legal action, and charge that they had conspiring with his Castilian enemy, much as Bernat de Cabrera had in the year before his death.[150] After writing his wife, he penned an angry letter to the urban estate of the Barcelona parliament, pointing out in specific terms how their selfish behavior was undermining his Valencia campaign which had just entered a critical stage. If they wanted to be thought of as his good subjects, they now had to stand with the clergy and nobles in doing their duty for king and country.[151] When the king received no response from the members

7 ELIONOR OF SICILY AS A WARTIME LEADER 183

of the urban estate, he fired off another letter to then, which promised that if they did not follow his earlier advice, he would loose on them "such a great punishment that it would be an example for all time."[152]

Whether Elionor knew of this correspondence or not, her troubles with the Barcelona assembly continued. On August 22, she met with the full *corts* "on the cloister grass" of the Franciscan monastery to hear that the estates would only agree to pay 55,000 *libras*, the collection of which they would largely control. To them, the *fogatges* from the earlier *corts* were now dead letters though the queen demand that the household taxes be paid in full. It the estates this was the cruelest of injustices.[153] Elionor, now seeming to have completely lost control of the assembly, prorogued it fourteen times in the next three weeks. When the *corts* finally reconvened on September 21, the rambunctious estates repeatedly hooted her down until her advisers and other officials were able to establish enough control so she could again address the assembly. Unfortunately, she was still acting for her husband who gave her a message to deliver to the estates. Pere III, it seems, had made a deal with the mercenaries who were streaming across the Pyrenees. They had to be paid by October 1 or the king was sure they would sell their services to Pedro I.

When Elionor gained control of the assembly again, she launched into a fifteen-minute speech considered by many to be the greatest parliamentary address of the fourteenth century. She reminded the Catalans of the almost sacred allegiance that bound them to their king. Since he and his brave troops were holding off Castilian attacks in Valencia at that very moment, the Catalans had no choice but to give these heroes the means with which to attain victory. If the companies did not receive this money and the Castilian king found out about it, the great victories Pere had won in Valencia would be undone and the commonwealth of his realms would be gravely endangered. At the end of this increasingly emotional appeal, Elionor confessed the "great anxiety, confusion, and sadness" she had suffered at the hands of the Catalans. It was now time for her to forget this, and for the estates to do their duty and vote their approval for the subsidy so long requested from them.[154] Having gained the upper hand by her simple but direct eloquence, she put the case to the members of the estates before they had time to disappear from the large room they faced her in for an extended lunch. She had the members of the clerical estate lined up and asked individually if they approved of her demand for money. When the churchmen gave in, the queen's victory swept over the noble and urban estates and within three days the elated queen had

184 D. J. KAGAY

gained the approval of the *corts* for all the subsidies requested of them. On December 15, the assembly formally approved of the grants before the king, his wife, and first son.[155]

Despite the problems Elionor encountered in the assemblies of 1364 and 1365, her fairness in hearing the different sides of issues brought before her and the unwavering support of the royal positions made her largely acceptable to both sides. It was not unusual, then, that we see the queen acting in the *corts* of Montblanc to have funds voted by the assembly collected and distributed by the deputies of the assembly and used to defend the Catalan coast. As a royal administrator, she had lived through the parliamentary changes that gave increased power to the members of the national assemblies at the coat of the royal government of which she was a part.[156]

NOTES

1. Joseph Ángelo Dávila, *História de Xerez de la Frontera*, ed Juan Abellán Pèrez (Helsinki, 2008), 87–88 (chap. 4); María Martínez Martínez, "Un medio vida en la frontera murciana-granadino (siglo XIIII)," *MMM* 13 (1986): 49–62; Manuel Rojas Gabriel, "El valor bélico de la cabalgada en la frontera de Granada (c.1350-c.1481)," *AEM* 31, no. 1 (2001): 295–328; A. Vazquez: "Una cabalgada de moros," *Aljaranda* 1 (1991): 8–10.

2. Donald J. Kagay, "The Defense of the Crown of Aragon During the War of the Two Pedros (1356-1366)," *The Journal of Military History* 71, no. 1 (January, 2007): 11–33, esp. 17–20.

3. Robert I. Burns, "The Significance of the Frontier in the Middle Ages," in *Medieval Frontier Societies*, ed. Robert Bartlett and Angus Mackay (1989; reprint (Oxford, 1996), 307–30; Francisco de Moxó y Montoliu, *Estudios sobre las relaciones entre Aragón y Castilla (SS. XIII–XV)* (Zaragoza, 1997), 141–49.

4. Abulafia, *Mediterranean Emporium*, 236; Western *Mediterranean Kingdoms*, 123–27, 179; Giunta, *Aragoneses*, 1:146–55; idem, "La politico mediterranea di Pietro il Cerimonioso, in *Pere el Cerimoniós i seva època*, ed. María Teresa Ferrer i Mallol (Barcelona, 1989), 59–76.

5. Ayala, *Pedro I*, 469–78 (1356, chaps. i–vi); Manuel Barrios, *Pedro I el Cruel: La nobleza contra su rey* (Madrid, 2001), 33–40.

6. Ayala, *Pedro I*, 473–75; María Teresa Ferrer i Mallol, "Causes i antecedents de la guerra dels dos Peres," *Boletín de la Sociedad Castellornse de Cultura* 63 (1987): 445–508, esp. 445–67; María Rosa Muñoz

Pomer, "Preliminares de la Guerra de los Dos Pedros en el Reino de Valencia," *AUA* I (1982): 117–34, esp. 121.

7. Ayala, *Pedro I*, 474 (1356, chap. iii); Zurita, *Anales*, 4: 289–292 (IX:iii).
8. ACA, CR, R. 1379, 12v–13v; Pere III, *Chronicle*, 2: 496–99; Estow, *Pedro*, 184.
9. *Usatges*, trans Kagay, 73, art. 35, fnt. 35.
10. Ayala, *Pedro I*, 474–75 (1356, chap. x).
11. Donald J. Kagay, "Army Mobilization," 95–115, idem, "War Financing in the Late-Medieval Crown of Aragon," *JMMH* 6 (2008): 119–48, esp. 124–25.
12. ACA, CR, R. 1379, f. 124v; *Documenta Selecta Mutuas Civitatis Arago-Cathalaunicae et Ecclesiae Relationes* [hereafter *DS*], ed. Johannes Vincke (Barcelona, 1936), 430 (doc. 565).
13. ACA, CR, R. 1184, f. 113; *DHC*, 87–88.
14. ACA, CR, R. 1380, f. 71; Pere III, *Chronicle*, 2:522–25 (VI:22–24; *DS*, 425–25 (doc. 561); Donald J. Kagay, "The Theory and Practice of Just War in the Late-Medieval Crown of Aragon." *Catholic Historical Review* [hereafter *CHR*] 591–610; Mario Lafuente Gómez, Devoción y patronazgo en torno al combate en la Corona de Aragón: Las commemoraciones á San Jorge de 1356," *Aragone en la Edad Media* 20 (2008): 427–44.
15. ACA, CR, R. 1149, f. 96v; *Epistolari*, 155 (doc. 21).
16. ACA, CR, R. 149, f. 96v; R. 1151, f. 65v R. 1379, f. 111v; 147–48v, 161r–v; Ayala, *Pedro I*, 478 (1357, chap. iii); Antonio Guitiérrez de Velasco, "La Conquista de Tarazona en la Guerra de los Dos Pedros (Año 1357," *CHJZ* 10–11 (1960): 69–98, esp. 83–88; Zurita, *Anales*, 4:316–17 (IX:vii).
17. ACA, CR, R. 1032, ff. 160r–v; R. 1382, ff. 81r–v; Ayala, *Pedro I*, 499–500 (1350, chap. xxii); Antonio Gutiérrez de Velasco, "La contaofensiva aragonesa en la Guerra de los Dos Pedros: Actitud militar y diplomática de Pedro IV el Cerimoniosos (años 1358 á 1362)," *CHJZ* 14–15 (1963): 7–30, esp. 16–17.
18. ACA, CR, R. 1383, ff. 179v–80; Ayala, *Pedro I*, 503–4 (1360, chaps. viii–ix.).
19. Ayala, *Pedro I*, 485 (1358, chap. ix).
20. Ibid., 494–95 (1359, chaps. xi–xii); ACA, CR, R. 1381, f. 232v; R. 1382, f. 19v; R. 1383, f. 58.
21. Ayala, *Pedro I*, 495 (1359, chap. xii); Pere III, *Chronicle*, 2:522–23 (VI:22); Donald J. Kagay, "The National Defense Clause and the Emergence of the Catalan State: *Princeps namque* Revisited," in *War*, Study I, 57–97, esp. 74–75; Zurita, *Anales*, 4:376–78 (IX:xxiii).
22. Ayala, *Pedro I*, 495 (1359, chap. xiii); Pere III, *Chronicle*, 2:525 (VI:25).

186   D. J. KAGAY

23. Ayala, *Pedro I*, 496 (1359, chap. xiv); Pere III, *Chronicle*, 2:526 (VI:25–26).
24. Ayala, *Pedro I*, 497 (1359, chaps. xvi–xix; Pere III, *Chronicle*, 2:526 (VI:26).
25. Ayala, *Pedro I*, 532 (1364, chap. iii); Pere III, *Chronicle*, 2:544–45 (VI:40).
26. Ayala, *Pedro I*, 532 (1364, chap. iii); Pere III, *Chronicle*, 2:546–48 (VI:40).
27. Ayala, *Pedro I*, 532 (1364, chap. iii); Pere III, *Chronicle*, 2:548–50 (VI:41). Lafuente Gómez, *Dos Coronas en Guerra*, 134-37; Zurita, *Anales*, 4:501–3 (IX:liv).
28. Ayala, *Pedro I*, 532 (1364, chap. iii); Pere III, *Chronicle*, 2:551–52 (VI:42–43).
29. Pere III, *Chronicle*, 2:552–53 (VI:44).
30. Ayala, *Pedro I*, 532 (1364, chap. iv); Pere III, *Chronicle*, 2:553–54 (VI:45); Zurita, *Anales*, 4:505–6 (IX:lv).
31. Ayala, *Pedro I*, 532 (1364, chap. iv); Pere III, *Chronicle*, 2:554 (VI:45). For Mediterranean mooring devices and sea winds, see: Robert I. Burns, S.J. "*Gegna*: Coastal Mooring in crusader Valencia," *Technology and Culture* 47 (2006): 777–86; Fernand Braudel, *The Mediterranean and the Mediterranean World in the Age of Philip II*, trans. Siân Reynolds, 2 vols. (New York, 1992), 1:257.
32. Ayala, *Pedro I*, 533 (1364, chap. vi).
33. Ayala, *Pedro I*, 533 (1364, chap. vii); Pere III, *Chronicle*, 2:563–67 (VI:52)
34. ACA, CR, R. 727, ff. 16465v; R. 1210, ff. 47r–v; R. 1211, f. 63v; Ayala, *Pedro I*, 143 (1364, chap. vii).
35. Pere III, *Chronicle*, 2:548–50, 569 (VI:41, 55); Kagay, "Theory and Practice," 602.
36. Pere III, *Chronicle*, 2:569–71 (VI:41, 55–56); Zurita, *Anales*, 4:464–65 (IX:xlvi)
37. ACA, CR, R. 1149, f. 88; R. 1150, ff. 272r–v; R. 1381, ff. 37v–38; Ayala, *Pedro I*, 479 (1357, chap. vi); Pere III, *Chronicle*, 2:514–16 (VI:13–14).
38. ACA, CR, Varia, no. 68, f. 171; Ángeles Masiá i de Ros, *Relación castellano-aragonesa desde Jaime II á Pedro el Cerimonioso*, 2 vols. (Barcelona, 1994), 2;459 (doc. 271/115).
39. ACA, CR, Varia, no. 68, ff. 238–39v; Masiá i de Ros, *Relación*, 2:512–26 (doc. 231/153).
40. ACA, CR, R. 913, f. 46; R. 914, f. 126.
41. *Colección de las Cortes de los antiguos reinos de Aragón y de Valencia y del principado de Cataluña* [hereafter *CAVC*], ed. Fidel Fita and Bienvenido Oliver, 27 vols. (Madrid, 1896–1922), 3:1.

42. Jesús Lalinde Abadia, *Le institución virreinal en Cataluña* (Barcelona, 1964), 47–98; idem, "Virreyes," 100–2; Earenfight, "Maria of Castile, Ruler," 51.

43. José María Font y Rius, "The Institutions of the Crown of Aradon in the First Half of the Fifteenth Century," in *Spain in the Fifteenth Century 1369, 1516: Essays and Extracts by Historians of Spain*, ed. Roger Highfield, trans. Frances M. López-Morillas (New York, 1972), 169–92, esp. 180–81; Lalinde Abadia, "Virreyes," 101–2.

44. Aneas Hontangas, "Reines lloclinents," 15–16; Earenfight. "Maria of Castile, Ruler," 51; Miron, *Queens of Aragon*, 145; J.E. Martínez Ferrando, "Jaume II," in *Els Descendents de Pere el Gran* (Barcelona, 1980), 1.

45. Ruiz Domingo, "*Del qual tenim loch*," 322–23; Martínez Ferrando, Jaume II, 153–54.

46. Gutiérrez de Velasco, "Fortalezas," 9–15; Donald J. Kagay, "Border War as Handmaiden of National Identity: The Territorial Definition of Late-Medieval Iberia," *Journal of the Georgia Association of Historians* 28 (2009): 88–138, esp. 110; Ruiz Domingo, "*Del qual tenim loch*," 315–17.

47. ACA, CR, R. 1137, ff. 40–41; Roebert, "Nominations," *Mediaeval Studies* 80 (2018): 171–229, esp. 199–200 (doc. 1).

48. ACA, CR, R. 1071, ff. 40v–41; Roebert, "Nominations," 200–202 (doc. 2).

49. ACA, CR, R. 1137, f. 40; Roebert, "Nominations," 199: *eapropter de circumspeccione provida et providencia circumspecta maturoque discrecionis consilio ac aliis virtutibus vestri.*

50. ACA, CR, R. 1071, f. 40v; Roebert, "Nominations," 203: *alta et circumspecta providencia merito confidentes.*

51. ACA, CR, R. 1568, f. 1; Ruiz Domingo, "*Del qual tenim loch*," 311.

52. Ruiz Domingo, "*Del qual tenim loch*," 312–13.

53. ACA, CR, R. 1075, ff. 29v–30; Roebert, "Nominations," 202–3 (doc. 3).

54. ACA, CR, R. 970, ff. 186–89v; Roebert, "Nominations," 203–13 (doc. 4).

55. ACA, CR, R. 995, ff. 105–7v; Roebert, "Nominations," 214–21 (doc. 5)

56. ACA, CR, R. 1567, f. 120v; R. 1573, f. 18v; Ruiz Domingo, "*Del qual tenim loch*," 313–14.

57. ACA, CR, R. 1573, ff. 68–69v; Roebert, "Nominations," 221–24 (doc. 6).

58. ACA, CR, R. 1537, ff. 122r–v.; Roebert, "Nominations," 226–27 (doc. 7).

188   D. J. KAGAY

59. ACA, CR, R. 1584, f. 70v; Deibel, "Reyna Elionor," 449 (doc. 6); Roebert, "Nominations," 228–29 (doc. 8).
60. ACA, CR, R. 1566, ff. 107, 179v–180; R. 1567, ff. 25v, 43.
61. ACA, CR, R. 1566, ff. 40, 46, 97; R. 1567, ff. 25 v, 41, 136v–37.
62. ACA, CR, R. 1534, ff. 37v–38, 63v–64; R. 1566, ff. 45v–46, 97, 147v; R. 1567, ff. 41v–42,43, 139v.
63. ACA, CR, R. 1534, f. 121; R. 1566, ff. 73v, 81v; R. 1568, f. 71v.
64. ACA, CR, R. 1565, ff. 179r–v; R. 1566, ff. 85v, 148v–50v, 171v–72; R. 1567, ff. 28v–29, 37, 115v, 187r–v; R. 1570, ff. 34, 46v, 76r–v, 83r–v.
65. ACA, CR, R. 1566, ff. 81, 99v; R. 1567, ff. 112v, 115.
66. ACA, CR, R. 1566, f. 89v.
67. ACA, CR, R. 1566, 124v, 158 v; R. 1567, ff. 3v, 44v, 72, 133v.
68. ACA, CR, R. 1567, ff. 113v–15.
69. ACA, CR, R. 1568, f. 7v.
70. ACA, CR, R. 1568, ff. 9r–v. For Heredía's life and career, see, Anthony Luttrell, *Juan Fernandez de Heredía; Castellan of Amposta (1346-1377)* (Oxford, 1959).
71. ACA, CR, R. 1568, 10–11, 46r–v, 47v.
72. ACA, CR, ff. 106r–v, 107v; R. 1568, ff. 12r–v, 17v–18, 23r–v, 27–28v, 33–34, 38, 39–40, 45, 46. For the *fogatge*, see María Teresa Ainaga Andrés., "El fogaje aragonés de 1362: Aportació a la demografía de Zaragoza en el siglo XIV," *AEEM* 9 (1989): 33–59; Kagay, "War Financing," 134; J.M. Pons Guri, "Un fogatjament desconegut del l'any 1358," *Boletín de Real Academia de Buenas Letras de Barcelona* 30 (1963–1964): 322–498.
73. ACA, CR, R. 1568, ff. 32v–33.
74. ACA, CR, R. 1568, ff. 32, 43v.
75. ACA, CR, R. 1567, ff. 38v, 106r–v; R. 1568, ff. 45, 61r–v.
76. ACA, CR, R. 1567, ff. 84r–v, 139v; R. 1568, ff. 76v–77; R. 1579, f. 54.
77. ACA, CR, R. 1566, f. 97; R. 1567, f. 135; R. 1568, ff. 5v–6, 32r–v, 35r–v.
78. ACA, CR, R. 1566, ff. 107, 110, 115v, 161, f. 185; R. 1567, f. 18.
79. ACA, CR, R. 1567, f. 125; R. 1568, ff. 1r–v, 66.
80. ACA, CR, R. 1566, ff. 188r–v; R. 1567, ff. 117r–v, 133v.
81. ACA, CR, R. 1537, f. 46; R. 1567, f. 22v.
82. ACA, CR, R. 1566, f. 115.
83. ACA, CR, R. 1567, f. 139; R. 1568, f. 65v; R. 1578, ff. 36r–v, 59v–60; R. 1578, f. 32.
84. ACA, CR, R. 1566, f. 108v; R. 1567, ff. 22–24, 40r–v, 43v–44, 46.
85. ACA, CR, R. 1537, f. 51v; R. 1566, f. 157; R. !567. ff. 123v–24; 125, 127, 139; R. 1573, ff. 112v, 146.

7 ELIONOR OF SICILY AS A WARTIME LEADER 189

86. ACA, CR, R. 1566, ff. 131r–v; R. 1567, ff. 86–135; Kagay, "Shattered Circle," 124–25.
87. ACA, CR, R. 1566, ff. 108v, 176r–v; Kagay, "Shattered Circle," 130–31.
88. ACA, CR, R. 1536, f. 40bis; R. 1573, ff. 16v, 153v; Roebert, "Que nos tenemus," 263–65.
89. ACA, CR, R. 1568, f. 61, R. 1573, ff. 166v–67.
90. ACA, CR, R. 1569, f. 28; R. 1373, f. 190v; Ferrer i Mallol, "Tinença," 61 (doc. 18).
91. *Customs of Catalonia*, 2-, 5, 7, 20 (arts. 2, 5, 9, 22); A. M. Aragó Cabañas, "Las "tenentiae castrorum" del reino Valencia en la época ed Jaime II," in *Primer Congreso de Historia del Pais Valenciano* (Valencia, 1971), 569–70. For castle conteol, see *Usatges*, trans Kagay, 34–38.
92. ACA, CR, R. 1574, f. 94v; R. 1566, f. 81; Ferrer i Mallol, "Tinença," 3.
93. ACA, CR, R. 1566, f. 81; R. 1567, f. 72; R. 1569, ff. 27v–38v; Ferrer i Mallol, "Tinença," 60–62 (docs. 17, 19).
94. ACA, CR, R. 1387, ff. 19, 143v; Ferrer i Mallol, "Tinença," 7, 9.
95. ACA, CR, R. 1569, f. 108; R. 1578, f. 84; Ferrer i Mallol, "Tinença," 21–22, 62–63 (doc. 20).
96. ACA, CR, R. 1568, ff. 284–29; R. 1581, f. 118v; R. 1583, f. 178v. R. R. 1584, ff. 11–12v.
97. *Customs of Catalonia*, 60–61, art. 56.
98. ACA, CR, R.1569, ff. 22v–23; Ferrer i Mallol, "Tinença," 60 (doc. 16); Donald J. Kagay, "Defending the Western and Southern Frontiers in the War of the Two Pedros: An Experiment in Nation-Building," *Journal of the Georgia Association of Historians* 23 (2002): 77–107, esp. 89; idem, "Pere III's System of Defense in the War of the Two Pedros (1356-1366): The Aragonese Crown's Use of Aristocratic, Urban, Clerical, and Foreign Captains," *Studies in Medieval and Renaissance History*, Third Series, 7 (2010): 195–232, esp. 201.
99. ACA, CR, R. 1199, f. 404; R. 1210, f. 115; R. 1572, f. 2; Ferrer i Mallol, "Tinença, 63 (doc. 21); 66 (doc. 24); 67–68 (doc. 26).
100. ACA, CR, R. 1199, ff. 403r–v; R. 1566, ff. 158r–v; R. 1577, ff. 117r–v; Ferrer i Mallol, "Tinença," 21, 65 (doc. 23).
101. *Customs of Catalonia*, 2, 5, 7, 20 (arts. 2, 5, 9, 22). For castle conteol, see: *Usatges*, trans Kagay, 34–38.
102. ACA, CR, R. 1566, ff. 121v–22, 152r–v, 154; R. 1567, ff. 140v. 184v, 187; R. 1578, f. 53v.
103. ACA, CR, 1566, 153r–v; R. 1582, f. 92.
104. ACA, CR, R. 1537, f. 42; R. 1566, f. 154; Ferrer i Mallol, "Tinença," 68 (doc 27).
105. ACA, CR, R. 1566, ff. 158r–v; R. 1567, ff. 3v, 44v, 72, 129v; R. 1568, f. 53, 69v–70; R. 1581, f. 24v.

106. ACA, CR, r. 1566, f. 125; R. 1567, f. 107v; R. 1568, ff. 60v–61, 70v.
107. ACA, CR, R. 1567, f. 100v, 107; R. 1568, f. 28v.
108. ACA, CR, R. 1567, f. 73.
109. ACA, CR, R. 1568, ff. 34v, 47v, 55v–56v, 57–58v, 62v, 67–69, 70r–v, 72, 73, 76v–77.
110. ACA, CR, R. 1568, ff. 74–75.
111. Pere, *Chronicle*, 2:526–27 (VI:26); Zurita, *Anales*, 4:382 (IX:xxiv).
112. ACA, CR, R. 1567, f. 73v.
113. ACA, CR, R. 1568, ff. 2, 64, 66, 77, 78
114. ACA, CR, R 1567, ff. 66v, 107; R. 1568, ff. 13v–14, 71.
115. ACA, CR, R. 1568, f. 10v.
116. ACA, CR, R. 1568, ff. 46r–v, 52v–53, 62r–v
117. ACA, CR, R. 1568, ff. 11, 62r–v, 67r–v, 70v–71v.
118. ACA, CR, R. 1567, f. 123v; R. 1568, ff. 60v, 61v, 65v.
119. ACA, CR, R. 1568, ff. 3–4.
120. ACA, CR, R. 1568, ff. 10v, 47, 57v–58
121. ACA, CR, R. 1568, ff. 13v, 69v, 87r–v; Pedro Garcés de Cariñena, *Nobiliaria de Aragón* (Zaragoza, 1983), 170, 189.
122. . ACA, CR, F. 1568, ff. 1r–v, 5, 25–26, 30v–45v.
123. ACA CR, R. 1567, f. 83v.
124. ACA, CR, R. 1568, ff. 7r–v. Elionor expense scale per ship was the following: weapons, 2,000 libras; payment of crew of ten men for two months, 2,500 libras, fitting out two galleys of Narbonne. 2,500 libras; Loan to meet expenses, 3,000 libras; provisions including olive oil, vinegar, beans, cheeses, meat etc., 2,500 libras; Payment of money put up by Jacme dez Vilat, 1,000 libras; Salary for ten Catalan horsemen, 600 libras; messengers and mail, 700 libras; Interest for loaned money, 1,000 libras. Grand Total: 164,000.
125. ACA, CR, R. 1568, ff. 12r–v, 14v.
126. ACA, CR, R. 1568, f. 21v.
127. ACA, CR, R. 1568, ff. 23–24, 27, 30v–31, 36v.
128. ACA, CR, R. 1568, ff. 30r–v, 32r–v, 39v–40.
129. ACA, CR, R. 1568, ff. 23v, 24, 27, 30v–31.
130. ACA, CR, R. 1568, ff. 32v–34v, 46; Sobreques, *Barons*, 144–45.
131. ACA, CR. R. 1568, ff. 36r–v, 39r–v, 42v, 73v–74v.
132. ACA, CR, R. 1567, ff. 106–7; R.1568, ff. 23, 36v–37, 38, 40v–41v, 73–74.
133. ACA, CR, R. 1568, ff. 2–3, 15–16v, 17, 18–19, 22–23.
134. ACA, CR, R. 1566, f. 73v; R. 1567, 86v; R. 1568, ff. 45v, 47v–48, 50v–51, 61v.
135. ACA, CR, ACA, R. 1567, 101r–v; R. 1568, ff. 3–6v.

136. ACA, CR, ff. 13, 19–20v, 21v, 27v, 38r–v, 52r–v, 62. The breakdown for Gerona and its surroundings ran as follows: Gerona: 25 rowers and crossbowmen; Sant Feliu de Guixols: 3 seamen; Palomera,: 4 men; Campredon: 10 men: Figures: 10 men; Villages of the Count of Ososa, County of Empuries, Viscounty of Rochbertí and the lands of P. De Montcada: 3 men; Castles of Besalú, county of Osona and Empuries: 12 men; Castles pf the Vicarate of Campredon and Ripoll: 20 men; P. de Montcada: 10 men; Castle of Rocabertí: 15 men; Fief of Ripoll and Babares: 2 men.

137. ACA, CR, R. 1568, ff. 61v–62.

138. ACA, CR, ACA, 15, 17v, 24v; Mott, *Sea Power*, 218–24.

139. ACA, CR, R. 1568, ff. 13v–14, 15r–v, 17v, 21 v, 24r–v, 37v, 51.

140. ACA, CR, R. 1573, f. 13; R. 1574, f. 108v.

141. ACA, CR, R. 1534, f. 141v; R. 1547, f. 98v. For Valencian *Generalitat*, see José Martínez Aloy, *La Diputación de la Generalidad de Valencia* (Valencia, 1930); Font Rius, "Institutions," 176–77.

142. Pere, *Chronicle*, 2:542 (VI:37); *CAVC*, II:135–41; Donald J. Kagay, "The Parliament of the Crown of Aragon as Military Financier in the War of the Two Pedros," *JMMH* 14 (2016): 57–77, esp. 68; José Luis Martín, "Las cortes de Pedro el Ceremonioso," in *Pere el Cerimonióla seva época*, ed. María Teresa Ferrer i Mallol (Barcelona, 1989), 99–111, esp. 108.

143. *CAVC*, II:146–50 (art. 1); Kagay, "Parliament," 68; Martín, "Cortes," 108–9.

144. *CAVC*, II:168–70; Kagay, "Parliament," 68–69.

145. *CAVC*, II:170–80.

146. Ibid., 181–207; Pere III, *Chronicle*, 2:568–69 (VI:54); Kagay, "Parliament," 69.

147. *CAVC*, II:332–49; María Teresa, Ferrer i Mallol, "Les Corts de Catalunya i creació de la Diputació del General en el marc de la guerra amb Castilla (1359-1369)," *AEM* 334, no. 2 (2004): 875–939, esp. 918–28; M. Fibla Guitart, "Les Corts de Tortosa i Barcelona 1365. Recapte de donatiu," *Cuadernos de Historia Económica de Cataluña* 19 (1978): 97–121; Sánchez Martínez, "Negociación," 130–31.

148. *CAVC*, II:353–57; Fibla Guitart, "Corts," 100; Sánchez Martínez, "Negociación," 133–39; J.A. Sesma Muñoz, "Fiscalidad y poper. La fiscalidad centralizada como instrumento de poder en la Corona de Aragón," *Espacio, Tiempo y Forma* 1 [series III] (1988): 447–68, esp. 460.

149. *CAVC*, II:358–62.

150. ACA, R. 1206, ff. 22r–v; Sánchez Martínez, "Negociación," 158–59.

151. ACA, CR, R. 1208, ff. 33–34; Sánches Martínex, "Negociación," 141, 159–60 (doc. 3).

152. ACA, CR, R. 1208, f. 50v; Sánchez Martínez, "Negociación," 241–42, 160–62 (doc. 4).
153. *CAVC*, III:58–77; Kagay, "Parliament," 70.
154. *CAVC*, II:369–72; *Parliaments*, 27–33; Pere III, *Chronicle*, 2:572–73 (VI:57); Suzanne F. Cawsey, *Kingship and Propaganda: Royal Eloquence and the Crown of Aragon c.1200-1450* (Oxford, 2002), 116; Kagay, "Parliament," 69–70; Sánchez, Martínez, "Negociación," 145.
155. *CAVC*, II:372–76, 445.
156. ACA, CR, R. 1537, ff. 109v–10v.

CHAPTER 8

Elionor, a Personal Life

Despite the massive evidence of all sorts that remain to us, it is often difficult to draw an accurate picture of Queen Elionor. We have no portrait from which we can ascertain her appearance. The only remaining image of Pere III's third wife is the seal with which she marked many of her documents. This crucially important implement was made of red wax and shows the queen as a young and fairly slender woman standing before a canopy with the shields of Aragon and Sicily on either side. A circular legend runs around the edge spelling out her various titles in the following way: ALIENORA DEI GRA[CIA] REGINA ARAGONUM, VALENCIE, MAIORICARUM, SARDINIE ET CORSICI, COMITIS-SAQUE BARCHINONE, ROSSILIONIS ET CERITANIE.[1] This image which represents the power Elionor exercised gives us only an official representation of the woman this book deals with. To glean a fuller picture of the queen, we must look at her husband's view of a wife he clearly appreciated, whether he loved her or not. We can then apply this indirect form of assessment to the relationship she had with her children and her Sicilian siblings, the members of her court and household, the many religious charities she engaged in, the several building projects she took so much interest in second half of her reign, and finally to the entertainments she so clearly enjoyed. In this way, we can attain a much brighter view of the human being than her official image.

© The Author(s), under exclusive license to Springer Nature   193
Switzerland AG 2021
D. J. Kagay, *Elionor of Sicily, 1325–1375*, The New Middle Ages,
https://doi.org/10.1007/978-3-030-71028-6_8

194   D. J. KAGAY

1   THE CORONATION AND ELIONOR'S CHANGING ROLE AS QUEEN

While the ceremony was late in coming to the Crown of Aragon, by the thirteenth century, an unbroken line of such royal rites began and stretched down to Pere III and beyond. The ceremony was consistent until the fourteenth century, made up of several days of rites that began with an all-night vigil after which the sovereign was made a knight. Then the king-to-be came before a group of prelates who anointed him with holy oil and then gave him two of the principal symbols of his royal authority, the orb and scepter. Finally, the metropolitan of Catalonia or Aragon, either the archbishop of Tarragona or Zaragoza, performed the most important act of the ceremony, the placing of the crown on the king's head. Thereafter, the man who might serve in that post for months or even years, now officially held the title. His first act was to swear to all his realms that he would protect his subjects and their laws. This ceremony normally took place in the great castle and gothic cathedral at Zaragoza.[2]

The standard for the Aragonese coronation during the first thirteenth century was set outside of Aragon and even outside of Spain when Pere I was crowned as Aragonese king in 1214 by Pope Innocent III (r.1198–1216); he had the ceremony repeated at Zaragoza in the next year. The difficulty with this movement toward coronation was that it had established an unfortunate precedent of making the Aragonese sovereign the pope's vassal. Since Jaume I, Pere I's son, had spent so much of the first part of his reign in establishing the royal authority, he shied away from coronation because of the limitations it could impose on his power.[3]

Despite the actions of the Conqueror, the rites by which Aragonese kings were made had come into full operation by the time of Jaume I's death in 1276. His immediate descendants, however, starting to make seminal changes to the rites which in themselves altered the king's role and made room for his queen. Perhaps under the influence of his bride, Constanza, Pere II, Jaume's son, did not avoid coronation, undergoing it "with honor and great solemnity" on November 15, 1276, at Zaragoza[4] Like his father, though, the prince complained about a crucial part of the rite he was about to undergo—his physical crowning by the archbishop of Zaragoza. Though he allowed this part of the ceremony to go forward, he was clearly not happy about it, and moved to prevent any legal prejudice to his successors by the archbishop's formal placement of the crown on the new king's head. Pere did begin changes to the rite. Indeed, he did crown his wife, a Sicilian princess, who like Elionor, had extremely strong feelings about her royal title to her island homeland.[5]

Alfons II shared his father's concerns when on Easter, April 14, 1286, he was crowned at Zaragoza by his cousin, Bishop Jaime of Huesca. He, too, accepted the crown from his cousin, but disallowed any clerical over-lordship. Instead, he accepted the crown "neither from the Church nor against the Church." The ritual act would thus not be prejudicial to his successors.[6] Jaume II, Alfons's brother, had served as king of Sicily from 1285 and when he acceded to the Crown of Aragon in 1291, called the Aragonese to a *cort general* which met on September 24–26 at the Cathedral or San Salvador in Zaragoza, hosting 112 Aragonese nobles and representatives from twenty-five cities and towns of the realm. On the first day of the assembly, Jaume attained his second kingship by passing through a rite about which he made few complaints. After receiving the crown, he swore to uphold the "good estate" of the Crown of Aragon.[7]

Alfons III, the son of Jaume II and hero of the Sardinian campaign (1322–1323), carefully planned his coronation in a way that showed that he and the not the church was fully in charge. The days before the ceremony were filled were jousting and other entertainments engaged in by the vast number of knights. The new knights Alfons had recently dubbed expanded the throng of great men who several days before the coronation engaged in mass combats and even a primitive form of bull fighting.[8] If these entertainment elements were not enough, the king had much more to show his people when he took the crown.

The ceremony took place on April 3, 1328, in the usual site of the Cathedral of San Salvador in Zaragoza. One of the many guests, the great warrior, and chronicler, Ramon Muntaner, has left a very lengthy and detailed description of the ritual which the king had clearly planned out in some detail before it took place. On Holy Saturday (April 2), when it was getting dark, a massive crowd carrying candles and causing a thundering racket with drums and other noisemakers, moved from Zaragoza's great castle, the Aljafería, to the cathedral. The king had told the attendees to trim their beards and dress in their best apparel. This huge crowd, looking very much like an army from the great number of weapons its members carried, followed the king's horse as he moved toward the cathedral, just behind a wagon with five large burning torches attached to it. Like a

196   D. J. KAGAY

modern football crowd, this swaying audience kept up the din with staccato cries of "Aragon" and the names of the baronial houses from which many of the audience had come.

The very size of this raucous crowd was noteworthy but could not outpace the wonder of the ceremony to follow on Easter morning. As the Aragonese archbishop and his attendants readied themselves for mass by donning their rich vestments, Alfons put on similar clerical garb: a surplice and a luxuriously decorated royal robe (dalmatic) and the stole, a strip of colorful silk studded with "pearls and precious stones," worn exactly as the greatest clerics in the cathedral did–around the neck and over the shoulders. Before the service had begun, Alfons had his sword and crown put on the high altar, ready to be used when the rite reached its crucial point. During the Mass, the king signaled his son, Prince Pere, and nephew, Prince Ramon Berenguer, to each bring him one of his spurs to put on. He then took up the sword before laying prostrate before the altar. Then rising, he strapped on his scabbard, and removed the sword from it. He then brandished it three times against all his enemies and did the same to protect his defenseless subjects. The archbishop then proceeded to anoint the king's shoulder and right arm. After this, Alfons totally broke with tradition and, without the help of anyone, clerical, or lay, put a gorgeous and remarkably expensive crown on his head and then picked up the golden orb and scepter. In so doing, he had declared himself king.[9]

Since Pere III played an integral part in his father's coronation and the knightly ceremonies that proceeded it,[10] it is not unusual that he attempted to slavishly follow that path of coronation that his father had so skillfully laid out and the great chronicler, Muntaner, had described in such florid detail. With the death of his father on January 24, 1336, the new king began to prepare for his own coronation which traditionally would extend over Easter Saturday and Easter Sunday morning, which in that year fell on April 6 and 7. The complexities built into his new office, however, soon stood in the way of tradition. Since the young king had just fallen under interdict for not making an annual payment to the papacy which recognized its superior feudal position over Sardinia and Corsica, the king had to scramble to clear up this potentially disastrous beginning to his reign.[11]

Though this was rapidly settled, Pere was thrown into confusion by Catalan demands that he go to Barcelona and swear to uphold the *Usatges* and the region's other traditional laws. Pere quickly decided that the coronation was the first order of business and swore that he would not leave Zaragoza until it took place.[12] With all these problems solved, the coronation took place a week later in the traditional sites within the center of the Aragonese capital. Mimicking the movements of his father from eight years before, Pere crossed from the Aljafería to the cathedral of San Salvador with a number of prelates from Aragon and Sardinia as well as his closest baronial advisers. When they entered the ecclesiastical building, the king went before the large altar and began to pray "with great devotion." After some hours of this, his elder companions left the twenty-year-old monarch to sleep in the sacristy and then spent the rest of the night "joyfully singing and playing games."[13]

On the next morning, as the clerics were preparing for Mass, Pere dressed himself with the type of vestments his father had worn at his coronation, including a richly decorated dalmatic robe and a stole. He had admitted his concern that the rapidly approaching ceremony could be plagued with "great perils and many scandals," and, as it turned out, he did not have long to wait for these to materialize. When the Mass was about to begin, and all the principals were probably still in the sacristy, the archbishop begged for the reestablishment of the traditional element in the ceremony, which would allow him to take up the crown and place it on the king's head. Pere would not hear of it and his advisers considered it prejudicial to royal power. Looking for any kind of fall-back position, the churchman begged to be able to straighten the crown once Pere had placed it on his own head. Looking for a facile compromise, Pere agreed, knowing full well he was shortly going to go back on his word—an unfortunate trait he was justifiably known for throughout his reign. After they had all come out of the sacristy, the king bluntly informed the prelate that neither he nor anyone else "of any rank" would touch or help the king with the crown. Like his father, the newly minted king put on the crown and then took up the orb and scepter, slowly left the cathedral, mounted his horse, and rode at the head of a large procession to the Aljafería. There the celebration went on for several days, Pere keeping the palace doors open for anyone who wished to enter and dine. According to his officials, 10,000 visitors availed themselves of this opportunity within the first day of royal generosity.[14]

What does this small history of Aragonese coronations actually have to do with Pere III's view of himself as an Aragonese sovereign, and for our purposes, how is Elonor or any other queen of the Crown of Aragon

198   D. J. KAGAY

connected to this crucial change in the structure of royal power posited by the striking changes inserted into coronation practices of the Barcelona's dynasty in 1328 and 1336. Both queries take us into Stephen Greenblatt's concept of "Self-Fashioning," which attempts to determine how the identity of individuals and the influence of authority inter-act in creating new identities, and from them, new institutions.[15]

Pere III, as a reader of history and profound admirer of many of his predecessors on the Aragonese throne like his great-great grandfather Jaume I and great-grandfather, Jaume II, spent much of his adult life in trying to bring about changes in his personal identity and in that of the cluster of realms he inherited and those he brought under his control after becoming king. As far as coronation went, his actions at Zaragoza in 1336 were hardly revolutionary, but replicated very closely the actions of his father in 1328, which did not guarantee a change in Aragon's coronation norms, since his two sons, Joan and Martí, could very easily have gone back to the old ways of becoming king. This was to be prevented by a general guide, published in 1353, of how all future Aragonese coronations would be conducted. This directive, entitled "An Ordinance Made by the Most Distinguished and Excellent Prince and Lord, Sir Pere III, King of Aragon, Concerning the Manner by which Aragonese Kings shall be Consecrated and Crown Themselves" (*Ordinació feta per lo molt alt e molt excellent prícep e senyor lo senyor en Pere Terç, rey d'Aragó, de la manera con los reys d'Aragó e faran consagrar e ells mateys se coronaran*), made certain that future coronations would not be carried out according to the will of each individual Aragonese sovereign, but instead in line with the ceremonial directives laid out by Pere himself for all future generations to follow. The ceremonial whim of Alfons III and his son had now become a ritual norm.[16]

This type of making official what had always simply been customary was not new with Pere III but, in many ways, marked his reign. More than merely a "friend of ceremonies and etiquette," the king repeatedly attempted to make the unregulated in administration, the history of his realms, the functioning of kingship, and feudal lordship in his realm fully regulated. His well-earned nickname, "the Cerimonious," reflects an intellect that was hardly the home of the new and untested, but one that recognized good ideas of others and attempted to make them part of the intellectual and political inheritance he left to his successors.[17]

With a mind often busy gathering ideas which would later be incorporated into much larger intellectual structures, Pere III's involvement of his wife in the new norms of coronation commenced by his father and formalized by his own efforts is hardly surprising. What is surprising, however, is that it took so long to draw one of his mates into the new coronation norms. After all, when Elionor came along, Pere had already gone through two wives, the first of whom had given him healthy heirs, albeit female ones. Neither, however, from the happenstance of what children they bore or the undreamt of results of a pandemic, proved suitable for the crown. Elionor, the mother of two healthy boys within the first seven years of marriage, however, proved a perfect candidate for the arena of coronation, an honor that very few Aragonese queens received, despite the ruling of Pope Innocent III in 1205 that queens were as worthy of coronation honors as were their royal husbands. If this was true, however, only one other queen in the Barcelona dynasty, the other Sicilian, Constanza, had received the honor.[18]

This expression of royal honor only came to Elionor after the birth of her first son, Joan, on St. John's Day (December 27, 1351). In the next few months Pere, his wife, and young son traveled to Zaragoza, Barcelona, and Valencia where the heir-apparent received oaths of allegiance from his three future realms. The king had intended to have this ceremony during the Aragonese *cortes* called at Zaragoza in the beginning of September but was forced to put it off for unspecified "just reasons and causes." Many of those planning to attend were now invited to be in Zaragonza on September 5 where they would tender their oaths of allegiance to his son. Since the prince was barely six months old, Pere planned to speak for his son and accept the oaths of allegiance tendered to him.[19]

Though the queen was not mentioned in regard to the September 5 meeting, she certainly knew that the king was planning her "happy coronation" because throughout the preceding summer she repeatedly asked her Aragonese and Catalan towns for help in financing the celebrations that would accompany the ceremonies in honor of herself and her son.[20] Pere was also planning for the great event. In early April, he wrote the archbishop of Zaragoza, asking that he obtain from the papacy the "apostolic indulgence issued concerning the coronation and anointing of the Aragonese king."[21] He also wrote to a Jewish silversmith of Lerida to produce a new, extremely lavish crown, orb, and scepter for his wife. After serving in the queen's coronation, the crown was pawned in 1363 to meet war expenses.[22]

Joan's crowning ceremony and that of his mother probably both took place on September 5 in the cathedral of the Holy Savior (San Salvador) in Zaragoza shortly after the Aragonese *cortes* had convened. The crown prince remained so interested in the oath of allegiance rendered to him in the 1352 ceremony that after his father's death in 1387 he had his protonotary sift through the archives, presumably so the Aragonese could take the same oath to Joan that they had with Pere.[23] Though no contemporary documentary record of the coronation ceremony of the queen and her son survived, several mentions of the rite are found in Pere's letters of the time.[24]

A complete record of the ceremony of September 5, however, appeared in the ordinance published on January 20, 1353, which used the coronation of the preceding year as an updated version of the Aragonese ceremonial of 1200.[25] In the profusely illustrated document, Elionor is shown surrounded by the archbishop of Zaragoza and other clergy kneeling before her husband who is carrying out her anointment and coronation. Like her Sicilian predecessor, Constanza, she was formally endowed with the symbolic power of the crown and the ruling implements which reinforced his own claim to royal power. As Pere III explained in his ceremonial, his queen's new crown represented much more than the precious materials it was made or the sublime workmanship that brought it into being. Instead it signified the limitless authority which all royals had in doing good for their people.[26]

From one point-of-view, while expressing his appreciation for his wife's presentation to him of a healthy son, Pere III's coronation of his wife reinforced his own power. The rite also implied the political and administrative partnership that Elionor had formed with her husband. He recognized this union on eight occasions between 1358 and 1374 by granting his wife the authority of the lieutenancy general. The coronation was indeed an honor that greatly pleased Elionor because it stated undeniably how important the king thought she was. In 1381, six years after her death, however, the king granted the same honor to the "unscrupulous and beautiful widow," Siblia de Fortià.[27] The reasons for the two ceremonies were clearly different. There could be no comparison between a hard-headed administrator and a play-girl of Aragonese court society. Yet, they both engaged in persistent "self-fashioning." One attained the royal identity she had sought for decades, while the other with little apparent effort occupied Pere's bed, but was never taken seriously as queen.

Elionor, like Constanza, came from the political cockpit that was medieval Sicily. Before her whirlwind marriage and departure from the land she had always called home, the princess harbored a wish that she could follow her father as the next Sicilian king, and never gave it up through her entire career as Aragonese queen until she was in sight of her death. This long-lived and quite emotional desire to become the royal head of her family was not to be, but it spurred her success as wife, mother, and administrator in the new realms that she would call home for over two decades. Her persistence and unwavering self-confidence as a princess provided the fuel for advancement from a successful wife and mother to a ferocious defender of her evolving political position who could prove a dangerous adversary for such power-brokers as Bernat Cabrera, Enrique de Trastámara, and even her husband himself. The drive for control in her Sicilian family impelled Elionor in very much the same way in her Aragonese life. For the queen, then, "self-fashioning" was hardly a new thing, but a drive for power that she refashioned in her adult years.

2   Elionor and Her Two Families

As we have seen, Elionor's Sicilian family was largely composed of weak men and strong women. After the death of her grandfather, Federico III, in 1337, the male holders of royal authority were weak in carrying out their duties, often because of ill-health. The only powerful male ruler she knew was her uncle, Duke Giovanni of Athens and Neopatria, who held together Sicily's royal government until the late 1340s. Her brothers, Ludovico, and Federico, who served as Sicilian kings, were both sickly and weak-willed. Though Elionor never saw them again, she never ceased her mail connections, which continually advised them to stand firm against the baronial cliques that dominated Sicily at the time. Her sisters, Constanza and Euphemia, were women of character like the Aragonese queen, taking much the same role as she did in advising and representing their Sicilian family. They both served as regents before their royal brothers came of age. Two other sisters, Beatrice and Blanche, married; only the first, however, had a child. After moving to eastern Spain, Elionor saw none of her relatives again, except for Beatrice, Euphemia, and Violante, as well as the illegitimate sons of Ludovico.[28] As the years passed, she was effected by a deepening homesickness to see her dwindling family and the homeland she still loved.[29]

While Elionor's relations with her own family are much better documented, the written sources leave large gaps in discerning her true feelings for her husband and their three surviving children. Her emotional connection to her husband, who also happened to be her uncle, is not revealed to any depth by surviving love letters or communications of any kind that would show their true feelings for each other. The only hint at such emotional connections rests in the written greetings of the many official letters that passed between them. The queen thus repeatedly refers to the king as her "most dear husband and lord," and the king responds by referring to her as "our most dear wife united to us by a conjugal bond" or "our most dear consort." In the formal communication between the two, we find nothing that directly reveals more intimate feelings. Pere's wild happiness is apparent at the birth of his first son and only daughter.[30] We see the queen's fear and concern for her husband during the naval war of 1359 and the Valencian campaigns of 1364–1365. Her happiness and appreciation was clearly apparent during the 1352 coronation. In most other descriptions of their relationship, their feeling for each other are either not expressed or only come through indirectly.

As was usual in most royal courts in the later Middle Ages, a distinct disconnect often existed between a queen- mother who maintained her own court and her children who were quickly packed off to separate quarters, complete with wet nurses, tutors, and a complete miscellany of other servants. With Pere and Elionor, their firstborn, Joan, seemed destined to accede to a brilliant royal career, but for his lackluster and unassuming personality. In the first weeks after her son's birth, the queen seemed a prototypical new mother who spent 40 *sous* of Barcelona to buy her son a silver teething ring surrounded with a small circlet of silver bells as well as a large number of silk outfits of various colors.[31] The queen seemed drawn back into her own Sicilian upbringing by feeding her little body *nocatuli*, a Sicilian type of pablum made principally from almond powder, water, rice, and sugar.[32] Within three weeks of his birth, Joan was taken into one of the large chamber in the royal palace at Perpignan and underwent a ceremony—probably seemingly interminable to him—by which he was declared duke of Gerona and count of Cervera. When he reached his fifteenth birthday, he could claim this valuable territory as his own, but until that time it would be controlled by his mother.[33]

Before he was four, the young prince was trundled off to Gerona with a corps of nannies, servants, and advisers. He was to stay there every summer between July and September. Even before that, much to

Elionor's opposition and disgust, her young son was largely under the control of her husband's principal adviser, Bernat de Cabrera, who would remain as the prince's mentor until his fifteenth birthday.[34]

As the Gerona summer vacations continued over the next few years, the king and queen received reports on the crown prince's health and intellectual advancement. In late July 1354, the king's governess, Catalan de Llança reported that her charge, despite an earlier fever, had arrived at Gerona "in sound and good disposition of his person."[35] In the next year, the crown prince, entering his fifth year, began to ride and was given a wax seal to mark the letters he would soon be dictating and writing for himself. This process that would mark the rest of Joan's life was already in operation when he sent his mother a letter. We do not know the text, and yet the overjoyed reaction to the missive by the king and queen was immediate. Elionor inserted the precocious epistle in a letter to her husband. He joyously responded to his wife that he was pleased to receive the dictated note which presaged an increase and growth of his [son's] person and understanding. Soon, the king predicted, he "will know things that are pleasing to God and to us."[36] By 1356, Joan's first governess, Cathalan de Llanca, had died and was to be replaced by another, Constanza de Puigvert, who would now be in charge of Joan and his new baby brother, Martí. When the crown prince reached his sixth birthday, his mother gave him a "silver saddle" to recognize his new skills as a horseman.[37]

As Joan moved into his teenage years, his mentor, Cabrera had less control and influence over the crown prince, who now began to take up the rule of the territories of his duchy and county. In the meantime, the king had introduced his son to various types of hunting, a pastime that he soon became adicted to and would remain a dominant activity throughout his adult life, thus providing his royal nickname, "the Hunter" (*el Caçador*). Joan also became a devotee of chivalric literature and an employer of countless troubadours. He was also all but mesmerized by the influence of astrology, spending a great amount of money on astrological books and practitioners of a science that both he and his father thought essential to royal success.[38]

With the establishment of these interests which occupied Joan for the rest of his life, it became obvious as the crown prince grew toward adulthood, that a great royal career did not await him. He disappointed his father for his lackluster military showing in the conflict with Castile and his mother for his administrative carelessness and the unbridled drive to exact from the Jewish and Muslim *aljamas* he ruled over uncustomary amounts of money for uncustomary reasons. Despite his failings, the duke of Gerona did not often prove dangerous to his royal parents, but, instead, could be relied on to carry out some of the more unpleasant tasks they assigned to him, but often only after firing a battery of complaints at them. After Joan's mother finally broke the power of her long-time enemy, Bernat de Cabrera, by putting him on trial for treason in 1364, and influencing a guilty verdict from a tribunal that she headed, the queen seemed to enjoy the last drop of vengeance by ordering Joan to carry out the punishment phase of the trial. Though the crown prince had been a close friend of Cabrera and his son, the count of Osona, he did very little to help the accused father and son, but put off his tutor's death for some weeks, despite being inundated with many letters "under secret seal" from his increasingly exasperated mother who time and again called for her enemy's execution. In the end, however, Joan, never strong enough to hold out against his mother for long, had his adviser of many years executed on July 26, 1364, at Zaragoza.[39]

When Joan finally married on December 17, 1370, his mother had hopes that her first son would eventually grow into his role as king. His queen, the French princess, Matha de Armagnac, was of such a sweet character that both of her in-laws loved her dearly.[40] Although Joan still feared opposing his father, he seemed more than willing to disagree with his mother by talking down to her in a way that probably infuriated her. When in 1371, he received a letter from his in-law, Count Joan I of Empúries, asking for help in imprisoning his wife, Elionor's sister, Blanca, the crown prince immediately started talking like an adult to his mother. He warned her to think before she acted if she wanted to maintain her offices and really behave as a helper to her sister. Shortly after this when his mother told him that her fever and serious cold had not improved, he seemed to finally understand his mother's frailty. Later when he heard that his mother's condition was better, he actually seemed overjoyed and begged Elionor to take better care of herself. His leave-taking shows in some way the emotion his mother's illness had brought out in her son: "Lady, your humble first-born, kissing your hands and feet, commends himself to your grace and blessing."[41] Finding out how really sick she was from her servants, the crown prince told his mother how truly sorry he was about her condition. If she would only watch what she ate and stay away from "foods that are contrary and not profitable," her life would be extended and, as Joan said, to his mother, "your life is very important to many men, especially to me."[42]

Even though Elionor did not live to see her first son wear a crown, she surely knew what her adopted cluster of realms would be in for. From his laziness, disinterest in government, and pointless stubbornness, Joan as king earned the stinging nickname, "the Neglectful" (*El Descurat*). Despite his poor royal reputation, he would take a second wife, Violante de Bar, in 1380, who surely must have reminded him of his mother. From her "forcefulness, decisiveness, and political savvy," the new queen quickly attained the post of lieutenant general and did everything possible to override her husband's all too obvious "indecision, laziness, and stubbornness."[43]

Because of their age or ill-health, Elionor's other children were not as often in her correspondence as Joan was. Her youngest son, Alfonso, who died before his second birthday, is hardly mentioned at all. Her daughter and namesake, "the very beautiful creature" who caught the eye of Enrique II's son, Juan, is known much more from her life in Castile than as an Aragonese princess. Only a few incidents tie the queen to her daughter. In 1367, after Enrique II's loss at Nájera and his escape into France, the fugitive's chancellor led his family on a harrowing journey out of Castile and into Aragon. Elionor was completely caught up in these frightening events since her nine-year-old daughter, even then the intended of Prince Juan, was in this party.[44] Despite the princess's long engagement with Enrique II's son, Queen Elionor increasingly opposed the match and did so down to her death. Pere III even seemed increasingly influenced against the union, but eventually gave into it because of the great money he had spent against foreign enemies and the faithful support long offered him by Enrique II.[45]

Elionor's second son, Martí, was clearly the apple of the queen's eye. Even her husband, who occasionally gave family matters short shrift, remarked that his wife loved Martí "with all her heart."[46] His stout frame and darker complexion reminded his mother of her Sicilian background, and unlike her other children, she seemed to actually enjoy his company. She was also very close to his intended, María de Luna, whose household the queen had managed since María was a very small girl. The queen watched over Martí and his bride-to be and provided a powerful example for both. As the duke of Montblach, Martí served both his mother and father in performing official duties such as escorting his sister, Elionor, to her wedding in Castile in 1376. Martí's mother spent a good part of

206   D. J. KAGAY

his early life in interacting with purchasing agents who worked to keep the prince's household supplied. As her death approached, she exerted as much pressure as she could to leave her second son all of her inheritance rights to Sicily. After his own son, Martí the Young died in 1309, Martí served as king of Sicily from 1409 to 1410.[47]

3   COURT LIFE

As the ultimate head of her own court and household as well as those of her children until they came of age, Queen Elionor faced an unending set of administrative duties every day. Though normally based in Barcelona, her court moved across Catalonia, Aragon, and northern Valencia, and on one occasion established itself on the rebellious island of Sardinia. This queenly establishment was the core of many other administrative lines. Money originating as revenues from the queen's urban vassals was then carefully accounted for by the royal administrative office of the *masetre racional*. Other officials then transported these funds sometimes over long distances in locked money-boxes on mule back to Elionor's court.[48] Because of this plodding life-line, the queen was frequently called on to pay for lost, stolen, or worn out mules and horses that served her officials.[49] A constant expense that was essential for the production and transport of messages, cost money on the front end with scribal fees and a set amount for each day it took for the messengers to make delivery.[50] While Elionor was normally at the mercy of the broader royal government for the funds that supported her own court administration, she occasionally went into business for herself by obtaining licenses from her husband or his officials to export wheat and barley.[51] She also borrowed money from Christian and Jewish moneylenders, finding some of them so essential to her finances that she hired them to serve as permanent functionaries.[52]

The queen's expenditures for matters large and small was watched over carefully by her treasurer and adviser, Berenguer de Relat, who taught her how money was to be spent and accounted for in Aragonese administrative circles. From this training, Elionor became a stickler for the issuance of payment orders and receipts in all transactions she and her officials engaged in. For one looking into Elionor's expenditures, the careful financial records of her court are a godsend. They reveal the expenses for short trips made by her porter, and the settlement of bills for the service of a court doctor, nanny of her children, trumpeter, troubadour, baker, falconer (along with the cost of a lost falcon), and doctor, as well as "sculptors and purveyors in stone."[53] Perhaps, one of her most important purchases—at least for her children—was 15 pounds of sugar candy and 20 pounds made from honey. Surprisingly, such purchases were listed with cosmetics and incense which may have been sold at the same shop.[54]

Many of the queen's purchases underlined the kind of court Elionor managed. Since her courtly establishment had little to do with the entertainment of foreign visitors and diplomats, it focused mostly on the table and other entertainments. Unable to equal the king's state dinners which accommodated up to 300 guests who consumed vast amounts of beef, chicken, bacon, eggs, bread, wine, and desserts,[55] the queen's courtly meals could only occasionally approach the level of her husband's culinary efforts with fine wine and interesting dishes. Although at times dining separately from each other, the queen sat down at the same table with her husband, especially when he was entertaining important guests. Though each court had different cooks, bakers, pastry chefs, and butlers, many of these could be combined for the larger occasions.[56]

Unlike Pere who, at least theoretically, attempted to set financial limits for the amount of wine and food consumed at this table, Elionor seemed to impose no such financial limitations on her table, regaling her guest with many different types of wine, plentiful loaves of white bread, several courses made up of domesticated fowl, eggs, hunted birds like crane, quail, pigeon, and partridge, salted or fresh fish, and other seafood such as cod, sardines, lobster, and squid, vegetables including Brussels sprouts, asparagus, greens, lettuce, peas, beans, and chickpeas. Elionor's cooks produced a number of sauces with the many spices and herbs she kept her kitchens supplied with.[57] Consulting with her kitchen staff, the queen planned most of the evening meals, often surprising her officials with specialties from their home regions. She spoiled her daughter, her husband's daughter, and perspective daughter-in-law with various candies, some from her own Sicilian homeland. Elionor utilized purchasing agents for all the courts she controlled. For supplying her table, this official, who was often away from the court in doing his duty, spent up to 250 *sous* of Barcelona a day on all the comestibles needed to supply the queen and her fellow diners.[58]

4   ELIONOR'S RELIGIOUS CHARITIES

One of the principal activities medieval queens engaged that was not always in tandem with their royal husbands was the support of the poor and of important institutions of the church, especially monasteries. Such activities are obvious in the careers of Iberian queens before and after Elionor. Alfonso X in his legal code, *Espéculo*, numbered as one of the key qualities of a royal wife a true sense of piety that would induce her to support the institutions of the church and care for the poor and unfortunate members of the realm. Castilian royal wives such as Leonor in the twelfth century and Berenguela and Violante in the thirteenth expanded cathedrals for the celebrations of new saints, founded and repaired monasteries, and regularly made donations to the poor and those afflicted by disease. María of Castile, wife of Alfons IV (r. 1416–1458), who served with a great political skill for long periods when her husband was fighting in Italy, made the protection of the poor and of destitute widows one of her prime ruling directives.[59]

A good deal of Elionor's non-committed money was employed in large sums through her chaplain or almoner in projects that were labeled by her court officials as "pious causes." Of these expenditures, the most regular were monthly payments to her almoner for feeding or clothing thirteen poor men or women during certain religious holidays. She also spent large sums on the decoration of local churches and the various chapels she had built in royal palaces throughout the Crown of Aragon. She filled the reliquaries of these edifices with expensive relics of Iberian and European saints and equipped them with candles and missals for the altars. Some of the royal money under her control also went to the repair of frontier churches that were often damaged during the war. Her money thus served to reestablish such institutions as true places of worship, but also to make them into points of defense against Castilian attacks. She also used her funds to build small chapels for her own use within the most important royal palaces.[60]

The queen utilized most of these religious funds to repair and expand monasteries from most of the principal orders. Some of these projects were so large and expensive that they could only be adapted to her budget by payment through installments. These enterprises normally came into the hands of the queen's almoner who distributed the pious funds once a year or every four months. The queen sometimes took up the donation process on her own, especially when she dealt with small monasteries or houses of lesser-known orders. This type of giving, which could apply to any worthy cause, was called a donation made "for piety or the love of God."[61] Elionor made many of these smaller grants (often under 100 *sous*) to monastic houses that belonged to orders that had a minor presence in the Crown of Aragon. These included the Augustinians, Carmelites, Cistercians, Dominicans, Mercedarians, and the Trinitarians, all of which were major monastic orders, but with a smaller footprint in Iberia. Surely the smallest of these organization was the "Order of Penitence of Jesus Christ," to which the Aragonese queen made only one tiny contribution, 12 *sous*.[62]

Some monasteries and convents scattered across the Crown of Aragon were the "pet projects" of Queen Elionor who took control of the funding of these sites without the help of her almoner. In these institutions, she engaged in large construction projects which took several years to complete. The most important of these were Santa María de Sixena, a Hospitaller site in the province of Lerida, as well as the monasteries of Santa Clara in the Aragonese cities of Calatayud and Teruel. The Aragonese queen's interest in this last site is demonstrated by the great amount of money she spent on moving the community and effectively rebuilding a new site in another location. Although one scholar attributed the founding of the monastery to Elionor in 1336, he also counted her as Pere III's fourth wife, but in both cases he was incorrect. The queen was not in Spain until 1349 and when she was in Iberia, she served as the Pere III's third wife.[63] There is some evidence that such an institution existed outside Teruel's walls, but had moved within the city walls from the early 1350s, and from that time stood as one of the Aragoese queen's principal monastic projects.

Elionor apparently informed Teruel's city council during this time that she wanted a monastery of the Saint Clares to be founded within their walls. The queen wished this action to be taken "secretly for our honor and service."[64] At about the same time that the queen had referred this matter to the urban authorities of Teruel, she broached the subject with the highest Franciscan official in Aragon on March 12, 1350. In turn, he sent several monks to the Aragonese city to instruct the women destined to serve in the monastery of the Clares. Though Elionor's part in this was kept secret, she and her treasurer had over 3,000 *sous* transferred to the members of Teruel's urban council without specifying how the money was to be used. This was the first installment of over 17,000 *sous* of Jaca designed for the Teruel institution.[65]

210   D. J. KAGAY

Not until the Castilian conflict petered out in 1366 did the Teruel project begin to reach some stage of completion. On May 8, when the fighting against Pedro I had completely died down, Elionor moved to have the monastery formally reestablished in the choir of the institution's newly build church. At this point, she regularly began to spend large sums of money to decorate the monastery buildings and establish a small library.[66] The institution began its new life when the abbess and her nuns formally took up residence on June 4, 1369. Most of them had come from northern Aragon and some had originated in the monastery of the Clares in Zaragoza. Though the Aragonese monarch was also involved in the Teruel project, it had originated and was carried to completion by his wife who continued pumping money into the monastery after its foundation in 1367. In the next year, she arranged to have annual grants made by the city of Teruel to the Clares and eventually had the revenues from the lucrative salt pits of Arcos turned over to the institution.[67] Never standing still with this project, the queen influenced Pope Gregory XI (r 1370–1378) to instruct the archbishop of Zaragoza to grant to the Clares at Teruel an annual sum of 100 libras of Tours. She transferred to the Teruel institution goods confiscated from those declared guilty in some legal suits and made occasional grants to serve its specific needs. From this generosity, the Teruel monastery regularly supported twenty nuns.[68]

From Elionor's first years of involvement with the Clares of Teruel in the 1350s, the members of the monastery did not forget their benefactors, the royal couple, offering prayers and masses for Elionor's parents and for the king and queen themselves. With the death of its stalwart supporter in 1375, the financial health of the institutions began to decline.[69] As with all of her religious charities, the queen was clearly moved by religious motives, but, in carrying out these projects, displayed time and again the same determination and people skills that made her a great administrator.

5   Elionor's Dream Palace

Queen Elionor's long support of churches, monasteries, and other religious institutions, some of which had been severely damaged during the long struggle with Castile, had given her invaluable experience in dealing with builders, a great number of craftsmen, and suppliers of construction materials. She had shown this clearly in her long involvement with the monastery of the Saint Clares in Teruel and several frontier churches in

Aragon and Valencia. Her connection as the feudal lady of many castles throughout the Crown of Aragon also led to a surprising understanding of how these structures were built and ultimately disintegrated. In effect all the buildings she was familiar with required the same skills and materials for construction and were all effected in much the same way by the peninsula's broad temperature ranges and varieties of liquid and solid precipitation as well as temperatures.[70]

Like many Iberian and other European queens, Elionor very quickly got used to the noise and filth associated with the seemingly unending repairs required to keep royal buildings safe and liveable. Since many of these structures had been put up in the twelfth century or before, they were often in need of extensive repair. As the fourteenth-century dawned, however, many of the changes in the royal families' edifices had more to do with new building styles than the complete shoring up of a decrepit site. Pere III and Elionor increasingly wanted privacy with doors that could be locked and windows that could be opened and looked through. This is not to say that they ignored extensive rebuilding in the Crown of Aragon's royal buildings. Not matter why such construction was necessary, the queen as royal administrator was invaluable in putting necessary building materials in the hands of skilled craftsmen. She was also adept at raising money and unskilled labor for such works from the communities in which royal palaces were located. In the 1360s and 1370s, she spearheaded such repairs in royal buildings at Huesca and Tarragona.[71]

Elionor's building projects that were closest to her daily life were those that effected the structures she lived in for most of her queenship. She had spent the first part of her royal career in what was called the "Old" or "Larger" palace in Barcelona. It was located in a square, the Plaza del Rei (Plaça del Rei), and still stands across from the cathedral (*Seu*), and the Palace of the Viceroys (Palacio de los Virreyes) which was the former location of the Archivo de la Corona de Aragón.[72] The palace which the queen lived in for the first two decades of her life was built on the site of an earlier Visigothic structure which from the late-eleventh century had served as the residence for the counts of Barcelona.[73]

Like the Tower of London, the Old Palace flanked by stretches of disintegrating Roman wall and surrounded by internal and exterior towers looked very much like a castle ready to defend itself in an impending war. Remodeled and repaired by his immediate predecessors, Pere continued this process by subdividing earlier halls around the central square of the building, converting them to a chapel and meeting rooms. The king also

212 D. J. KAGAY

had his bedroom remodeled with large windows from which he could see the Mediterranean. He also added a large chimney to warm portions of the living quarters. The king's greatest architectural achievement for the Old Palace was the "Great Hall" which served as a formal meeting site for the Catalan *corts* as well as a banqueting hall. It was completed with a ring of statutes of the counts of Barcelona and kings of Aragon. Pere also equipped the building with a storage site for his burgeoning archive and work rooms for his scribe. He also had secure rooms built for royal weapons and jewelry.[74] By the time Elionor arrived to take up occupancy, the Old Palace was most assuredly showing its age. It was cold and damp and her husband's repairs and remodeling did little to improve the crowded nature of the building which seemed to get more crowded every day.[75]

The king slowly decided that the aged palace was not worth the time and money to improve it and so started looking for another place to house himself, his wife, and children. He had hoped to build a new palace near the "shipyards (*drassanes*) and the harbor, but quickly found property near the sea too expensive.[76] After consulting with his wife, the king on January 30, 1367, bought the old Palace of the Templars which was eventually turned over to the Hospitallers. By February 1, Elionor hired Guillem Carbonell, a master builder, at an annual salary of 200 *sous* of Barcelona a year. She gave him the right to make all the necessary purchases for the project, but sternly warned him that "whatever was spent should appear in the [project] accounts."[77] The plot that the queen had bought would eventually be surrounded by terraces that were completely covered with greenery. The old complex also contained the Chapel of the Blessed Mary which was built in 1246.[78]

A year after the royal couple purchased the Palace of the Templars, construction began in earnest while the royal family began moving its possessions out of the larger palace which was now reserved for public use. During this time, Elionor began preparing for her own chamber by having her treasurer, Berenguer de Relat, take charge of a "large cauldron" which had been in the castle of Tortosa and have it transferred to the queen's new bathroom. Even before the construction commenced, the royal family had neighbors who occupied many of the small out-buildings of the complex. Interestingly, one of these dwelling would ultimately be occupied by Pere III' fourth wife, Sibilla de Fortía, after the king's death in 1387.[79] As often happens in such large-scale construction projects, the money set aside for repairing or tearing out ruined parts of the building complex was quickly consumed. New funds were forthcoming from the royal treasury, but Pere, being Pere, instructed the workers to save everything that could be reused. At the same time, his wife seemed more than happy to spend royal funds to pay the salary of her talented gardener and that of the men who made and buried upright 303 pillars to mark of the queen's newly planted garden.[80]

As the construction continued, the queen had a private chapel built between the main structure and the outer wall. On the upper floors, the rooms of Prince Martí, his intended, María de Luna, and Pere III's first daughter, Juana, were fashioned by closing in scaffolding and fitting it with a roof. The building's great Hall of the Knights was shored up and neighboring rooms were transformed for new uses, the most important of which was a large kitchen. After the church of the Temple was repaired, the queen had another chapel built near her own quarters. The king had a large space on the grand floor converted into his own rooms. This so-called White Chamber was fitted with broad windows, each of which was fitted with a seat. Not far from this, Pere subdivided the area into several offices for himself and his subordinates. Other rooms, fitted with shelves and tables, served as archive sites. The king also stored books and weapons in the same area.[81]

The furnishings in the palace were extremely simple and painfully utilitarian. People sat on stools and chairs that were precious only by their rarity. Only the queen enjoyed some little luxury in this regard with a beautiful and rare walnut folding chair. In many parts of the palace, closets were a rarity, normally to be replaced by chests, which also served the fortunate function of being seats for more than one person. Only the largest rooms were equipped with fireplaces and wall hangings to fight off winter cold. In these public areas, small tables stood here and there to provide room for reading more than for eating. As the night came on, the denizens of the palace carried burning tapers or were guided by wide candles in bulky iron holders.[82]

During the first years of construction, Elionor remained extremely busy in decorating the large rooms and her own quarters. In the last years of her life, she put her administrative skills to work by forcing a stone mason of Gerona to deliver long-awaited stone columns and seeing to the prompt delivery of 120 double beams and jousts. She employed one of her scribes in keeping a suitable record of the funds she laid out in the palace project and instructed her treasurer to see to the rapid payment of this important official. During this hectic period, she had attempted

214   D. J. KAGAY

to find a quiet place where she could continue her administrative career by ordering Berenguer de Relat, her treasurer, to have a "writing room" constucted in his own home. This site was to be equipped with tables and shelves that would accommodate copies of the documents they had finished or were in the process of doing so.[83]

When the queen was finally able to occupy her new quarters in the smaller palace, she slept on a canopy bed constucted from two mattresses which was closed in with three curtains. In the winter months, she slept under a fur coverlet. Her quarters included a small chapel as well as a wardrobe which contained some of her dresses. Many of the others may have been stored in one or more of the small houses in front of the Palace of the Temple. A pantry was also near to the queen's quarters. Despite all these improvements, the queen was never able to have the new latrines she wanted but had to rely on older privies. Even with all these changes within her new home, Elionor's attention very often seemed directed to her pleasure garden and the regular payment of the gardeners that tended it. In February 1375, a little over a month before she died, she arranged to pay a new gardener, a Sicilian at that, who drew a yearly salary of 300 *sous* of Barcelona. He was to prune all of the fruit trees so that when they would properly bear, and her servants could pick some of the product for use on the queen's table.[84]

After the queen's death, the smaller palace was finished with the construction of a great hall like that which her husband had built in the old palace. This project was carried to completion by the master builder, Jaume Landrich, between 1376 and 1378.[85] In its repaired state, the Palau Menor existed for another five centuries as the center of the Requesans family. By 1855, the palace complex had fallen into such ruin that only the central patio and the old chapel beside it were the only standing structures. The entire structure was sold the next year and converted into modern housing.[86]

Like her life with Pere III, Elionor's portion of the Smaller Palace was much smaller than her husband's, and in some ways on the periphery of their palace life. The queen had lived this kind of existence for many years, and from it gained a portion of control over her own life. She could now have space that was completely hers and away from the center of government that her husband dominated. Her autonomous space was close to her beloved son, Martí and María de Luna, his bride-to-be whom the queen also loved. It was also a center from which she could work in close harmony with her important advisers, a good many of whom were

Siciilian. From it, she could function as an important administrator in her husband's government. The true tragedy of the queen's dream palace was the short time she had to live there. From her occupancy of the site in 1368 she had under seven years to live there.

6   ELIONOR AS A PERSON

If as Robert Fossier explains, man is merely "an animated being who normally lives in an airy environment composed… of oxygen, nitrogen, and hydrogen," the question of when this upright mammal gains a personality is a question difficult for history to answer, especially in regard to humankind that lived or sometimes merely survived in the Middle Ages.[87] For Queen Elionor, we may try to fish the murky waters of Freud and Neo-Freudians, but would any of it be ultimately recognizable to the queen or the courtly world she lived in and often dominated?[88] Indeed, the concept of personality did exist in the high and later Middle Agers, but had more to do more with a representation rather what kind of person he or she was.[89] The noun *persona*, on the other hand, has a broad number of meanings which starts with the idea of a unique individual and proceeds to the appearance, identity, legal status, qualifications, standing and complex of personal traits which, in modern term, largely defines a personality.[90]

With Elionor and her husband's much revered great-great grandfather, Jaume I, the issue of personality is perhaps best explained by the modern literary and anthropological theory of self-fashioning which explored a broad complex of actions of every sort which past individuals engaged in to advance their reputation and position as a public person. Jaume I was a perfect example of this kind of individual advancement for the entire Crown of Aragon. An orphan who saw his father killed and dishonored at the battle of Miret (1214), he was a self-made man who rode victory in battle to a broadening glorious reputation while still quite young, portraying this success as the result of his "partnership with God."[91] In effect, his personal claim to "power and advancement" had much less to do with his actions than with the "works of God." and of "all the heavenly court."[92] This correct view of military glory made victory on the battlefield, especially if the enemy happened to be Muslim, one of many different types of "good works" a Christian could perform. This alone gave a man a "good reputation," and this alone is why he called for all

216   D. J. KAGAY

his successors to attend to their reputation by engaging in the good works of battle, even if victory was not their final result.[93]

This lesson of personal honor in furtherance of the importance of God was not lost on Queen Elionor. Even though she longed for political power and had done so before she left Siciliy, she all but immediately understood that these "masculine" ruling goals had to be suppressed, and replaced with the successful fulfillment of her role as a wife. When she carried out her wifely duties by presenting her husband with three healthy children in under a decade, Elionor immediately looked for new political accomplishments that were ostensibly in full service to Pere. As a talented administrator, she exercised power in a way she had longed to do before she had left Sicily. Yet, on the surface, her accomplishments were all in furtherance of her husband's authority and not her own. Yet, during the hectic and frightening naval campaigns of 1359, when the Aragonese king was away from his realms and in pursuit of the Castilian fleet, the Aragonese queen showed the full extent of her administrative talent. Like Jaime I, she had displayed her governmental skill, but in service of her marriage and her husband rather than for her own advancement. But for the sad case of Bertran de Cabrera, the queen's unsullied record as faithful wife and royal official would have escaped untainted from later writers who referred to Queen Elionor as the "image of evil" because of her central position in the Cabrera execution.

Because of her upbringing in what had become a minor and steadily declining, Sicilian court, her transfer to an Aragonese courtly organization which stood with Castile in the upper rungs of Iberian realms was very much a political, social, and cultural step-up. Spending much of her early life as queen at Perpignan and Barcelona, she was surrounded by extensive pleasure gardens which she never tired of and a number of castles and palaces that were colorfully decorated with all kinds of works of art. They were literate zones in which books and even state documents were readily available. All these accouterments of the royal life she had married into delighted the queen but the gardens large and small that queen walked through regularly seemed to please her the most.[94]

Though having lived a royal life for her first twenty-three years, the poverty and lessening power of the of her first family made Elionor especially serious about all kinds of jewelry, including regalia. Her concern is understandable since two years after she had left Sicily, she was still attempting to gain control of jewels that were still being held by the

Sicilian baronial officials or had been pawned by the Sicilian queen-mother. Though she produced a list of these precious objects, she never seemed to regain control of them.[95] Less than a year after her wedding, she made up for this bitter disappointment by buying, presumably from her operating funds, 60 large and small pearls, 32 sapphires, three rubies, and a golden statue of the Blessed Virgin Mary, the price of which came to over 3,000 *sous* of Barcelona. Not surprisingly after her earlier experience, the young queen insisted that the "jewels that we have bought and received justifiably" could just as justifiably be kept in her chambers.[96]

Like all royal families, that of Pere III and Elionor used jewelry and regalia to demonstrate their wealth, but also as a source of ready cash. The queen occasionally turned to pawning a portion of her jewels to gain money for some specific purpose. This was normally for only a short time and was carried out with Barcelona bankers, with which the queen had long-term financial relationships.[97] Elionor did not enter into such transactions from personal concerns, but because of her husband's desperate need. In 1357 and four years later, she pawned jewelry and crowns to raise the money Pere needed to pay his troops fighting against Pedro I of Castile.[98] As the queen got older and more careful, she had extensive lists of her valuables drawn up and checked before she pawned them. To ease her mind and free it for other matters, she increasingly gave her officials the responsibility of guarding her precious items of all sorts.[99]

Despite a growing obesity that Elionor suffered during and after her child-bearing years, the Aragonese queen was exceedingly well-dressed and was skillful at maintaining this reputation until her last years. The queen's wardrobe was extensive but was always evolving. The outer garments consisted of different weights of fabric used to produce winter and summer outer garments. The *cota*, a short type of outer covering; the *cota ardia* and *ajuba*, brightly colored doublets that often decorated with complex designs, were the principal types of clothing worn by women and men of the upper classes. The *cartapeu*, though like the other types, was an exclusively feminine garment. All these clothes were decorated with emblems fashioned from gold thread and were closed with pearl buttons. Those designed for winter were fringed with rabbit and ermine fur. Though the sleeves were normally simple, they could be fringed with silk material of different colors and billowed out to a broader circumference. For much of the early Middle Ages, only royals and those of the upper rungs of the nobility could afford this extremely elegant and busy apparel. From the thirteenth century, however, the wealthier townsmen

218   D. J. KAGAY

could afford to wear similar fashions and buy them for their wives and daughters. Despite royal and urban sumptuary laws that attempted to reserve the use of such fancy fashion for the circle of old power, the styles slowly radiated downward well into the fifteenth century. Internal garments, underwear covered with a "cloak" (*mantell*) did not undergo such expensive changes since they had no social statement to make.[100]

From only a narrow view of the queen's wardrobe in 1366, we can see how much of her budget went to the purchase of clothing and how clever she was in altering the dresses she already had. In the second half of her reign, Elionor continued to buy garments retail, but greatly increased her control over the price of her clothes by buying bolts of cloth directly, and then working with tailors who had long made dresses according to her design. In this way she attained completely new garments or renewed old ones. These changes grew increasingly necessary in her first decade when she went through four pregnancies and in the last decade as her stoutness increased. She utilized the same connections that provided for her garments to see to the production of clothes for her small children and shirts for Joan when he was a teenager.[101] She may even have influenced her husband's choice of garments when a cold snap in mid-November caught him without a coat and he ordered a peach-colored garment without fur to be made. Elionor had such good connections with the suppliers of many different colors of cloth that she quickly provided the specific material her husband preferred.[102]

The queen's most memorable garments were those she wore on memorable occasions. On September 5, 1352, she wore a silk dress decorated with gold embroidery which was covered with a red silk dalmatic that was fastened with four buttons made of gold thread. Except for its color, it was similar to the one her husband wore in the same ceremony when he put a crown on her head.[103] At the marriage of crown prince and Matha d'Armagnac on April 28, 1373, at the cathedral (*Seu*) in Barcelona, the groom's mother wore a blue silk *ajuba* decorated with pearls drawn out in an eagle motif, reflecting her coat-of-arms.[104] At Martí's wedding with María de Luna, on June 13, 1372, at the ancient church of Santa María del Mar in Barcelona, the Queen Mother wore a silk *ajuba* worked with gold thread and pearls in designs displayed in other gowns of the queen.[105] At her death in April 20, 1375, at Lerida, the queen was served by a shroud of 56½ inches of good linen.[106]

Queen Elionor's affection for beautiful jewelry and clothes points to a person who not only loved fine things, but also knew how to use their monetary value to support the realm she was married into and had long served. History has been unkind to Pere III's third wife in that it has left no certifiable portrait of the queen save for the seal image with which we began this chapter. On this official implement of 1349, the "regal figure stands in royal robes, wearing her consort's crown, her scepter in the right hand and the orb in the left."[107] Besides being an idealized image, the seal is also a political one. The only means of gaining some idea of the Aragonese queen's appearance is to look at her offspring, Joan, Martí, and Elionor. The appearances of Joan and Princess Elionor look a great deal like their father with sharp chins and narrow noses. Martí, the child that the queen "dearly loved," had a darker, Mediterranean complexion, a broad nose, wide-set eyes, and was stout from a young age. Her second child, might thus give the modern researcher an idea of the queen's appearance. Described as a slim and pretty princess by the royal ambassadors who helped arrange the Sicilian marriage, the queen, through the effects of four pregnancies in a fairly short time and perhaps the incipient effects of the kidney disease that ultimately cost her life, bore from the Barcelona populace the nickname "the fat queen." Her obesity increased as she aged, as did her sleeping disorders and kidney problems.[108]

Despite the steady advancement of her health problems, the queen was consistently carried forward by a vibrant spirit that served her well in private and public life. It is hardly clear if Pere III harbored any great love for his wife; what he did demonstrate was a repeated recognition of Elionor's intelligence, determination, and capabilities to gain what she wanted through direct attack or stealth. He increasingly depended on these talents, especially during his years of war with Castile and Sardinia when Elionor showed herself to be effective and dependable purveyor of desperately needed "food, medicines, and [other] provisions" to his armies.[109] There are hundreds of examples of the queen's governmental and courtly accomplishments, but what do they tell us of what kind of person she was.

Unfortunately, there are far fewer examples of what kind a person Elionor was. In some ways, her personal portrait is obscured by her. In some ways, her personal portrait is obscured by her official reputation. The darkest part of this record, the Cabrera affair, shows a women whose thirst for power and jealousy of her husband's most important adviser who was also put in a similar position with her first son made her a very skilled and ruthless enemy. Admittedly, her political drive and feeling of envy at having her role as a teacher of her first son led to actions that stained her reputation in her own era and in generations to come. As late as 1908, Salvador Sanpere i Miguel in his *Les Dames de Aragó* characterized both of Pere III's last two wives, Elionor and Sibília de Fortià., as the "image of evil" because of their underhanded political activities.[110] With the third queen, this assessment may be modified by the great loyalty she had to her family and to the Aragonese government for most of her life as queen. As Deibel points out, we are not able to tell when and to what degree, the queen's lingering illness affected her official and personal behavior.[111]

Because of the spotty record of the queen's personal life, we can make very few comments about her true personality except those that we have drawn indirectly from chronicle and manuscript sources. We know that she was a literate person from the great number of letters she read, commented on, and had sent out in her own name. She could also write, and occasionally included notes she had penned in larger missives prepared by her scribes. From the few books that are connected to her, she seemed to have an interest in medicine–perhaps reflecting her steadily advancing illnesses–and in religious works that she focused on increasingly during her later years, when her public piety was exercised for all to see. Her quick mind recognized those with greater stores of knowledge than her own and rewarded intellects such as Ferrer Sayoll and Bernat Metge. The latter, the author of *Lo Somni*, modeled his work after what he had seen in the queen's court and in that of her son Joan. In effect, what the poet wrote of was the steady disintegration of a government that Elionor had worked so hard to maintain and pass on to her descendants.[112] Can we attribute these failures to the third queen herself or were her efforts unable to overcome a mate whose cold and aloof character as well as his "absolute lack of scruples" cast a "tragic atmosphere" over the entire royal court.[113]

NOTES

1. ACA, COLLECIONES, Sigilografia, Sellos penpientes desprendidos, 285.
2. Antonio Durán Gudiol, "El rito de la coronación del rey en Aragón," *Argensola* 103 (1989): 17–37, esp. 34–37; Carmen Orcástegui Gros, "La Cornonación de los reyes de Aragón. Evolución politico-ideológica y ritua," in *Homenatge a Don Antonio Durán* (Huesca, 1995), 633–37, esp. 633–36; Bonifacio Palacios Martín, *La coronación sw los reyes de Aragón, 1204–1410, Aportción al estudio* (Valencia, 1975), 20–21.

8 ELIONOR, A PERSONAL LIFE 221

3. Aurell, " Strategies," 25–26; Durán Gudiol, "Rito," 18–20; Orcástegui Gros, "Coronación," Gros, "Coronación," 639–40; Palacios Martín, *Coronaciones*, 78–80, 299–301 (doc. 2).

4. *The Chronicle of San Juan de la Peña: A Fourteenth-Century Official History of the Crown of Aragon*, trans. Lynn H. Nelson (Philadelphia, 1991), 70 (chap. 36).

5. Jerónimo Blancas y Tomas, *Coronaciones de los serenísimos reyes de Aragón* (Zaragoza, 1864), 17–18; Durán Gudiol, "Rito," 25; Palacios Martín, *Coronaciones*, 78–80, 303–4 (doc. 7).

6. Durán Gudiol, "Rito," 26–27; Palacio Martín, *Coronaciones*, 122, 308 (doc. 12).

7. ACA, CR, R. 25, ff. 313–16v; R. 90, ff. 7v–8; Durán Gudiol, "Rito," 27; Palacios Martín, *Coronaciones*, 309 (doc. 13).

8. For early bullfighting, see: Elena Lourie, "A Fifteenth-Century Satire on Jewish Bullfighters," *Proceedings of the World Congress of Jewish Studies* 1 (1977): 129–139; Timothy Mitchell, *Blood Sport: A Social History of Spanish Bullfighting* (Philadelphia, 1991).

9. *The Chronicle of Muntaner*, trans. Lady Goodenough, 2 vols. (Nendeln, Liechtenstein, 1967), 2:716–26 (chaps. 296–7; Pere III, *Chronicle*, 1:168–69 (I:37–39); Aurell, "Strategies," 26–28; Aurell and Serrano-Coll, "Self Coronation," 78–79; Orcástegui Gros, "Coronación," 641–43.

10. *The Chronicle of Muntaner*, 2:721, 724 (chaps. 296–97).

11. Josep Rius Serra. "L'arquebisbe de Saragossa, canceller de Pere III," *Analecta Sacra Tarraconensia* 8 (1932): 1–63, esp. 10–12.

12. Pere III, *Chronicle*, 1:190–92 (II:3–5).

13. Ibid., 1:194 (II:8).

14. Ibid., 1:195–99 (II:15); Aurell, "Strategies," 28–29, 36–37; Durán Gudiol, "Rito," 31; Orcástegui Gros, "Coronación," 643–44; Palacios Martín, *Coronaciones*, 217, 243.

15. Stephen Greenblatt, *Renaissance Self-Fashioning from More to Shakespeare* (Chicago, 1980), 4–5.

16. *Ordinacions de la Casa i Cort de Pere el Ceemoniós*, ed. Francisco M. Gimeno, Daniel Gonzalbo, and Josep Trenchs (Valencia, 2009), 241–66; Aurell, "Strategies," 38–39; Aurell and Serrano Coll, "Self-Coronation," 77–84.

17. Kagay, "War," 2–79; Ferran Soldevila, *Història de Catalunya*, 3 vols. (Barcelona, 1934), 1:342.

18. Riera i Sans, "*Coronació*," 486.

19. ACA, CR, R. 1498, ff. 32–35v; Riera i Sans, "*Coronació*," 487.

20. ACA, CR, R. 1565, ff. 23r–v, 29r–v; 36, 41r–v, 44v, 53v; Riera i Sans, "*Coronació*," 488.

21. ACA, CR, R. 1066, ff. 29r–v; Riera i Sans, "*Coronació*," 488.

22. ACA, CR, R. 1571, ff. 98v–99; Riera i Sans, "*Coronació,*" 489.
23. ACA, CR, R. 1952, f. 57; Riera i Sans, "*Coronació,*" 490, ftn. 21.
24. ACA, CR, R. 1066, f. 103v; Riera i Sans, "*Coronació,*" 490.
25. Durán Gudiol, "Rito," 20–22.
26. Aurell and Serrano-Coll, "Self-Coronation," 85–88, 91–92; Riera i Sans, "*Coronació,*" 491; Marta Serrano-Coll, "Los signos del poder; *regalias* somo cumplemento a los emblemos del uso inmediato," *Emblemata* 17 (2011): 129–54, esp. 134.
27. Miron, *Queens of Aragon*, 196–97; Zita Rohr, "Lessons for My Daughter: Self-Fashioning Stateswomanship in the Late-Medieval Crown of Aragon," in *Self-Fashioning*, 46–78, esp. 49–48.
28. For further details, see Chapter 4.
29. Pere III, *Chronicle*, 2:590–91 (Appendix 2).
30. Ibid., 2: 456 (IV; 66; 2:518) (VI:18).
31. Joseph María Roca, *Johan I d'Aragó* (Barcelona, 1929), 1, 4, 9.
32. Ibid., 8, 421 (doc. 1).
33. ACA, CR, R. 1804, f. 21, Roca, *Johan I*, 5.
34. ACA, CR, R. 1145, f. 88v; R. 1538, 4v, 69; Roca, *Johan I*, 6, 419–20 (doc. 2).
35. Roca, *Johan I*, 21.
36. ACA, CR, R. 1148, f. 79v; Roca, *Johan I*, 22.
37. Roca, *Johan I*, 24–25.
38. Roca, *Johan I*, 25; Michael A. Ryan, *A Kingdom of Stargazers: Astrology and Authority in the Late-Medieval Crown of Aragon* (Ithaca, NY, 2011), 117–27, 138–47.
39. *CDACA*, 34: 275–76, 368–69; Pere III, *Chronicle*; 2:558 (VI:47); Roca, *Johan I*, 29.
40. Miron, *Queens of Aragon*, 209–11; Roca, *Johan I*, 66.
41. ACA, CR, R. 1735, ff. 6v–7; R. 1736, f. 30; Roca, *Johan I*, 162–63.
42. ACA, CR, R. 1741, f. 63; Roca, *Johan I*, 164
43. Bratsch-Prince, "Politics," 7–8, 14; Miron, *Queens of Aragon*, 214–16; Soldevila, *Historia*, 1:380.
44. ACA, CR, R. 912, ff. 165v–66; R. 913, ff. 222–23; F. 914, f. 166.
45. Pere III, *Chronicle*, 2:590–91 (Appendix 2–3).
46. Ibid., 591 (Appendix 3).
47. ACA, CR, R. 1567, ff. 27v–29; R. 1569, ff. 8v–9, 13v; Pere III, *Chronicle*, 2:591–92, 595 (Appendix 3–4); Núria Silleras-Fernández, *Power, Piety, and Patronage in Late-Medieval Queenship* (New York, 2008) 20-29-30; Tasis i Marca, *Pere el Cerimoniós*, 198.
48. *Quatre Llibres*, 99, 172, 182.
49. ACA, CR, R. 1567, f. 131r–v, 181v; *Quatre Llibres*, 97, 99–100, 148, 171–73, 175.
50. *Quatre Llibres*, 171–73, 175.

51. ACA, CR, R. 1567, f. 41.
52. ACA, CR, R. 1577, f. 177v; R. 1583, ff. 47, 164; Deibel, *Reyna Elionor*, 436–37.
53. ACA, CR, R. 1079, f. 73; R. 1563, f. 40; R. 2565, f. 127; R. 1566, ff. 81, 85v; R. 1567, f. 53v; R. 1568, ff. 32r–v, 38; R. 1570, ff. 85v–86; *Documents per l'historia de la cultura catalana mig-eval*, ed. Antonio Rubio i Lluch (Barcelona, 1908, 1921), 1:148, 209 (docs. 46, 214); *Quatre Llibres*, 179, 197, 201, 227.
54. *Quatre Llibres*, 105, 117.
55. María Carmen Carlé, "Alimentación y abastrciminto," *CHE*, 61–62 (1977): 246–341, esp. 279; E. Piedrafita, "La alimentación en Aragón en el siglo XIII: El modelo clerical y nobiliario," *RHJZ* 80–81 (2005–2006): 99–132, esp. 114.
56. Deibel, "Reyna Elionor," 402–3.
57. Deibel, "Reyna Elionor," 403; Juan Vicente García, "Alimentación y salud en la Valencia medieval. Teorías y prácticas," *AEM*, 43/1 (enero-junio de 2013): 115–58, esp. 135.
58. Deibel, "Reyna Elionor," 404.
59. María del Carmen García Herrero, "La dama modélica del cuatro cientos en la correspondencia del María de Castilla, Reina de Aragón (1416–1458)." *Cuadernos de CEMYR*, 23 (2015): 27–48, esp. 41; Vann, "Medieval Castilian Queenship," 126, 134–35, 142.
60. ACA, CR, R. 1537, f. 63; R. 1567, ff. 53v; 129v–130; R. 1574, ff. 4; 151, 168-r–v; R. 1575, f. 69; *Quatre Llibres*, 96, 108, 179; Deibel, "Reyna Elionor," 422–24.
61. Deibel, "Reyna Elionor," 424; Roebert, "*Idcirco*," 52–57.
62. Roebert "*Idcirco ad instar*," 66–69; *Quatre Llibres*, 179.
63. Roebert, "Leonor de Sicilia," 146.
64. ACA, CR, R. 1563, ff. 88–89; Roebert, "Leonor de Sicilia," 147.
65. Roebert, "Leonor de Sicilia," 148; idem, "*Idcirco ad instar*," 67.
66. ACA, CR, R. 1565, f. 34v; R. 1574, ff. 47r–v; Roebert, "Leonor de Sicilia," 148.
67. ACA, CR, R. 914, f. 97v; R. 1577, f. 106v; Roebert, "Leonor de Sicilia," 151–55.
68. ACA, CR, R. 1580, ff. 9r–v; R. 1583, ff. 108r–v; Roebert, "Leonor de Sicilia," 155–56, 158, 162.
69. Roebert, "Leonor de Sicilia," 164–65, 169, 171–72.
70. W.B. Fisher and H. Bowen-Jones, *Spain: An Introductory Geography* (New York, 1966) 130–31, 153–55, 172–74, 192–93.
71. ACA, CR, R. 1567, f. 176; R. 1575, f. 99v; R. 1580, ff. 12, 22.
72. Burns, *Society*, 24; Udina Martorell, *Guía*, 85–93.
73. Francesc Carreras Candi, *Geografia general de Catalunya. La ciutat de Barcelona* (Barcelona, 1916), 273–75; Stephen P. Bensch, *Barcelona and Its Rulers, 1096–1291* (Cambridge, 1995), 33–34.

74. Anna María Adroer i Tasis, *El Palau Reial Major de Barcelona* (Barcelona, 1979), 17–18, 31–33.
75. Ibid., 150–51.
76. Anna María Adroer i Tasis, "Un Palau Reial frustrat," in *II Congrés de Història del Pla de Barcelona*, 2 vols. (Barcelona, 1990), 2:135–43.
77. ACA, CR, R. 1575, ff. 47v–48; Anna Adroer i Tasis, "El palau de la Reina Elionor: Un monument desparagut," *Lambard: Estudis d'art medieval* 6 (1991–1993): 247–61, esp. 247–48.
78. Adroer i Tasis, "Palau de la Reina Elionor," 248.
79. ACA, CR R. 1579, f. 41v; Adroer i Tasis, "Palau de la Reina Elionor," 249.
80. ACA, CR, R. 1575, f. 176; R. 1577, f. 9v; Adroer i Tasis, "Palau de la Reina Elionor," 251.
81. Adroer i Tasis, "Palau de la Reina Elionor," 251–53.
82. Deobel, "Reyna Elionor," 411; Adroer i Tasis, "Palau de la Reina Elionor," 257.
83. ACA, CR, R. 1575, ff. 92, 105; R. 1579, f. 141; R. 1581, f. 158v; Adroer i Tasis, "Palau de la Reina Elionor," 255.
84. ACA, CR, R. 1584, ff. 1224-v; Adroer i Tasis, "Palau de la Reina Elionor," 253–54, 257.
85. Daniel Cid Moragas, "La respauració del desaparegut palau reial menor de Barcelona a través del llibre d'obrael cas de la sala major (1376–1378)," *Acta historica et archaeologica medievalia* !8 (1997): 397–425.
86. Pere Molas Ribalta, "El Palau Menor de Barcelona, center de sociabilitat nobiliária," 52 (2009–2010): 203–16, esp. 216.
87. Fossier, *Axe and Oath*, 2.
88. Sigmund Freud, *The Ego and the Id* (London, 1942); Abraham Maslow and Robert Frager, *Motivation and Personality* (New Delhi, 1987); Eugene Taylor, *The Mystery of Personality* (New York, 2009).
89. J.F. Niermeyer, *Mediae Latinitatis Lexicon Minus* (Leiden, 1976), 792.
90. Ibid., 789–92.
91. Robert I. Burns, S.J, "The Spiritual Life of James the Conqueror King of Arago-Catalonia, 1208–1276: Portrait and Self-Portrait," *CHR* 62 (1976): 1–35, esp. 10; Kagay, Jaime I," 103.
92. *BD*, 75 (chap. 52); Kagay, Jaime I," 103.
93. *BD*, 32, 84 (chaps. 16, 60); Burns, "Spiritual Life," 18.
94. ACA, CR, R. 1155, f 16v; R. 1179, f. 48v; *DHC*, 26–28.
95. ACA, CR, R. 1563, ff. 143, 144 r–v.
96. ACA, CR, R. 1563, f. 97.
97. ACA, CR, R. 1566, ff. 171v–72; R. 1567, ff. 187r–v.
98. ACA, CR, R. 1152, f. 172; R. 1197, f. 184; R. 1567, ff. 28v–29, 115v; *DHC*, 59–60.
99. ACA, CR, R. 1567, 28v–29, 37, 53v

8 ELIONOR, A PERSONAL LIFE   225

100. Aymerich Bassols, "Riques Vestidures," 25–30; María Isabel Gascón, "La vida cotidiana de tres reinas de la corona de Aragón s través de los libros de cuentas," *Pedralbes* 24 (2004): 13–54, esp. 26–27.
101. ACA, CR, R. 1742, f. 4; *Quatre Llibes*, 74; Aymerich Bassols, "Riques Vestidures," 41–42; Roca, *Johan I*, 264–65.
102. ACA CR, R. 1180, f. 124; *DHC*, 43 Aymerich Bassols, "Riques Vestidures,"42.
103. Aymerich Bassols, "Riques Vestidures," 33–34; Diebel, "Reyna Elionor," 413–14.
104. Aymerich Bassols, "Riques Vestidures," 34.
105. *Quatre Llibres*, 31; Aymerich Bassols, "Riques Vestidures," 35.
106. *Quatre Llibres*, 73; Aymerich Bassols, "Riques Vestidures," 40; Deibel, "Reyna Elionor," 393.
107. Miron, *Queens of Aragon*, 195–96.
108. *Epistolari*, 101; Ayrmerich Bassols, "Riques Vstidures," 38; Tasis i Marca, *Pere el Cerimoniós*, 92; Lorenzo Valla, *Historia de Fernando de Aragón*, trans. Santiago López Moreda (Madrid, 2002), 133.
109. Pere III, *Chronicle*, 2:485 (V:37).
110. Salvador Sanpere i Miquel, *Les Dames d'Aragó* (Barcelona, 1908), 15.
111. Deibel, "Reyna Elionor," 385.
112. Ibid., 385–87. For Metge as a government leader and the break down of the government he worked in, see: Donald J. Kagay, "Poetry in the Dock: The Court Culture of Joan I on Trial (1396–1398)," in *War*, Study XI, pp. 48–99, esp. 55–57; Alexandra Beauchamp, "Conseillers scélérats et mauvaisL le Roi d'Aragon, ses conseillers et le conseil à la fin du XIVe siècle," *Anales de la Universidad de Alicante. Historia medieval* 19 (2015–2016): 176–91, esp. 190–91.
113. d'Abadal. i Vinyals, Pere el Cerimoniós, 183–84; J.N. Hillgarth, *The Spanish Kingdoms 1250–1516*, 2 vols. (Oxford, 1976), 1:342–43; Kagay, "Treasons," 40; Tasis i Marca, *Pere el Cerimoniós*, 9–10.

CHAPTER 9

Elionor's Last Days

1 THE QUEEN'S FINAL SADNESS

At the end of her life, María of Castile, the most famous Aragonese queen of the fifteenth century, bared her sadness in a letter which talked of her "infirm body and unquiet solitude." In this missive that recounted her decades of royal service, the queen's pen seemed to reawaken the "sorrow and anger" caused by the long absence of her husband, Alfons IV (Alfonso V) (r. 1416–1458). She effectively stifled these feelings until the last period of her life when she foresaw a "great tribulation of the heart," that she could not avoid, but had to face, head-on.[1]

Although Elionor's husband was never away to the same extent as María's, the Sicilian queen met her fifth decade facing the same kind of impaired health and sorrow from a disintegrating relationship with her mate. At least in political terms, the royal couple seemed at the height of their shared power with the execution of the queen's main rival, Bernat Cabrera, in 1364.[2] After the shameful accomplishment of Cabrera's execution, the Aragonese king and queen began the long process of pulling apart from each other. In some ways, this divide widened because of their children. The crown prince viewed his mother as more of a rival than his father because the power she drew from some of her holdings stood in the way of his advancement in Valencia the realm he ruled over as governor.

© The Author(s), under exclusive license to Springer Nature Switzerland AG 2021
D. J. Kagay, *Elionor of Sicily, 1325–1375*, The New Middle Ages,
https://doi.org/10.1007/978-3-030-71028-6_9

227

An even more public disagreement centered on her daughter and namesake and a marital union with Prince Juan, son of Enrique de Trastámara, who eventually assumed the royal title of Castile as King Enrique II. This union had been in the works since the early 1360s. Though Pere held it up for some time in hopes of gaining from his prospective in-law long hoped for Castilian frontier land, fortresses, and towns, he eventually acceded to the nuptials. His wife, however, never seemed to trust Trastámara when he was her husband's captain and maintained this distrust when he became Castilian king. According to Pere, Elionor would not consent to the union because of her fresh memory of the "great trouble and harm" Enrique had committed against the Crown of Aragon. On numerous occasions, she thus still openly hated the Castilian king and "was furious when she even heard him mentioned."[3] Her opposition continued right up until her death with no real possibility of changing the marriage plans that went steadily forward. Pere and Enrique thus worked out some minor issues between themselves which led to a marriage agreement between Prince Juan of Castile and Princess Elionor of Aragon. The marriage between the two, who had known and were infatuated with each other since childhood, took place at Soría on June 18, 1375, some two months after Queen Elionor's death.[4]

In the last years of her life, Elionor harbored fond hopes of seeing her Sicilian homeland again, not as a tourist, but in company of a large armada that her husband was planning to unleash on the island to maintain at least some Aragonese control over it. With Federico IV's death in 1374, Sicily came under the tangential control of María, the daughter of Pere's own offspring, Constanza. To protect his granddaughter and his own claim to the island, Pere gathered a fleet of thirty galleys and twenty-four support ships. As this armada was being mustered, armed, and provisioned, the king, surely no Jaume I, a sovereign who had served as a battlefield commander until his death at age sixty-eight, eventually decided he was no longer "in condition to suffer [military] toils" and so cancelled the enterprise. Queen Elionor, who was overjoyed at the prospect of seeing her homeland again, suffered bitter disappointment when her hopes were dashed. This sorrow pointed unerringly to her death, even though her husband reported in his chronicle that his wife had dealt with this disappointment by "restraining her desire with patience."[5]

The passing of his wife of so many years in the spring of 1375 did not seem to affect the Aragonese king in any way, except perhaps with a sense of relief. Within a very short period, Pere III had found another love interest, the young widow, Sibilla de Forcía, who had become the elderly monarch's mistress before the end of 1375. Whether this relationship started before Elionor's death is not clear, but this was possible since Sibilla's first husband, Artal de Foces, was the queen's chamberlain, giving his young wife the possibility of access into both the queen and king's courts. By the late fall of 1375, the king's relationship with the young widow was obvious for all to see from the large grants the king had made to her. Whatever talents the young lady possessed, they did not include literacy or education of any sort. This did not stop the clearly infatuated Pere from marrying Sibilla and arranged for her a coronation ceremony identical to that which Elionor had enjoyed twenty-three years before. Though dead and buried, Elionor was not forgotten, especially when her replacement gained increasing public power by her husband's grant of a lieutenancy. Joan, especially, saw this action as a clear insult to his mother's memory and took out his vengeance on his father's fourth wife after he himself wore the crown.[6]

2   Last Days and Aftermath

The physical problems that eventually cost Queen Elionor her life began to manifest themselves in a lethal form in the last months of her life. In September 1367, she became extremely ill during a trip with her husband that forced her to put up at the Aragonese village of Pina de Ebro for several days. This kind of "wasting" (*magra*) was nothing new with the queen who seems to have suffered with intestinal problems since she was a girl. This "long illness" as described in her death notice, was most probably some form of what today is called Chronic Kidney Disease (CKD). This condition may have been complicated by her growing obesity which became apparent during her pregnancies and was seemingly passed on to her second son, Martí. As this disease seemed to increase in the last decade of her life, Elionor would have experienced a number of symptoms, but perhaps not at the same time. The most usual of these would have been decreased urine production, fluid retention, swelling of feet and ankles, shortness of breath, nausea, and a lessening of mental acuity. When this long-tern kidney condition intensified in the queen's old age–at least by medieval standards—Elionor very well may have faced a lethal case of nephritis which could have swelled her body and led to kidney failure.[7] If such an eventuality had occurred, the queen's last days which would

230   D. J. KAGAY

have brought death ever closer would have been marked by intense pain, diarrhea, and vomiting before she took her last breath.

Unfortunately, even with these possibilities, the details of Queen Elionor's last days are skimpy at best. We know that she died in Catalan city of Lerida on Friday, April 20, 1375, some two weeks after Easter. At terce (approximately 9am), she "returned her soul to her creator, dying after a long illness."[8] Pere III's official announcement of his wife's demise is even more clipped. Writing in his chronicle, the king simply remarked: "at this time, there passed from this life, the Queen, Dona Elionor, our wife and the daughter of the king of Sicily."[9] Though on June 12, 1374, the Aragonese queen had specified that she wanted to buried in the Cistercian monastery of Poblet "in the diocese of Tarazona," this wish was not immediately fulfilled and the queen was initially buried where she had died in consecrated ground at Lerida. Two years later in 1377, the king, for whatever reason, ordered his "deceased consort" to be exhumed from her crypt at Lerida by a monk of Poblet. This was only to occur after an apothecary of the city, who had perhaps served as one of the queen's officials, had examined her cadaver and reported back to the king concerning its condition. After this formality, the queen's body was moved to the monastery of the Saint Clares in Barcelona, one of the female religious houses she had supported during her lifetime. Only after seventeen years had passed did Elionor finally get her to wish when her remains were transferred to Poblet and she was buried to the right of her only husband. The foreign queen had finally entered the pantheon of Aragonese rulers.[10]

3   ELIONOR'S WILL

We hear of the Aragonese queen's will-making activity as early as 1365 when Pere III assured his wife and the executors she had named that the castles, villages, and rents that supported her court would be included in her will.[11] When this document was ready, its terms were formally proclaimed in the "large chamber" of the smaller palace on June 12, 1374, some ten months before her death. After specifying her executors, Elionor laid out their primary duties as taking possession of all her property and holding them until they were released to all the persons named in the document. If necessary, the executors could sell some of the queen's possessions. The resulting fund would come under the control of Berenguer de Relat, Elionor's trustworthy treasurer and adviser. A formal written version of the will was produced by the royal protonotary, Ferrer

Sayol, who returned one copy to the queen and had another registered in the royal archive.[12]

The first section of the queen's will contained a series of bequests to her husband and children. To Pere, she left two bolts of silk ornamented with gold and silver thread, a "certain psalter," an "apple of gold," a number of crosses, one of which was made of gold and "decorated with pearls and precious stones," as well as portraits of St Michael, Elijah, and Enoch which had been in her private chapel. The crosses were to pass down to the crown prince after the king's death. Elionor also bequeathed to her husband her palace and "pleasure garden, near the former headquarters of the Military Temple."[13]

To her first son, Joan, the queen left a golden case encrusted with pearls and rubies, which contained a sliver of the True Cross and part of the "Crown of Thorns of Our lord, Jesus Christ," an item his mother had received from the King of France. She also left him a golden *armorium* or host container, her canopy bed from the "White Chamber," which she had brought from Sicily, an image of eagles (her heraldic symbol) which she kept in her archive, the revenues of the Valencian towns of Alcoy, Barxell, Bocaryente, Biar, Lliria Gorga, Onteniente, and Travadell, one of her crowns of gold which was "better and larger...and "was made with pearls and precious stones." She also gave Joan and his wife, Matha, vases from her chapel decorated with portraits of Saint Michael and Saint Nicholas. These had also been in her chapel. Elionor may not have fully trusted her first-born and so warned him not to touch the Valencian revenues until her executors approved while specifying which of the bequests were to be shared with his wife and male heir if he managed to have one.[14]

The queen left to her "most dear son," Martí, a number of jewels used in her chapel, gold and silver chalices, and patens, a monstrance which contained precious stones in the shape of a garland, a silver box, a bed and its fittings, which, like that of the White Chamber, the queen had brought from Sicily, a wooden cross of the Lord from the queen's chapel, a gold cross encrusted with sapphires, a great emerald, four great pearls, and sixteen small ones.[15] Martí's sister, Elionor, received as her dowry 60,000 *libras* of Barcelona, the details of which were in her dowry agreement. This surely pleased the queen who had so much trouble in attaining her own dowry funds.

She would also have the revenues from certain "castles, towns, and villages" discussed in a special instrument. Elionor warned her executors and her husband that the princess's bequests were to come to her immediately after the queen's death. Even as she prepared for her own death, Elionor still held on to the hope that the Castilian wedding would not go forward. If it did not materialize, she wanted half of the dowry funds to got to her namesake and the other half to Martí, but none of it to the Castilian bridegroom, Prince Juan. Besides these large sums of money, Elionor gave to her daughter a silver bowl, other kitchen utensils, candle sticks, and bolts of woolen and silk cloth decorated with precious stones. These all were to be equally divided between the princess and her brother, Martí. For her daughter to enjoy for herself alone, the queen gave a golden chain, a bed with its fittings which Elionor had taken on some of her travels, twelve silver bowls and plates, a velvet dress, and sixty golden statues of castrated rams that were encrusted with precious stones.[16]

Elionor's relics that were not kept in gold or silver containers were to be divided between the princess and the queen's second son. Those that were sheathed in reliquaries would be divided between the princess and the monastery of the Saint Clares at Teruel. Many of the queen's towns and villages scattered between Catalonia and were to be divided between Pere and the crown prince. The general question of the rents from such sites would be decided by the executors. The queen also established a standard of succession in regard to manner these revenues would come to her children. If Joan died without a male heir, Martí would accede to them. If the same situation happened to him, the princess and her heirs would take control of such rents. Princess Elionor would also receive money drawn from other Valencian revenues.[17]

Besides the formal bequests that the Aragonese queen had made, her will contained many codicils which confirmed or changed earlier grants to the members of the family. As far as the revenues of the Valencian towns and castles went, the executors were to take control of this money immediately after Elionor's death, settle all her financial obligations and see to final revenue collections owed her. Only then would these rents be divided among the queen's children. Knowing her sons, Elionor warned them not to dare or presume to take control of these Valencian funds before the executors did. Once the Valencian sites were distributed to the heirs, their inhabitants were bound to swear "oaths of fealty and allegiance" to the heirs.

The executors would act as proxies in such ceremonies and serve as officials in these communities until the heirs appointed their own men. The executors were bound to maintain their "grace and honor" in all these administrative activities. Immediately after Queen Elionor's death, her four deputies were also bound to take immediate control of all her "jewels, gold and silver vases, precious stones, pearls, clothes, cloth, animals, equipment of her chamber as well as all [other] moveable goods." These would then be sorted and delivered to the proper parties. Treasurer Relat would carry out this process, but if he refused to do so, Joan would be tasked with the choice of a man of "good reputation" for the job. No matter who assumed this responsibility, he would be charged with the distribution of all of the queen's jewels among the executors who then would have them delivered to the proper party in line with the bequests.[18]

The queen's previous pious causes were carefully described and extended as individual codicils. The monastery of the Saint Clares at Teruel received 70,000 *sous* of Jaca to build a hospital, another "new structure," and support six presbyteries. The abbess would collect 200 *sous* of Barcelona from royal funds each year to help support the institution. The queen also granted 300 *sous* of Barcelona to support a priest for the monastery; the abbess would also administer this bequest. Another fund of 2,000 *sous* of Jaca was settled on the Teruel institution to offer masses for the queen after her death. Sale of Elionor's property to certain Jews would feed the fund designated to aid the Teruel institution. Rents from a Teruel citizen would also provide a sum of 6,000 *sous* of Jaca to act as an operating fund for the monastery. Despite this inflow of money, the queen had a judge of Teruel review all purchases that the abbess made with it.[19]

The queen also took precautions for her soul after death by ordering that alms should be given for the support of 700 paupers, twelve priests, and 15 scholars within the bishopric of Barcelona. She attempted to maintain her good reputation after her death by arranging to have her tomb decorated with a covering of cloth of gold which bore the insignia of the Aragonese royal house. Elionor also left money so on the day of her death 100 paupers, each paid 15 *sous* of Barcelona, would accompany her coffin to its burial place if this was to be in Barcelona. If the tomb was elsewhere, they would be paid a small fee to pray for her soul. Once a year, her executors were to arrange a procession of 25 paupers, each of whom had received at least 12 *sous* of Barcelona and a certain amount of grain for their efforts. Prince Martí was to draw all funds needed for the ceremony from the rents owed by a Barcelona freehold, but it is clear that such a processions could not have taken place before 1377 when the queen's body was in fact in the Catalan capital. Whether any of these pious clauses were actually carried out as Queen Elionor wished is not known.[20]

The codicils concluded with a list of individual grants to be paid as soon after Elionor's death as possible. She began with further gifts to her two families; namely monetary grants to her two sons for the children they might have, jewels for her stepdaughter, Joanna, and to the queen's younger sister of the same name, and money for Federico IV's illegitimate son.[21] She also gave varying sums to a long list of Sicilian and Iberian officials to repay them for the many "damages and expenses" they incurred.[22] Elionor had also made instructed the board of executors to have all her current officials remain in place until their fate could be decided by the king. She formally gave a great deal of power to these four deputies so "everything held in our mind" would be carried out in exact terms.[23]

4   LAST WORDS

As we have stated before, Eleanor of Provence, a thirteenth-century queen of England, and Elionor of Sicily, a fourteenth-century queen of Aragon, led similar lives even though they lived in different centuries. They both came from under-funded families filled with strong women and weak men. Marriage for both was a road to a better-funded if not a more secure life. Their husbands were hardly accomplished military men, but they both possessed a determination that often saw them to victory or at least to safety. The queens often seemed able to out-think and out maneuver their husbands, but both began to lose this advantage in their later years. They both died away from the great burial place reserved for the royal families they were a part of. With Eleanor, her place of last repose was the nunnery of Amesbery, and not a site of honor in Westminister Abbey; with Elionor, the road to final burial was a pilgrimage from Lerida, to the Barcelona monastery of the Saint Clares, and only a decade later to the emerging royal pantheon of Poblet. Both these tales of the queens after death imply a kind of grateful forgetfulness among their husbands and sons who had to honor their wives or mothers with a final sign of respect. Despite final signs of disrespect or carelessness the living royals were occasionally guilty of, we may characterize both queens in the way one modern historian did for the English one: "Her reign was marked by strife, and she had certainly made mistakes, but through it all her energy was unflagging, and her dreams large."[24]

NOTES

1. García Herrero, "Dama Modiílica," 40.
2. Pere III, *Chronicle*, 2:544, 556–58 (VI:39, 47).
3. Ibid., 2:589–90 (Appendix 3).
4. Ibid., 2: 581–83, 589–90 (VI:63; Appendix 2); Ayala, 560, Chap. 17.
5. Ibid., 2:586–90 (Appendix 1–2); Giunta, *Aragoneses*, 199–200.
6. Núria Silleras-Fernández, "Money Isn't Everything. Concubinage, Class, and the Rise of Sibi ≠ la de Fortiá, Queen of Aragon (1377–87)," in *Women and Wealth in Late Medieval Europe*, ed. Theresa Earenfight (New York), 67–88, esp. 67–68, 70, 76; Miron, *Queens of Aragon*, 196–207; Tasis i Marca, *Pere el Cerimoniós*, 105–9.
7. "Acute Nephritis,". https://www.healthline.com/health/acute-nephritic-syndrome. Accessed August 14, 2020; "Interstitial Nephritis" (n.d.). https://www.mountsinai.org/health-library/diseases-conditions/interstitial-nephritis. Accessed August 14, 2020; "Your Kidneys and How They Work" (2014). https://www.niddk.nih.gov/health-information/kidney-disease/kidneys-how-they-work. Accessed August 14, 2020.
8. ACA, CR, R. 1537, f. 139; R. 1585, f, 23v.
9. Pere III, *Chronicle*, 2:582–83, (VI:64).
10. Deibel, "Reyna Elionor," 394; Miron, *Queens of Aragon*, 195.
11. ACA, CR, R. 1536, ff. 75–76v.
12. ACA, CR, R. 1537, ff. 139–141v.
13. ACA, R. 1537, ff. 142–43v.
14. ACA, CR, R. 1527, ff. 144–45v; 151.
15. ACA, CR, R. 1537, ff. 138r–v, 145v–146.
16. ACA, CR, R. 1537, ff. 146v–150v.
17. ACA, CR, R. 1537, ff. 151–155v.
18. ACA, CR, R. 1537, ff. 156v–161v.
19. ACA, CR, R. 1537, ff. 162–63v, 166–69. Elionor made similar grants to the monasteries of Saint Clares at Calatayud and for the upkeep of several Catalan cathedrals and a number of hospitals. ACA, CR, R. 1537, 169v–171v
20. ACA, CR, R. 1537, ff. 165r–v; 167r–v, 171–172v.
21. ACA, CR, R. 1537, ff. 172v–173.
22. ACA, CR, R. 1537, ff. 173–74.
23. ACA, CR, R. 1536, ff. 176r–v.
24. Goldstone, "Four Queens." 306–307.

Notes on Aragonese Money

The coinage mentioned in Queen Elionor's accounts and letters first sprang from an imitation of gold coinage issued at Cordoba in the eleventh and twelfth centuries which eventually emerged in Aragon and Catalonia as *sous* made up a silver–copper alloy (*vellón*) and solidified into two coinage types minted at different sites; namely, the *sou* (*solidus*) of Barcelona and that of Jaca. Each was divided into *dinars*. A similar coin developed in Valencia after Jaume I's conquest of the region in 1238. The purchasing power of the three coins differed with the *sou* of Barcelona possessing the most and the Valencian the least. Another small coin that Elionor mentioned was the *morabetín*, a Christian imitation of an Almoravid gold coinage type. From 1340, Pere III had introduced the gold *florin*, an imitation of the principal coinage of Florence, which, however, did little to displace the earlier *sou* type.[1]

---

[1] A.M. Balaguer, "La moneda de oro del Reino de Aragón en las Edades Media," *Acta Numismática* 13 (1983): 137–65; Burn, *Society*, 108–9; M. Crusafont i Sabater and A.M. Balaguer, "La numismátic navarro-aragonesa alto medieval: Nuevas hipótesis," *Gaceta Numismática* 81 (1986): 35–66; M. Crusafont i Sabater, "Del morabatín almorávide al florin. Continuidad o ruptura en la Cataluña medieval," in *I Jarique de Estudios Numismática Hispano-Arabes* (1988): 191–200.

© The Editor(s) (if applicable) and The Author(s), under exclusive license to Springer Nature Switzerland AG 2021
D. J. Kagay, *Elionor of Sicily, 1325–1375*, The New Middle Ages, https://doi.org/10.1007/978-3-030-71028-6

BIBLIOGRAPHY

PRIMARY SOURCES

The Book of Deeds of James I of Aragon: A Translation of the Medieval Catalan "Llibre delos Feyts". Translated by Damian Smith and Helena Buffery. Aldershot, Hampshire: Ashgate, 2003.

"Chronica Adefonsi Imperatoris." In *The World of El Cid: Chronicles of the Spanish Reconquest*. Translated by Simon Barton and Richard Fletcher. Manchester University Press, 2000. 148–263.

"Chronica Adefonsi Imperatoris." In *The World of El Cid: Chronicles of the Spanish Reconquest*. Translated by Simon Barton and Richard Fletcher. Manchester: Manchester University Press.

The Chronicle of Muntaner. Translated by Lady Goodenough. 2 vols. Nendeln, Liechtenstein: Kraus Reprint Limited, 1967.

The Chronicle of San Juan de la Peña: A Fourteenth-Century Official History of the Crown of Aragon. Translated by Lynn H. Nelson. Philadelphia: University of Pennsylvania, 1991.

Colección de las Cortes de los antiguos reinos de Aragón y de Valencia y del principado de Cataluña. Edited by Fidel Fita and Bienvenido Oliver, 27 vols. Madrid: Real Academis de Historia, 1896–1922.

Cronache Siciliane inedito delle fine de medioevo. Edited by Francesco Giunta. Palermo: Della Società Sicilana per la storia patria, 1955.

Documenta Selecta Mutuas Civitatis Arago-Cathalaunicae et Ecclesiae Relationes. Edited by Johannes Vincke Barcelona: Biblioteca Balmes, 1936.

Documents Historichs Catalans del Sigle XIV: Colleció de cartas familiars Correspponents als trgnats de Pere del Punyalet y Johan I. Edited by Josep Coroleu. Barcelona: Imprempta La Renaixwnsa, 1889.

© The Editor(s) (if applicable) and The Author(s), under exclusive license to Springer Nature Switzerland AG 2021
D. J. Kagay, *Elionor of Sicily, 1325–1375*, The New Middle Ages,
https://doi.org/10.1007/978-3-030-71028-6

240 BIBLIOGRAPHY

Documents per l'historia de la cultura catalana mig-eval. Edited by Antonio Rubio i Lluch. Barcelona: Institut de Estudis Catalans, 1908, 1921.

Els quatre llibres de la reina Elionor de Sicilia a l'Arxiu de la Cadedral de Barcelona. Edited by Margarida Anglada, M. Àngels Fernandez, Concepció Petit Cibirain. Barcelona: Fundació Noguera, 1992.

Epistolari de Pere III. Edited by Ramon Gubern. Barcelona: Editorial Barchino, 1955.

Las Siete Partidas. Translated by Samuel Parsons Scott. Edited by Robert I. Burns. S.J. 5 vols. Philadelphia: University of Pennsylvania Press, 2001.

Liber Feudorum Maior. Edited by Francisco Miguel Rosell. 2 vols. Barcelona: CSIC, 1945.

López de Avala, Pero. "La Crónica del Don Pedro." In *Cronicas de los reyes de Castilla.* Edited by Cayetano Rosell, 3 vols., Biblioteca de Autores Españoles, 66. Madrid: M. Rivadeneyra–Editor, 1875, 1:401–593.

López de Meneses, Amada. *Documentos acerca de la Peste Negra en la dominion de la Corona de Aragón.* Zaragoza: Escuela de Estudios Medievales, 1956.

Ordinacions de la Casa i Cort de Pere el Ceemoniós. Edited by Francisco M. Gimeno, Daniel Gonzalbo, and Josep Trenchs. Valencia: Universitat de Valencia. 2009.

Pere III of Catalonia (Pedro IV of Aragon), *Chronicle.* Translated by Mary Hillgarth, Introduction by J.N. Hillgarth. 2 vols. Toronto: Pontifical Institute of Mediaeval Studies, 1980.

The Usatges of Barcelona: The Fundamental Law of Catalonia. Translated by Donald J. Kagay. Philadelphia: University of Pennsylvania Press, 1994.

SECONDARY SOURCES

Aberth, John. *From the Brink of the Apocalypse: Confronting Famine, War, and Death in the Later Middle Ages.* New York: Routledge, 2001.

Abulafia, David. *Frederick II: A Medieval Emperor.* London: Allen Lane. The Penguin Press, 1988.

Adroer i Tasis, Anna María. "El palau de la Reina Elionor: Un monument desparagut." *Lambard: Estudis d'art medieval* 6 (1991–1993): 247–61.

———. "Un Palau Reial frustrat." In *II Congrés de Història del Pla de Barcelona.* 2 vols. Barcelona: Np, 1990.

Ainaga Andrés, María Teresa. "El fogaje aragonés de 1362: Aportació a la demografía de Zaragoza en el siglo XIV." *AEEM* 9 (1989): 33–59.

Almeida Rodrigues, Ana Maria Seabra de. "Between Husband and Father: Queen Isabel of Lancaster's Crossed Loyalties." *Imago Temporis. Medium Aevum* 3 (2009): 205–18.

BIBLIOGRAPHY 241

Alvira Cabrer, Martín. "De Alarcos á las Navas de Tolosa: Idea y realidad de la batalla de 1212." In *Alarcos 1195: Actas de Congreso Internacional Comemeraticva de VIII Centenario de Batalla de Alarcos*. Edited by Ricardo Izquierdo Benito and Francisco Ruiz Gómez. Ciudad Real: Universidad de Castilla-La Mancha, 1996. 254–64.

Aneas Hontangas, Marina. "Les reines lloctinents a Corona d'Aragó." PhD dissertation, University of Barcelona, July, 2014.

Ángelo Dávila, Joseph. *História de Xerez de la Frontera*. Edited by Juan Abellán Pèrez. Helsinki: Academia Scientiarum Fennica, 2008.

Aragó Cabañas, Anton M. "Las escribanías reales catalano-aragonesas de Ramon Berenguer IV á la minoría de Jaume I." *Revista de archivos, bibvliotecas y museos* 80 (1977): 421–44.

———. "Las "tenentiae castrorum" del reino Valencia en la época de Jaime II." In *Primer Congreso de Historia del Pais Valenciano*. Valencia: Np, 1971. 569–70.

Aurell, Jaume. *Authoring the Past: History, Autobiography, and Politics in Medieval Catalonia*. Chicago: University of Chicago Press, 2012.

———. "Strategies of Royal Self-Fashioning: Iberian King's Self-Coronations." In *Self-Fashioning and Assumptions of Identity in Medieval and Early Modern Iberia*. Edited by Laura Delbrugge. Leiden: Brill, 2016. 18–45.

Bachman, Clifford R. *The Decline and Fall of Medieval Sicily: Politics, Religion, and Economy in the Reign of Frederick III, 1296-1337*. Cambridge: Cambridge University Press, 1995.

Baer, Yitzhak. *A History of the Jews in Christian Spain*. Translated by Louis Schoffman. 2 vols. Philadelphia: The Jewish Publication Society, 1992.

Balaguer, A.M. "La moneda de oro del Reino de Aragón en las Edades Media." *Acta Numismática* 13 (1983): 137–65.

Balaguer, Federico. "La Chronica Adefonsi Imperatoris y la elevación de Ramiro al Trono Aragnés." *EEMCA* 6 (1952–1953): 7–33.

Barrios, Manuel. *Pedro I el Cruel: La nobleza contra su rey*. Madrid: Temas de Hoy, 2001. 33–40.

Beauchamp, Alexandra. "Conseillers scélérats et mauvaisL le Roi d'Aragon, ses conseillers et le conseil à la fin du XIVe siècle." *Anales de la Universidad de Alicante. Historia medieval* 19 (2015–2016): 176–91.

Bensch, Stephen P. *Barcelona and its Rulers, 1096-1291*. Cambridge: Cambridge University Press, 1995.

Bildhauer, B. *The Curse of Eve, the Wound of the Hero: Blood Gender and Medieval Literature*. Philadelphia: University of Pennsylvania Press, 2003.

Bisson, Thomas N. *The Crisis of the Twelfth Century: Power, Lordship, and the Origins of European Government*. Princeton, NJ: Princeton University Press, 2009.

242 BIBLIOGRAPHY

———. "The Organized Peace in Southern France and Catalonia, ca. 1140-ca. 1230." *AHR* 82 (1977): 290–303.

———. "The Problem of Feudal Monarchy: Aragon, Catalonia, and France." In *Medieval France and Her Pyrenean Neighbors: Studies in Early Institutional History*. London: The Hambledon Press, 1989. 237–55.

———. "Ramon de Caldes (c. 1135-1199): Dean of Barcelona and King's Minister." In *Medieval France*. 187–98.

———. *The Black Death*. Edited and Translated by Rosemary Horrox. Manchester: Manchester University Press, 1994.

Blancas y Tomas, Jerónimo. *Coronaciones de los serenísimos reyes de Aragón*. Zaragoza: Imprent del Hospicio, 1864.

Bofarull y Moscaro, Prospero. *Los condes de Barcelona vindicados*. 2 vols. Barcelona: Imprenta de J. Oliveres y Monmany, 1936.

Born, Lester Kruger. "The Perfect Prince: A Study in Thirteenth- and Fourteenth-Century Ideals." *Speculum* 3, no. 4 (October, 1928): 470–504.

Bratsch-Prince, Dawn. "The Politics of Self Representation in the Letters of Violant de Bar (1365-1431)." *Medieval Encounters* 12, no. 1 (2006): 2–25.

Braudel, Fernand. *The Mediterranean and the Mediterranean World in the Age of Philip II*. Translated by Siân Reynolds. 2 vols. New York: HarperCollins, 1992.

Bresc, Henri. "Palermo in the 14th-15th Century: Urban Economy and Trade." In *A Companion to Medieval Palermo: The History of a Mediterranean City from 600 to 1500*. Edited by Annliese Nef. Leiden: Brill, 2013. 235–67.

Bruzelius, Caroline. "Queen Sancia of Majorca and the Convent Church of Sta. Chiara in Naples." *Memoirs of the American Academy of Rome* 40 (1995): 69–100.

Burns, Robert I. *The Crusader Kingdom of Valencia: Reconstruction of a Thirteenth-Century Frontier*. 2 vols. Cambridge, MA: Harvard University Press, 1967.

———. "*Gegna*: Coastal Mooring in crusader Valencia." *Technology and Culture* 47 (2006): 777–86.

———. *Medieval Colonialism: Postcrusade Exploitation of Islamic Valencia*. Princeton, NJ: Princeton University Press, 1975.

———. "The Paper Revolution in Europe: Crusader Valencia's Paper Industry: A Technological and Behavior Breakthrough." *Pacific Historical Review* 50 (1981): 1–30.

———. "The Significance of the Frontier in the Middle Ages." In *Medieval Frontier Societies*. Edited by Robert Bartlett and Angus Mackay. 1989; Reprint. Oxford: Clarendon Press, 1996.

———. *Society and Documentation of the Crusader Valencia*, Vol. 1 of *Diplomatarium of the Crusade Kingdom of Valencia: The Registered Charters of*

BIBLIOGRAPHY **243**

its Conqueror, Jaume I, 1257-1276, 4 vols. to date. Princeton, Princeton University Press, 1985 to date.

———. "The Spiritual Life of James the Conqueror King of Arago-Catalonia, 1208-1276: Portrait and Self-Portrait." *CHR* 62 (1976): 1–35.

———. "*Stupor Mundi*, Alfonso X the Learned." In *Emperor of Culture: Alfonso X the Learned of Castile and His Thirteenth-Century Renaissance*. Edited by Robert I. Burns, S.J. Philadelphia: University of Pennsylvania Press, 1990. 1–13.

Bynum, Caroline Walker. *Jesus as Mother: Studies in the Spirituality of the High Middle Ages*. Berkeley: University of California Press, 1982.

Cabazuelo Pliego, José Vicente. "Las communidades judías del mediodía valenciana, De la vitalidad á la supervivencia." *MMM* 29–30 (2005–2006): 75–104.

Campón Gonsalvo, Julia. "Consequencias de la guerr ad los Dos Pedros en el condado." *AUA* 8 (1990–1991): 57–68.

Canet Aparisi, Teresa. "La aministración real y los antecedentes históricos de la audencia moderna." *Estudis: Revista de Historia Moderna* 32 (2006): 7–40.

Carlé, María. Carmen"Alimentación y abastrciminto." *CHE* 61–62 (1977): 246–341.

Carmen García Herrero, María del. "La dama modélica del cuatro cientos en la correspondencia del María de Castilla, Reina de Aragón (1416-1458)." *Cuadernos de CEMYR* 23 (2015): 27–48.

Carreras Candi, Francesc. *Geografia general de Catalunya. La ciutat de Barcelona*. Barcelona: Np, 1916.

Castor, Helen. "Exception to the Rule." *History Today* 60, no. 10 (October 2010): 37–43.

Cawsey, Suzanne F. *Kingship and Propaganda: Royal Eloquence and the Crown of Aragon c.1200-1450*. Oxford: Clarendon Press, 2002.

Chejne, Anwar G. *Muslim Spain: Its History and Culture*. Minneapolis: The University of Minnesota Press, 1974.

Cid Moragas, Daniel. "La respauració del desaparegut palau reial menor de Barcelona a través del llibre d'obrael cas de la sala major (1376-1378)." *AHAM* 18 (1997): 397–425.

Collins, Roger. *The Arab Conquest of Spain, 710-797*. London: Blackwell, 1989.

Comas-Via, Mireia. "Widowhood and Economic Difficulties in Medieval Barcelona." *Historical Reflections/Réflexions Historiques* 43, no. 1 (Spring 2017): 93–103.

Crawford, Anne. "The Queen Council in the Middle Ages." *English Historical Review* 116, no. 469 (November 2001): 1193–1211.

Crusafont i Sabater, M. "Del morabatín almorávide al florin. Continuidad o ruptura en la Cataluña medieval." *Jarique de Estudios Numismática Hispano-Arabes* I (1988): 191–200.

244   BIBLIOGRAPHY

Crusafont i Sabater, M. and A.M. Balaguer. "La numismátic navarro-aragonesa alto medieval: Nuevas hipótesis." *Gaceta Numismática* 81 (1986): 35–66.

D'Abadal y de Vinyals, Ramón. *Pere el Ceremoniós i els inicis de la decadència political de Catalunya.* Barcelona: Edicions 62, 1972.

Deibel, Ulla. "La Reyna, Elionor de Sicilia." *Memorias, Real Academis de Buenas Letras de Barcelona* 10 (1928): 355–452.

Diago Hernando, Máximo. "La movilidad a ambos lados de la Frontera entre las Coronas de Castilla y Aragón durante el siglo XIV." *Sefarad* 63 (2003): 237–82.

Dillard, Heath. *Daughters of the Reconquest: Women in Castilian Town Society 1100-1300.* Cambridge: Cambridge University Press, 1984.

Dozy, Reinhart Pieter Anne. *Spanish Islam: A History of the Muslims in Spain.* Translated by Francis Griffin Stokes. 1913; Reprint. London: Frank Cass, 1972.

Dualde Serrano, Manuel and José Camarena Mahiques. *El Compromiso de Caspe.* Zaragoza: Institución "Fernando el Católico," 1980.

Durán Gudiol, Antonio. "El rito de la coronación del rey en Aragón." *Argensola* 103 (1989): 17–37.

Earenfight, Theresa, "Absent Kings: Queens as Political Partners in the Medeiival Crown of Aragon." Edited by Theresa Earenfight. *Queenship and Political Power in Medieval and Early Modern Spain.* Aldershot, Hampshire: Ashgate, 2005. 33–51.

———. *The King's Other Body: María de Castile and the Crown of Aragon.* Philadelphia: University of Pennsylvania, 2010.

———. "María of Castile, Ruler or Figurehead? A Preliminary Study in Aragonese Queenship." *MS* 4 (1994): 45–61.

———. "Political Culture and Political Discourse in the Letters of Queen Matía." *La coronica* 32, no. 1 (Fall, 2003): 135–52.

Elias, Norbert. *The Court Society.* Translated by Edmund Jephcott. New York: Pantheon Books, 1983.

Epstein, Stephan R. "Cities, Regions, and the Late Medieval Crisis: Sicily and Tuscany Compared." *Past and Present* 130 (February, 1991): 3–50.

———. *An Island for Itself: Economic Development and Social Change in Late-Medieval Sicily.* Cambridge: Cambridge University Press, 2003.

Estow, Clara. *Pedro the Cruel of Castile, 1350-1369.* Leiden: E.J. Brill, 1995.

Fernández Armesto, Felipe. *Before Columbus: Exploration and Colonization from the Mediterranean to the Atlantic, 1229-1492.* Philadelphia: University of Pennsylvania Press, 1987.

Ferrer i Mallol, María. "Causes i antecedents de la guerra dels dos Peres." *Boletín de la Sociedad Castellornse de Cultura* 63 (1987): 445–508.

———. "Les Corts de Catalunya i creació de la Diputació del General en el marc de la guerra amb Castilla (1359-1369)." *AEM* 334, no. 2 (2004): 875–939.

BIBLIOGRAPHY 245

———. *Entre la paz y la guerra. La corona catalano-aragonesa y Castille en la baja Edad Media*. Barcelona: Institució Milá Fontanals, 2005. 338–40.

———. "La organización militar en Cataluña en la Edad Media." *Revista de Historia Militar*, Special Issue (2001): 119–222.

Fibla Guitart, M. "Les Corts de Tortosa i Barcelona 1365. Recapte de donatiu." *Cuadernos de Historia Económica de Cataluña* 19 (1978): 97–121.

Fisher, W.B. and H. Bowen-Jones. *Spain: An Introductory Geography*. New York: Frederick A. Praeger Publisher, 1966.

Flood, John. *Representations of Eve in Antiquity and the English Middle Ages*. New York: Routledge, 2011.

Font y Rius, José María. "The Institutions of the Crown of Aradon in the First Half of the Fifteenth Century." In *Spain in the Fifteenth Century 1369, 1516: Essays and Extracts by Historians of Spain*. Edited by Roger Highfield. Translated by Frances M. López-Morillas. New York: Harper and Row Publishers, 1972. 169–92.

Fossier, Robert. *The Axe and the Oath: Ordinary Live in the Middle Ages*. Translated by Lydia G. Cochrane. Princeton: Princeton University Press, 2007.

Freud, Sigmund. *The Ego and the Id*. London: Hogarth Press. 1942.

Gaibrois del Ballesteros, Mercedes and Ana del Campo Gutíerrez. *María de Molina*. Pamplona: Urgoiti DL, 2011.

Gambero, Luigi. *Mary in the Middle Ages: The Blessed Virgin Mary in the Thought of Medieval Latin Theologians*. Milan: Edizioni San Baolo, 2000.

García, Juan Vicente. "Alimentación y salud en la Valencia medieval. teorías y prácticas." *AEM* 43, no. 1 (enero-junio de 2013): 115–58.

García Gallo de Diego, Alfonso. *Manual de historia del derecho español*, 2 vols. Madrid: Gráca ministrativa, 1967.

———. "La sucesión al trono de Aragón." *AHDE* 36 (1966): 5–188.

Gascón, María Isabel. "La vida cotidiana de tres reinas de la corona de Aragón s través de los libros de cuentas." *Pedralbes* 24 (2004): 13–54.

Giunta, Francesco. *Aragoneses y catalanes en el Mediterráneo*. Translated by Juan Bignozzi. Barcelona: Editorial Ariel, S.A., 1989.

———. "La politico mediterranea di Pietro il Cerimonioso." In *Pere el Cerimoniós i seva època*. Edited by María Teresa Ferrer i Mallol. Barcelona: CSIC: Institució Milà i Fontanals, 1989. 59–76.

Goldstone, Nancy. *Four Queens: The Provençal Sisters Who Ruled Europe*. New York: Penguin Books, 2007.

———. *Joanna: The Notorious Queen of Naples, Jerusalem & Sicily*. New York: Phoenix, 2010. 389–92.

Gómez, Miguel. "Alfonso III and the Battle of Las Navas de Tolosa." In *King Alfonso VIII of Castile: Government, Family and War*. Edited by Miguel

246 BIBLIOGRAPHY

Gómez, Damian Smith, and Kyle C. Lincoln. New York: Fordham University Press, 2019. 143–71.

González, Luís. "Primeras resistencias contra el lugarteniente general-virrey en Aragón." *AEM* 8 (1989): 303–14.

Goodman, Jennifer R. "The Lady with the Sword: Philippa of Lancaster and the Chivalry of the Infante Dom Henrique (Prince Henry the Navigator)." In *Queens, Regents, and Potentates*, 149–65.

Grant, Lindy. *Blanche of Castile*. New Haven, CT: Yale University Press, 2016.

Greenblatt, Stephen. *Renaissance Self-Fashioning from More to Shakespeare*. Chicago: University of Chicago Press, 1980.

Grisez, Germain. "Mary, Mother of Jesus, Sketch of a Theology." *New Black-friars* 78, no. 920 (October, 1997): 418–24.

Gubern i Domench, Ramon. "Notas sobre la reducció de la *Cronica* de Pere el Cerimoniós." *Estudis Romanics* 2 (1949–1950): 135–43.

Gutiérrez de Velasco, Antonio. "La contaofensiva aragonesa en la Guerra de los Dos Pedros: Actitud militar y diplomática de Pedro IV el Cerimoniosos (años 1358 á 1362)." *CHJZ* 14–15 (1963): 7–30.

———. "Las fortalezas aragonesas ante la gran ofensiva castellana en la guerrs de los dos Pedros." *CHJZ* 12–13 (1961): 9–15.

Hamann, Bryon Ellsworth. *Bad Christians, New Spains, Catholics and Native Americans in a Mediterranean World*. London: Routledge, 2020.

Heuben, Hubert. *Roger II of Sicily: A Ruler Between East and West*. Translated by Graham A. Loud and Diane Milburn. Cambridge: Cambridge University Press, 2002.

Hillgarth, J.N. *The Spanish Kingdoms 1250-1516*. 2 vols. Oxford: Clarendon Press, 1976.

Hollister, C. Warren and John W. Baldwin. "The Rise of Administrative Kingship and Philip Augustus." *AHR* 83, no. 4 (October, 1978): 867–905.

Honeycutt, Lois. "Female Succession and the Language of Power in the Writings of Twelfth-Century Churchmen." In *Medieval Queenship*, 189–201.

———. "Medieval Queenship." *History Today* 39, no. 6 (June, 1989): 16–22.

———. *An Idea of History: Selected Essays of Américo Castro*. Edited and Translated by Stephen Gilman and Edmund L. King. Columbus, OH: Ohio State University Press, 1977.

Howell, Margaret. "The Resources of Eleanor of Provence as Queen Consort." *EHR* 102, no. 403 (April, 1987): 372–93.

Johnston, Mark D. "Parliamentary Oratory in Medieval Aragon." *Rhetorica: A Journal of the History of Rhetoric* 10, no. 2 (Spring, 1992): 99–117.

Kagay, Donald J. Army Mobilization. Royal Administration and the Realm in the Thirteenth-Century Crown of Aragon." In *Iberia and the Mediterranean World*. Edited by Paul E. Chevedden, Donald J. Kagay, Paul G. Padilla, and Larry E. Simon. 2 vols. Leiden: Brill, 1996. 2:95–115.

———. "Battle-Seeking Commanders in the Later Middle Ages: Phases of Generalship in the War of the Two Pedros." In *The Hundred Year War (Part III): Further Consequences*. Edited by L.J. Andrew Villalon and Donald J. Kagay. Leiden: Brill, 2013.

———. "Border War as Handmaiden of National Identity: The Territorial Definition of Late-Medieval Iberia." *JGAH* 28 (2009): 88–138.

———. "Defending the Western and Southern Frontiers in the War of the Two Pedros: An Experiment in Nation-Building." *JGAH* (2002): 77–107.

———. "The Defense of the Crown of Aragon During the War of the Two Pedros (1356-1366)." *The Journal of Military History* 71, no. 1 (January, 2007): 11–33.

———. "The Dynastic Dimension of International Conflict in Fourteenth-Century Iberia." *MS* 17 (2008): 77–96.

———. "Jaime I of Aragon: Child and Master of the Spanish Reconquest." *JMMH* 8 (2010): 69–108.

———. "The National Defense Clause and the Emergence of the Catalan State: *Princeps namque* Revisited." In *War*, Study I. 57–97.

———. "The Parliament of the Crown of Aragon as Military Financier in the War of the Two Pedros." *JMMH* 14 (2016): 57–77.

———. "Pere III's System of Defense in the War of the Two Pedros (1356-1366): The Aragonese Crown's Use of Aristocratic, Urban, Clerical, and Foreign Captains." *Studies in Medieval and Renaissance History*, Third Series, 7 (2010): 195–232.

———. "Poetry in the Dock: The Court Culture of Joan I on Trial (1396-1398)." In *War*, Study XI. 48–99.

———. "Rule and Mis-rule in Medieval Iberia." In *War, Government, and Society in the Medieval Crown of Aragon*. Aldershot, Hampshire, 2007. Study IV. 48–66.

———. "A Shattered Circle: Eastern Spanish Fortifications and Their Repair During the 'Calamitous Fourteenth Century'." In *War*, Study III. 11–35.

———. "The Theory and Practice of Just War in the Late-Medieval Crown of Aragon." *CHR*, 591–610.

———. "The Theory and Practice of War and Government Practiced by King Pere III "the Ceremonious" of Aragon (1336-87)." *MS* 27, no. 1 (2019): 63–85.

———. "The "Treasons" of Bernat de Cabrera: Government, Law, and the Individual in the Late-Medieval Crown of Aragon." *Mediaevistik* 13 (2000): 39–54.

———. "Two Towns Where There Once Was One: The *Aldea* and Its Place in Urban Development of the Aragonese Middle Ages." *The Journal of the Rocky Mountain Medieval and Renaissance Association* 14 (1995): 33–43.

248 BIBLIOGRAPHY

———. "War Financing in the Late-Medieval Crown of Aragon." *JMMH* 6 (2008): 119–48.

Kennedy, Hugh. *Muslim Spain and Portugal: A Political History of al-Andalus.* London: Longman, 1996.

King, P.D. *Law and Society in the Visigothic Kingdom.* Cambridge: Cambridge University Press, 1972.

Kinkade, Richard. "Alfonso X, *Cantiga* 235 and the Events of 1269-1278." *Speculum* 67 (1992): 284–323.

———. "Violante of Aragon (1236?-1300): An Historical Overview," *Exemplaria Hispanica* 2 (1992–1993): 1–37.

Kosto, Adam. "The *Liber Feudorum Maior* of the Counts of Barcelona: The Cartulary as an Expression of Power." *Journal of Medieval History* 27 (2001): 1–22.

Lacave Riaño, José Luis. "Los judíos en España medieval." *Historia* 16, no. 58 (1981): 49–61.

Ladurie, Emmanuel Le Roy. *Montaillou: The Promised Land of Error.* Translated by Barbara Bray. New York: George Braziller, Inc., 1978.

Lafuente Gómez, Mario. "Devoción y patronazgo en torno al combate en la Corona de Aragón: Las commemoraciones á San Jorge de 1356." *AEEM* 20 (2008): 427–44.

———. *Dos Coronas en Guerra. Aragón y Castilla (1356-1366).* Zaragoza: Grupo de Investigaciómn C.E.M.A., 2012.

Lalinde Abadía, Antonio. "Vivveys y lugartientes medievales en la Corona de Aragón." *CHE* 31–32 (1960): 98–172.

Lalinde Abadia, Jesús. *Le institución virreinal en Cataluña.* Barcelona: CSIC, 1964.

Ledesma Rubio, Maria Luisa. "El Patrimonio real en Aragón a fines del siglo XIV: Los dominos y rentas de Violante de Bar." *AEEM* [Ejemplar dedicado á estudios de economía y sociedad (siglos XII a XVI)] 2 (1979): 135–70.

L'Hermite-Leclercq, Paulette. "The Feudal Order." In *Silences of the Middle Ages* vol. 2 of *A History of the Women in the West.* Edited by Christiane Klapisch-Zuber. 5 vols. Cambridge, MA: Harvard University Press, 1992. 202–66.

Lizondo, M. Rodrigo. "La Unión valenciana y sus protaginistas." *Liganzas* 7 (1975): 133–66.

Lomax, Derek W. *The Reconquest of Spain.* London: Longmans, 1978.

López de Meneses, Amada. "El canciller Pero López de Ayala y los reyes de Aragón." *EEMCA* 8 (1967): 189–264.

López Rodríguez, Carlos. "Orígenes del Archivo de la Corona de Aragón (En tiempos, Archivo Real de Barcelona)." *Hispania* 226 (mayo-augusto, 2007): 413–54.

Lourie, Elena. "A Fifteenth-Century Satire on Jewish Bullfighters." *Proceedings of the World Congress of Jewish Studies* 1 (1977): 129–39.

BIBLIOGRAPHY 249

MacDonald, Robert I. "Law and Politics: Alfonso's Program of Political Reform." In *The World of Alfonso the Learned and James the Conqueror: Intellect and Force in the Middle Ages*. Edited by Robert I. Burns, S.J. Princeton, NJ: Princeton University Press. 150–99.

Madurell i Mazrimon, Josep. *El paper a les terres caralans: contribuciío a la seva història*. 2 vols. Barcelona: Fundacio Salvador Vives Casajuana, 1972.

Madurell Marimón, Josep Maria. "Una Concordia entre Pedro el Cerimonioso y María de Portugal, Infanta de Aragón." *AHDE* 41 (1971): 425–38.

Maravall, José Antonio. *Estudios de historia de pensamiento español*. New York: Ediciones Cultura Hispanica, 1970.

Martín, José Luis. "Las cortes de Pedro el Ceremonioso." In *Pere el Cerimonióla seva época*. 99–111.

Martin, Therese. "The Art of a Reigning Queen as Dynastic Propaganda in Twelfth-Century Spain." *Speculum* 80 (2005): 1134–71.

———. "Fuentes de Potesdad para reinas e infantes. El infantazgo en los siglos centrales de la Edad Media." *AEM* 46, no. 1 (enero-junio de 2016): 97–136.

Martínez, Fancisco. "El tercer casmiento de Pedro el Cerimanioso." In *III Congreso de história de la Corona de Aragón dedicado al periodo comprendido entre la muerte de Jaime I y la proclamación del rey don Fernanso de Antequera*. 3 vols. Valencia: Imprenta del hijo de F. Vives, 1923–1928. 1:542–77.

Martínez Martínez, María. "Un medio vida en la frontera murciana-granadino (siglo XIIII)." *MMM* 13 (1986): 49–62.

Masiá i de Ros, Ángeles. *Relación castellano-aragonesa desde Jaime II á Pedro el Cerimonioso*. 2 vols. Barcelona: CSIC, 1994.

Maslow, Abraham and Robert Frager. *Motivation and Personality*. New Delhi: Pearson Education, 1970.

McCrank, Lawrence J. "Documenting Reconquest and Reform: The Growth of Archives in the Medieval Crown of Aragon." *American Archivist* 56 (Spring, 1993): 256–318.

Meyerson, Mark D. *Jews in an Iberian Frontier Kingdom: Society, Economy, and Politics in Morvedre, 1248-1391*. Leiden: Brill, 2004.

Mineo, E. Igor. "Palermo in the 14th-15th Century: The Urban Society." In *Companion*. 269–96.

Miron, E.L. *The Queens of Aragon: Their Lives and Times*. London: Stanley Paul and Company, 1914.

Miret y Sans, Joaquin. "Negociations de Pierre IV d'Aragon avec la cour de France (1366-1367)." *Revue Hispanique* 13, no. 43 (1905): 76–135.

Mitchell, Linda E. "The Lady as Lord in Thirteenth-Century Britain." *Historical Reflections/Réflexions Historiques* 18, no. 1 (Winter, 1992): 71–97.

Mitchell, Timothy. *Blood Sport: A Social History of Spanish Bullfighting*. Philadelphia: Philadelphia University Press, 1991.

250 BIBLIOGRAPHY

Molas Ribalta, Pere. "El Palau Menor de Barcelona, center de sociabilitat nobiliária." 52 (2009–2010): 203–16.

Mollat, G. The "Babylonian Captivity" of the Medieval Church. Translated by Janet Love. New York: Harper & Row Publishers, 1963.

Monter, William. The Rise of Female Kings in Europe, 1300-1800. New Haven, CT: Yale University Press, 2012.

Moxó y Montoliu, Francisco de. Estudios sobre las relaciones entre Aragón y Castilla (SS. XIII-XV). Zaragoza: "Institución Fernando el Católico," 1997.

Mundo, Anscari M. "El pacte de Cazola de 1179 i el "Liber feudorum maior." Notes paleogràfiques I diplmàtiques." In Jaime I y su época, 3 vols. Zaragoza: Institución "Fernando el Católico," 1979-1982. Comunicacions 1 y 2: 119–29.

Muñoz i Soria, Nuria. "Las Cartes de la Reina Elionor de Sicilia." PhD dissertation, University of Barcelona, 1985.

Muñoz Pomer, María Rosa. "Preliminares de la Guerra de los Dos Pedros en el Reino de Valencia." AUA I (1982): 117–34.

Nelson, Janet L. "Medieval Queenship." In Women in Medieval Western European Culture. Edited by Linda E. Mitchell. New York: Garland Publishing, Inc., 1999. 179–207.

Norman, Diana. Siena and the Virgin: Art an Politics in a Late Medieval City-State. New Haven, CT: Yale University Press, 1999.

O'Callaghan, Joseph F. A History of Medieval Spain. Ithaca, NY: Cornell University Press, 1975.

———. "The Ideology of Government in the Reign of Alfonso X of Castile." Exemplaria Alfonsina I (1991–1992): 1–17.

———. The Learned King: The Reign of Alfonso X of Castile. Philadelphia: University of Pennsylvania Press, 1993.

———. "The Many Roles of Medieval Queens: Some Examples from Castile." In Queenship and Political Power in Medieval and Early Modern Spain. Edited by Theresa Earenfight. Aldershot, Hampshire: Ashgate, 2005. 21–32.

Oldfield, Paul. "The Imprint on Medieval Southern Italy." History 3, no. 3 (July, 2008): 312–27.

Olivar Betran, Rafael. Bodas reales de Aragón con Castilla, Navarra y Portugal. Barcelona: Alberto Martin, 1949.

Orcástegui Gros, Carmen. "La Cornonación de los reyes de Aragón. Evolución politico-ideológica y ritual." In Homenatge a Don Antonio Durán. Huesca: Instituto de Estudios Altoaragonese, 1995. 633–48.

Orsi Lázero, Mario. "Estrategia, operaciones y logística wn un conflicto mediterráneo. La revuelta del juez de Arborea y la "Armada y Viatge" de Pedro el Ceremonioso a Cerdeña (1353-1354)." AEM 38, no. 2 (julio-diciembre, 2008). 921–68.

BIBLIOGRAPHY 251

Palomeque Torres, Antonio. "Contribución al estudio del ajercito en los estados de la reconquista." *AHDE* 15 (1944): 205–551.

Parsons, John Carmi. "Mothers, Daughters, Marriage, Power: Some Plantagenet Evidence, 1150-1500." In *Medieval Queenship*. Edited by John Carmi Parsons. New York: St. Martin's Press, 1998. 63–78.

Pelikan, Jeroslav et al. *Mary: Images of the Mother of Jesus in Jewish and Christian Perspective*. Minneapolis, MN: Fortress Press, 2005.

Pernoud, Régine. *Blance of Castile*. Translated by H. Noel. New York: Putnam, 1975.

Piedrafita, E. "La alimentación en Aragón en el siglo XIII: El modelo clerical y nobiliario." *RHJZ* 80–81 (2005–2006): 99–132.

Pons Guri, J.M. "Un fogatjament desconegut del l'any 1358." *Boletín de Real Academia de Buenas Letras de Barcelona* 30 (1963–1964): 322–498.

Quatriglio, Giuseppe. *A Thousand Years in Sicily: From the Arabs to the Bourbons*. Translated by Justin Vitiello. Mineola, NY: Legas, 2005.

Ray, Jonathan. *The Sephardic Frontier: The 'Reconquista' and the Jewish Community in Medieval Iberia*. Ithaca, NY: Cornell University Press, 2006.

Recuro Lista, Alejandro. "Doña Leonor: infanta castellana, reina aragonesa y elemento de discordia en las relaciones castellano-aragonesas en la primera mitad del siglo XIV." *Estudios Medievales Hispánicas* 2 (2013): 221–49.

Riera i Sans, Jaume. "La Coronació de la Reina Elionor (1352)." *AHAM* [Homenatge a la profesora Dra Carmen Batlle Girart] 26 (2005): 485–92.

Rius Serra, Josep. "L'arquebisbe de Saragossa, canceller de Pere III." *Analecta Sacra Tarraconensia* 8 (1932): 1–63.

Roberts Gaventa, Beverly. *Mary: Glimpses of the Mother of God*. Columbia, SC: University of South Carolina Press, 1995.

Roca, Joseph María. *Johan I d'Aragó*. Barcelona: Casa prov. De Caritat, 1929.

Rodon Binue, Eulalia. *El lenguaje técnico def Feudlism en el siglo XI en Cataluña: Contribución al este de latin medieval*. Barcelona: CSIC, 1957.

Roebert, Sebastian. "*'Idcirco ad instar illius Zerobabell templum domini rehediff-icantis'*, La politica monastica de Elionora di Sicilia." *Edad Media. Revista de Historia* 18 (2017): 49–74.

———. "Leonor de Sicilia y Santa Clara de Teruel: La foundación reginal de un convento de clarisas y su primer desarrollo." *AEM* 44, no. 1 (enero-junio de 2014), 141–78.

———. "The Nominations of Elionor of Sicily as Queen-Lieutenant in the Crown of Aragon: Edition and Commentary." *Mediaeval Studies* 80 (2018): 171–229.

———. "*'Que nos tenemus a dicto domino rege pro camera assignata,'* The Development, Administration of the Queenly Estate of Elionor of Sicily (1349-1375)." *AEM* 46, no. 1 (enero-junio de 2016): 231–68.

252 BIBLIOGRAPHY

Rohr, Zita. "Lessons for My Daughter: Self-Fashioning Stateswomanship in the Late-Medieval Crown of Aragon." In *Self-Fashioning*. 46–78.

Rojas Gabriel, Manuel. "El valor bélico de la cabalgada en la frontera de Granada (c.1350-c.1481)." *AEM* 31, no. 1 (2001): 295–328.

Rovira i Sola, Manuel. "Notes documentales sobre alguns effectes de la presa de Barcelona per al-Mansur." *AHAM* 1 (1980): 31–45.

Rubin, Miri. *Emotion and Devolution: The Meaning of Mary in Medieval Religious Cultures*. Budapest: CEU Press, 2009.

Ruiz Domingo, Lledó. "'*Del qual tenim loch*,' Leonor de Scilia y el origen de la lugartenencia feminina en la Corona de Aragón." *Medievalismo* 27 (2017): 303–26.

Runciman, Steven. *The Sicilian Vespers: A History of the Mediterranean World in the Later Thirteenth Century*. London: Penguin Books, 1961.

Ryan, Michael A. *A Kingdom of Stargazers: Astrology and Authority in the Late-Medieval Crown of Aragon*. Ithaca, NY: Cornell University Press, 2011.

Sablonier, Roger. "The Aragonese Royal Family Around 1300." In *Interest and Emotion: Essays on the Study of Family and Kinship*. Edited by Hans Medick and David Warrean. Cambridge: Cambridge University Press, 1984. 210–39.

Sánchez Albornoz, Claudio. "El aula regia y las asambleas políticas de los godos." *CHE* 5 (1945): 5–110.

Sánchez Martínez, Manuel. "Negociación y fidcalidad en Cataluña a mediados de siglo XIV: Los Cortes de Barcelona de 1356." In *Necociar en la Edad Media/Négocier en la Moyen Âge. Actas de Colquio celedrada en Barcelona las dias 14, 15, 16 de Octubre de 2004*. Edited by María Teresa Ferrer i Mallol, Jean-Marie Moeglin; Stéphane Pequinot, and Manuel Sánchez Martínez. Barcelona: CSIC: Institución Milá y Fontanals, Depto de Estudios Medievales; Casa de Velásquez (Madrid); Université de Paris XII (Val de Marne, 2005). 123–64.

Sanpere y Miquel, Salvador. *Las Damas d'Aragó*. Barcelona: Col. Biblioteca Popular de la Acenç, 1908.

Santamaria, Alvaro. "La expansion político-militar de la corona ad Aragón bajo la dirección de Jaime I: Baleares." In *Jaime I y su época, X congreso de história de la Corona de Aragón*. 3 vols. Zaragoza: "Institución Fernando el Católico," 1979. Ponencias. 93–149.

Segura Graiño, Cristina. "Derechos sucesorios al trono de las mujeres en la corona de Aragon." *Mayurga* 22, no. 2 (1989): 591–99.

———. "Las mujeres de la sucesión á la corona de Castilla en la Baja Edad Media." *Estudios de Edad Media* 12 (1989): 205–14.

Serrano-Coll, Marta. "Los signos del poder; *regalias* somo cumplemento a los emblemos del uso inmediato." *Emblemata* 17 (2011): 129–54.

Sesma Muñoz, José Ángel. *La corona de Aragón. Una introcucción critica*. Zaragoza: Caja de Ahorros de la Inmaculada de Aragón, 2000.

BIBLIOGRAPHY 253

———. "Fiscalidad y poper. La fiscalidad centralizada como instrumento de poder en la Corona de Aragón." *Espacio, Tiempo y Forma* 1 [series III] (1988): 447–68.

Shadis, Miriam. *Berenguela of Castile (1180-1246) and Political Womwsn in the High Middle Ages.* New York: Palgrave Macmillan, 2009.

Shatmiller, Joseph. *Shyllock Reconsidered; Jews, Moneylending and Medieval Society.* Los Angeles: University of California Press, 1983.

Silleras-Fernández, Núria. "Money Isn't Everything. Concubinage, Class, and the Rise of Sibila de Fortiá, Queen of Aragon (1377-87)." In *Power, Piety, and Patronage in Late-Medieval Queenship.* New York: Palgrave Macmillan, 2008. 67–88.

Smith, F. Darwin. *The Life and Times of James I the Conqueror, King of Aragon, Valencia, and Majorca, Count of Barcelond and Urgel, Lord of Montpellier.* Oxford, 1894.

Soifer Irish, Maya. *Jews and Christians in Medieval Castile: Tradition in Medieval Castile: Tradition, Coexistence, and Change.* Washington, DC: Catholic University of America, 2016.

Soldevila, Ferran. *Els primer temps de Jaime I.* Barcelona: Institut de Estudis Catalans, 1968.

Sitges, J.B. *la muerte de D. Bernardo de Cabrera.* Madrid: Establecimiento tipográfico "Sucesores de Rivadenera," 1911.

Stalls, William Clay. "Queenship and the Royal Patrimony in Twelfth-Century Iberia: The Example of Petronilla of Aragon." In *Queens, Regents, and Potentates* Edited by Theresa M. Vann. Dallas, TX: Academia Press, 1993. 49–61.

Starkey, David. *Magna Carta: The Medieval Roots of Modern Politics.* New York, 2015.

Tasis i Marca, Rafael. *Pere el Cerimoniós i els seus fills.* 1957: reprint; Barcelona: Edicions Vicens-Vives, S.A., 1980.

———. *La vida dei Rei En Pere III.* Barcelona: Editorial Aedos, 1949.

Tausiet, María. *Urban Magic in Early Modern Spain: Abracadabra Pmnipotens.* Translated by Susannah Howe. New York: Palgrave Macmillan, 2014.

Taylor, Eugene. *The Mystery of Personality: A History of Psychodynamic Theories.* New York: Springer, 2009.

Tcach, César. "Las aljamas de la Corona de Aragón y su organización interna (siglo XIV)." *El Olivo: Documentación y estudios para el diálogo entre Judíos y Cristianos* 13, no. 29–30 (1981): 245–70.

Thomas, George Anthony. "The Queen's Two Bodies: Sor Juana and New Spain's Vicereines." *Hispania* 92, no. 3 (September, 2009): 417–29.

Titone, Fabrizio. *Governments of the Universitates. Urban Communities of Sicily in the Fourteenth and Fifteenth Centuries* Turnhout: Brepols, 2009.

254 BIBLIOGRAPHY

Traggia, Joaquim. "Illustración del reynado de Don Ramiro II." *Memorias del Real Academia de História* 3 (1799): 497–592.

Trenchs Odena, Josep. "La escribanía de Ramón Berenguer III (1097-1131): Datos para su estudio." *Saitabi* 31 (1984): 11–36.

———. "Las escribanías reales catalanoaragonesas de Ramón Berenguer IV á la minoría de Jaime I." *Revista de archivos, bibliotecas y museos* 80 (1977): 421–42.

———. "Los escribanos de Ramón Berenguer: Nuevos datos." *Saitabi* 29 (1979): 5–20.

———. "Jaime Saccora y la escribaní de Jaume I." *Jaume I y su època* 2:607–21.

Udina Martorell, Federico. *El archivo condal de Barcelona en los siglos IX-X. Estudio crítico de sus fundos.* Barcelona: CSIC, 1951.

———. *Guía hustórica y descriptiva del Archivo de la Corona de Aragón.* Madrid: Ministerio de Cultura, 1986.

Valla, Lorenzo. *Historia de Fernando de Aragón.* Translated by Santiago López Moreda. Madrid: Alkal, 2002.

Valls i Subirà, Oriols. *Paper and Watermarks in Catalonia.* 2 vols. Amsterdam: Paper Publication Society, 1970.

VanLandingham, Marta. "The Hohenstaufen Heritage of Costanza of Sicily and the Mediterranean Expansion of the Crown of Aragon in the Later Thirteenth Century." In *Across the Mediterranean Frontiers, Trade, Politics: and Religion.* Edited by Dionisius A. Agius and Ian Richard Netton. Turnhout: Brepols, 1997. 87–104.

———. *Transforming the State: King, Court, and Political Culture in the Realms of Aragon (1213-1287).* Leiden: Brill, 2002.

Vann, Theresa M. "The Theory and Practice of Medieval Castilian Queenship." In *Queen, Regents, and Potentates,* 125–47.

Vazquez, A. "Una cabalgada de moros." *Aljaranda* 1 (1991): 8–10.

Villalon, L.J. Andrew and Donald J. Kagay. *To Win and Lose a Medieval Battle: Nájera (April 2, 1367), a Pyrrhic Victory for the Black Prince.* Leiden: Brill, 2017.

Warren, W.L. *King John.* Berkeley, 1978.

Wasserstein, David. *The Rise and Fall of the Party-Kings.* Princeton, NJ: Princeton University Press, 1985.

Woodacre, Elena. "Ruling and Relationships: The Fundamental Basis of the Exercise of Power? The Impact of Marital and Familial Relationships on the Reigns of the Queen's Regnant of Navarre (1274-1517)." *AEM* 46, no. 1 (enero-junio de 2016), 167–201.

———. "The She Wolves of Navarre." *History Today* (June, 2012): 48–51.

Ziegler, Philip. *The Black Death.* New York: Harper & Row, Publishers, 1969.

Zurita y Castro, Jeronimo. *Anales de Aragon.* Edited by Angel López Canellas, 9 vols. Zaragoza: "Institución Fernando el Católico," 1969–1985.

INDEX

A
adalid, 45
Alagorça, 128
Albornoz, Ferran Gomez de Albornoz, captain, 176
Alfonso I of Aragon, 5
Alfonso IX of León, 28
Alfonso X, 7
Alghero, 84
Aljamas, 134–137, 139
aljamas (Jewish)
  Barcelona, 95, 96, 98, 105
  Borja, 96
  Cervera, 96, 98, 105
  Gerona, 96, 98
  Lerida, 96, 98, 103
  Teruel, 98
  Valencia, 96, 106
  Vilafranca, 96, 98
Almudevar, 132
Anagni, treaty, 44
Andalusia, 25
Andrew of Hungary, 31, 32
Aneas Hontangas, Marina, 15, 21

Anglesola, Galceran de, Pere III's ambassador, 56
Aragonese kings
  Alfons I, 27, 33
  Alfons II, 36
  Ferran I, 34
Aragonese Royal Court
  early medieval, curial ordinances
    Alfons II, 112, 114, 115, 117
    Jaume II, 113–116
    Pere II, 113–115, 117
    Pere III, 116, 117, 128, 130, 136
  early medieval, *curia regis*, 114
  Officials
    butler, 112, 118
    chamberlain, 111, 112, 115, 118
    chancellor, 112, 113, 116, 118
    constable, 112
    grammarian, 112
    maeste racional, 114, 115, 117, 118, 124
    professor, 112

© The Editor(s) (if applicable) and The Author(s), under exclusive
license to Springer Nature Switzerland AG 2021
D. J. Kagay, *Elionor of Sicily, 1325–1375*, The New Middle Ages,
https://doi.org/10.1007/978-3-030-71028-6

256 INDEX

steward, 112
Visigothic predecessor
   aula, 111, 113
   household, 111
Aragón River, 95
Araviana-Castilian defeat, 1359, 149
Arborea, Judges of, Sardinian rulers, 83
Arcadells, 126
Archivo de la Corona de Aragón
   Alfons I, 5
   Alfons II, 5, 8
   Chapel of Santa Agueda, 8
   Frederick II, 2, 8
   Jaume I, 3, 6, 8
   Jaume II, 8, 14
   location, 5, 7
   origins, 30
   Pere II, 2, 7, 8
   Ramon Berenguer IV, 5, 7, 19
   Ramon de Caldes, 6, 19
Arraona, castle, 104
Ausona, 130
Avignon, 77, 78, 81
Aymerich Bassols, Montse, 15, 21

B
Bachman, Clifford, 14, 20
Balearic Islands, 11
Barcelona, 42, 47, 49–52, 56
Barcelona *corts*, 1364, 159
Barcelona *corts*, 1365, 151
battles, 44
   Benevento, 36
   Las Navas de Tolosa, 25, 28
   Sicilian Vespers, 31, 36
Benevento, 36
Berenguela, Leonese queen, 92
Berenguer Carbonell, ambassador, 68, 76, 81
Berenguer de Relat, 206, 212, 214

Berga, 102
Bernardi, 130
Biescas, 95
Birta, castle, 96
Bishop Gui de Boulogne, papal legate, 155
Black Death, 24, 29, 95, 135
Blanche of Castile, French queen, 92
Blasco de Alagon, 71, 73, 84
Blasco de Heredía, ambassador, 74
Boccaccio, Giovanni, 33
Bordeaux, 24, 37
Bordeaux
   French kings
      Charles IX, 23
Breda, monastery, 130, 133
Burgo, Palan, townsman, 128
Burriana, 48

C
Cabrera, Bernat, Aragonese official, 101
Cabrera, Bernat, royal advisor, 130–134
Calatayud, 126, 130, 132, 135
Caliphate of Córdoba, 42
Caltabellota, treaty, 44
Camprodón, 121
Campromis de Caspe, 34
Candanchú, 95
canon law, 112
Cardinal Guillaume de la Jugie, papal legate, 155
Castelhabib campaign, 1365, 154
Castellón, 48
Castilian civil war, 1366–1369, 155
Castilian kings
   Alfonso VI, 27, 35
   Alfonso VIII, 28
   Alfonso X, 25, 27, 28, 38
   Alfonso XI, 24, 29

Enrique I, 28, 30
Fernando III, 28, 29
Pedro I "the Cruel", 29, 39
Sancho IV, 28
Castro, Felipe de, noble, 104
Catalonia, 41–44, 52
Catania, 73, 75
churches, Elionor's support, 208, 210
clergy, Elionor's suppot, 200
Cocentaina, 104
Collioure, 94
Commeracions de Pere Albert, 167
Compromise of Caspe, 47
Constanza, Aragonese princess, 97
Constanza, Aragonese queen, 43, 46, 50, 53–55
Corsica, 45
Costum de Espanya, 167, 169
Count Bernardi de Osona, 132
Count Enrique de Trastámara, 102, 104, 149, 163, 174
Count Ramon Berenguer IV of Barcelona, 112, 131
Count Ramon Berenguer IV of Province, 93
court cuisine, 202
court life, 206

D
Deibel, Ulla, 13, 20

E
Ebro River, 49
Edward III of England, 24
El Bayo, castle, 96
Elche, 126, 135
Eleanor of Anjou, English queen, 54, 55
Eleanor of Provence, Enclish queen, 92, 93
Eleanor of Sicily

dower rights, 92, 93
dowry, 91, 93–95
exchange of properties, 91
finances of last years, 99
lack of revenues, 92
military salaries, 100
royal grants, 97, 101, 104
wedding gifts, 91
Elionor and Sicily
connextions with Sicilian family, 67
diplomacy
1349 Aragonese naval attack, 74
Castile, 78, 85
Genoa, 83, 85–87
Naples, 69, 76, 78, 81–83
Sardinia, 75, 79, 81, 85
Venice, 86
dowry dispute, 69–71
drive for Sicilian throne, 69, 80, 81
Giunta, Francesco, Sicilian historian, 77, 87
Neopolitan attacks, 66, 80
relations with major Sicilian cities, 67, 73
relations with Sicilian kings, 73
Sicilian king, 79
Sicilian officials, 70, 72
Elionor as War Administrator
castles
Camarasa, 167
Cubells, 167
Marmillar, 167
Montcada, 167, 169
St Pol, 167
command of castellans
discipline, 163
payment of companies, 161, 163, 174
transfer of companies, 174
naval campaign-1359
arming galleys, 150

258 INDEX

fitting out ships, 176, 179
transport of ships, 170
urban centers affected
Alcoy, 175
Crevillente, 168, 173
Elche, 173, 175
Huelamo, 176
Lliria, 165, 167
Peñaguila, 167
Tarazona, 145, 165–167
Teruel, 165, 167
Elionor' character
deep affection, 218
children, 205, 206
officials, 206, 208
servants, 202, 204, 214
final depression, 227
homesickness for Sicilian homeland,
201
jealousy, 219
Cabrera affair, 219
stubbornness, 205
Elionor of Sicily
administrative records, 10, 21
archives, 10
brothers, 51, 55, 58
coverage in medieval chronicles, 2,
3, 11
dower rights, 56
dowry, 56, 57
good works, 55
marriage contract, 49
marriage in Valencian, 51, 52,
57–59
marriage proposal, 56, 57
parents, 49
Sicilian life, 56, 58, 59
Sicilian ruling rights, 46, 54
sisters, 46, 51, 57, 58
trip to Valencia, 43
upbringing, 24, 57, 202, 216
Elionor of Sicily, administrator

chamberlain, officials
Castelló, Ramon de, 118
Copons, Ramóa de, 118
Ripoll, Beremguer, 118
chancellor, officials
Bishop Romeus de Cescomes
of Lerida, 118
Carbonell, Berenguer, 118
Oliver Guillem d', 118
Puig, Bernat de, 118
Serra, Guillem d', 118
Vallseca, Jaume de', 118
maestre racional, officials
Berenguer de Relat, 119
Conill, Bernat, 119
Fernández de Heredia, Blasco,
119
Sayoll, Ferrer, 119
Sos, Jaume de, 119
Spelunca, Geralt, 119
mayordomos, officials
Pagara, Ramón de, 118
Rajadell, Joan Berenguer de,
118
Elionor's appearance and style
clothes, 217, 218
jewels, 216–218
seal portrait, 219
Elionor's coronation
coronation of Elionor, 1352
Pere's formulation of new
Aragonese coronation, 197
coronation of Sibilla de Fortía,
1381, 212
description of last two
coronations-1328-1336,
196, 198
history of Aragonese coronations,
194, 197
Elionor's final illness
death, 228, 229, 231–234

April 20, 1375-Lerida, 9:00am,
230
lingering illnesses and increasing
obesity
Chronic Kidney Disease, 229
increasing obesity, 229
three burials
Lerida, 234
Poblet, 230, 234
Saitn Clares, Barcelona, 230,
234
Elionors Last Will and Testament
bequests
children, 231
husband, 231, 232
members of Sicilian family, 232
much of property converted
to money, especially for
Princess Elionor's dowry,
231, 232
codicils, pious causes, 233
churches, 232
conditions, queen's financial
support in exchange for
prayers at her funeral and
on specified saints day,
161, 230
monasteries, 235
poor people, 92
priests, 233
Drawn up, 1365, 230
Made official,1374, 230
Elionor's loss of control over Sicily
now ruled by her niece, Queen
María, 228
Elionor's negative relations with Pere
III and Encique II of Castile,
120, 134
Elionor's oppositions to marriage of
Princess Elionor and Prince Juan
of Castile, 228

Elizabeth of Carinthia, Sicilian queen,
54, 58
Epstein, Stephan, 14, 21

F
Federico III of Sicily, 14
Finke, Heinrich, 10, 13
Flor, Roger de, 45
French kings
Charles VIII, 28
Philippe III, 30
Philippe VI, 29, 30
frontier, Aragonese, 148, 161, 173,
174
frontier, Castilian, 148
frontier, Valencian, 160
Fueros of Aragon, 112

G
Genoa, 54, 123
Gerona, 117, 129, 130, 133, 135
Gerona, Berenguer de, townsman,
127
Gilabert, Ferrer, royal official, 129
Giunta, Francesco, 87–90
Great Western Schism, 32
Guerrea, Lop de, Pere III ambassador,
56

H
Hospitallers, 7, 9
Howell, Margaret, 93
Huesca, 125, 127, 137, 138

I
Ibiza, 11, 96

J
Jaca, 95, 97–99, 103

260 INDEX

Játiva, 104
Joan, Aragonese prince, 117
Joanna I of Naples, 12
Joanna, Navarrese queen, 49, 50, 66, 83
Joan, Prince, 198–200, 202–205, 218–220
John of Gaunt, 30
justicia, urban official, 94

K
kings
  Aragonese, 111–114, 116, 118, 124, 128
    Alfons II, 114, 115, 117
    Alfons III, 8, 47, 48, 83
    Jaume I, 113, 117, 130, 134, 135
    Jaume II, 65, 83
    Pere II, 65
  Castilian, 3, 7, 47, 85, 86, 121, 134, 147, 148, 151, 153, 155, 158, 162, 166, 171, 180, 183, 228
    Pedro I, 78, 82, 83, 85–87
  English, 112
    Henry I, 112
  French, 112, 130
    Philippe III Augustus, 112
  Majorca, 117
    Jaume IV, 123
  Navarre, 120, 132
    Charles II, 132
  Sicilian
    Federico IV, 66, 76
    Ludovico I, 66–76, 82, 84
    Pietro II, 65, 70
  Tunis, 44
    Abu-al-Husan, 81
kings and princes
  Aragonese

Alfons III, 47, 48
Jaume I, 41–43
Jaume II, 44, 45, 47, 54, 58
Martí I, 46
Pere II, 43, 44, 54
Pere III, 41, 46, 47, 51, 53
Byzantine, 45
  Michael IX, 45
Castilian
  Alfonso XI, 48, 51
  Fernando (Ferran), princr, 100, 101
  Fernando III, 41, 42
  Fernando IV, 47
  Fernando, prince, 48
  Pedro I, 42, 49, 97, 100–102
English
  Henry III, 92, 93
  John I, 92
Majorcan kings
  Jaume II, 43
Sicilian
  Charles I of Anjou, 43
  Federico III, 44, 54, 55
  Federico IV, 46, 50
  Ludovico, 94
  Martí the Younger, 46
  Pietro II, 54, 55

L
Las Navas de Tolosa, 41, 42, 59
Lauria, Roger de, 44
Leges Palitinae, 116
Leonor of Castile, Aragonese queen, 47, 48, 51–53, 100, 101
Leonor of Portugal, Portuguese queen, 95
Liber Feudorum Maior, 6, 18, 19
Lliria, 97, 98, 102, 103, 123, 125, 127, 137
Lope de Luna, Archbishop of Zaragoza, 49

INDEX   261

Louis of Taranto, 32
Luera, 127
Lugidor, Sardinia cape, 85
Lull, Domenic, urban official, 126

M
Magna Carta, 92
Majorca, 6, 7, 9
Majorcan kings
    Jaume III, 32
    Jaume VI, 32
Malta, 44
Manresa, 87
Maria de Luna, 11
María, Narraese queen, 46, 49, 50, 52
María of Navarre, Navarrese queen, 95
Martí, Aragonese prince, 120, 121
Martí I, 2, 4, 16, 17
Martínez Ferrando, Jesus Ernesto, 10
Martin IV, pope, 44
Martí, Prince, 198, 203, 205, 206, 213, 214, 218, 219
Matha de Armignac, Aragonese princess, 120
Medieval Queens
    Aragonese
        Constanza, 29, 30, 35–37
        Petronilla, 33, 34
    Castilian
        Berenguela, 28
        Blanca, 28
        Blanche de Bourbon, 29
        Violante, 25, 28, 29
    causes of death, 29, 31–37
    children, 24–26, 29, 34, 36, 37
    languages, 24, 25
    lifestyle, 23, 24, 27
    Mediterranean
        Elvira, 35
        Joanna I, 31

        Margaret, 35
        Sancia of Mallorca, 31
    mistresses
        Blanche de Bourbon, 29
        Juana de Castro, 29
        Leonor de Guzman, 29
        María de Molina, 29
    Navarrese
        Juana I, 30
        Juana II, 30
    princesses
        Joan, 24
Mediterranean kings
    Charles I of Anjou, 60
Messina, 54, 56, 58, 66, 67, 73, 75, 82, 83
Minorca, 96
Miron, Berenguer, townsman, 129
monasteries, Elionor's support, 208, 210
Mongrí, Guillem de, 43
Montblanc, castle, 98
Montcada, castle, 99
Muñoz i Soria, Nuria, 13, 20
Murcia, 28
Muret, battle, 42
Murviedro, 48, 52, 102, 103, 106, 121, 123, 131, 135
Murviedro peace, 1363, 155
Murviedro siege, 1365, 154

N
Nájera, battle, 105
Naples, 27, 31, 32, 39, 44, 54
New Palace, Barcelona, 202, 212
noblemen
    Count Joan of Empuries, 50
    Count Ramon Berenguer III of Barcelona, 42
    Duke Giovanni of Athens, 55
    Duke William of Athens, 45

262 INDEX

Elector Rupert II of the Palatinate, 55
Palici, Mateo de, 58
nobles
Count Pedro de Montcada, 66, 75
Count Pedro de Ribagorza, 71
Duke Barnabò of Naples, 80
Duke Federico of Athens, 66, 71, 75
Duke Galeazzo of Naples, 80
Duke Giovanni of Athens, 65, 70, 74
Mostaça, Jaume, 75
Orlando of Aragon, 77
Palermo, 67, 72–75
Plizzi, Mateo de, 74
Sassari, 84

O
Old Palace, Barcelona, 211, 212
Olot, 121
Ordinacions, 116
Orihuela campaign, 1364–1365, 154
Otto of Brunswick, 32

P
Palermo, 44, 54
Peace and Truce of God, 112
Peñaguila, 97
Pere III, 193, 194, 196–198, 200, 205, 209, 211–214, 217, 219, 220
administrative records, 12, 13, 15
Cronica, 3, 4
Perpignan, 50, 95
Philippa of Lancaster, Portuguese queen, 92
Philippe d'Evreux, 30
Poblet, monastery, 50, 53
Podiolo, Guillem Bernat de, royalofficial, 129

poor, Elionor's support, 205, 208
popes
Clement VI, 31
Post-Traumatic Stress Disorder, 32
Princeps namque, 131
Princess Elionor, 219
Puig de Santa María, 97, 102, 103
Pyrenees, 145, 170, 183

Q
Queralt, Pedro de, townsman, 117

R
Raviolos, 125
Relat, Berenguer de, Aragonese official, 98, 104, 107
Riera i Sans, Jaume, 14, 21
Ripoll, 118, 121
Robert the Wise, 31
Roebert, Sebastian, 15, 16, 21
Roger II, 35, 36, 40
Roig, Guisbert, urban official, 129, 130
Roman law, 112
Roussillon, 94, 96, 108, 123, 131
royal official, 216
royal servants, 202, 204, 214
Ruiz Domingo, Lledó, 15, 21
rustling, 146

S
Sabadell, 104, 127, 128
Saint Clares, Terue, monastery, 209, 210
Sánchez Martínez, Manuel, 14, 21
San Feliu de Quíxols, 129
San Lucár de Barrameda, 147
Sardinia, 45–47, 96, 98, 99
Segura, 145, 150, 151
Seville, 25

Sibilla de Fortia, Aragonese queen, 92, 106
Sicilian kings
    Charles I of Anjou, 31, 36
    Robert the Wise, 31
    Roger II, 35, 36
    William I, 35
Sicilian Vespers, 113, 117
Siete Partidas, 27, 39, 91, 107
slavery, 146
solonot, 153
St. Clares-Messina, monastery, 58

T
Tamarite de Litera, 51
Tarazona, 94, 95, 97–99, 103
Tarrega, 100, 102, 105
Temple of Templars, 212
Teresa de Entenca, Aragonese queen, 47
Terrer-1361, peace, 155
Teruel, 94, 95, 98, 99, 103, 119, 120, 123–125, 128, 135
Tudela, 49
Turia River, 95
Turibas, Martin de, townsman, 127

U
Ugo of Valencia, bishop, 59
Unión, 45, 48, 51, 52, 96
Urban V, pope, 124
Usatges of Barcelona, 112

V
Valencia, 3, 6, 7, 9, 11, 12, 14, 113–115, 117, 121, 122, 125, 134, 135
Valencia campaign, 1364–1365, 151, 182
Valladolid, 29
Venice, 54
Vilagrassa, 100, 102, 103
Violante de Bar, Aragonese queen, 92

W
War of Sicilian Vespers, 113
War of the Two Pedros, 10, 16, 96, 99, 100, 103, 106, 108, 145, 171, 184

Z
Zaragoza, 50, 53, 119, 134

Printed in the United States
by Baker & Taylor Publisher Services